Children of Color

*Psychological Interventions
with Minority Youth*

Jewelle Taylor Gibbs
Larke Nahme Huang
and Associates

Forewords by
Congressman George Miller
and Stanley Sue, Ph. D.

Children of Color

Psychological Interventions with Minority Youth

Jossey-Bass Publishers · San Francisco

CHILDREN OF COLOR
Psychological Interventions with Minority Youth
   by Jewelle Taylor Gibbs, Larke Nahme Huang, and Associates

Copyright © 1989 by: Jossey-Bass Inc., Publishers
                      350 Sansome Street
                      San Francisco, California 94104
                                  &
                      Jossey-Bass Limited
                      Headington Hill Hall
                      Oxford OX3 0BW

Library of Congress Cataloging-in-Publication Data

Gibbs, Jewelle Taylor.
   Children of color : psychological interventions with minority
youth / Jewelle Taylor Gibbs, Larke Nahme Huang, and associates :
forewords by George Miller and Stanley Sue. — 1st ed.
       p.   cm. — (The Jossey-Bass social and behavioral science
series)
   Includes bibliographies and index.
   ISBN 1-55542-156-3 (alk. paper)
   1. Child psychopathology. 2. Children of minorities—United
States—Psychology. I. Huang, Larke. II. Title. III. Series.
   [DNLM: 1. Ethnic Groups—psychology—United States. 2. Mental
Health Services—in adolescence—United States. 3. Mental Health
Services—in infancy & childhood—United States. WA 305 G443c]
RJ499.G47   1989
618.92'89—dc 19
DNLM/DLC
for Library of Congress   88-46098
                                                              CIP

Manufactured in the United States of America

The paper in this book meets the guidelines for
permanence and durability of the Committee on
Production Guidelines for Book Longevity of the
Council on Library Resources.

JACKET DESIGN BY WILLI BAUM
FIRST EDITION

HB Printing   10 9 8 7 6 5 4

Code 8930

The Jossey-Bass
Social and Behavioral Science Series

To my beloved parents
Margaret Taylor Hancock and the late Reverend Julian Augustus Taylor
whose high expectations
inspired two generations of Black youth to achieve

To my family
Christina Lee Huang and Kevin Nahme Huang
for timely inspiration and constant distraction
and
E. Kirk Huang
for loving companionship and rejuvenating enthusiasm

Contents

Foreword

Over the last several decades, we in the United States have witnessed dramatic changes that have profoundly affected our young people and their families demographically, economically, socially, and psychologically and that pose enormous challenges to which the nation must respond.

Perhaps nowhere are these changes more evident and compelling than in the rapidly increasing cultural and demographic diversity of our citizenry. Minority group members—Blacks, Hispanics, American Indians, and Asians—constitute 14 percent of all adults in the country and 20 percent of children under 17. By the year 2000, it is projected that one-third of all school-age children will fall into this category.

This changing demographic tapestry in the United States promises not only the richness that diversity brings but also many difficult challenges in extending the American dream to all of our citizens. Historically, minorities have found themselves at the bottom of the economic and social order. They are disproportionately represented among the poor, the unemployed, the homeless, the sick, the inadequately educated, and those who are ill-prepared for full participation in American life. For minority children, the toll has been even greater. Infant mortality in the Black community is double that in the White community, and the gap is widening. Half of all Black children and one-third of all Hispanic children live in poverty. School dropout rates for minority youth remain at alarming levels, with rates reaching more than 60 percent in some urban areas.

Concomitant economic changes and increasing isolation of minority communities compound the challenges. The number of blue-collar manufacturing jobs is declining—jobs that allowed past generations of minorities and immigrants to climb into the economic mainstream. The opportunities now available to minority adults increasingly are in low-paying service-sector jobs that provide far fewer opportunities for upward mobility.

In addition, we have seen an upswing in race-related violence and other racially motivated incidents in diverse communities around the country. Apart from their tragic personal significance, incidents of racial antipathy give us important lessons about larger economic and demographic trends in our society and about the environments in which our children are growing up.

Children of color face daily challenges to their success and self-esteem. In investigations by the U.S. Select Committee on Children, Youth, and Families, we have documented the disparate treatment of minority and White children with mental health problems. The understanding and treatment of children's mental health is still in its infancy in America. Nearly ten million children suffer from mental health problems that need attention. Yet, an estimated 70 to 80 percent of these children get inappropriate mental health services or no services at all. For children of color, the problems are even more severe. Due to a mental health system that is poorly funded and all too frequently insensitive to race and ethnic origin, minority children are often misdiagnosed and mistreated, if they are treated at all.

The importance of addressing these issues cannot be overstated: They must be at the core of America's agenda. This book provides an important contribution in defining and making more visible these concerns, which have remained under wraps for far too long. Children are our future, and we must give them the opportunity to do a good job of it. They and the nation deserve no less.

February 1989   Congressman George Miller
                                Chairman, Select Committee
                                on Children, Youth, and Families
                                U.S. House of Representatives

Foreword

Hodgkinson (1983) has indicated that in the next few years, the motive for working with and knowing about ethnic minority groups will be not political liberalism or obligation but enlightened self-interest. It is obvious that the interest of all is served by an ability to work with diverse ethnic populations: The population of American society is increasingly diverse, and if we are to achieve economic, social, educational, and democratic ideals, we must develop multicultural knowledge and skills. In the mental health field, the need for enlightenment is particularly acute. Many minority individuals experience stress, which contributes to adjustment problems and psychopathology, but we lack adequate institutional resources and mental health services to address their problems. There are many economic, sociocultural, and political reasons why these problems continue to exist. For mental health professionals, one major barrier to attending to these problems has been inadequate knowledge and training.

Many of us who have studied the effect of ethnicity on mental health are frequently asked such questions as: What are the cultural values of particular ethnic groups? How do cultural conflicts affect mental health? What assessment instruments are valid to use with these groups? Must psychotherapeutic techniques be modified to be effective with minority clients? What is meant by the term *culturally sensitive therapist?* Do minority group members demonstrate a great deal of heterogeneity? What kinds of psychotherapeutic and societal interventions are required to address the mental health needs of ethnic minorities? In view of the growing diversity of U.S. society, how can we plan for the future?

In this book Jewelle Taylor Gibbs, Larke Nahme Huang, and their colleagues address some of these questions with respect to minority children and families. The work is a significant contribution for several reasons: First, because little has been written about minority children, researchers, practitioners, and decision makers often must operate without much knowledge of the issues involved. This book provides an up-to-date analysis of the state of knowledge and developmental/ecological and intervention issues. Second, the book is strongly oriented toward both scholars and practitioners. Researchers should find many of the ideas amenable to further study; practitioners will gain a better understanding of how to assess and treat minority children. While no simple answers are given, the cultural, sociopolitical, and clinical contexts presented by the various contributors should enable practitioners to better work with members of diverse cultural groups. Third, unlike many books of readings that lack integration and coherence, this book consists of chapters in which a standard format is used in discussing issues, and the authors illustrate their ideas with case studies. Particularly interesting are the analyses of specific cases by the different contributors. These analyses provide a most enlightening lesson in how cases can be meaningfully approached by experts who have broad knowledge of cultural diversities and the issues of psychological assessment and intervention. No longer do we have to restrict our discussions about work with culturally diverse clients to abstract admonitions. We now have an adequate knowledge base and the expertise to begin to truly respond to the needs of ethnic minority groups.

February 1989   Stanley Sue, Ph. D.
                             Professor of Psychology
                             University of California, Los Angeles

Reference

Hodgkinson, H. L. "Guess Who's Coming to College?" *Academe*, 1983, *69*, 13–20.

Preface

Minority children and adolescents are the most rapidly growing segment of the youth population in America; yet, very little literature is available to enlighten clinicians, educators, health professionals, and social workers about their problems and needs. While training graduate students in clinical psychology and social work, we recognized the need for a comprehensive book on the psychological assessment and treatment of minority children and adolescents, a group woefully neglected in the recent proliferation of textbooks on minority mental health. Most of these recent books focus on the mental health problems of minority adults and the implications of ethnicity for family therapy, even though all the major ethnic minority groups are characterized by disproportionately youthful populations compared with the White majority. Our experiences as teachers, supervisors, and consultants further emphasized the need for a book that would encompass theoretical, empirical, and clinical perspectives on the assessment and treatment of minority youth.

To date, no single book addresses the unique problems and special needs of minority children and adolescents with psychological and behavioral problems. The knowledge base about minority populations has been expanding, but this knowledge has only recently been effectively translated into a few comprehensive handbooks for use in clinical intervention and training of mental health and human service professionals. Because the population of non-White and Spanish-speaking youth in the United States is rapidly increasing and is expected to reach 30 percent of all youth by the year 2000, the need for educational and clinical resources relevant to this group is clearly evident. In fact, minority youth now make up over 50 percent of the student population in many large urban school districts, with concomitant increases in academic and behavioral problems, which teachers and counselors are unprepared to handle effectively. Thus, this book is designed to meet the needs of educators and professionals in the mental health and human service professions, such as psychiatry, psychology, social work, psychiatric nursing, and counseling.

Goals of This Book

Children of Color fulfills several goals and will be useful in a wide variety of clinical, professional, and educational settings. First, its primary purpose is to present a well-balanced discussion of the issues involved in clinical assessment and treatment of minority children and adolescents from six major ethnic groups and two emerging special population groups. The various contributors cover a range of interventions, from psychodynamic to social cognitive to systems-oriented, with an ecological perspective providing a common thread across groups and serving to integrate the conventional with the more culturally based methods of intervention.

Second, a comparative, cross-cultural approach informs each chapter, enabling the reader to compare selected topics (for example, socialization practices, identity formation, coping strategies, assessment issues, treatment approaches) across ethnic groups.

Third, the book reflects a major commitment to an ecological perspective that recognizes the significant impact of social and environmental factors, such as poverty, discrimination, immigration, and family structure, on the adaptation and coping patterns of minority children and adolescents. We strongly believe that some knowledge of a group's history in the United States, traditional value system and family organization, and current demographic realities is essential for accurate clinical assessment and effective intervention with youth from diverse ethnic backgrounds. For this reason, relevant background information is briefly summarized for each minority group in order to provide a sociocultural context that justifies the recommendations for differential strategies of assessment and treatment.

Regrettably, this book could not include every ethnic minority group. We have decided to focus on children and adolescents from six of the larger groups in the United States—Black Americans, Chinese Americans, Japanese Americans, American Indians, Mexican Americans, and mainland Puerto Ricans—and two emerging groups, Southeast Asian refugees and biracial youth. The six ethnic groups have been, historically, the largest minority groups with the longest period of residence in this country; more literature and a greater range of reliable sources are available for writing about these groups; and they represent a broad range of demographic, linguistic, and acculturation situations. For example, in terms of population trends, Chinese Americans are a rapidly increasing group, while Japanese Americans are stabilizing and perhaps even declining because of high rates of out-group marriage. The route of entry to the United States varies from American Indians, who were indigenous, to Black Americans imported as slaves, to Japanese Americans and Chinese Americans imported as laborers, to the most recent Southeast Asians, who were initially admitted as political refugees. Along with these differences in migration history, the groups display a continuum of acculturation, which is reflected in linguistic and cultural patterns ranging from the bilingualism of many second-generation Spanish-speaking Americans to the rapid assimilation of many third-generation Japanese Americans.

It is important to underscore the wide diversity *within* each ethnic group. Attitudes, behaviors, and values of individual members are strongly influenced by their degree of acculturation, their socioeconomic status, and their ties with ethnic institutions and communities. For example, first- and third-generation Japanese Americans may be less alike than middle-class Japanese Americans and White Americans. As you read our contributors' descriptions of the traditional history, culture, and mental health attitudes and beliefs of these ethnic groups, keep in mind that each group is in the process of continual change and adaptation to the dominant society and that these generalizations are not equally applicable to all its members.

Separate chapters address the unique problems of two emerging groups in the youth population—refugee youth from Southeast Asia and biracial adolescents. Although the clinical literature contains very little about these two groups, they are a rapidly growing segment of the youth population in this country, and we believe they pose particular challenges to mental health practitioners who may be unfamiliar with their cultural and social experiences. These two chapters offer an initial attempt to consolidate the ethnographic, developmental, clinical, and empirical literature that provides useful information for clinicians who work with these youth.

Many other minority groups, of course, have more recently grown in size and made significant contributions to our society, such as Koreans, Filipinos, Cubans, Central Americans, West Indian Blacks, and Pacific Islanders, among others. Limitations of space and inadequate data bases on children's mental health issues have kept us from including all these minorities. However, throughout this book there are sections on assessment and treatment that will have some relevance for these groups, as well as many references to publications that are directly applicable to them.

In planning the topics to be included, we decided to present thorough coverage of selected treatment modalities rather than to produce a survey text with a superficial coverage of all modalities of treatment for minority children and adolescents. Since most of these youth are seen in outpatient clinics and practice settings, the authors focus on appropriate individual and family treatment modalities. Few authors address the issues of residential treatment or hospitalization, since these are specialized settings that frequently involve medication and more restrictive forms of intervention. Finally, psychological testing is not covered in this book because the issues of testing minority youth have been effectively addressed in many other textbooks.

Overview of the Contents

The twelve chapters are organized to reflect natural group-ings within the broad category of ethnic minority populations as well as historical differences in their relationship to the domi-nant culture. The first chapter, by Jewelle Taylor Gibbs and Larke Nahme Huang, provides an introduction to the book and an overview of the issues. In this chapter we describe the pur-pose and goals of the book, its conceptual framework, and its integrative cross-cultural perspective.

Nine topical chapters follow, each focusing on a particu-lar minority group or special population. Authors of these chap-ters are psychologists who have both personal and professional knowledge and extensive clinical experience with the ethnic groups they describe. The content of these chapters adheres to a similar format: demographic data, epidemiological data on inci-dence of psychological and behavioral disorders (where avail-able), historical information about entry/migration to the United States, significant issues of family structure and functioning, sociocultural issues in assessment (attitudes, values, and beliefs about mental health and illness, symptom patterns, and help-seeking and utilization patterns), and implications for effective intervention strategies and treatment techniques. Each author presents case vignettes to illustrate the role of sociocultural fac-tors in the assessment of symptomatology, defensive strategies, and coping behaviors in emotionally troubled minority children and adolescents, for the purpose of developing treatment tech-niques and alternative intervention strategies.

In Chapter Two, Larke Nahme Huang and Yu-Wen Ying describe the mental health issues for Chinese American children and adolescents and provide a unique model of "active exchange" in intervention with these youth and their families.

Donna K. Nagata focuses in Chapter Three on the impli-cations of bicultural identity for Japanese American children, who are particularly vulnerable to parental and societal pres-sures to fulfill the expectations of the "model minority" stereo-type as they cope with the dual pressures of normative develop-mental tasks and acculturation.

In Chapter Four, Teresa LaFromboise and Kathryn Graff Low propose a combination of indigenous and Western therapeutic methods to treat the psychological and behavioral problems of American Indian youth, whose problems often result from the poverty, social isolation, and cultural discontinuities of reservation or urban life.

In Chapter Five, LaRue Allen and Shayda Majidi-Ahi emphasize the resilience and adaptability of Black American children, whose psychosocial development is frequently affected by poverty and racial discrimination.

Jewelle Taylor Gibbs builds on this theme in Chapter Six in describing the psychosocial problems of Black American adolescents, whose behavioral disorders often mask underlying psychological problems that are exacerbated by their disadvantaged socioeconomic status.

In Chapter Seven, Oscar Ramirez points out the dual impact of biculturalism and bilingualism in the psychosocial development of Mexican American children, who often find themselves in conflict between the traditional Latino values of their parents and the values of contemporary Anglo society.

Jaime Inclán and D. Gloria Herron touch on similar themes in Chapter Eight in describing the mental health issues for Puerto Rican youth. As in the previous chapter, the authors emphasize the importance of involving the family in any treatment program for a Latino child or adolescent.

Larke Nahme Huang presents an overview in Chapter Nine of the adjustment issues facing Southeast Asian refugee and immigrant children, who have experienced multiple separations and losses, forced relocation, and pressures for rapid acculturation to an unfamiliar society.

In Chapter Ten, Jewelle Taylor Gibbs examines the implications of biracial ethnicity for the psychosocial adjustment of adolescents, whose identity development may be made more difficult by conflicts about their dual racial heritage.

Chapter Eleven illustrates the diverse ways in which several contributing authors view a standardized case of a child or adolescent, depending on their particular sociocultural contexts and therapeutic modalities. The objective of this chapter is to highlight how clinicians' cultural sensitivity can influence their conceptualization of a case, their diagnostic assessment, and their treatment recommendations, particularly when they are taking into account the sociocultural background of the child or adolescent client.

In Chapter Twelve, Huang and Gibbs integrate the common themes developed in the topical chapters, highlighting the similarities and differences in mental health issues among the various groups of minority children and adolescents. We also propose an ecological model of clinical inquiry and assessment appropriate for minority children and adolescents, who share certain characteristics that set them apart from the dominant majority. Finally, we present a set of recommendations for further research on the mental health of minority youth, greater expansion and improvement in the training of mental health professionals to treat minority clients, and significant restructuring of the mental health delivery system to meet the needs of the growing minority population.

In summary, we feel that *Children of Color* is an important contribution to the field of minority mental health for three reasons: It will fill a significant gap in the clinical literature on the treatment of minority children and adolescents, because no such book is currently available; it will be valuable for use in the training of all mental health and human service professionals, many of whom are required to gain knowledge of ethnic minority groups for their licensing examinations in psychiatry, psychology, social work, and marriage and family counseling; and it will be extremely useful for mental health and human service professionals in all public and private agencies, which, according to current demographic projections, will serve an increasingly higher proportion of minority youth and their families well into the twenty-first century.

We should add one caveat to our readers that our goal is not to create "experts" or "specialists" in the field of minority mental health but to provide an introduction to, and a way of understanding, the mental health problems of minority youth. We hope that this book will not only expand the knowledge base of clinicians who work with these youth but also increase their sensitivity to the similarities and differences within and among groups in our society.

Children of color constitute one of the fastest-growing segments of the population, and yet social scientists have paid little attention to their development, educators have demonstrated little understanding of their special needs, and mental health professionals have shown little awareness of their special problems. It is our hope that this book will make an initial contribution to increasing the understanding of their needs, improving the assessment of their mental health, and developing more effective methods of intervention and treatment for their behavioral and psychological disorders.

February 1989   Jewelle Taylor Gibbs
                                                   Stanford, California

                                                   Larke Nahme Huang
                                                   Potomac, Maryland

Acknowledgments

Children of Color truly represents a collaborative undertaking, not only of the contributing authors, but also of many others who made direct and indirect contributions to the project. First, we would like to thank the contributing authors, whose enthusiasm and cooperation sustained us through the challenges inherent in such a project. We would also like to express our appreciation for the encouragement and support of Dean Harry Specht and other colleagues in the School of Social Welfare, University of California, Berkeley.

We are grateful for the advice and counsel of Sheldon J. Korchin and colleagues in the Psychology Clinic, University of California, Berkeley. A special thanks to Forrest B. Tyler of the University of Maryland, whose knowledge and ideas instilled precious life values and the wisdom of diversity.

We owe thanks to several research assistants who assisted with the research on our chapters in this book, including Helen Ahn, Kathryn Chun, Holly Danforth, Alice Hines, Karen Huang, Mary Leong Lam, Huong Mai Le, Lawrence Liese, Martha Sue Skinner, and Alberta Wu. We also want to acknowledge the helpful comments and insights offered by graduate students in our courses on minority mental health from 1981 through 1988. We further express our thanks to James Steele, Norma Harrison, and all of the office staff who were so cooperative in facilitating our work in countless ways. To Gracia Alkema, our editor at Jossey-Bass, we express our deep appreciation for her belief in this project, her consistent support and patience, and her prompt and insightful feedback.

Our special thanks to Sharon Ikami, who typed several versions of this manuscript with such professionalism, patience, and graciousness. We wish also to acknowledge the indirect contributions of the professors who taught us and the clinicians who supervised us during our graduate and postgraduate training in clinical and community psychology at the University of California, Berkeley (J.T.G.), Yale University (L.N.H.), Mt. Zion Hospital in San Francisco (J.T.G.), Stanford University (J.T.G.), George Washington University Medical Center (J.T.G.), and Langley Porter Psychiatric Institute, University of California Medical Center, San Francisco (L.N.H.).

We are grateful to our families and friends for their unwavering support and sustenance throughout the two years of our intense involvement in this project: Leonard and Dorothy Nahme, Andrew and Diana Huang, Donna N. Salcetti, Scott Ren Nahme, Earnestine Singletary, Phyllis Elperin Clark, and all of the Taylor clan and the Gibbs extended family in the San Francisco Bay area. To our respective spouses, James and Kirk, and to our children, Geoffrey, Lowell, Christina, and Kevin, we owe a special debt of gratitude for their patience and forbearance.

Finally, this volume is the culmination of a joint effort between two friends and colleagues from different ethnicities and backgrounds. We have learned much from and about each other, and in the spirit of diversity, our own lives have been enriched and the bonds of friendship and knowledge strengthened through this relationship.

J.T.G.

L.N.H.

The Authors

Jewelle Taylor Gibbs, a clinical psychologist, is associate professor at the School of Social Welfare, University of California, Berkeley. She received her A.B. degree *cum laude* from Radcliffe College and subsequently was awarded an M.S.W. degree in social work, an M.A. degree in psychology, and a Ph.D. degree in clinical psychology from the University of California, Berkeley. Prior to her academic career, Gibbs was employed as a clinical social worker for five years at Cowell Student Health Center, Stanford University. She has served on the board of directors of the American Orthopsychiatric Association, as well as on the editorial board of the *American Journal of Orthopsychiatry.* She is currently a member of the Advisory Board of the National Resource Center for Children in Poverty. A former fellow at the Mary I. Bunting Institute at Radcliffe College, Gibbs was the recipient of the 1987 McCormick Award from the American Association of Suicidology for her contributions in the area of minority suicide. The author of numerous chapters and journal articles on adolescent psychosocial problems and minority mental health issues, she is also the editor of and major contributor to *Young, Black and Male in America: An Endangered Species* (1988).

Larke Nahme Huang, a clinical-community psychologist, currently on leave for childrearing, was assistant professor at the School of Social Welfare, University of California, Berkeley. Huang received her A.B. degree with high honors from the University of Maryland and her M.S. and Ph.D. degrees in psychology from Yale University. She completed a two-year clinical fellowship at the Langley Porter Psychiatric Institute of the University of California Medical School, San Francisco. Her research and teaching interests include cultural pluralism and minority mental health issues, as well as the acculturation process for minority children and refugees. Her clinical practice includes both Asian and non-Asian young adults, adolescents, and families and clinical supervision of psychology interns. Huang has served as a grants reviewer for the National Institute of Mental Health, as cochair of the Advisory Board for the National Asian American Psychology Training Center, as a consultant for the Head Start In-Depth Validation Program, and as a member of the Governor's Advisory Committee on the Policy Implications of California's Increasing Minority Populations.

LaRue Allen, a clinical psychologist, received her A.B. degree *cum laude* from Radcliffe College and her Ph.D. degree in clinical-community psychology from Yale University. She is currently associate professor of psychology at the University of Maryland's College Park campus. Allen is also a faculty affiliate at the Bush Center for Child Development and Social Policy at Yale University and conducts research on coping and adjustment in children and adolescents with a special focus on developmentally disabled and chronically ill children.

D. Gloria Herron, a native of Cuba, received her B.S. degree from Indiana University and her M.S. degree in psychology from Purdue University. She is currently a doctoral candidate in clinical psychology at Fairleigh Dickinson University. Herron completed a two-year clinical internship at New York University–Bellevue Medical Center in New York City. On completion of her Ph.D. degree, she plans to work with children and families and to serve the Hispanic community.

Jaime E. Inclán, a clinical psychologist with a private practice specializing in family therapy, received his B.A. degree from Georgetown University. A native of Puerto Rico, he later received his Ph.D. degree in clinical psychology from New York University, followed by postgraduate training in family therapy. Since 1983, Inclán has served as director of the Roberto Clemente Family Guidance Center at Gouverneur Hospital, New York City, and he is currently clinical assistant professor of psychiatry at the New York University School of Medicine. He has held appointments as a member of Governor Cuomo's Commission on the Future of Mental Health, as vice-president of the Association of Hispanic Mental Health Professionals, and as a member of the board of directors of the American Orthopsychiatric Association. Inclán is the author of numerous articles on family therapy training and minority mental health.

Teresa D. LaFromboise, a counseling psychologist, received her master's degree from the University of North Dakota and her Ph.D. degree in counseling psychology from the University of Oklahoma. She is currently assistant professor of counseling psychology in the School of Education, Stanford University. Her area of specialization is social skills training for American Indian bicultural competence.

Kathryn Graff Low is a doctoral candidate in counseling psychology at the School of Education, Stanford University. Low received her master's degree from Harvard University and is currently an intern in the Department of Behavioral Medicine at Stanford University.

Shayda Majidi-Ahi received her Ph.D. degree in clinical psychology from the Department of Psychology, University of Maryland, College Park. She is currently a postdoctoral fellow at the Massachusetts Mental Health Center in Boston.

Donna K. Nagata, a clinical psychologist, received her Ph.D. degree in clinical psychology from the University of Illinois, Champaign–Urbana. She is currently assistant professor of psychology at Smith College. Nagata has a part-time private practice specializing in the treatment of children and also conducts research on Japanese Americans and family interaction.

Oscar Ramirez, a clinical psychologist, received his B.A. degree from the University of Texas, Austin, and his M.A. and Ph.D. degrees in clinical psychology from the University of Michigan, Ann Arbor. Ramirez is currently clinical assistant professor of psychiatry at the University of Texas Health Science Center, San Antonio. He also has a private practice specializing in work with children, adolescents, and families, with a particular emphasis on child sexual abuse.

Yu-Wen Ying, a clinical psychologist, is currently assistant professor at the School of Social Welfare, University of California, Berkeley. She received her B.A. degree *magna cum laude* from Barnard College of Columbia University. Ying, a native of Taiwan, received her doctorate in clinical psychology from the University of California, Berkeley, after which she completed a postdoctoral internship at Mount Zion Hospital and Medical Center in San Francisco. Ying, who has a small private practice, conducts research on Asian American mental health issues.

Children of Color

*Psychological Interventions
with Minority Youth*

1

A Conceptual Framework for Assessing and Treating Minority Youth

Jewelle Taylor Gibbs
Larke Nahme Huang

The field of minority mental health has grown rapidly since it was fostered by the community mental health movement in the late 1960s. Although the movement has spawned dozens of books on a range of minority mental health issues, nearly all these books have focused on the problems of minority adults and families. Minority children and youth, despite their growing numbers in the population, have generally been neglected in the mental health literature.

Between 1960 and 1985, the proportion of non-Whites in the United States population has increased dramatically. Demographers predict that non-White and Spanish-speaking youth under age 18 will constitute 30 percent of the nation's youth population in the year 2000 and 38 percent by 2020 (U.S. Bureau of the Census, 1987). These population changes and projected trends result largely from four factors: increased immigration from Latin America, Asia, and the Caribbean, higher birthrates of these immigrant groups and resident minority groups, increased longevity of the minority population, and lower birthrates of the resident White population.

1

These population trends have created a "demographic imperative" for the social institutions that serve youth to modify their traditional programs and services in order to serve these minority youth more effectively (Ozawa, 1986). The impact of this changing population has already been felt by schools, social services, health and mental health agencies, juvenile probation services, and all other family- and youth-oriented programs. For example, non-White youth constituted over 50 percent of the public school population in California by the fall of 1988 and well over half the students in many large urban school districts throughout the country ("Anglos Becoming School Minority," 1988). As the population of minority youth continues to grow, it has become increasingly clear that most of the human service and mental health professionals who serve them do not have adequate information, applicable training, or appropriate resources to address their problems and needs. This gap is particularly acute in urban areas, where high rates of poverty among minority groups contribute to social isolation and social disorganization, further magnifying ethnic and cultural differences (Edelman, 1987; Wilson, 1987).

In 1978 the President's Commission on Mental Health noted that low-income minority children and adolescents were particularly at risk for psychological disorders and behavioral problems because of their low socioeconomic status, their often stressful environments, and their lack of access to mental health services. A decade later, this situation has not measurably improved, and children of color are still triply disadvantaged by their ethnicity, their poverty, and their social isolation (Children's Defense Fund, 1987; Rodgers, 1986).

Our purpose in this book is to provide a balanced and comprehensive overview of psychological intervention with minority children and adolescents experiencing psychological and behavioral problems. Toward this end, we will (1) provide basic demographic and sociocultural information about these minority youth, (2) present data on the incidence of behavioral and psychological disorders in these groups, and (3) propose an ecological and culturally sensitive framework for psychosocial assessment and treatment of these youth. Rather than presenting a comprehensive survey of all possible treatment modalities for children and adolescents, we concentrate on clients seen in outpatient clinical settings, where the great majority of these young people are treated.

We focus on school-age children and youth from age 5 through age 21 in several major ethnic minority groups in the United States: Asians, Blacks, Hispanics, and Native Americans. In recognition of the diversity within the Asian and Hispanic populations, separate chapters are devoted to two of the largest ethnic groups within each of these categories—Chinese American and Japanese American youth representing Asians, and Mexican American and mainland Puerto Rican youth representing Hispanics. In addition, there are chapters on the unique experiences and problems of refugee children from Southeast Asia and of biracial children and adolescents.

We chose these particular groups for several reasons. First, the six ethnic groups are among the largest minority groups with a long period of residence in the United States. Second, there is a significant data base on these groups, which includes ethnographic, demographic, empirical, and clinical studies. Third, these groups represent a continuum of acculturation from the most assimilated (Japanese Americans) to the least assimilated (American Indian), with a wide spectrum between these extremes, reflecting different patterns of migration, different degrees of bilingualism, and different levels of adaptation to mainstream customs, values, and behaviors. Additionally, these groups represent contrasting demographic trends, from Chinese Americans and Hispanic Americans, who are rapidly increasing in the population, to Japanese Americans and Black Americans, who are stabilizing or declining in numbers or as a proportion of the population.

Each of these groups harbors great diversity in migration history, socioeconomic status, level of acculturation, life-style, values, and behaviors. While acknowledging this diversity, we have emphasized the shared history, cultural traditions, and social experiences of each of these groups vis-à-vis the dominant society. There may be greater differences between some Hispanic and non-Hispanic Blacks, for example, or between American Indians from different tribal backgrounds, than between some members of these groups and some White Americans. It is not our intention to create or reinforce stereotypes or myths about any of these groups but, rather, to present the available information that will inform mental health clinicians about some central characteristics of a group's cultural heritage so that they can deliver more effective and culturally sensitive services to its youth and their families.

Our Conceptual Framework

This book is organized around three primary conceptual perspectives: a developmental perspective, an ecological perspective, and a cross-cultural, or minority mental health, perspective.

Developmental Perspective. The developmental perspective provides a framework for examining the influence of race and ethnicity on the psychosocial tasks of growing up in American society. Although maturational processes are undeniably universal and occur with only minor variations across racial and cultural groups, many social science researchers have shown that these processes are subject to wide ethnic variations in their behavioral manifestations, their symbolic meanings, and their societal responses (Phinney and Rotheram, 1987).

Erikson (1959) proposes that there are five psychosocial stages from birth to late adolescence, each one posing a specific developmental challenge for the growing child to master. The outcome of each stage is determined by an interaction of the individual's personality attributes, relationships with significant others, and opportunities available in the environment. Successful resolution of the psychosocial crises in the first five stages depends on a favorable interaction of these three variables and will result in a balance of the sense of trust over mistrust in the infant, autonomy over shame and doubt in the toddler, initiative over guilt in the preschool child, industry over inferiority in the latency-aged child, and identity consolidation over identity diffusion in the adolescent. In discussing these psychosocial crises, Erikson points out that children from minority and low-income backgrounds may experience more difficulties in achieving these positive outcomes because of prejudice, discrimination, or barriers to full opportunity for personal growth.

It is important to note two major contributions of Erikson's theory to the study of minority children and youth, as well as to recognize certain limitations in the theory. First, this framework enables mental health clinicians to evaluate the child's level of psychosocial development at various ages on the basis of certain salient characteristics such as independence, competence, interpersonal skills, and sense of personal identity. Second, the framework is useful for assessing the child's relationships with significant others (such as parents, teachers, and peers) and adjustment to the environment (for example, home, school, and community).

Although Erikson's stage-related theory of psychosocial development is quite relevant for children reared in nuclear families in highly industrialized societies, it may be less applicable to children reared in extended families in nonindustrial societies where different psychosocial outcomes might be emphasized. Awareness of this potential bias is an important caveat in assessing specific characteristics in children of recent immigrants and those reared on reservations or in other culturally homogeneous environments.

A second major limitation of Erikson's theory is its assumption that the self-concept and the self-esteem of minority children are significantly affected by the stigma of membership in a devalued ethnic group. This assumption is contradicted by the work of Mead (1934), who proposes that a child develops self-esteem and a self-concept from the reflected appraisals of family and close relatives and friends and not from the broader society, which only later affects the adolescent leaving the relative social insulation of his or her family and ethnic community. Recent surveys of the literature on the self-esteem of minority children and adolescents support the view that their self-esteem is as high as or higher than their White peers' (Powell, 1985; Rosenberg and Simmons, 1971; Taylor, 1976).

In spite of these limitations, Erikson's conceptual scheme provides the clinician with a framework for viewing important areas of psychosocial growth and development. By complementing this scheme with the ecological and cross-cultural perspectives, the clinician will obtain a more comprehensive and differentiated view of minority youth.

Ecological Perspective. The ecological perspective as proposed by Bronfenbrenner (1979) is useful in viewing the growing child and adolescent as an active agent in a series of interlocking systems, ranging from the microsystems of the family and the school to the macrosystem of governmental social and economic policies. Each of these systems poses risks and opportunities for the child or adolescent interacting with the environment at successive developmental stages. This ecological perspective is especially relevant in analyzing the impact of poverty, discrimination, immigration, and social isolation on the psychosocial development and adjustment of minority children and youth.

Recent research on poor families has shown that poverty has a negative impact on nearly all aspects of their children's lives, including nutrition, health care, housing, education, and recreation (American Public Welfare Association, 1986; Rodgers, 1986; Schorr, 1986). When children are both poor and members of ethnic minorities, the negative and long-term impact of poverty increases significantly (Wilson and Aponte, 1985; Committee for Economic Development, 1987; Edelman, 1987). Recent immigration status and language problems are additional sources of stress for children of immigrants and refugees, who must cope not only with adjustment to a strange new culture but also with the loss of their native land and indigenous culture (Sluzki, 1979).

Historical, economic, and political realities shape the macrosystem of minority youth. For example, Asian and Hispanic immigrants are often compared to European immigrants of the late nineteenth and early twentieth centuries, but these contemporary non-White immigrants and their children encounter a very different set of attitudes and experiences from the dominant society than the earlier waves of White immigrants. Second, structural changes in the economy and technological changes in the work force have resulted in high unemployment among minority adults, many of whom lack the education or skills to compete in a highly industrialized urban economy (Wilson and Aponte, 1985). Third, since the demise of the War on Poverty, political attitudes have become more conservative, and there has been a backlash against affirmative action programs in employment and higher education. All these trends have hit low-income minority families hard, acting as stressors that diminish their ability to provide a stable and nurturant environment for their children (Edelman, 1987). In spite of these ecological stressors, these families have shown remarkable resilience, creativity, and competence in meeting the tasks of socializing their children in an often hostile and alien environment.

The ecological perspective is also useful in assessing a child's psychosocial functioning in the family, the school, the peer group, and the community. The impact of these systems on minority youth cannot be overestimated, since they form the setting for socialization. As Huang points out in Chapter Nine, in families who have recently immigrated, children and adolescents are often in conflict between two competing sets of values and norms, which require them to develop one set of behaviors in the family setting and another set in school and community settings. When these behaviors are diametrically opposed, emotional stress inevitably results. It may be expressed in somatic symptoms, behavior disorders, school adjustment problems, delinquency, depression, or suicidal behavior.

Cross-Cultural Perspective. The cross-cultural perspective, developed by anthropologists to establish a comparative framework for the analysis of all human societies, assumes that all behavior has meaning and serves some adaptive function; behavior is also governed by a set of rules and norms that promote stability and harmony within a society. Dysfunctional or deviant behavior, as defined by the group, disrupts group functioning and must be regulated by some type of institutionalized control mechanism, such as shamans, spiritualists, faith healers, or mental health practitioners (Price-Williams, 1975).

Many minority mental health researchers have used this cross-cultural perspective to provide a comparative context for viewing psychological phenomena among diverse ethnic groups in the United States (Green, 1982; Jones and Korchin, 1982; Marsella and Pedersen, 1981). Although these efforts are still in their infancy, research on mental health in a variety of ethnic groups has encompassed a wide range of topics, including attitudes toward mental health and mental illness; belief systems about the causes of mental illness and dysfunctional behavior; differential symptomatology, defensive patterns, and coping strategies; help-seeking behaviors; utilization of services; and responsiveness to treatment.

Ethnicity and Mental Health

Research on minority mental health has documented the numerous ways that ethnicity influences the psychological well-being of minority adults and families, but little attention has been paid to its influence on the developing child and adolescent, with a few notable exceptions (see, for example, Powell, Yamamoto, Romero, and Morales, 1983; Phinney and Rotheram, 1987). Obviously, such influences are mediated to children through their parents and other significant adults in their immediate social environment.

First, ethnicity shapes the child's belief system about what constitutes mental health and mental illness, encompassing both general criteria and specific behaviors.

Second, ethnicity influences the child's manifestation of symptoms, defensive styles, and patterns of coping with anxiety, depression, fear, guilt, and anger. Some ethnic groups reinforce "acting in" neurotic symptoms, others reward "acting out" characterological symptoms, and still others reward somatic symptoms. Children learn patterns of illness and dysfunctional behavior that are culturally reinforced and tolerated.

Third, ethnicity largely determines help-seeking patterns that parents use to seek relief for children or adolescents with dysfunctional behaviors or symptoms. Parents may, for example, consult a priest or minister, a spiritualist or native healer, an herbalist or acupuncturist, or a tribal council or family elder.

Fourth, ethnicity is a major factor shaping the way the child or adolescent utilizes and responds to treatment. Initial

· how is ethnicity a major factor in shaping the way an adolescent utilizes and responds to treatment?

level of trust and openness, attitude toward self-disclosure, willingness to discuss certain topics, motivation to participate in insight-oriented treatment—all these aspects of the treatment relationship are filtered through the screen of ethnicity.

Sue and Sue (1977) have identified three sets of variables that are important to assess in minority clients: culture-bound variables, language-bound variables, and class-bound variables. These variables are particularly relevant for children and adolescents, whose daily lives are circumscribed by their family and community experiences. In order to conduct an adequate assessment of the young client, the clinicians should have some knowledge of the family's cultural background, attitudes, norms, and child-rearing practices; some familiarity with the family's language, immigration history, belief systems, and level of acculturation; and an understanding of how socioeconomic status affects the family's life-style, community experiences, opportunities, and aspirations.

Ethnicity, Social Class, and Adaptation. The term *ethnicity* has been defined in a variety of ways, but it will be used here to mean membership in a group of people "who share a unique social and cultural heritage that is passed on from generation to generation" (Mindel and Habenstein, 1981, p. 5). Green (1982, p. 9) further points out that "members of an ethnic group believe themselves to be distinctive from others in some significant way." Race and ethnicity are not identical, but they often overlap, as with Chinese Americans or Black Americans. Hispanics, in contrast, are defined by their common cultural heritage (Latin American) and their language (Spanish), but they may be White, Black, or Indian or a mixture of all three.

Membership in an ethnic group provides a cultural identity and a set of prescribed values, norms, and social behaviors for an individual. Ethnic identity provides a significant framework through which the growing child views the self, the world, and future opportunities. It also gives meaning to the child's subjective experiences, structure to interpersonal relationships, and form to behaviors and activities. For example, ethnicity may be a determining factor in what kind of family a child grows up in, what language she will speak first, what kind of neighborhood she lives in, what church she attends (if any), what school she attends, and what role models are available.

Ethnic identity, when combined with membership in a minority race, creates a dual challenge to a child or adolescent. In a country where the dominant majority is Caucasian, there are many White ethnic groups, such as the Jews, the Poles, the Irish, and the Italians (Mindel and Habenstein, 1981). Members of these groups can practice their cultural customs in their homes and their places of worship, but they can also blend into the mainstream social institutions, such as schools, businesses and professional activities, and government. However, minority groups of color are visibly identified by their physical or linguistic differences. Minority groups have been defined as "those groups that have unequal access to power, that are considered in some way unworthy of sharing power equally, and that are stigmatized in terms of assumed inferior traits or characteristics" (Mindel and Habenstein, 1981, p. 8). Minority status has historically been associated with a more restricted range of options in education, employment, and life-style, as well as reduced opportunities for mobility and success in the wider society (Omi and Winant, 1986). Thus, children growing up in minority families are not only exposed to different family dynamics, school experiences, and community responses than children from White families, but they are also confronted with social and economic barriers that profoundly influence their opportunities.

Social class is another dimension that describes and defines the child's world by ascribing a particular position and value to his family's socioeconomic status (SES). The family's SES will largely determine the child's social environment, life-style, level of education attained, and occupational aspirations. For an adolescent, social class will also influence choice of friends, activities, and social roles. Thus, membership in a social class provides boundaries within which the growing child and adolescent will experience a restricted range of opportunities, choices, and challenges in particular social contexts.

In American society there is an important interrelationship between ethnicity, race, and social class. High status is associated with membership in White, Anglo-Saxon, middle-class families; low status is associated with membership in non-White, ethnic minority, lower-class families. It follows that children and adolescents in many Asian, Black, Hispanic, and Indian families are triply stigmatized in American society because they differ from the ideal norm in three major respects: They are non-White by race (except for Spanish-speaking Whites), non–Anglo-Saxon by ethnicity, and predominantly non-middle-class by socioeconomic status.

An Interactive Model. It is obvious that the developmental, ecological, and cross-cultural perspectives overlap considerably and may be conceived more parsimoniously as three interacting dimensions of the child's life experience. We propose that ethnicity is the overarching dimension that provides the child with a framework for perceiving and responding to the world; shapes the child's personal and social identity; establishes values, norms, and expectations for appropriate behaviors; and defines parameters for choices and opportunities for the child's social, educational, and occupational experiences. Ethnicity is a major influence on the child's socialization in the family, providing the structures through which developmental tasks are mediated. Moreover, ethnicity has a significant impact on the way the child is perceived and treated in the school, by peers, and in the broader community.

It is also important to point out that parents from different ethnic groups may use different criteria to measure independence, competence, and interpersonal skills, and they may differentially value these behaviors as relevant or irrelevant to the child's successful adaptation to the social environment. Thus, their child-rearing practices reflect broad diversity in the techniques used to socialize children according to the belief system, values, and norms of their ethnic group. DeAnda (1984) has described the process of bicultural socialization, through which minority parents teach their children how to function in two distinct sociocultural environments. She posits six factors that influence the outcome of this process of dual socialization: (1) the degree to which the two cultures share norms, values, perceptions, and beliefs, (2) the availability of cultural translators, mediators, and models, (3) the amount and type of corrective feedback provided by each culture about one's behaviors in that culture, (4) the congruence of the minority individual's conceptual and problem-solving style with that of the mainstream culture, (5) the individual's degree of bilingualism, and (6) the degree of similarity in physical appearance to the mainstream culture. DeAnda's model of bicultural socialization illustrates how the developmental, ecological, and cross-cultural frameworks can be combined to understand the socialization of ethnic minority children.

Implications for Assessment

An understanding of these three overlapping perspectives offers a comprehensive framework for the clinician to assess the five major domains of the functioning of the child or adolescent: individual level of psychosocial adjustment, relationships with family, school adjustment and achievement, relationships with peers, and adaptation to the community (Oldham, Looney, and Blotcky, 1980; Looney and Lewis, 1983).

Individual Psychosocial Adjustment. There are a number of areas in which variations in individual development have significant implications for the child's psychosocial adjustment and, therefore, implications for psychological evaluation. These areas are physical appearance, affect, self-concept, and self-esteem; interpersonal competence; attitudes toward autonomy; attitudes toward achievement; management of aggression and impulse control; and coping and defense mechanisms.

• *Physical appearance.* In evaluating the physical appearance of the minority child or adolescent, the clinician must bear in mind that low-income minority children often suffer from malnutrition, which causes stunted growth, low hemoglobin levels, and skin and hair problems (Kovar, 1982; Egbuono and Starfield, 1982). Diet can also affect energy level, sleep, and elimination, so a complete physical examination may be indicated to rule out physiological causes of emotional and behavioral problems. In addition, variations from the preferred Anglo norms in height, weight, or physique can cause stress for minority children and adolescents.

• *Affect.* Affective expression in children is influenced by cultural norms, so that some children appear to be more animated while others are more reserved. Culturally appropriate norms of expressing affect should not be confused with lack of affect or depressed affect. Similarly, direct eye contact between children and adults is discouraged in some ethnic groups, so that looking away should not be interpreted as a sign of disrespect or evasiveness.

• *Self-concept and self-esteem.* Groups vary in the value they attach to particular characteristics and abilities, which become the sources of self-concept and self-esteem for the child and adolescent. It is important for the clinician to know the differential value placed on specific attributes within each ethnic group in order to evaluate the minority youth's criteria for self-evaluation.

• *Interpersonal competence.* Ethnic groups also vary in the values attached to certain kinds of interpersonal skills. Behaviors that are highly valued and reinforced in one group may be considered inappropriate in other groups. Clinicians should be familiar with the norms of interpersonal competence in each group in order to determine whether a child or adolescent is behaving in appropriate ways in his or her sociocultural milieu.

• *Attitudes toward autonomy.* Parents in different ethnic groups place differential emphasis on early training for independence and later encouragement of adolescent autonomy. In evaluating parental attitudes toward autonomy, the clinician must have sufficient knowledge of the ethnic values toward independence training at each level of development in order to determine whether the family has respected or violated its own cultural norms concerning the development of autonomy, whether the family's norms are in serious conflict with the norms of the child's school or community environment, and whether the degree of dependence or autonomy is adaptive within the youth's overall life situation (Phinney and Rotheram, 1987).

• *Attitudes toward achievement.* Cultural attitudes toward educational achievement vary widely among ethnic groups as a function of historical traditions, philosophical systems, opportunity structures, and school-related experiences.

Groups that have been cut off from their original cultures through slavery or forced relocation have been divorced from a meaningful connection with their past cultural achievements. Subjected further to continuing barriers to social mobility, these parents frequently subscribe to the value of education but find it difficult to demonstrate the connection between education and occupational success to their children. Often the achievement motive will be expressed in other ways for these youth, and their aspirations will be shaped accordingly.

In evaluating achievement attitudes and behaviors in minority youth, the clinician should not only examine traditional channels of educational achievement but should also include other areas such as sports, music, and social relationships. When minority youth are referred for academic or behavioral problems in the classroom, their failure often reflects low teacher expectations, chaotic school environments, inflexible or inappropriate curricula, or inappropriate placement (Reed, 1988). The clinician should assess achievement motives, interests, aptitudes, and abilities and try to determine how best to facilitate a match between the client's motives and abilities and the available role models and opportunities.

• *Management of aggression and impulse control.* There is great ethnic variation in the socialization practices that families use to teach children how to channel their aggressive and sexual impulses. Some minority parents typically induce shame in order to teach children appropriate ways to manage their impulses; others prefer to induce guilt in order to achieve the same goal. Still other parents use harsher methods of discipline to create external sanctions for inappropriate expressions of aggression and sexuality. These different approaches have implications for the development of internal controls, the ability to delay gratification, and the choice of subliminatory channels.

• *Coping and defense mechanisms.* Parents from different ethnic groups employ culturally prescribed strategies to teach children how to cope with anxiety. The two basic strategies are to reinforce externalizing (acting out) behaviors or internalizing (acting in) behaviors as a defense against anxiety. The clinician should be familiar with the cultural preference in handling anxiety, the defense mechanisms that are reinforced, and the adaptive strategies that are used to handle stress.

An important caveat cannot be stated too frequently throughout this book: The clinician should always use knowledge about a child's ethnic background as a *general* guide to psychosocial assessment but should always be mindful of the individual child's unique characteristics, situation, symptoms, defenses, and coping strategies.

Family Relationships. Roles and functions of children in families vary according to the family's structure, size, traditions, communication patterns, and expectations, all of which are influenced by ethnicity and social class (Mindel and Habenstein, 1981; McGoldrick, Pearce, and Giordano, 1982). Sex and birth order of the child frequently impose a set of norms and expectations that prescribe appropriate behaviors and attitudes for that child. Physical characteristics such as skin color, physical or mental disability, and certain personality traits may be irrelevant to the child's status in some families while highly salient in others. Socialization practices in the preschool years result in a broad spectrum of parent/child and sibling relationships in minority families (Phinney and Rotheram, 1987).

Family relationships in some ethnic groups tend to be defined in terms of age and sex-role hierarchies, with a strong emphasis on filial obedience to parental authority, respect for elders, acceptance of male authority, loyalty to the extended family, and strong conformity to community norms and expectations. Other ethnic groups are characterized by greater egalitarianism in age and sex roles; greater emphasis on shared household responsibilities, individual decision making, and flexibility in marital roles; and moderate conformity to community norms and expectations.

In some ethnic families, children assume household chores and child care at earlier ages than is the norm among Anglo families. These roles should not be confused with the premature "parentified" role often assumed by the first-generation immigrant child, who may serve as an interpreter and mediator between parents and the dominant society. "Parentified" children are also found in single-parent families, where they may provide emotional support and companionship as well as household help to an overstressed parent. The clinician should be able to distinguish between children who are fulfilling supportive roles in accordance with their age and abilities and those who are acting inappropriately as substitute parents.

If family communication patterns are hierarchal and children are discouraged from expressing their opinions or engaging in free-flowing conversations, they may have some problems adapting to the teacher's expectations of verbal participation in the classroom. Traditional communication patterns in some ethnic families, for example, are not wholly compatible with the demands of the American educational system, which rewards assertive behavior, verbal fluency, and competitiveness in students (Committee for Economic Development, 1987).

Parental use of authority and disciplinary practices, which varies considerably among different ethnic groups, is reflected in the ways in which their children respond to authority and rule setting. The child who does not fit the ideal cultural familial norm may be scapegoated and identified as "the problem child" or "the difficult child" and may be perceived as the rule breaker and the norm violator.

School Adjustment and Achievement. As the second major institution of socialization for latency-aged children and adolescents in American society, school is an important arena for the evaluation of a child's adjustment. There are four broad areas in which the child's school adjustment should be measured: psychological adjustment to the school setting, behavioral adjustment in the school setting, academic achievement, and relationships with peers.

• *Psychological adjustment.* Minority children, particularly those from low-income families, often experience difficulties making the transition from home to school. A number of factors may account for their problems with this transition: parental lack of education, negative parental attitudes or experiences with the school system, lack of familiarity with the norms and expectations of the classroom, language problems, and social-class differences (Dokecki and others, 1975). In latency-aged children, this lack of fit between the child's background and the school environment may be reflected in separation anxiety, school phobia, somatic symptoms, sleeping and eating problems, enuresis, and depression.

In adolescents, school phobia or truancy may actually represent fear of a violent or chaotic school environment or fear of social rejection due to some cultural, racial, or economic difference from the majority of the student body. For many minority adolescents, the transition from elementary school to the middle school or junior high school is stressful because they leave a neighborhood school where they form a majority of the students for a larger school where they may become a numerical minority, a process that is repeated in the transition from junior high to high school. Rosenberg (1979), discussing the stress of being a minority adolescent in a dissonant social context, points out how this situation can impair a teenager's self-concept and self-esteem. Such a transition also typically requires the adolescent to become accustomed to a new set of criteria for evaluating academic competence, social skills, and extracurricular abilities. These new standards of evaluation can create considerable anxiety and depression for minority students who have previously excelled in their own neighborhood schools but must adjust to new criteria, which generally place them at an initial disadvantage. School psychologists and social workers who evaluate students for placement in special classes need to take these various factors into account in order to avoid the misidentification of minority students, who are overrepresented in classes for students with emotional problems and learning disabilities (Reed, 1988; Mercer, 1975; Samuda, 1975).

• *Behavioral adjustment.* Minority children and adolescents are also overrepresented in special education classes for children with behavior problems (Reed, 1988; Mercer, 1975; Rivers and others, 1975). While some children are socialized to internalize their anxiety through symptoms of depression, withdrawal, somatization, and phobic behaviors, other children are reinforced for externalizing their anxiety through fighting, acting out, and delinquent behaviors. The incidence of school violence, delinquency, substance abuse, and gang activity is much higher in inner-city schools than in middle-class urban and suburban schools (Children's Defense Fund, 1987; Committee for Economic Development, 1987). More students display disruptive behaviors in the school setting, there are more disciplinary problems for teachers, and there are fewer mental health professionals to handle the referrals. When these students are referred for problem behaviors, the clinician should conduct a careful assessment of their home situation (some do not have adequate sleeping or study facilities), their nutrition (some are hyperactive or lethargic because of poor diets), their family situation (some are victims of child abuse, family violence, or absent parents), and their health status (some have undetected vision, hearing, or other physical problems) (Kovar, 1982; Children's Defense Fund, 1987; Powell, Yamamoto, Romero, and Morales, 1983). A careful evaluation of these students will reveal that behavior problems are usually symptomatic of more serious underlying psychological and physical problems that are often chronic and have been neglected because of poverty, lack of access to health care, and, in some cases, parental unawareness.

  • *Academic achievement.* Low-income minority children and adolescents have generally not performed as well as their majority classmates on standardized achievement tests, in Carnegie units earned toward high school graduation, or in grade-point averages (Reed, 1988; Committee for Economic Development, 1987). As a result, these minority students have had particular difficulties in achieving parity with the non-Hispanic White students in the public school system. This book will not tackle the controversy of the use of intelligence tests with minority students; other researchers have discussed the problems of norms and the inappropriate use of these tests with children from culturally different backgrounds (Mercer, 1975; Samuda, 1975; Snowden and Todman, 1982). Through these test results, many minority students are mislabeled as educationally handicapped, placed in remedial classrooms, and channeled into educational programs that are neither challenging nor useful. This misplacement probably contributes to the feelings of alienation among many minority students, who have higher dropout rates and higher rates of expulsions and suspensions than White students (Reed, 1988; Children's Defense Fund, 1987).

Clinicians assessing the academic performance of minority youth should pay careful attention to their verbal skills (they may have much greater fluency in their native language), their attitudes toward school (they may feel stigmatized by placement in a special education class), their motivation for learning (they may see no relation between school and the "real world"), their study habits (they may not have a safe and quiet place to study at home or a schedule for studying), and their level of family support (their parents may not be able or willing to assist in and reinforce efforts to succeed academically). Since poor academic achievement is more often a consequence of cultural, social, and environmental factors than of lack of ability, a sensitive clinician can identify factors that impede the performance of minority students and can develop an intervention plan to improve their academic skills.

• *Relationships with peers.* Finally, the child's relationships with peers in the school setting should be evaluated, since it is easier to obtain independent ratings of peer interactions in the school than in the community setting. The clinician should assess the child's ability to form friendships, to display empathy, to engage in cooperative and competitive activities in the classroom and in extracurricular activities, to manage aggressive and sexual impulses, and to engage in socially appropriate same-sex and mixed-sex activities.

As minority children move into adolescence and enter schools with more heterogeneous student bodies, they are more likely to become aware of their particular ethnic or minority status and its associated degree of desirability. Biracial and bicultural adolescents may have particular problems with joining a peer group, since they do not fit into the rigid ethnic categories that define peer-group membership in adolescence. At this stage, it is also important to assess the formal and informal labels and identity of a peer group to which the adolescent belongs, as these labels supply valuable clues to the teen's self-perception and preferred activities. The minority teenager's choice of extracurricular activities and the level of involvement is also an important clue to self-confidence, sense of competence, and degree of comfort in relating to peers.

Relationships with Peers in the Community. In addition
to the child's peer relations at school, relationships with peers in
the neighborhood and community should also be evaluated. Minority children and adolescents very often have two sets of peer
relationships, one in the school setting and another in the community setting. The latter peers are more likely to be from their
own ethnic group in their immediate neighborhood, attending
their church and participating in their community activities (for
example, Black History Week, Chinese New Year's, Cinco de
Mayo Festival). Thus, the usual question about having a best
friend should include school and neighborhood to determine
the primary locus of the child's peer affiliations. Minority children who are social isolates at a predominantly White school
may be sociometric stars in their segregated neighborhood.
Moreover, adolescents are more mobile and can select their
friends from a wider geographical area, so inquiries should be
made about the scope of their social networks. For teens referred for problem behaviors, substance abuse, or delinquency,
the clinician should determine whether these behaviors represent individual maladaptation or whether they represent conformity to the peer-group culture of many inner-city ghettos
and barrios. The choice of intervention for a teenager who is a
socialized delinquent will be very different than for one who is
an antisocial delinquent (Gibbs, 1982; Gold and Petronio, 1980).
Assessment of peer relationships should focus on the social
skills of the adolescent as defined by the ethnic group—that is,
using whatever criteria that group uses to measure social competence, group acceptance, and group leadership.

In the area of peer relationships, sexual relationships in
adolescents are an important area of assessment. The clinician
should inquire about dating practices, sexual preference, involvement in sexual activity, attitudes toward contraception,
knowledge about sexually transmitted diseases, and issues of
intraracial versus interracial dating, particularly for biracial and
bicultural youth.

Adaptation to the Community. The latency-aged minority child's experiences in the community usually revolve around
church activities, youth groups, and language schools. Involvement in these activities should be assessed to obtain a complete

picture of the child's areas of interest, mobility in the community, sense of security about nonfamily activities, behavioral adjustment, and quality of relationships with other adult authority figures. Minority children are sometimes token members of community groups, including children's drama, dance, and music groups, which can be prestigeful for their parents but stressful for them. They are sometimes scapegoated by other children who subtly reward them for assuming the role of the group's clown, rebel, or victim. Alternatively, a meaningful community activity can provide the minority child with a sense of competence and special skills that may not be available in the school or home situation. It is important for the clinician to determine the role and function of the child in community activities, which can either enhance development or siphon off energy that could be more productively directed in the regular school setting.

The adolescent's role in the community expands to include the possibility of work, organized sports and arts activities, and volunteer activities. If a teenager has a part-time or full-time job, it may be essential to assess job performance, interaction with employers and co-workers, and management of money. Minority adolescents often have problems finding jobs, and this difficulty affects their sense of self-worth and their ability to develop good work habits (Sum, Harrington, and Goedicke, 1987; Larson, 1988). If the adolescent is involved in any major activity such as an athletic team, a drama group, a rock band, or a volunteer group, the clinician should assess the impact of this activity on self-concept, sense of competence, and educational and occupational aspirations. The clinician should also determine whether this involvement has created any family conflicts, affected academic performance, or contributed to any dysfunctional behavior such as delinquency or drug abuse.

Implications for Treatment

The distinction between assessment and treatment is often artificial, since many clinicians believe that treatment begins with the first contact with the client. For the sake of this discussion, the assessment process is separated from treatment on the assumption that some children and adolescents will not be referred for psychological treatment but instead will be offered alternative options, such as medication or environmental modification of a family, school, or peer system.

A number of studies have shown that minority clients have higher dropout rates than Whites in the initial stages of treatment. Clinicians should therefore be particularly alert to the issues of involving minority children and youth in the treatment process after an initial diagnostic assessment and treatment recommendation has been completed (Sue, 1977). Clinicians who adopt the multidimensional conceptual framework outlined earlier will be more effective in selecting and implementing appropriate interventions for minority youth. If these youth are referred for psychological treatment, we propose that certain issues must be addressed irrespective of the therapist's theoretical framework or the treatment modality (for example, individual, group, or family treatment). These issues, though common to all therapeutic encounters, take on special significance in the treatment of children of color, and they will be discussed in depth in the following chapters. A brief summary below will highlight the salient issues in culturally sensitive treatment of these youth.

Entry into Treatment. The clinician's initial task is to relieve the child's anxiety and fears about treatment, particularly for minority youth, who are less likely than White youth to have experience with and knowledge about therapy. These clients may also enter treatment with negative attitudes about the helping professions, based on their families' previous experiences with the health and social welfare bureaucracy. Moreover, they may be concerned about being stigmatized by their families, teachers, and peers as "crazy," since formal mental health treatment is still a source of shame and embarrassment for many minority families.

Clinicians have found several strategies to be effective in their initial contacts with these clients. First, some minority youth respond favorably to an informal, friendly style wherein the clinician chats with them to put them at ease. Called *personalismo* by Hispanics and "interpersonal competence" by others, this approach defuses anxiety and establishes initial rapport (Muñoz, 1982; Gibbs, 1985). Other youth, however, may prefer a more formal style of authority. Second, the traditional sex- and age-role relationships of the particular ethnic group should be respected if a child is initially interviewed with the family; this signals the family that the clinician understands and respects their cultural norms, even if the family does not actually conform to those norms. Third, clinicians should offer a brief explanation of therapy, its similarity to familiar roles of healers in the culture (for example, *curandero*, medicine man), and the expectation that it will bring some symptom relief to the client (Acosta, Yamamoto, and Evans, 1982; Frank and others, 1978).

Establishing a Relationship. Having overcome the initial barriers to treatment, the clinician faces the next challenge of establishing a therapeutic alliance with the minority youth. Major issues in the development of this relationship are establishing trust, facilitating open communication, and negotiating boundaries. Trust is a central issue in the treatment of minority clients, who have often been misperceived, mislabeled, and mistreated by other helping professionals. These clients frequently express some degree of "cultural paranoia," initially behaving with suspicion and skepticism in clinical encounters (Gibbs, 1985; Ridley, 1984). Clinicians should consciously communicate warmth and acceptance of these clients, who may be expecting a distancing and superior attitude.

To facilitate open communication of information and feelings, the clinician should be willing to share some limited personal information. Minority clients will vary in their degree of self-disclosure, but generally they are not as comfortable as Anglo clients in discussing their inner feelings and the intimate details of their lives. By respecting their pace of discussing culturally sensitive topics, the clinician will gradually build rapport and increase the clients' level of self-disclosure over the course of treatment.

As the treatment relationship develops, it will be important for the clinician to negotiate boundaries within which the treatment will occur. These boundaries are an extension of the treatment contract, but they focus more specifically on the client's expectations of the therapist. Since many of these clients are unfamiliar with the therapeutic process as well as the relationship, it is important for clinicians to emphasize confidentiality, to define the relationship in business rather than social terms, and to structure sessions with flexible but clear guidelines. Negotiating boundaries in treatment of minority youth and their families is a process of mutual accommodation between the clinical concerns of the therapist and the cultural norms of the clients.

A Look Forward

Children of color are a population at risk for behavioral and psychological problems because of their minority status, their often low socioeconomic status, and their limited access to health and mental health services. Yet, in spite of their greater vulnerability to problematic outcomes, the majority adapt successfully to their environments and grow up to function effectively as adults. Obviously, many of these children enjoy protective factors that provide effective buffers against the stresses of poverty, prejudice, and social isolation. These protective factors may include extended families, supportive kin and social networks, strong religious beliefs, and traditional sources of help or healing.

The remainder of this book is organized to reflect the experiences of minority groups who have followed different historical pathways in American society. The next nine chapters each focus on a different minority group or special population. Each contributor employs the three primary conceptual perspectives described earlier—developmental, ecological, and cross-cultural—with varying levels of emphasis, but all of them are committed to a person-in-environment approach to the issues in assessment and treatment of minority children and adolescents. This multidimensional conceptual framework allows each author to analyze the interaction of sociocultural, developmental, and environmental factors.

The first two of these chapters describe Chinese American and Japanese American youth, groups categorized by Mindel and Habenstein (1981) as "early-arriving ethnic minorities" because they first immigrated to the United States before 1900. The next four chapters describe American Indians, Black Americans (children and adolescents), and Mexican Americans, categorized by these authors as "historically subjugated but volatile ethnic minorities" because of their history of forced relocation, slavery, or exploited labor. A chapter on mainland Puerto Ricans, categorized as a "recent and continuing ethnic minority," follows. Finally, two chapters concern Southeast Asian refugee youth and biracial adolescents, whom we categorize as "emerging special populations."

The next chapter is a unique attempt to provide a cross-cultural comparison of clinical material. We discuss the responses of the various contributing authors who were asked to comment on a child or adolescent clinical case, with only the ethnicity of the client and the clinician varied. This chapter shows how clinicians' cultural sensitivity can influence their conceptualization of a case, their diagnostic assessment, and their treatment recommendations, particularly when they take into account the sociocultural background of the child or adolescent client.

In the concluding chapter, the similarities and differences among the minority groups are discussed with a view toward implications for a culturally sensitive approach to assessment and treatment of minority youth in general. Three other important issues are also discussed in the final chapter: the need for further research on minority mental health issues, the need for expanded and improved training programs for mental health professionals, and the need for major changes in the mental health service delivery system to meet the needs of this population.

At this point we do not have sufficient valid and reliable data about some ethnic groups to constitute the "final word" on their mental health status, problems, or needs. Yet, as minority populations continue to increase, we cannot wait for more years of research to provide this information in order to address their mental health needs. We believe that this book represents an initial step in helping mental health practitioners and educators to understand how ethnicity and socioeconomic status affect the psychosocial development and adaptation of minority youth. Although we hope clinicians will gain a better understanding of these youth and their families, we must caution them that they will not become experts in minority mental health simply by reading this book. Ideally, clinicians will become more knowledgeable about the particular ethnic groups they serve and more sensitive to the similarities and differences among all human groups.

Children of color are rapidly increasing in American society, and yet they remain misunderstood, mislabeled, and mistreated. This book is a modest effort to increase the understanding of their needs, to improve the assessment of their problems, and to develop more effective methods of intervention and treatment for their behavioral and psychological disorders.

References

Acosta, F. X., Yamamoto, J., and Evans, L. A. *Effective Psychotherapy for Low-Income and Minority Patients.* New York: Plenum, 1982.

American Public Welfare Association. *One Child in Four.* New York: American Public Welfare Association, 1986.

"Anglos Becoming School Minority." *San Francisco Chronicle,* August 22, 1988, p. 1.

Bronfenbrenner, U. *The Ecology of Human Development: Experiments by Nature and Design.* Cambridge, Mass.: Harvard University Press, 1979.

Children's Defense Fund. *A Children's Defense Budget.* Washington, D.C.: Children's Defense Fund, 1987.

Committee for Economic Development. *Children in Need: Investment Strategies for the Educationally Disadvantaged.* New York: Committee for Economic Development, 1987.

deAnda, D. "Bicultural Socialization: Factors Affecting the Minority Experience." *Social Work,* 1984, *29,* 101–107.

Dokecki, P. R., and others. "Low Income and Minority Groups." In N. Hobbs (ed.), *Issues in the Classification of Children: A Sourcebook on Categories, Labels, and Their Consequences.* Vol. 1. San Francisco: Jossey-Bass, 1975.

Egbuono, L., and Starfield, G. "Child Health and Social Status."
    Pediatrics, 1982, *69,* 550–556.

Edelman, M. W. *Families in Peril: An Agenda for Social Change.*
    Cambridge, Mass.: Harvard University Press, 1987.

Erikson, E. H. "Identity and the Life Cycle." *Psychological Is-
    sues,* 1959, *1* (1).

Frank, J. D., and others. *Effective Ingredients of Successful Psy-
    chotherapy.* New York: Brunner/Mazel, 1978.

Gibbs, J. T. "Personality Patterns of Delinquent Females: Eth-
    nic and Sociocultural Variations." *Journal of Clinical Psy-
    chology,* 1982, *38,* 198–206.

Gibbs, J. T. "Treatment Relationships with Black Clients: Inter-
    personal Versus Instrumental Strategies." In C. Germain
    (ed.), *Advances in Clinical Social Work Practice.* Silver Spring,
    Md.: National Association of Social Workers, 1985.

Gold, M., and Petronio, J. "Delinquent Behavior in Adoles-
    cence." In J. Adelson (ed.), *Handbook of Adolescent Psy-
    chology.* New York: Wiley, 1980.

Green, J. W. *Cultural Awareness in the Human Services.* Engle-
    wood Cliffs, N.J.: Prentice-Hall, 1982.

Jones, E. E., and Korchin, S. J. (eds.). *Minority Mental Health.*
    New York: Praeger, 1982.

Kovar, M. G. "Health Status of U.S. Children and Use of Medi-
    cal Care." *Public Health Reports,* 1982, *97,* 3–15.

Larson, T. E. "Employment and Unemployment of Young
    Black Men." In J. T. Gibbs (ed.), *Young, Black, and Male in
    America: An Endangered Species.* Dover, Mass.: Auburn
    House, 1988.

Looney, J. G., and Lewis, J. M. "Competent Adolescents from
    Different Socioeconomic and Ethnic Contexts." *Adolescent
    Psychiatry,* 1983, *11,* 64–74.

Marsella, A. J., and Pederson, P. B. (eds.). *Cross-Cultural Coun-
    seling and Psychotherapy.* Elmsford, N.Y.: Pergamon Press,
    1981.

McGoldrick, M., Pearce, J. K., and Giordano, J. (eds.). *Ethnicity
    and Family Therapy.* New York: Guilford Press, 1982.

Mead. G. H. *Mind, Self, and Society.* Chicago: University of Chi-
    cago Press, 1934.

Mercer, J. "Psychological Assessment and the Rights of Children." In N. Hobbs (ed.), *Issues in the Classification of Children: A Sourcebook on Categories, Labels, and Their Consequences.* Vol. 1. San Francisco: Jossey-Bass, 1975.

Mindel, C. H., and Habenstein, R. W. (eds.). *Ethnic Families in
America: Patterns and Variations.* (2nd ed.) New York: Elsevier, 1981.

Muñoz, R. F. "The Spanish-Speaking Consumer and the Community Mental Health Center." In E. E. Jones and S. J. Korchin
(eds.), *Minority Mental Health.* New York: Praeger, 1982.

Oldham, D. G., Looney, J. G., and Blotcky, M. "Clinical Assessment of Symptoms in Adolescents." *American Journal of
Orthopsychiatry,* 1980, *50,* 697-703.

Omi, M., and Winant, H. *Racial Formation in the United States:
From the 1960's to the 1980's.* Boston: Routledge & Kegan
Paul, 1986.

Ozawa, M. "Nonwhites and the Demographic Imperative in Social Welfare Spending." *Social Work,* 1986, *31,* 440-446.

Phinney, J. S., and Rotheram, M. J. *Children's Ethnic Socialization: Pluralism and Development.* Newbury Park, Calif.:
Sage, 1987.

Powell, G. J. "Self-Concepts Among Afro-American Students in
Racially Isolated Minority Schools: Some Regional Differences." *Journal of the American Academy of Child Psychiatry,* 1985, *24,* 142-149.

Powell, G. J., Yamamoto, J., Romero, A., and Morales, A. (eds.).
The Psychosocial Development of Minority Group Children.
New York: Brunner/Mazel, 1983.

President's Commission on Mental Health. *Mental Health in
America: 1978.* Vol. 1. Washington, D.C.: U.S. Government
Printing Office, 1978.

Price-Williams, D. R. *Explorations in Cross-Cultural Psychology.*
San Francisco: Chandler and Sharp, 1975.

Reed, R. "Education and Achievement of Young Black Males."
In J. T. Gibbs (ed.), *Young, Black, and Male in America: An
Endangered Species.* Dover, Mass.: Auburn House, 1988.

Ridley, C. R. "Clinical Treatment of the Nondisclosing Black
Client: A Therapeutic Paradox." *American Psychologist,*
1984, *39,* 1234-1244.

Rivers, L. W., and others. "Mosaic of Labels for Black Children." In N. Hobbs (ed.), *Issues in the Classification of Children: A Sourcebook on Categories, Labels, and Their Consequences.* Vol. 2. San Francisco: Jossey-Bass, 1975.

Rodgers, H. R. *Poor Women, Poor Families.* Armonk, N.Y.: M. E. Sharpe, 1986.

Rosenberg, M. *Conceiving the Self.* New York: Basic Books, 1979.

Rosenberg, M., and Simmons, R. *Black and White Self-Esteem: The Urban School Child.* Rose Monograph Series. Washington, D.C.: American Sociological Association, 1971.

Samuda, R. *Psychological Testing of American Minorities: Issues and Consequences.* New York: Dodd, Mead, 1975.

Schorr, A. *Common Decency: Domestic Policies After Reagan.* New Haven, Conn.: Yale University Press, 1986.

Sluzki, C. "Migration and Family Conflict." *Family Process,* 1979, *18* (4), 379–390.

Snowden, L., and Todman, P. A. "The Psychological Assessment of Blacks: New and Needed Developments." In E. E. Jones and S. J. Korchin (eds.), *Minority Mental Health.* New York: Praeger, 1982.

Sue, D. W., and Sue, D. "Barriers to Effective Cross-Cultural Counseling." *Journal of Counseling Psychology,* 1977, *24,* 420–429.

Sue, S. "Community Mental Health Services to Minority Groups: Some Optimism, Some Pessimism." *American Psychologist,* 1977, *32,* 616–624.

Sum, A., Harrington, P. E., and Goedicke, W. "One-Fifth of the Nation's Teenagers: Employment Problems of Poor Youth in America, 1981–1985." *Youth and Society,* 1987, *18,* 195–237.

Taylor, R. L. "Psychosocial Development Among Black Children and Youth: A Reexamination." *American Journal of Orthopsychiatry,* 1976, *46,* 4–19.

U.S. Bureau of the Census. *Statistical Abstract of the United States: 1987.* (107th ed.) Washington, D.C.: U.S. Department of Commerce, 1986.

Wilson, W. J. *The Truly Disadvantaged.* Chicago: University of Chicago Press, 1987.

Wilson, W. J., and Aponte, R. "Urban Poverty." *Annual Review of Sociology,* 1985, *11,* 231–258.

2

Chinese American Children and Adolescents

Larke Nahme Huang
Yu-Wen Ying

A chapter on psychological problems in the Chinese American population may seem surprising to some, since Asian Americans in general use mental health services very seldom and since most professionals in the field have had minimal, if any, contact with Chinese American clients. Add to this the popular media stereotype of Asians as the "model minority," and one is justifed in asking, "Do such problems actually exist in this community?" The answer, of course, is yes, but unfortunately, utilization rates and media stereotypes obscure the reality. The Special Populations Task Force of the President's Commission on Mental Health (1978) concluded that ethnic minorities are underserved or inappropriately served by existing mental health services and that utilization rates are not reliable indicators of need in minority communities. Ethnic minority clients often find mental health services strange, intimidating, stigmatizing, and not particularly helpful. In the past, Chinese Americans tended to use mental health services only as a last resort, when family and community resources had been exhausted.

In addition, cultural definitions of mental health problems vary considerably within the Chinese community and most dramatically between Asian and Western cultures. These conceptualizations often direct one's search for resolution, so that if the disorder is thought to result from weak will or organic factors, a teacher, elder, or physician may be sought rather than a psychiatrist, psychologist, or mental health worker. These unconventional help-seeking patterns further obfuscate the true incidence of psychological disorder in this population.

Finally, the "model minority" stereotype oversimplifies the issues for Chinese Americans and obscures important realities in the community. Without a doubt, some Asian Americans, some Chinese Americans, have "made it" socially and economically. However, many have not. Although Chinese Americans have among the highest median family incomes of many ethnic minorities, they are also underemployed and are receiving lower salaries than other people doing comparable work. In the 1970s, the poverty rate for Chinese Americans in New York City was 15 percent, 4 points higher than the national rate (Chen, 1981). Chinese American youth, in particular, suffer under this stereotype, as it obscures the heterogeneity among this population and places undue stress and expectations on them.

The objective of this chapter is to familiarize the reader with the Chinese American population in the United States and to highlight mental health issues and intervention strategies for children and adolescents in that population. This is a task "easier said than done," as Chinese Americans are an extremely heterogeneous group—socially, politically, and culturally. Although it is impossible to provide a picture of the "typical Chinese American," it is reasonable to try to present a framework for examining the Chinese experience in America. One such framework that allows for multiple levels of analysis is an ecological systems approach (Bronfenbrenner, 1979), which enables one to examine the interaction between individual and environment. So, for example, to understand the experience of Chinese American youth in this country, it is necessary not only to understand child-rearing strategies of Chinese and Chinese American parents but to comprehend the impact of restrictive immigration laws in the 1900s, of miscegenation and exclusion laws, which were only recently repealed in the 1960s, and of racism and discrimination. These larger societal issues have an impact on Chinese American families, the composition of these families, their descendants, and the community as a whole. Similarly, Confucian traditions, passed from one generation to the next, though becoming increasingly diluted and "Westernized," still impose an Eastern philosophy of order on the family. Although these events and traditions will have varying impact depending on the degree of acculturation, they represent levels of analysis critical to an understanding of Chinese American youth and their manifestation of psychological problems.

To begin to understand these youth, it is first necessary to obtain an overview of the Chinese in the United States, critical events in their history and patterns of migration, and traditions carried from China that have influenced family formation in this country.

The Chinese in America

According to the 1980 census, there are 812,178 Chinese residing in the United States. Of these, 37 percent are native-born and 63 percent are foreign-born (U.S. Bureau of the Census, 1983b). These statistics indicate a population still in the process of acculturating and establishing a Chinese American culture, where the migration process is still a fresh experience and integration of the "old" with the "new" is still ongoing. The rate of immigration has significantly increased since the elimination of quotas on immigrants from Asia in 1965, and it is expected to continue to rise into the next century.

Geographically, the majority of the Chinese American population is found along the West and East coasts, primarily in and around major metropolitan centers. Forty percent live in California; 27 percent in the northeastern states, with 20 percent in New York State; 11 percent in the South; 9 percent in the North Central states; and 12 percent in Hawaii (U.S. Bureau of the Census, 1983a).

The median age of Chinese Americans is 29.6 years. Youth make up 30 percent of the population, with a fairly even distribution across the ages (U.S. Bureau of the Census, 1983a).

Education is highly valued within this culture. This is

demonstrated in the high percentage of school enrollees at all ages. Of persons 25 years and older, 71.3 percent are high school graduates, and the median number of school years completed is 13.4. Seventy-five percent of males over 25 and 67.4 percent of females have completed high school (U.S. Bureau of the Census, 1983b). Yet, in contrast to these statistics, 11 percent of Chinese Americans are illiterate, a percentage seven times that for Whites and three times that for Blacks (Chen, 1981).

Socioeconomically, Chinese Americans span a wide range, some families living at or below the poverty level and others among the most wealthy of the general population. Median household income in 1980 was $19,561. Of 250,585 households, 31,022 households (12 percent) exist on an income less than $5,000; at the other extreme, almost 20,000 households make over $50,000 (U.S. Bureau of the Census, 1983b). Except for Southeast Asian refugees, the Chinese have the highest number of persons living below the poverty level of all Asian groups in the United States.

Chinese Migration, Culture, and Family

History and Patterns of Migration

The history of Chinese migration to the United States is a very sporadic, uneven one. Chinese first arrived in this country in 1820 in extremely small numbers. The catalyst for increased migration was the discovery of gold in California in the 1840s in conjunction with increasingly harsh living conditions in China due to oppressive, feudalistic control by the Manchu dynasty, repeated floods and famine, and ongoing civil wars. These immigrants and those to follow came with the intent of making a fortune in America, the "Gold Mountain," and then returning to China (Sung, 1967). Most of these immigrants were from areas around Hong Kong, Macao, and Guangdong (Canton) province and were Cantonese-speaking males.

These earliest immigrants were received with little animosity and much indifference. However, as the United States entered its own economic downturn in the late 1870s and as the numbers of Chinese immigrants increased into the thousands, anti-Chinese sentiment grew. It culminated in the Chinese Exclusion Act of 1882, which was the first legislation to ban a particular race from entering the United States. In 1924 the Oriental Exclusion Act banned all immigration from Asia. During the period from 1890 to 1945, more Chinese left than entered the United States. Those remaining lived under the oppression of the exclusion laws, suffering innumerable humiliations, racial violence, loss of property and livelihood, and sometimes loss of life. In spite of the hostile environs, many Chinese elected to stay in the United States, but in order to do so they needed to change their status from laborers (who were targets of deportation) to merchants or businessmen. Chinatowns became the basis for this economic conversion, drawing on traditional structures such as clans and family associations to organize an urban economic community built on the service industries, such as restaurants, small shops, domestic work, and laundries (Chen, 1981; Lyman, 1976).

The next wave of immigrants reflected the changing social structure in China. When imperial China fell in 1911, a new middle class consisting of businessmen and entrepreneurs emerged. These families, as well as affluent landowners, began to send their children overseas to obtain an American or European education or to establish an overseas branch of the family business. These new immigrants came from a wealthier social class, usually spoke a different dialect than the earlier Chinese from Guangdong, often originated from such cosmopolitan cities as Shanghai, were better educated, and did not settle in Chinatowns. They had little in common with the earlier settlers, and so the two groups initially had minimal interaction. However, like the earlier immigrants, many of these immigrants were sojourners who intended to return to China and, with their modern education, secure prestigious positions in their provinces. With the Communist takeover of China in 1949, these immigrants were stranded overseas and became unintended permanent residents in the United States.

In 1965, in the midst of the civil rights movement, the Immigration and Nationality Acts Amendments ended legislated discrimination and resulted in yet another wave of immigrants. Some of these post-1965 immigrants were unskilled laborers, but many were from middle-class or affluent families, speaking Mandarin rather than the Cantonese dialects, sometimes fluent in English, and possessing higher-level skills and education. They usually came via Hong Kong or Taiwan and attempted to establish themselves in businesses, industry, and professions for which they had been trained (Chen, 1981). Although many of these immigrants eventually became successful, they often suffered a period of underemployment or downward mobility because their training or degrees were initially less valued than and noncompetitive with comparable degrees in the United States.

Culture and Family Traditions

Although Chinese American families show much diversity and variation, the following discussion will convey some of the historical and cultural antecedents for Chinese American family structure. The nature and structure of the Chinese family derived from Confucian philosophy, which dictated a sense of order and a prescription for role relationships within Chinese society. Guidelines for specific family relationships, patterns of communication, and negotiations with the outside world were delineated with the goal of harmonious existence in society (Lin, 1938).

Family Roles. Confucian ethics placed a strong emphasis on roles within the family and the proper behavior associated with each role. Obligations, responsibilities, and privileges of each role were clearly delineated according to a vertical, hierarchal role structure with the father as the undisputed head. His authority was unchallenged, and he was the recipient of total respect and loyalty from all family members. In return, he assumed maximum responsibility for the family's social status and economic well-being. The mother was responsible for the emotional nurturance and well-being of the family, her primary role being to serve the father and raise the children. She was accorded respect from her children, although her role was less removed and distant than the father's. She would often intercede with the father on behalf of the children. Mothers were generally discouraged from taking on work roles outside the family (Shon and Ja, 1982).

Gender and birth position were also associated with certain duties and privileges. Sons were more highly valued than daughters; family lineage was passed through the male, while females were absorbed into the families of their husbands. The first-born son, the most valued child, received preferential treatment as well as more familial responsibilities. The prescriptive roles for daughters were less rewarding, as females often did not come into a position of authority or respect until they assumed the role of mother-in-law.

These family roles were predominant in imperial, feudal China. Of course, as China has modernized, these roles have altered radically. Similarly, in acculturated Chinese families in the United States, only derivatives of these rigidly defined roles remain. For example, females are not entirely relegated to subservient roles. Fathers are often the figurative heads of families, especially when dealing with the public, while the mother may in fact be the driving force in the family and the decision maker behind the scenes. First sons continue to be highly valued, but the discrepancies between the sexes in duties and privileges, though still there, are not so glaring.

The extended family, rather than the nuclear family, was the primary family unit in China. The process of migration disrupted these family relationships, but many Chinese in America have attempted to reconstruct this kinship network. For some, the extended family is clearly identified as an important source of social and sometimes financial support. However, for some highly Westernized families, the extended family may also be experienced as a burden and a restriction on one's autonomy.

Patterns of Communication. Congruent with a rigid system of role relationships, rules of communication were governed by the attributes of the parties involved. Within families, usually gender and age governed the degree of open expression allowed, the initiator of conversation, the structure of the language used, and the topics to be addressed. Communication was often indirect, and outright confrontation was eschewed. Even today, expression of emotion is generally frowned on; suppression of undesirable thoughts or emotions is highly valued. These rules for communication contrast markedly with American values of expression and the tendency to "speak your mind" or "let it all hang out" (Shon and Ja, 1982).

Obligation, Shame, and "Face." In contrast to the Western concept of contractual obligation and reciprocity, the unspoken and obligatory reciprocity in interaction is of paramount importance in Chinese culture and continues to be evident among Chinese in America. Obligations are determined by one's role (for example, the obligation of the child to the parent, or filial piety) or incurred through acts of kindness or helpfulness. Behavior is often dictated by a sense of obligation or a desire to avoid being in a position of obligation.

Shame and loss of face are similarly guiding principles of behavior and powerful motivating forces for conforming to societal or familial expectations (Shon and Ja, 1982). Even truthfulness and honesty in the abstract are secondary to "saving face" for oneself and others. Bringing shame on one's family is avoided at all costs. Ability to place the group's or family's wishes above one's individual desires is held as a virtue. Given that interdependence is the foundation of Chinese culture, everything an individual does is viewed as a reflection on the family as a whole.

Mental Health Issues
for Chinese American Children and Adolescents

The literature on psychological and behavioral disorders in Chinese American children and adolescents is quite limited, as Asian Americans, in general, have not been the focus of systematic inquiry concerning mental health issues. Several studies of Chinese American adults examine psychiatric hospitalization rates, patterns of service utilization, and comparison of inpatients and outpatients (Berk and Hirata, 1973; Brown, Stein, Huang, and Harris, 1973; Sue and McKinney, 1975); however, none of these studies looks at the youth population. Even the Special Populations Task Force of the President's Commission on Mental Health, which submitted an extensive report on the mental health of Asian/Pacific Americans in 1978, neglected to examine the mental health needs of Chinese American youth.

The County of Los Angeles Department of Mental Health (1985, 1986) reports serving a total of 652 Chinese American clients during the 1984–85 fiscal year, of whom 97 were children under age 18. For the following fiscal year, the number rose to 873, and of these 115 were children under 18. Diagnostically, these clients ranged from adjustment disorder to psychotic disorders. Unfortunately, the specific diagnostic breakdown for these Chinese American children is not available.

Data from various urban community mental health service agencies and programs provide a better diagnostic picture. At the Asian Community Mental Health Services, in Oakland, California, sixteen Chinese American children and adolescents were seen during the 1987–88 fiscal year (D. Li-Repac, personal communication, Aug. 8, 1988). Of these, six were under age 13 and ten were between 13 and 17; six were female and ten male. Diagnostically, three suffered from disorders usually first evident in infancy, childhood, or adolescence, two from schizophrenic disorder, one from a psychotic disorder not elsewhere classified, three from affective disorder, and seven from adjustment disorder.

At San Francisco's Galileo High School Adolescent Program, fifty adolescents (twenty-nine males and twenty-one females, aged 14 to 20) were seen during the 1987–88 school year (L. Lee, personal communication, July 28, 1988). Of these, fifteen received a diagnosis of adjustment disorder with depressed mood; twelve, adjustment disorder with mixed emotional features; seven, adjustment disorder with mixed disturbance of emotions and conduct. The remaining sixteen met criteria for a variety of other disorders, ranging from anxiety disorder to schizophrenic disorders. The major precipitating factors appeared to be immigration adjustment and change of school.

At the Asian Bicultural Clinic of Gouverneur Hospital in New York City, fourteen adolescents (aged 12 to 19) were seen for suicidal gestures/attempts during 1985–1988 (Ma, Cohen, and Yeung, 1988). Six were male, eight female; six were U.S.-born and eight were foreign-born (mostly from Hong Kong).

Their diagnoses ranged from affective disorder (seven clients), schizoaffective disorder (two), schizophrenic disorder (one), and atypical psychosis (one) to adjustment disorder (two) and life circumstance problem (one). Eight of the adolescents made one suicidal gesture/attempt during this time period, and the other six made two or three. The precipitating events were family conflicts (four), problem relationships with the other sex (three), school adjustment (three), psychotic delusion (three), and conflict with peers (three).

These data provide a rough picture of the range of psychological difficulties experienced by Chinese American children and adolescents. However, the relatively small numbers of Chinese American youth in these programs are likely to reflect underutilization of the services and thus give only an incomplete picture. Our limited information on the psychological problems of Chinese American youth makes it necessary to extrapolate from other areas of the literature that may bear on the experiences of these children and their mental health. Three such areas are studies of migration and relocation of youth, self-concept studies, and empirical personality studies.

Touliatos and Lindholm (1980) compared the incidence of psychological disturbance in American-born Caucasian children and in children of foreign-born parents. Within the sample of ninety-seven children of foreign-born parents, forty-two were of Chinese, Japanese, or Southeast Asian descent. Some of these children were American-born, some foreign-born. The types of disorders examined were conduct problems, personality problems, inadequacy/immaturity problems, socialized delinquency, and psychotic symptomatology. In all five areas, the children of foreign-born parents showed less psychopathology than the native-born Caucasian children. Further analysis revealed that children of Chinese, Japanese, or Southeast Asian descent exhibited significantly fewer disorders in the conduct problems and inadequacy/immaturity areas than native-born Caucasian children.

The results of this study are consistent with Aronowitz's (1984) review, which concluded that immigrant children do not necessarily show a higher incidence of disorder than their native

peers. None of the studies that Aronowitz reviewed focused specifically on Chinese children; however, his conclusions about
immigrant children in general may be pertinent. Acknowledging
that the incidence of disorder is not greater for immigrant children, he nevertheless documented that when disorders do occur,
there is a certain predictability. These children tend to present
with anxiety and depression and conduct disorders rather than
acute psychiatric symptoms. An extensive survey of West Indian
children in London revealed that conduct disorders among the
immigrant children were manifest almost entirely at school and
not at home (Rutter and others, 1974). The authors suggested
that this may be due to possible learning difficulties at school,
racial discrimination, and high pupil turnover in the predominantly immigrant schools.

The developmental literature indicates that relocations
may be stressful for children (Garmezy and Rutter, 1983). The
subjective experience and manner of coping are, of course, related to the developmental stage of the child. For the latency-
age child or adolescent, relocations or migrations are experienced directly and may represent a significant loss and, at least,
temporary instability and uncertainty. Anxiety and depression
may initially outweigh the excitement associated with the
move. For the infant and toddler, the relocation is more often
experienced through the parents. As long as the parents remain
constant figures in the child's life, the impact of a move may be
less dramatic. However, the anxiety experienced by the parents
may be inadvertently transmitted to the young child. Rutter
(1983) indicates that children may be affected by their parents'
attitude and psychological state as well as by any actual event.
Thus, a relocation may still have a dramatic impact on the very
young child, though indirectly experienced.

Children and adolescents may assume rather passive roles
in the early stages of migration and then become quite active
and mobilized in the later stages. They generally have little say
in the decision-making process and the actual arrangements for
migrating; however, once in the new country, they tend to
acculturate more rapidly and then assume a more active role in
the family. These children become "parentified," assuming roles

that previously had been those of their parents. Because of their more rapid ease with the new language, they become the negotiators of the outside world for their parents. They do the shopping, they pay the bills, they answer the telephone; they are their parents' interpreters. For some children, this new role may be novel and exciting. However, when prolonged, it can become burdensome and tedious and a threat to the traditional configuration of roles within the family.

Ou and McAdoo (1980) examined the self-concept, ethnic preference, and cognitive development of American-born latency-age children of Chinese immigrant parents. The children in this study generally had high self-concept, low anxiety, and high cognitive functioning. A child's mental health was related to the parents' attitude toward their heritage. For the older (fifth- and sixth-grade) boys, the more Chinese spoken between parent and child, the higher the boys' anxiety. Additionally, the more positive parents' attitudes were toward Chinese culture, the lower the older boys' self-concept. The researchers concluded that speaking English in the home lowered the boys' anxiety because it lessened the bicultural and bilingual pressure on the child. The findings on self-concept may reflect the uncertainty and difficulty for the latency-age bicultural child in establishing a sound self-concept. While the parents may demonstrate a strong attachment to the Chinese culture, the older boys in this sample may be more acculturated to mainstream American society, resulting in some confusion over self-concept.

In a similar vein, Hisama (1980) speculated about the relation between immigrant acculturation patterns and psychological disorders manifested by children. In traditional Asian families, children may be expected to give unquestioning obedience to their parents and strive at any cost for the academic excellence expected of them. Their parents remain unacculturated, creating a substantial gap between the home and school environments. Hisama indicates that the children of these families will tend to internalize their distress, thus manifesting more anxiety reactions, psychosomatic disorders, and school phobia. In contrast to these families, the marginal family is characterized by uncertainty in identification with the new and old cultures. Unquestioning obedience to parents is not present in these families. Role relationships within the family have become confused and disorganized. In these families, the children may tend to externalize their anxiety and manifest behavioral disorders.

For adolescent immigrants, problems seem to center on self-concept, identity conflicts, and generational conflicts with parents. Although these are typical issues confronting adolescents, migration seems to exacerbate these normal developmental conflicts (Aronowitz, 1984). Studies of minority immigrants reveal self-depreciation and low self-worth among these adolescents (Nann, 1982; Osborne, 1971), many of whom feel driven to make the difficult choice between the values and identities of their old and new cultures. These conflicts and role stresses may result in deviant behavior and, occasionally, serious psychopathology (Naditch and Morrissey, 1976).

First-born males in Chinese American families are under extreme pressure and may be especially vulnerable to psychological disorders (Hisama, 1980). This point is reiterated by Lee (1982), who states that the positions of oldest son and youngest daughter are associated with the highest rates of psychopathology in Chinese American culture. Oldest sons are expected to provide emotional support to the mother, assume responsibility for the educational and character development of younger siblings, and bring honor and financial support to the family. The youngest daughter may resent being left with responsibility for the parents as her older siblings leave home as well as the unequal treatment she receives in comparison with her brothers. As the youngest, she may also be the most acculturated and the most vulnerable to cultural conflicts and disagreements with her parents.

Empirical personality studies of Chinese American college students found them to be more inhibited, conventional, and socially withdrawn than their White American counterparts (Sue and Kirk, 1973). A study using the MMPI revealed Chinese American college students in Los Angeles to have problems with dependency, inferiority feelings, ruminations, somatic complaints, and limited social skills (Sue and Sue, 1974). Sue and Frank (1973) report that Chinese American college students suffer from more stress than nonminority American students and tend to feel more isolated, lonely, rejected, and anxious. The results of these studies must be interpreted with caution, as the norms for the assessment instruments used were established with White, middle-class populations.

In the past, cultural restraints against aggression have contributed to a relatively low rate of juvenile delinquency. In recent years, however, this rate has been rising, with a particularly marked increase in more aggressive offenses such as assault and robbery (Abbott and Abbott, 1973; Sue, Sue, and Sue, 1983). In San Francisco, where approximately 12 percent of the population is Chinese American, 5 percent of the 8,000 juvenile offenders each year are identified as Chinese American (Millard, 1987). As Chinese American youth become more acculturated, parental authority begins to erode and constraints against aggression become less effective. Parents are often distracted from family issues as they try to make a living in the new country; frequently both parents work, a change from the previous role structure, so that there is less direct supervision in the home. For adolescents living in Chinatown, which has all the characteristics of an urban ghetto, the unemployment rate among youth is high, and the impoverished conditions and poor housing are glaring. The arrival of immigrant youth who possess little or no English and no job skills compounds the existing problems.

The phenomenon of gangs among Chinese American youth, which often receives sensational coverage by the news media, is becoming increasingly alarming to the Chinese community. The process of gang formation in the Chinese community is not unlike that in other communities; however, the gangs' involvement in criminal activities, including assault and extortion within the community, intermittently brings them into the public limelight (Fong, 1968). The antecedents for this behavior are similar to the socioenvironmental conditions associated with delinquency, in conjunction with a poor self-image resulting from language problems, poor academic performance in school, self-depreciation internalized from the outside dominant community, and provincial rivalries stemming from place of birth.

This discussion has focused primarily on immigrant and

first-generation youth. Later generations of Chinese American youth will be more acculturated; however, they may retain some ethnic traditions and differences in cultural values. Their manifestations of disorder and attitudes regarding mental health may be more similar to those of mainstream American youth, but ethnic identity issues are frequently involved. Identity conflicts may be the primary presenting problem or may be interwoven with other psychological disorders.

Sociocultural Issues in Assessment

Clinicians working with children and adolescents are generally in agreement that working with the family system and the school system facilitates effective psychological treatment (Pothier, 1976; Reisman, 1973). The following ecological approach to assessment focuses on the individual person system, the family system, and, briefly, the school and societal systems. For each of these interacting subsystems, relevant sociocultural factors will be presented as they are key to an accurate interpretation of the data.

The Individual Person System

The categories of data for an assessment of Chinese American youth may be similar to those used with White American youth, with the addition of two dimensions: level of acculturation and immigration history. However, the actual data may have very different meaning when examined in a sociocultural context.

Level of Acculturation. Level of acculturation is an extremely significant factor, as it will affect the interpretation of data obtained throughout the assessment. A recent immigrant child may be very unfamiliar with American customs and values and may possess a distinctly Chinese world view. Chinese values, traditions, and behavior may be the standards for this child. For a child who is third-generation and very Westernized, however, ethnic differences may be minimal. English may be spoken in the home and values may be very Americanized. Excessive attention to cultural explanations will be inappropriate in this situation. Somewhere in the middle range is the bicultural child who incorporates both Chinese and American values and behaviors. For some children, biculturalism engenders stress and even psychopathology when the values come into conflict. Others, however, negotiate competently between the two cultures, mastering both and skillfully employing situation-appropriate behaviors.

Immigration History. The child's age at the time of immigration and resettlement may influence the degree of acculturation and socialization to American society. Usually, younger children adjust more rapidly than older children, who may experience more difficulty in acquiring the new language. Country of origin, socioeconomic status in that country, process of actual migration, and persons accompanying the child may also influence the ease of the transition and the adjustment of the child. While many children migrate with intact families, many others are sponsored by relatives in the United States and are joined later by their parents. Some children migrate with older siblings and are separated from parents for a long period. Readjustment to nuclear family life or to parents who are recent immigrants and unacculturated may be the source of much disharmony in the newly reunited family. Although this factor may not seem to be as critical for American-born Chinese children, it is important to understand the immigration history of their parents or grandparents. Many Chinese parents immigrate to America for the futures of their children. This becomes a powerful dynamic in the family, and the burdens and responsibilities placed on the children to justify the parents' sacrifices play an important role in these children's development.

Physical Appearance. For children, any deviation from the norm may garner undesired attention. Conformity in appearance and behavior is highly valued. For the Chinese American child, who differs in physical appearance and, depending on degree of acculturation, may also differ in dress, behavior, and mannerisms, this may be a point of conflict or sensitivity. In addition, the generally smaller physique of Chinese American children makes them vulnerable to the "heightism" so prevalent in American society (Okie, 1988).

Speech and Language. The importance of language as an issue will vary depending on degree of acculturation. It is important to assess the degree of fluency in English and Chinese, especially if this may be affecting competence in schoolwork. For the American-born child, language may not be as critical an issue, although assessing its role in family dynamics would be important. The combination of monolingual parents with bilingual children may upset the traditional role configurations within the family. Additionally, a child's rejection of the culture of origin is often associated with refusal to speak the native language, much to the chagrin and displeasure of the parents or grandparents.

Affect. What is often considered excessively restrained or nonexpressive affect in Chinese Americans may in fact be culturally appropriate. Overt expression of feelings is encouraged in Western culture but not in Chinese culture. On the contrary, suppression of emotion, particularly in public situations, is highly valued. Expression of affect, especially negative affect, is thought to reflect poor upbringing. Again, this is related to degree of acculturation. The highly expressive Chinese American child may be behaving culturally appropriately if from a very Americanized family or if highly adapted to Western manners.

Interpersonal Relations. The quality of relatedness to other children and adults must be examined for appropriate dependence, affection, closeness, and separation. In contrast to the "rugged individualism" espoused by American society, interdependence, and often prolonged dependence, within the Chinese family is highly encouraged. Acknowledgment of role relationships and associated "proper" behavior contribute to a sense of formality, especially when adults are involved. For example, Chinese children are expected to address all adults by a formal title, such as Uncle, Aunt, Mr., or Mrs., not by first names.

Attitude Toward Self. This category includes one's feelings about oneself, stability of self-identification, self-esteem, and sense of competence. Studies of minority children conducted before the civil rights movement of the 1960s often found negative self-images (Brody, 1968; Clark and Clark, 1947). More recent studies have generated mixed results. Many Chinese American children have experienced some sort of ethnicity-related insult, internal or external, to their sense of self. This may range from simple yet painful teasing at school to recurrent ethnic-derogatory comments by other significant persons, which become internalized by the child, to total denial of one's ethnicity.

Anxiety and Patterns of Defense. The degree of anxiety, the way it is manifest, and under what conditions are important to assess. With children in general, and Chinese American children in particular, the earliest manifestations are often somatic concerns and complaints, sleep and appetite disturbances, and disruptions in school performance. Given the importance placed on academic excellence in the Chinese culture, this last is a frequent presenting problem.

Issues of Sexuality. For adolescents, it is important to assess how sexuality is manifest and its role in family dynamics. Sexuality remains a taboo subject in many Chinese American families. A therapist must treat this topic with much discretion and develop a strong alliance with the family before broaching issues of sexuality.

The Family System

In working with Chinese American children or adolescents, it is important for the treatment program to involve the family, as this is the critical unit of social organization in this culture.

Acculturation. In addition to the typical "generation gap" within families, Chinese American families may experience "acculturation gaps." Individual members may adapt to a new environment at quite different rates. In recent immigrant families and even some second-generation families, parents are much more reluctant to accept the values and behaviors of the American culture than their children, who readily become "Americanized" in dress and behavior and, subsequently, in values. These different rates of acculturation are often the source of family disharmony.

Stage in Migration History. Sluzki (1979) identifies five discrete stages in the migration process, each of which is associated with different types of family conflict and coping patterns. The first two stages are preparation and the actual act of migration. The third stage, a period of overcompensation, is characterized by a heightened level of activity focused on survival and the satisfaction of primary needs.

The fourth stage is a stormy, crisis-ridden period of decompensation. The family is confronted with the task of reshaping its new reality and maximizing its compatibility with the new environment. Family members may also begin to step back and take a more realistic view of their situation. Disappointment may be acknowledged, and realization of the losses associated with leaving their homeland may penetrate the defense system that initially spawned the period of overcompensation.

The final stage involves a clash between generations, which is often both intercultural as well as intergenerational. Offspring raised in the United States often clash dramatically with their parents in terms of values, norms, and behaviors. It is in these latter two stages that families are most prone to have contact with mental health services.

Attitudes About Mental Health. When explaining mental disorders, Chinese rarely draw on psychological causes. Explanations usually involve social, moral, or organic factors (Ishisaka and Takagi, 1982; Tseng and McDermott, 1981). In social explanations, the individual is seen as the victim of some unfortunate and uncontrollable circumstance. Fate may be implicated in this event, as opposed to individual factors. In moral explanations, mental disorder is considered a punishment for a violation of values. For example, a violation of filial piety or bringing shame to the family may trigger mental disorder. Guilt arises from transgressions of interpersonal obligations deriving from cultural traditions. Occasionally, the misconduct of one's ancestors may lead to misfortune in later generations. This is exemplified in the popular belief that "one wrong marriage leads to three generations of disorder." Finally, organic and genetic explanations are probably the most common. Physical disease or an imbalance of yin and yang, two basic life forces, is seen as the source of mental disorder. Somatic explanations are consistent with the Eastern concept of unity of mind and body, which links physical and emotional functioning.

Pattern of Help Seeking. Consistent with the foregoing explanations for mental disorder, Chinese Americans rarely approach formal psychological helpers except as a last resort. Intrafamilial help from family elders or extended family members is often considered more appropriate because of fears of what might happen to the disordered individual if the problems are revealed to outside authorities and also because of the powerful sense of family shame and obligation.

Family Communication. As discussed earlier, what may appear to be formal and somewhat stilted communication may in fact be culturally determined. Patterns of communication are often indirect, not free-flowing, and roles are not egalitarian. A reluctance to disclose family problems may not be "resistance" but, rather, culturally appropriate propriety and attempts to "save face."

Socioeconomic Status. Chinese Americans span the entire socioeconomic range, and one often finds multiple wage earners within a household. This category of data may be important in assessing resources available to the family and may also shed light on the role arrangements within the family as they relate to occupational status. Particularly for recent immigrant families, traditional wage-earner relationships may be disrupted, generating disharmony within the family.

Support System. It is also critical to assess the degree to which this family is isolated or integrated within its community. If the family is most comfortable with traditional Chinese culture, does it interact with other families with similar values, or is it isolated among primarily non-Asian families? Or, if it is highly assimilated, does it maintain any ties with the Chinese American community and culture? The support network in which a family is embedded may affect identity development and conflict for its children and adolescents.

The School System

Racial/Ethnic Composition. Is the child or adolescent the only Chinese American student in the class? American-born or foreign-born? Is this of significance to the child? For some children, it is isolating and intimidating. For others who are more acculturated, it is of no consequence. However, the way the child experiences peer relationships and internalizes the views of peers is important to assess, as it may strongly influence the child's attitudes toward him- or herself.

Attitudes of the Teacher. The stereotype of the Chinese American student as bright, conscientious, and quiet is extremely pervasive. Although stereotypes may contain seeds of reality, they are nevertheless harmful and limiting to individual growth. Unfortunately, many teachers may have expectations of Chinese students based on these stereotypes. Recently, with the influx of immigrants, many Chinese students are entering school with limited English skills. Teachers in port-of-entry areas are becoming frustrated and annoyed with the difficulties in, and the lack of support services for, dealing with these students. Some teachers are tired of teaching "foreigners." Other teachers minimize cultural differences and expect these students to mirror White, majority students. They would like assertive, active participants in class, not realizing that this expectation may contrast with the child's home environment, where quiet, obedient behavior is expected. The Chinese American student in this situation must negotiate between the conflicting expectations of the two settings.

Societal Issues

The attitude of American society toward its minority populations fluctuates in relation to a number of factors, politics and economics being primary ones. Growth of civil rights, development of affirmative action policies, encouragement of minority businesses, and endowment of scholarships for minority students may be the priority of one administration, only to be rapidly discarded by the succeeding one. Most recently, Asian groups in the mid 1980s have been the targets of considerable anti-Asian sentiment. At the college level, Asian American students are facing a backlash in response to their increasingly successful penetration of exclusive colleges and universities. This has resulted in unofficial yet discriminatory quotas on admissions (Nakao, 1987) as well as negative attitudes and anti-Asian bias among non-Asian students and college personnel. Other sources of hostility include the growth and proliferation of Asian American small business, the mounting trade deficits with Japan and Taiwan, numerous stories heralding Asian American superachievers in education, and the increasing visibility of Asian Americans moving into previously all-White or all-Black communities (Fong, 1987). This growing resentment has resulted in a resurgence of violence toward Asian Americans.

Chinese American children and adolescents, though not always immediate victims of this violence, are often unknowing and unintended victims. This hostility penetrates systems in which these children are direct or indirect participants—schools, families, peer groups, parents' places of employment, neighborhood playgrounds, and communities. Even though there may be no obvious link between this societal attitude and a youngster's psychological disorder, it is important to examine the larger societal issues that may form the backdrop for the child experiencing difficulties.

Intervention and Treatment

In the psychological treatment of Chinese Americans, it is necessary but not sufficient to understand sociocultural factors. The therapist must go beyond cultural awareness to an understanding of how these factors translate into concrete therapeutic behaviors. The following discussion will use clinical cases to illustrate pertinent issues in two phases of the therapeutic process: entering treatment and establishing the working alliance. The cases are taken from the caseload of the first author, a Chinese American female psychologist.

Entering Treatment. For many Chinese Americans, contacting mental health services represents a "last ditch" effort to resolve the problem. Usually, other sources of help have been exhausted, as the following case example illustrates.

Rose was an 18-year-old adolescent who had immigrated from China with her parents as a young child. She was brought to an inpatient mental health crisis unit by her mother and 17-year-old brother with the assistance of a mental health outreach worker. At intake, she was hostile and belligerent and needed to be restrained. She was disheveled and unkempt, was disoriented, and had delusions of meeting Chairman Mao in Chinatown. She was angry at her parents for "incarcerating" her and claimed she had important appointments to keep.

Rose's mother spoke only Toishanese, so a history was obtained using the brother as translator. The mother noted a gradual deterioration in Rose's behavior following completion of high school about one and a half years earlier. At that time she became sullen and withdrawn, lost all friendships, and had difficulty maintaining a job in the family's small restaurant. She began using makeup in a garish fashion, staying out late at night, and verbally abusing her mother. The precipitating incident for admission to the crisis unit was increasingly bizarre behavior in the home followed by a physical assault on her mother.

During the first six months of Rose's deterioration, the mother had sought help from an acupuncturist, relatives, the family doctor, and a minister. When nothing seemed to relieve the problem, the family, very ashamed and desperate, began to lock Rose in her room. It was during this eight-month period that she would escape at night and wander the streets. Her brother would find her, usually quite delusional, and bring her home. Rose's mother was quite tearful as she provided this history; the brother seemed nonexpressive but tense. After completion of the intake procedure and medical exam, it was discovered that Rose was six to seven months pregnant. The mother and brother said they were totally unaware of this.

This case vividly illustrates the difficulty with which some Chinese Americans approach formal mental health services. Rather than seek help from unfamiliar sources, this family had lived with their daughter's deteriorating condition for over a year with limited resources and no formal assistance. It was not until she became unmanageable that they sought help. By that time, the daughter had become so psychotic that inpatient treatment was required. The family's reluctance to seek help reflected their feelings of shame and embarrassment, their lack of familiarity with mental health services, and their defensive pattern of denial, which they also mobilized in regard to Rose's sexuality and pregnancy. For the therapist or mental health worker, it is critical to understand the significance of the family's decision to come to the crisis unit: the profound sense of failure, the loss of face, and the exposure of inner family problems that may provoke feelings of guilt and uneasiness. Conversely, the family may also be yearning for relief and a close supportive relationship. Appreciating this ambivalence may be crucial to the therapeutic relationship.

This case also highlights the role of interpreter. Although family members may often be used for expedience, there is always a potential conflict of interest. It is therapeutically more advantageous to have an interpreter experienced in psychological issues, owing to the difficulty of translating English expressions or emotional terms into Chinese. It is important to use the same interpreter, if possible, and to reassure the client of confidentiality. In addition, it is often useful to schedule pretherapy sessions with the interpreter to establish a relationship, discuss the translation format, and allow the interpreter to raise questions (Lee, 1982).

Another issue in the entering phase of treatment is the *therapist's credibility* in the eyes of the Chinese American client. In the minority mental health literature, there has been much discussion about the therapist/client match: Should Asian clients see Asian therapists, should Blacks see Blacks, and so forth? Sue and Zane (1987) have provided a useful reformulation based on ascribed credibility (the position or role one is assigned on the basis of sex, age, and expertise) and achieved credibility (the therapist's skills involving culturally appropriate interventions and general therapeutic skills). Traditionally, in Asian cultures, women have been subordinate to men and youth to elders; hence, a young female would have a low ascribed status in contrast to an elderly male. In the entering phase of treatment, the young, female therapist must rapidly demonstrate effective therapeutic skills in order to attain a higher achieved credibility and maintain the client in therapy.

Mrs. Wong, an immigrant from Hong Kong, traveled one hour to the university mental health clinic for evaluation and treatment of her child, who was manifesting behavior problems. In opposition to a referral from the school, she bypassed the bi-culturally staffed neighborhood psychiatric clinic. When she was assigned to a Chinese American therapist at the university clinic, she was very disappointed, refused to see this therapist, and indicated that she wanted to see one of the "real" doctors like Dr. Smith.

Mrs. Chu brought her 6-year-old son to the university mental health clinic at the urging of her family doctor, who speculated that the child was developmentally delayed. She was very relieved to be assigned a Chinese American therapist. She immediately and tearfully described her son's problems as well as her own personal and family difficulties in adjusting to life in the United States.

In these two cases, the therapist's ascribed status had different implications. For Mrs. Wong, expertise was associated with being White, as is the case in Hong Kong, a British colony, where one may be socialized to believe this and where, in fact, British people are "in power." If the therapist's ascribed status as a Chinese American interferes with Mrs. Wong's attempts to engage in therapy, this should be acknowledged, and perhaps another therapist should be assigned the case. An underlying issue is whether to deal with Mrs. Wong's internalized feelings of self-devaluation and ethnic inferiority or to respond to her overt wishes. In this initial stage, the subjective experience of the client is crucial, and if one is to engage the family in treatment, responding to her expressed wishes will be necessary. An additional issue in this case may be Mrs. Wong's concerns with confidentiality, reflected in her traveling beyond her familiar community to one where no one would recognize her.

In contrast, Mrs. Chu valued the opportunity to meet with a Chinese American therapist. This facilitated her rapid self-disclosure and immediate engagement in therapy. For her, the therapist's ethnicity was associated with a high level of ascribed credibility.

Establishing the Working Alliance. A major problem in the treatment of Chinese Americans is their tendency to drop out after the initial sessions. They often do not see the efficacy of "talking," nor do they experience any sense of personal relief or connection with the helping services. For these reasons, the working alliance needs to be reconceptualized as an *active exchange* where the clients immediately feel there is reciprocal giving and receiving, where they are gaining something definite as a result of their participation in the interaction. For example, extensive evaluations or lengthy history-taking sessions may often result in parents' removing the child from treatment because they feel they have gained nothing in exchange for their time and information. Some of the components in this "active exchange," on the client's part, include willingness to come to therapy, disclosing information and feelings, listening to the therapist, and providing some form of payment for services. The therapist's part in this "exchange" includes willingness to share information about one's credentials and personal qualifications, providing education about the therapeutic process and the mental health system, giving reassurance, empathizing with the client's pain and frustrations, accepting the client's formulations of the problem, and acknowledging appropriate social and cultural etiquette. This reciprocity, or mutual exchange, enables the client to feel an immediate and direct benefit from the treatment. The following case will illustrate this reciprocity.

Wei Lee, a 19-year-old male, was referred to the therapist by an inpatient mental health crisis unit for follow-up treatment on an outpatient basis. Wei's diagnosis was paranoid schizophrenia. Many of his delusions were race-related; his feelings of persecution were based on being Chinese American and being rejected by his surrounding community. After one session with Wei, and with Wei's consent, the therapist invited his parents to meet with her. Mr. and Mrs. Lee, immigrants from China, had resided in the United States for over twenty years, and both worked as civil servants for the city government. They were a rather traditional couple, Mr. Lee being the clear, dominant authority and Mrs. Lee being silent, in the background, and considerably more emotional. Wei was their fourth child and had been born in the United States.

Although Mr. and Mrs. Lee recognized the bizarre behavior of their son, they expressed anger and frustration toward the mental health system. They said that very little information had been shared with them, there was no discussion of his diagnosis or treatment plan, and after he was discharged, Wei returned home, again became withdrawn, and stopped his medications. They reported that this was Wei's second hospitalization in two years and the pattern was exactly the same. Their questions remained unasked and unanswered, and Wei had refused to continue treatment.

The therapist discussed the diagnosis and range of possible implications, answered questions about the hospitalization and the mental health system, discussed insurance and disability payments, and employed the parents as "collaborators" in the treatment plan. She acknowledged the boundaries and limits of confidentiality in the individual therapy with Wei, but she also invited any calls or questions from the parents. She listened and empathized with their frustrations with their son and the mental health system and acknowledged Mrs. Lee's concerns about possible relations between events during her pregnancy and Wei's disorder. This meeting went beyond the designated fifty minutes.

For three and a half years, the therapy with Wei continued with the support of his parents. The payment of a reduced fee was shared by Wei and his parents. Wei learned to identify environmental and personal factors that triggered his delusions and developed methods to cope with them. He began to be able to distinguish reality-based racism from his own projections. No further meetings were held with his parents, although they initiated telephone contact with the therapist about once a month. Wei made considerable gains, lived independently, worked as a grocery clerk, and visited his family regularly.

In working with children and their families, it is important to establish a working relationship with the parents, as they can "make or break" the therapy. In this case, the therapist "exchanged" information, education, and supportive empathy for parental support of the treatment. She acknowledged Mrs. Lee's emotion-filled hypotheses about her son's illness while presenting other possible theories and hypotheses, based on her own expertise, for Mrs. Lee to consider. She clarified the treatment process in a clear, nonpatronizing manner and engaged the parents as "partners" in the treatment. They felt comfortable in calling whenever they had questions or concerns but did not pry into the specifics of Wei's therapy sessions, accepting the therapist's limits regarding that. In contrast to previous therapists, who had attempted to disengage Wei from his family with the implication that they were not "therapeutically" good for him, this therapist tried to specify behaviors that would help or hinder Wei's progress. In conjunction with Wei and his parents, she reached the conclusion that an independent residence with regular visits home for meals would be in Wei's best interest and would satisfy the cultural value of family interdependence.

In the "active exchange" with Wei, the therapist provided the following: support, empathy, and constancy; acknowledgment of his delusions and methods for gaining control over them; acceptance of his belief that racism was partly responsible for his condition; and an examination of his relevant settings—work, residence, and family—and factors in each that triggered his decompensation. Together they outlined methods for coping with those factors. For Wei's part of the exchange, he disclosed conflicts, difficult emotions, and his previously private and protective delusions, and he complied with the overall treatment plan. The alliance with Wei and his parents was grounded in a mutual exchange and a sense of reciprocity. Each participant dispelled any feeling of obligation by actively "giving" and "providing" in the relationship.

The appropriate pacing of self-disclosure and the management of communication are a delicate process with Chinese American clients. Personal disclosure of problems is antithetical to the cultural value of preserving "face" and keeping one's troubles contained within the family. In group or family therapy, often used with adolescents, this is particularly problematic, as the Chinese American adolescent, perhaps already feeling guilty for needing special treatment, is asked to reveal problems to a group of strangers, in direct contrast to family norms. Thus, the adolescent may feel doubly conflicted. Disclosure of family problems may also have different implications for various family members, as seen in the next case.

Mrs. Chow requested therapy for her family because of her 14-year-old son's outbursts in the home, his poor school grades, and her concerns that he would become a "delinquent." Their first session was with a Chinese American female therapist. Mrs. Chow and her son did most of the talking. She focused on her son's unmanageable behavior, speaking angrily toward him, and then began blaming the father for his inability to control his son. The son, experiencing severe identity conflicts, also seemed angry and accused his father of being too "Chinese-y." His father remained quiet, contributing little to the interaction. However, the family failed to return for subsequent sessions, never directly canceling the session with the therapist but leaving messages with excuses in response to the therapist's inquiries.

In this case, the therapist had lost control of the session, and the rapidity of disclosure had resulted in a "loss of face" for the father. The public humiliation by his son and his wife made it too difficult for him to return or to allow his family to return. The therapist failed to manage communication with respect to the cultural hierarchy and did not intercede quickly enough to stem the verbal abuse from son to father. The father, receiving nothing positive in this "exchange," refused to participate. Additionally, the therapist's low ascribed credibility as a young female further impeded the development of a therapeutic relationship.

In the cases presented so far, the concept of "active exchange" to establish a working alliance has focused primarily on the parents. This concept is also pertinent to the therapeutic relationship with the child or adolescent. In this situation, the "active exchange" may involve using tangible, specific techniques such as roleplaying, global assessment scaling, or play therapy.

Michael, a 17-year-old Chinese American high school senior born in the United States, was referred to an outpatient adolescent crisis unit by his school counselor for depression and suicidal ideation. Michael was failing in several subjects, was repeatedly absent or late for school, and was sleeping much of the time.

Michael's parents (his mother had immigrated from Taiwan over twenty years earlier; his father was American-born) were both successful professionals. They said, "There's nothing wrong with us or with Michael's younger brother and sister, so what's wrong with Michael?" The parents expected their children to be doctors and were frustrated and angered by Michael's academic failure. Michael was the first-born son and received the most pressure from the parents.

The therapist arranged a family meeting and then met several times with the parents, met regularly with Michael in individual sessions, and had regular phone contact with his school counselor. In the session with the parents, the "active exchange" involved the following: In response to their indirect queries, the therapist shared her academic and professional qualifications, knowing that education and advanced degrees were particularly meaningful to this couple and would raise her "ascribed credibility"; she underscored the importance of diminishing pressure on Michael and gently introduced more realistic expectations for their son (who was not interested in becoming a doctor and lacked the requisite academic record), guiding them toward recognition of Michael's other areas of strength. The parents reciprocated with support of Michael's therapy and attempts to adjust their expectations for Michael. Empathically, the therapist guided them through the process of grieving as they relinquished their unrealistic aspirations for Michael.

The individual work with Michael involved psychodynamic therapy supplemented with behavioral techniques. It was important that an "active exchange" with Michael produce meaningful gains early in the relationship. The therapist validated his interests and empathized with the pressure he endured from his parents. Michael became most animated and excited when talking about enrolling in a course to become a volunteer firefighter but would occasionally become unrealistic and impassively state his goal of becoming a neurosurgeon (his parents' wishes). He ventilated his own frustrations and his envy of his younger brother, who was enrolled in an academically exclusive high school. Michael's dreams and fantasies revealed a very active fantasy life, internalized feelings of failure, and much aggression. The therapist noticed much disorganization in his task orientation and problem-solving style. To deal with his disorganization, the therapist used the Global Attainment Scaling (GAS) to accomplish different objectives. This was done with school attendance, focusing on getting to school on time more frequently, which was necessary in order to graduate. This technique was also used in relation to study habits. Michael was a socially awkward, highly introverted adolescent. Roleplaying was used to prepare him for upcoming social situations. In general, the therapy focused on discrete behavioral goals (important indicators of progress for both Michael and his parents) as well as in-depth work on emotional areas.

The "active exchange" was a critical process in this therapy. Both Michael and his parents needed to experience benefits from therapy as soon as possible. Early on, Michael experienced relief from anxiety, understanding from an adult, validation for his interests, and some success using the GAS. As Michael's attendance improved and the number of hours spent sleeping diminished, his parents also noted these changes and continued support of his therapy. Michael's case also illustrates the destructiveness of the media stereotype of the Asian American "whiz kids" (Brand, 1987). Parents expect this stereotype and place unrealistic and injurious academic pressure on their children. For Michael, this was an added stress compounding already serious emotional problems.

For many Chinese American children, play therapy may be a useful vehicle for dealing with the problem of self-disclosure and saving face, as the following case illustrates.

Billy was a 9-year-old fourth-grader, referred for disruptive behavior in school, marked deterioration in academic performance, and difficult behavior at home. He had been born in the United States of parents who had immigrated from China as adolescents. Billy was the shortest boy in his class.

Billy repeatedly brought homework into the playroom. He ignored the toys, concentrated on doing his homework, and engaged in minimal communication with the therapist. He would occasionally ask the therapist to correct his homework. The therapist began to use the homework as a vehicle for communication. Eventually, Billy admitted that he was coming here as punishment and that he thought the therapist was a teacher or some kind of tutor. After the therapist's role was clarified, Billy began to move toward the toys. Over several sessions, he played with army men who were all repeatedly killed by a single "hero." Probing revealed this hero to be "a big White guy and new in town," while the other men were all different colors and not as smart. Symbolically, the play revealed Billy's poor self-esteem and conflicts around being a new Chinese American boy in a predominantly non-Asian, suburban school. Further play revealed anger toward his parents for removing him from his old neighborhood and friends, most of whom were also Chinese American.

Because Billy could not directly talk about these issues or express anger toward his parents to a stranger, play served as a face-saving modality. Unlike verbal disclosure, symbolic play does not provoke guilt or shame for revealing family difficulties or secrets to an outsider. Some children initially have difficulty using the play materials. Most commonly, Chinese American children view the therapist as a teacher, and bringing in homework is sometimes even encouraged by parents, who may not be familiar with the therapeutic process. A decline in academic performance is often a first indicator of problems and, for some Chinese parents who stress academic excellence, a most impor-

tant symptom to alleviate. When using play therapy, it is important to educate parents about its efficacy, as they may often
view it as frivolous and not educational or healing.

Billy's case also illustrates that cultural identity conflicts
may be the core problem or may be entangled with the main
presenting problem. His feelings of not fitting in and of feeling
inferior and different generated much anger and hostility, which,
in turn, interfered with his schoolwork and his relations with his
parents.

Summary and Conclusions

Chinese Americans are a very diverse population within
the United States. They come from different provinces of China
and countries in Asia, they speak different dialects, their descendants are quite variable in their degree of acculturation to
American society, and their manifestations and conceptualizations of psychological disorders are numerous. Among Chinese
American youth, psychological problems span the entire range
from severe psychotic illness to quasi-normative adolescent
identity conflicts. However, what is striking is the degree to
which ethnic and racial issues are interwoven with the presenting disorder. The psychotic delusions often involve themes of
racial persecution; the adolescent identity conflicts involve
questions of "Am I Chinese or American? Where do I fit? Where
do I belong?" Consequently, in treating these youth, it is important to understand the dynamic blending of generic and culture-
specific features.

An ecological perspective is conducive to a fuller understanding of the disorders of these youngsters. The individual
psychodynamics are intertwined with the primary cultural and
social unit, the family; in turn, the family continually negotiates with outside institutions, whether they are schools, of-
fices, neighborhoods, or family associations. As the case studies
illustrate, some families experience frustrating and bewildering
contact with mental health agencies. Therapists in these situations need to be guides for the youngster and family, not only
collecting data for an assessment but simultaneously unraveling

intersystem conflicts that contribute to the presenting psychological problems.

This chapter has offered a framework for intervention with Chinese American families, children, and adolescents. Although awareness of the culture is important for good intervention, it is not enough. A dynamic understanding of sociocultural factors in assessment, a knowledge of techniques for establishing therapist credibility, and a working alliance based on a reciprocal "active exchange" are essential for effective treatment.

References

Abbott, K., and Abbott, E. "Juvenile Delinquency in San Francisco's Chinese-American Community: 1961–1966." In S. Sue and N. Wagner (eds.), *Asian-Americans: Psychological Perspectives.* Palo Alto, Calif.: Science and Behavior Books, 1973.

Aronowitz, M. "The Social and Emotional Adjustment of Immigrant Children: A Review of the Literature." *International Migration Review,* 1984, *18* (2), 237–257.

Berk, B., and Hirata, L. "Mental Illness Among the Chinese: Myth or Reality?" *Journal of Social Issues,* 1973, *29* (2), 149–166.

Brand, D. "The New Whiz Kids." *Time,* Aug. 31, 1987, pp. 42–51.

Brody, E. (ed.). *Minority Group Adolescents in the United States.* New York: Krieger, 1968.

Bronfenbrenner, U. *The Ecology of Human Development: Experiments by Nature and Design.* Cambridge, Mass.: Harvard University Press, 1979.

Brown, T., Stein, K., Huang, K., and Harris, D. "Mental Illness and the Role of Mental Health Facilities in Chinatown." In S. Sue and N. Wagner (eds.), *Asian-Americans: Psychological Perspectives.* Palo Alto, Calif.: Science and Behavior Books, 1973.

Chen, J. *The Chinese of America: From the Beginnings to the Present.* New York: Harper & Row, 1981.

Clark, K., and Clark, M. "Racial Identification and Preference in Negro Children." In T. Newcomb and E. Hartley (eds.), *Readings in Social Psychology.* New York: Holt, Rinehart & Winston, 1947.

County of Los Angeles Department of Mental Health. *Client and Service Summary Statistics for the Period 07/01/84–06/30/85.* Los Angeles: County of Los Angeles Department of Mental Health, 1985.

County of Los Angeles Department of Mental Health. *Client and Service Summary Statistics for the Period 07/01/85–06/30/86.* Los Angeles: County of Los Angeles Department of Mental Health, 1986.

Fong, S. "Identity Conflicts of Chinese Adolescents in San Francisco." In E. Brody (ed.), *Minority Group Adolescents in the United States.* Baltimore: Williams & Wilkins, 1968.

Fong, T. "Asian Small Business Growth Becomes Lightning Rod for Anti-Asian Sentiment." *East/West News,* July 9, 1987, p. 1.

Garmezy, N., and Rutter, M. (eds.). *Stress, Coping and Development in Children.* New York: McGraw-Hill, 1983.

Hisama, T. "Minority Group Children and Behavior Disorders— the Case of Asian-American Children." *Behavior Disorders,* 1980, 5 (3), 186–196.

Ishisaka, H., and Takagi, C. "Social Work with Asian- and Pacific-Americans." In J. Green (ed.), *Cultural Awareness in the Human Services.* Englewood Cliffs, N.J.: Prentice-Hall, 1982.

Lee, E. "A Social Systems Approach to Assessment and Treatment for Chinese-American Families." In M. McGoldrick, J. K. Pearce, and J. Giordano (eds.), *Ethnicity and Family Therapy.* New York: Guilford Press, 1982.

Lin, Y. *The Wisdom of Confucius.* New York: Random House, 1938.

Lyman, S. "Conflict and the Web of Group Affiliation in San Francisco's Chinatown, 1850–1910." In N. Hundley (ed.), *The Asian American: The Historical Experience.* Santa Barbara, Calif.: Clio Press, 1976.

Ma, S. P., Cohen, N. L., and Yeung, W. "Assessing Suicide Risk Among Chinese-American Adolescents." Paper presented at annual meeting of the American Orthopsychiatric Association, San Francisco, Mar. 1988.

Millard, M. "Problem of Asian Juvenile Offenders Brings Outcry for Better System in S.F." *East/West News*, July 30, 1987, pp. 1, 8–9.

Naditch, M., and Morrissey, R. "Role Stress, Personality, and Psychopathology in a Group of Immigrant Adolescents." *Journal of Abnormal Psychology*, 1976, *85* (1), 113–116.

Nakao, A. "Thorny Debate over U.C.: Too Many Brainy Asians?" *San Francisco Examiner*, May 3, 1987, pp. A1, A12–13.

Nann, B. "Settlement Programs for Immigrant Women and Families." In R. Nann (ed.), *Uprooting and Surviving*. Dordrecht, Holland: Reidel, 1982.

Okie, S. "Children Reach for New Heights in Study of Growth Hormones." *The Washington Post*, October 31, 1988, pp. A1, A4.

Osborne, W. "Adjustment Differences of Selected Foreign Born Pupils." *California Journal of Educational Research*, 1971, *22*, 131–139.

Ou, Y. S., and McAdoo, H. "Ethnic Identity and Self-Esteem in Chinese Children." Unpublished report submitted to NIMH Center for Minority Group Mental Health Programs. Columbia, Md.: Columbia Research Systems, 1980.

Pothier, P. *Mental Health Counseling with Children*. Boston: Little, Brown, 1976.

Reisman, J. *Principles of Psychotherapy with Children*. New York: Wiley, 1973.

Rutter, M. "Stress, Coping and Development: Some Issues and Some Questions." In N. Garmezy and M. Rutter (eds.), *Stress, Coping and Development in Children*. New York: McGraw-Hill, 1983.

Rutter, M., and others. "Children of West Indian Immigrants: I. Rates of Behavioral Deviance and of Psychiatric Disorder." *Journal of Child Psychology and Psychiatry*, 1974, *15*, 241–262.

Shon, S., and Ja, D. "Asian Families." In M. McGoldrick, J. K. Pearce, and J. Giordano (eds.), *Ethnicity and Family Therapy*. New York: Guilford Press, 1982.

Sluzki, C. "Migration and Family Conflict." *Family Process*, 1979, *18* (4), 379–390.

Special Populations Task Force. *Report on the Mental Health of Asian/Pacific Americans Submitted to the President's Commission on Mental Health.* Washington, D.C.: U.S. Government Printing Office, 1978.

Sue, D., Sue, D. W., and Sue, D. M. "Psychological Development of Chinese-American Children." In G. J. Powell, J. Yamamoto, A. Romero, and A. Morales (eds.), *The Psychological Development of Minority Group Children.* New York: Brunner/Mazel, 1983.

Sue, D. W., and Frank, A. C. "A Typological Approach to the Psychological Study of Chinese- and Japanese-American College Males." *Journal of Social Issues,* 1973, *29* (2), 129–148.

Sue, D. W., and Kirk, B. "Differential Characteristics of Japanese-American and Chinese-American College Students." *Journal of Counseling Psychology,* 1973, *20,* 142–148.

Sue, S., and McKinney, H. "Asian-Americans in the Community Health Care System." *American Journal of Orthopsychiatry,* 1975, *45* (1), 111–118.

Sue, S., and Sue, D. W. "MMPI Comparisons Between Asian-American and Non-Asian Students Utilizing a Student Health Psychiatric Clinic." *Journal of Counseling Psychology,* 1974, *21* (5), 423–427.

Sue, S., and Zane, N. "The Role of Culture and Cultural Techniques in Psychotherapy: A Critique and Reformulation." *American Psychologist,* 1987, *42* (1), 37–45.

Sung, B. *Mountain of Gold.* New York: Macmillan, 1967.

Touliatos, J., and Lindholm, B. "Behavior Disturbance of Children of Native-Born and Immigrant Parents." *Journal of Community Psychology,* 1980, *8* (1), 28–33.

Tseng, W. S., and McDermott, J. *Culture, Mind and Therapy.* New York: Brunner/Mazel, 1981.

U.S. Bureau of the Census. *1980 Census of Population: General Population Characteristics, United States Summary.* Washington, D.C.: U.S. Government Printing Office, 1983a.

U.S. Bureau of the Census. *1980 Census of Population: General Social and Economic Characteristics, United States Summary.* Washington, D.C.: U.S. Government Printing Office, 1983b.

3

Japanese American
Children and Adolescents

Donna K. Nagata

Japanese American adults have typically been perceived as being successful, well acculturated, and mentally healthy, while their children are often seen as being obedient and educationally successful. However, mental health professionals have become increasingly aware that these perceptions are incomplete and inaccurate and that there has been a failure to recognize the impact of cultural and sociohistorical factors on the mental health of Japanese American parents and their children. The present chapter reviews literature on the assessment and treatment of Japanese American children and adolescents and their families. Since little is available on this topic, it is hoped that this chapter will provide an initial framework for understanding the complex issues presented by this population.

For the purposes of this chapter, the term *Japanese American* refers to a person who was born in the United States or who immigrated near the turn of the century. It does not include recent immigrants from Japan. Specific Japanese terms are used to identify generations of Japanese Americans. The "Issei" were the first generation of Japanese to come to the United States; the "Nisei," second-generation Japanese Americans, were born here. The offspring of the Nisei make up the third generation and are called "Sansei," while the fourth and fifth generations are referred to as "Yonsei" and "Gosei," respectively. Because anti-Asian immigration laws regulated the numbers of Japanese immigrants to the United States, there is an unusual degree of distinction between these generational categories. Most Issei immigrated between 1900 and 1924, and their American-born children, the Nisei, were generally born between 1910 and 1945 (Kitano, 1969b). In addition, there are some Japanese Americans who were American-born and therefore technically are Nisei but who also spent many of their early years in Japan. The term *Kibei* has been used to refer to these individuals. It is primarily the children and grandchildren of the Nisei or Kibei generation who constitute the current Japanese American youth population.

Demographic Data

In 1980 there were 716,000 Americans of Japanese ancestry in the United States, including 28 percent who were foreign-born (U.S. Bureau of the Census, 1983, Table 40). The geographical distribution of Japanese Americans reflects a strong concentration in the West (80.3 percent) as opposed to the Northeast (6.5 percent), Midwest (6.5 percent), or South (6.6 percent). Geographical location is an important variable to consider when reviewing the research literature. Although the two largest concentrations of Japanese Americans are in California (261,800) and Hawaii (239,700), a distinction must be made between these groups. Japanese Americans in Hawaii live in an environment with many Asian Americans, while mainland Japanese Americans live in a Caucasian-majority environment. In addition, the government-enforced incarceration of Japanese Americans during World War II affected nearly all those on the mainland, in contrast to much smaller numbers in Hawaii. The impact of these varied environments can be seen in the finding that Hawaiian Japanese Americans tend to preserve their Japanese culture to a greater degree than their mainland counterparts (Johnson, 1977; Kitano, 1969b). There are also important distinctions between different mainland cities with Japanese American populations. Gehrie (1976) points out that there are differences between Japanese Americans who grew up in Los Angeles, where there is an identifiable, concentrated Japanese American population, and in Chicago, where Japanese Americans are more widely dispersed. Sansei interviewed by Gehrie in Chicago, for example, perceived California Sansei as less individualistic and more sheltered within the Japanese American community.

Educationally, Japanese Americans are above the national average. Nearly all graduate from high school. In 1980 the U.S. census showed that 96.2 percent of Japanese Americans aged 16 to 17 at that time were enrolled in school. Over 96 percent of both male and female adults aged 25–29 years were high school graduates, and 26 percent of those 25 years or older had four or more years of college. In addition, the majority of Japanese American children under 18 were living at home with two parents. With a median family income in 1980 of $27,354, Japanese American families have one of the lowest poverty rates (4.2 percent) in the country. However, the "successful" economic picture of the Japanese Americans must be viewed with caution. A separate 1980 report published by the United States Commission on Civil Rights points out that Japanese Americans (and other Asian Americans) are actually underemployed (U.S. Commission on Civil Rights, 1980). The report cites a study conducted by Cabezas (1979) which found that college-educated Japanese American males in four major mainland cities (Chicago, Los Angeles, New York, and San Francisco) made several thousand dollars less than their majority non-Asian peers in 1970.

Although Japanese Americans were the largest Asian American group at the time of the 1970 census, they are currently the third largest. (As of 1980, the largest group is Chinese Americans, followed by Filipino Americans.) According to estimates from the Population Reference Bureau and Hawaii's East-West Center, by the year 2000, all Asian American groups except Japanese Americans will experience growth rates of 10 percent or more. The projection for the Japanese American population for 2000 is 856,619, or 8.7 percent of the total Asian American population. Hence, Japanese Americans are becoming an ever smaller proportion of the Asian American group.

Whereas in 1980 they constituted 20.7 percent of all Asian Americans, the percentage is expected to drop to 12.3 by 1990 and 8.7 by 2000 (Gardner, Robey, and Smith, 1985).

The census data reflect two important issues for Japanese American families. First, they illustrate how it is possible for stereotypes of Japanese American educational and economic success to be perpetuated. These stereotypes are then used by some to support the view that Japanese Americans are "problem free" and have assimilated well into American mainstream society. Information in the current chapter challenges this viewpoint. Second, the data reflect a cultural group whose proportion of representation in society is decreasing. This can have important implications for Japanese Americans' sense of community, identity, and role in the majority society. The current outmarriage rate is estimated to be greater than 60 percent (Kitano, Yeung, Chai, and Hatanaka, 1984). Many Japanese Americans worry that Japanese American culture and values will disappear altogether in the near future. In the meantime, the diminishing numbers of Japanese Americans also reduce the degree to which they can maintain the political power necessary to advocate for their community needs.

Utilization of Mental Health Facilities

To understand the mental health needs of Japanese American youth, it is useful to evaluate the degree to which this population is using current services. Unfortunately, a review of literature on the incidence of psychological and behavioral disorders in children revealed no comprehensive data published on Japanese American children and adolescents. This absence of information is not surprising, given that there is very little information on the mental health of Japanese Americans of any age (Kitano, 1969a). The data reported for Japanese Americans indicate that they rarely seek mental health services and are underrepresented in service utilization (Kitano, 1969a; Sue and Morishima, 1982; Uomoto and Gorsuch, 1984). Kitano (1969a), for example, found that admission rates to California state mental hospitals were proportionately much lower for Japanese

Americans than for Caucasian Americans. Similarly, Sue and McKinney (1975) found that although Japanese Americans made up 1.2 percent of the population in the Seattle area, they represented only 0.1 percent of the cases seen at community mental health centers there.

There are numerous problems with this "treated cases" method of estimating the mental health needs of any group (see Sue and Morishima, 1982). One major problem concerns the assumption that low utilization rates imply a low incidence of problems in the community. However, research indicates that it may be only the most distressed Japanese Americans who seek public services and that the absence of Japanese Americans in the mental health statistics reflects their culturally based hesitancy to use services, not their "superior" mental health (Kitano, 1969a; Sue and Morishima, 1982; Sue and Sue, 1974).

Rather than reflecting an absence of mental health problems, low utilization rates seem to indicate that Japanese Americans are reluctant to use the types of services for which such statistics are maintained. An informal study by Kitano (1969a) noted that Japanese American mental health professionals themselves agreed that Japanese Americans rarely use professional services for emotional problems. One possible reason is that they rely more on the extended family and informal structures for support (Kitano, 1969b). This would not be surprising, since the family unit is of central importance in Japanese American culture. Kim (1978) conducted a needs assessment of Japanese Americans in the Chicago area and found support for this hypothesis. She reported that the Japanese Americans in her study relied more heavily on private resources (for example, family, friends, relatives) than public resources (hospitals, doctors, police).

Attitudes toward utilization of mental health services may differ across generations, however. A recent study suggests that the supportive function of the Japanese American family for psychological problems may be less apparent today. Uomoto and Gorsuch (1984) examined the attitudes of second- and third-generation (Nisei and Sansei) Japanese Americans toward mental health and non–mental health referrals. Participants from

Seattle and Los Angeles were presented with vignettes describing various disorders (paranoid schizophrenia, major depression, and agoraphobia) and a fourth vignette describing marital and family problems. They were then asked to write two things they would do in response to each vignette. In contrast to earlier literature, family and friends were not seen as the primary source of referral. Referral to a mental health facility was at least as frequent as referral to family and friends for problems of schizophrenia, depression, and agoraphobia. Sansei were more likely to refer the cases in the vignettes to a psychiatrist or psychologist than Nisei. Hence, it is possible that the cultural variables mentioned previously may be less apparent in the mental health attitudes of today's Japanese Americans. All respondents in the study, however, were less likely to turn to mental health professionals for referral of marital and family problems. This is particularly important given that many child/adolescent problems are related to family issues.

The surrounding ethnic environment may also influence the likelihood that a Japanese American family will utilize services. Prizzia and Villanueva-King (1977) found that, in Hawaii, Japanese Americans reported less discomfort in seeking counseling at a community center than their Samoan, Filipino, Hawaiian, Chinese, and Caucasian American counterparts. Although this seems to contradict previously cited findings indicating that Japanese Americans would be reluctant to seek services, it may also be seen as evidence for the influence of ethnic environments. Japanese Americans, and Asian Americans in general, form a much larger proportion of the population in Hawaii. Accordingly, they may experience greater comfort in seeking services there, because the greater availability and visibility of Asian ethnic mental health workers make the services less alien and intimidating.

Epidemiological Data

Data on the incidence of specific problems among Japanese American children and adolescents are scarce. However, statistics gathered by the Clinical Information Service of the Department of Mental Health in Los Angeles, an area with a high concentration of Japanese Americans, illustrate the range of cases that have been treated (data provided through personal communication with S. G. Lubeck, May 7, 1987). A total of 879 Japanese American clients received public mental health services in Los Angeles County from 1985–86. Of this total, 12.5 percent ($N = 110$) were 21 years of age or younger. These 110 youth represented less than one tenth of 1 percent of the county's Japanese American population. The majority of clients from the youth group were between ages 13 and 21. More specifically, the breakdown by age was as follows: 5 clients aged 5 years old or less, 14 clients aged 6–12 years, 45 clients aged 13–18 years, and 46 clients aged 19–21 years. The most frequent mode of service was outpatient (94 cases), followed by inpatient (9 cases), day treatment (5 cases), and case-management/continuing care services (2 cases). Almost all clients aged 21 or younger who were seen for inpatient and day treatment services were 18–21 years of age.

The Los Angeles County statistics also showed that Japanese American boys (62 percent of total cases seen) were seen more frequently for outpatient care than girls. In addition, the most frequent primary diagnoses for Japanese American youth at the time of initiating outpatient services were adjustment disorders, conduct disorders, affective-related disorders, and schizophrenia-related disorders. Approximately 12 to 15 outpatient clients aged 21 or younger fell within each of these categories.

Overall, the Los Angeles County statistics reflect a very low incidence rate for Japanese American children and adolescents. The low incidence of referred Japanese American child and adolescent cases is also reflected in data reported by Sata (1983). Sata noted that information available through the Seattle public schools for 1974–75 reflected "extremely low" numbers of Sansei children who were identified as having behavioral or special education problems. In addition, of 1,458 Sansei students in the Seattle school district that year, only 2 were suspended.

It should be noted, however, that private mental health service utilization is not represented in either the Los Angeles or the Seattle data. Hence a true estimate of utilization would be higher. In addition, the low incidence rate does not mean that Japanese American children do not suffer from psychological difficulties. The low rates of documented treatment cases may actually reflect a tendency by Japanese American parents to deny or minimize certain behavioral problems in their children. Sata (1983), for example, points out that cases of hyperactivity may be infrequently reported for Japanese American children because their parents minimize the clinical significance of overactivity and inattention.

Very low rates of delinquency for Japanese American youth have also been reported (Kitano, 1967). The Los Angeles County probation figures for 1960 indicated that Japanese Americans had the lowest number of arrests of all comparison groups (White, Black, Chinese, and Native American). Kitano (1967) noted that those Japanese Americans who were delinquent were more likely to come from broken homes, to identify with their ethnic community, to be distant from their families, and to be essentially "marginal" socially. More recent investigations suggest that the low rates of the 1960s might have underestimated Japanese American juvenile arrests because of early intervention by Nisei parents to correct the problem. Since parental action can increase the likelihood that formal charges or further prosecution will be dropped, it seems likely that a higher proportion of Japanese American juveniles were engaged in delinquent behavior but that this was not reflected in formal arrest records (Sata, 1983). Data on the specific offenses committed by Japanese American juveniles were unavailable. However, Morales, Ferguson, and Munford (1983) report that the most frequent offenses committed by Asian Americans as a combined group were burglary, petty theft, auto theft/joyriding, and possession of marijuana.

Some information exists about alcohol and drug abuse. Japanese Americans have been observed to drink less alcohol than Caucasian Americans. However, increasing acculturation has resulted in an increase in alcohol consumption by Japanese American youth (Sue and Nakamura, 1984). Today's Sansei and Yonsei adolescents and young adults are more likely to drink than their parents or grandparents. Sue and Nakamura (1984) point out that a fourth-generation Japanese American adolescent has parents whose cultural attitudes and behavior toward alcohol are much closer to those of the more permissive American society. Hence, this adolescent may be more at risk for developing alcohol-related problems. Nakagawa and Watanabe's (1973) survey of drug use by Japanese Americans in Seattle junior and senior high schools also supports the hypothesis that current Japanese American youth may be more at risk for chemical abuse than previous generations. Of the Japanese American students polled, 29 percent reported having had some experience with drugs.

In contrast, Japanese American families remain underrepresented in statistics on child abuse. Dubanoski and Snyder (1980) reported that although Japanese Americans accounted for about 27 percent of the population in Hawaii in 1976 and 1977, only 3.45 percent of abuse and 4.65 percent of neglect cases were attributed to them. Interestingly, neglect was more common than abuse. The authors suggested that this finding may reflect the Japanese American family's emphasis on shame and ostracism as forms of punishment, as opposed to direct confrontations involving physical violence.

The lack of documented psychological or behavioral difficulties in Japanese American children and adolescents should not be seen as evidence for the absence of psychological problems. Sue and Morishima (1982) point out that psychological distress is not always presented in the form of pathology. It might also be reflected in a diminished degree of positive mental health or in a failure to live up to one's potential. There is evidence, for example, that Japanese American children aged 9–12 years have a less positive self-concept than their Caucasian American peers with respect to physical characteristics and that this dissatisfaction may endure into young adulthood (Arkoff and Weaver, 1966). Sata (1983) suggests that early adolescence and the onset of dating may present especially stressful times for Japanese American children. This is a time when the realities of their ethnicity may create difficulties (for example, encountering parents in other racial groups who have negative attitudes toward Japanese or Japanese Americans). The transition between high school and college may also be problematic. Emphasis by Nisei parents for their Sansei children to do well in school can create pressures on those who do attend college. Further, because of the high numbers of Japanese Americans attending college, a stereotype exists that all Japanese Americans are high academic achievers. Sata points out that those youth who do not go on to college may be at particular risk for emotional problems. Not only do they fail to live up to the stereotype of Japanese American success, but they are also more likely to be exposed to discrimination in the nonprofessional labor market.

Cultural and Family Characteristics

The lack of information on the incidence of diagnoses for Japanese American children and adolescents is reflective of a larger phenomenon—the lack of data on Japanese American mental health in general. Kitano (1969a) noted that it is curious that so little scientific interest in Japanese Americans has been generated. He hypothesized that perhaps this lack of interest can be attributed to the perception that Japanese Americans have been so successful in adapting to life in the United States. Stereotypes of Japanese Americans as the "model minority" have caused many people to assume that Japanese Americans are no different from nonminority Caucasian Americans. Yet, a brief glance at the history of the Japanese in this country shows that this is far from true.

Historical Perspectives of the Family. Japanese Americans first immigrated to the United States after 1885, when Japan first legalized emigration (Knoll, 1982). The major portion of Japanese immigration occurred between 1890 and 1924. This first generation of immigrants (the Issei) were young males who hoped to earn a fortune and return to Japan. Most did not return but settled in Hawaii and along the Pacific Coast, working as farm laborers. Issei men eventually requested wives from Japan, and the arrival of these Issei women marked the beginnings of the Japanese American family. The numbers of Japanese in America grew; by 1920 there were 111,000 people of Japanese ancestry. However, the Immigration Act of 1924 curtailed the relatively free immigration of all Asians, and fewer than 7,000 Japanese Americans came to the United States between 1925 and 1941 (Knoll, 1982). When World War II began in 1941, no Japanese were allowed into the country.

The children of the Issei were born in America, and most spent the larger part or all of their lives in this country. These second-generation Japanese Americans (the Nisei) were raised with a mixture of Japanese and American values. It was not unusual for a Nisei child to attend Japanese-language school immediately after American school every day or to go from speaking English at school to speaking Japanese at home. Because Japanese Americans tended to keep within their own community, the Nisei associated primarily with other Japanese Americans and hence were exposed to the same pressures to conform that the Issei experienced. Marriages for both the Issei and Nisei generations were also primarily within-group, because of anti-miscegenation laws as well as ethnic preference. For example, a law preventing intermarriage with Whites existed in California, where the majority of non-Hawaiian Japanese Americans were located, until 1948 (Tinker, 1982).

Laws preventing Japanese from marrying Whites represent only a portion of the discriminatory legislation and racism experienced by Japanese Americans in this country. Numerous immigration quotas and restrictions were applied to them, and it was not until the McCarran-Walter Act of 1952 that the Issei were allowed to apply for citizenship. The most blatant act of discrimination toward Japanese Americans took place during World War II when all persons of Japanese ancestry were removed from their homes along the West Coast and placed in internment camps for periods of up to four years. Following the bombing of Pearl Harbor in 1941, more than 110,000 Japanese Americans were ordered by the United States government to live in army barracks located in desolate desert areas of the country (Kitano, 1969b). Two thirds were U.S. citizens (primarily Nisei). They could take only what they could carry and were given little time to prepare for the move. Many had only twenty-four hours' notice that they were being evacuated. Most

Japanese Americans remained in the camps for an average of two to three years. The impact of this internment, as will be discussed later, was great (Nagata, 1987).

The third-generation Japanese Americans (the Sansei) differ markedly from their grandparents and parents, particularly with respect to outmarriage. Kitano, Yeung, Chai, and Hatanaka (1984) report that in 1979 in Los Angeles, Japanese American rates of outmarriage were 60.6 percent; half of these outmarriages were to non-Asians. This high rate of outmarriage is important to note, for it means that the structure of the present-day Japanese American family is qualitatively different in many ways. The child or adolescent of Japanese American ancestry today is as likely to come from a family where a second racial or cultural background is present as from a family where both parents are Japanese American.

Family Structure. Although Japanese American families have tended to remain intact, with low rates of separation and divorce, generational changes over time and outmarriage rates have certainly affected the nature of the family for this ethnic group. Even in families where both parents are Japanese Americans, it is impossible to predict the degree to which family structure and values brought to the United States by the Issei generation have been retained. Nonetheless, it is highly likely that the Japanese values of the Issei have, albeit perhaps indirectly, shaped important characteristics of the present-day Japanese American family. Therefore an overview of these values is useful.

The Issei who came to the United States had been raised entirely with Japanese concepts of social and familial structure. Kitano and Kikumura (1976) summarize key aspects of Japanese social structure that have been identified by Nakane (1970). These include the following: (1) an emphasis on *ie*, or the household unit, as the most important structure for early socialization and upbringing, (2) an emphasis on the group as opposed to the individual and on roles within the group structure, (3) the importance of loyalty, and (4) the importance of rank and status. In essence, the Japanese social structure for the Issei stressed high in-group unity, group consensus, and discouragement of individuality. Additional terms that are useful in understanding Japanese behavior include *on* and *giri*, which emphasize the importance of recognizing ascribed and contractual obligations, respectively, and *amae*, which is not directly translatable into English but very generally involves the concept of dependency and the need to be loved and cherished (Kitano, 1969b).

In comparing the structure of families in Japan and the United States, Yamamoto and Kubota (1983) describe the Japanese family as emphasizing the priority of the family group over the individual, vertical relationships, conformity to societal norms, and social control based on shame, guilt, and an appeal to duty and responsibility. In contrast, American families are seen as emphasizing individualism, equalitarian relationships, independent behavior in society, and social control based on love and punishment. Other characteristics of the Japanese American family seen as representative of Japanese values include a vertical structure with authority vested in the father and older males, duty and obligation stressed over love, an emphasis on prolonged family dependence, encouragement of obedience and conformity in children, and an emphasis on indirect, nonconfrontational techniques of parenting that rely on nonverbal communication (Kitano and Kikumura, 1976). In addition, Kitano (1969b) notes the importance of the extended family as a source of social support.

Enryo, a Japanese concept that means to be reserved, not to express one's wishes or preferences, and to defer to those in authority (Yamamoto and Kubota, 1983), has also influenced the Japanese American family. This can be seen in such behaviors as a reluctance to praise achievements, a hesitancy to speak out, or a reluctance to ask questions. *Gaman*, another Japanese term, is used to describe the importance of repressing or internalizing, rather than externalizing, emotions. In the Japanese American family, this is often demonstrated by an emphasis on keeping emotions such as anger or hostility inside. This, in conjunction with the value of nonconfrontational and indirect communication, serves to minimize overt outbursts of aggression.

Although the indirect communication style can be a

strength for the Japanese American family, it can be problematic around certain topics. Sexuality, according to Kitano (1969b), was rarely discussed between the Issei and Nisei generations, where a language difference created an obvious communication barrier. However, recent data from Abramson and Imai-Marquez (1982) suggest that even the Sansei generation, who do not have a communication barrier with their children, may experience difficulty in discussing sexuality within the family. According to their study, although the level of sex-related guilt has been decreasing with each successive generation, Japanese Americans, as a group, still express significantly greater sex-related guilt than Caucasian Americans. This research did not explore the relation between sex guilt and parental communication about sexual issues. However, it seems plausible that higher degrees of sex guilt would be associated with greater discomfort in discussing sexual matters.

Some characteristics of family role structure appear similar between Japanese and Japanese American families, while others have been adapted to the American life-style. For example, although the Issei father was structurally in the position of greatest authority, he was culturally disadvantaged in the United States and had to rely on his Nisei son or daughter to handle issues where communication outside the Japanese community was necessary (Kitano, 1969b). A number of researchers have pointed to the fact that each successive generation of Japanese Americans is more acculturated than the last, and today's Sansei are depicted as being much less influenced by Japanese values and more influenced by American values than their parents and grandparents (for example, Connor, 1974; Masuda, Matsumoto, and Meredith, 1970; Padilla, Wagatsuma, and Lindholm, 1985). At the same time, there is evidence that differences do remain between Japanese American and Caucasian American families. O'Reilly, Tokuno, and Ebata (1986) found that Hawaiian Japanese American parents differed from their Caucasian American peers in their rankings of valued competencies to be encouraged in children. While the Caucasian American parents ranked the characteristic "Self-directed" highest in importance, Japanese American parents rated "Behaves well" as most important. In another study, Caudill and Frost (1972) noted that although some behaviors of Sansei mothers from Hawaii resembled those of Caucasian American mothers more than those of mothers in Japan, the Sansei also retained characteristics of mothering that were more like the Japanese mothers' (for example, spending greater amounts of time carrying, lulling, and playing with their babies). Finally, although the Sansei are generally portrayed as being highly acculturated, this may not necessarily be true. Gehrie (1976) has suggested that the individualistic behaviors that some interpret as reflecting acculturation may actually be more reflective of the Sansei's mode of handling their anxiety about being different in a White-majority environment. Clearly, further research to explore the dynamics underlying observed behaviors of acculturation is necessary.

The Internment Experience. The preceding paragraphs highlight several important characteristics of the Japanese American family and the ways these traits have been perpetuated. However, the single most important historical event to influence Japanese American families and their retention of Japanese characteristics is perhaps the internment during World War II. Hence, this event warrants special attention.

Several researchers have discussed the psychological impact of the internment camps on the Japanese American family (for example, Morishima, 1973; Mass, 1986). These effects included a change in family structure due to barracklike communal conditions and disruption of normal family roles, severe economic loss, the psychological stress of being uprooted and incarcerated for a prolonged period, blatant questioning of one's national loyalty, and the experience of victimization and fearfulness for one's future. Mass (1986) has noted that the impact of these conditions on those who were interned was great and resulted in the adoption of defense mechanisms such as repression, denial, rationalization, and identification with the aggressor. Perhaps the most noticeable impact of the camps is how little the Issei and Nisei have discussed their experiences during the years they were interned. For forty years, an open discussion of the internment was absent. Some have attributed this silence to the hypothesis that the internees were similar to victims of rape

(Hansen and Mitson, 1974). Like rape victims, they had done nothing wrong and yet experienced shame and guilt for what had happened to them.

The impact of the internment extends beyond those who were incarcerated. As literature on children of survivors of the Holocaust demonstrates (for example, Danieli, 1982; Nadler, Kav-Venaki, and Gleitman, 1985), the children of those who underwent such severe and disruptive discrimination are likely to experience cross-generational psychological effects. One way in which the Sansei and Yonsei have been affected is through the child-rearing practices of their parents. Morishima (1973) noted that many Nisei parents who were interned indicated that they made a concerted effort to raise their children to be as "American" as possible. Given this context, it is not surprising that very few Sansei speak or understand Japanese. Kitano and Kikumura (1976) also point out that, as a result of the camp experience, Japanese Americans were especially concerned that their children not "rock the boat" or "stick out" in their communities. In essence, there was a strong desire for invisibility. Parental expectations of the younger generation have also been affected. Henkin (1985) suggests that the Nisei may have responded to racial discrimination in part through an emphasis on high achievement, which has created stress for the Sansei. Many Sansei may experience as shameful a level of accomplishment that other Americans might see as a success. A Sansei student, for example, may be embarrassed by a less than perfect A- grade-point average, while her Caucasian American peer would see this as outstanding. At the same time, Henkin notes, the Sansei are caught in a double bind between being as "American" as possible (which includes becoming independent) and remaining "Japanese" by following their parents' expectations to maintain close family ties.

My interview research indicates that the lack of parental communication about the internment has affected the Sansei. A hesitancy to discuss the topic created a sense of emotional distance for some and frustration for others. Although Sansei are eager to learn more about this part of their parents' lives, they are reluctant to ask, partly out of respect for their parents' privacy and partly out of fear of uncovering negative emotions or information within their family. Despite a lack of communication about the camps, the internment continues to be an important issue for many Sansei. One interviewee, for example, felt that his mother's camp experience had affected his upbringing. He stated: "I'm sure it affected how she dealt with that part of her life. . . . It shaped her temperament and instilled in her that her children need to succeed in life." This pressure, he noted, resulted in high expectations for success, expectations that both he and his sister found difficult to bear. Eventually, both sought therapy to help them deal with their difficulties.

The full extent to which the internment has affected the children in today's Japanese American families remains to be seen. What is apparent is that the internment has had an important impact on these families in multiple ways.

Sociocultural Issues in Assessment

As we have seen, Japanese Americans and their families are not likely to utilize public mental health facilities. Clinicians must therefore recognize that once a Japanese American child and family do seek services, their needs may be especially great, since they have already overcome important barriers to obtaining treatment. Assessment of Japanese American clients should recognize the importance of three basic areas of information: (1) client attitudes toward psychological problems and services, (2) therapist sensitivity to cultural issues in case conceptualization, and (3) the appropriateness of various assessment techniques.

Client Attitudes. The first area of information concerns the attitudes that a Japanese American client may have about psychological problems and seeking services. Kitano (1970) notes that the Issei brought with them from Japan a view of mental illness as something that is inherited and "taints" the bloodline. Because psychological problems were seen as a reflection of family and bloodline, a great deal of shame, or *haji,* may be associated with mental disturbances. This suggests the importance of assessing any concerns that a Japanese American family or client might have about confidentiality and seeking services. These concerns may not be expressed directly or verbally, however, and the therapist may wish to reduce a family's feeling of shame by actively recognizing the personal nature of the information being shared and reassuring them that this information will be held in confidence. It may be helpful to ask family members directly about their conceptualization of emotional problems and how they view the current presenting complaint.

Kitano (1970) also notes that Japanese Americans tend to view mental illness as inappropriate behavior or malingering. Recognizing this, a clinician should explore the degree to which parents feel a child's behavior problems are willful or manipulative. This would be particularly critical in cases that involve family therapy or collateral work with parents.

Japanese American clients may differ from non-Asian clients not only in their attitudes toward emotional difficulties but also in the very manner in which their complaints are presented. Sue and Sue (1974) noted that Japanese American college students tended to report more somatic complaints than their Caucasian American counterparts. Similarly, Kitano (1982) describes a study by Okano (1977) in which Japanese Americans from Los Angeles reported that they did not experience frequent emotional or psychological problems. The majority of respondents saw themselves as mentally healthy. They did acknowledge, however, that their major personal problems were related to their physical health. Japanese Americans, then, are more likely to express emotional difficulties through somatization, and a thorough assessment of both psychological and physical factors is especially important when working with these clients.

Therapist Sensitivity in Case Conceptualization. The issues presented above point to the importance of assessing the attitudes held by Japanese American children and families who seek services. However, therapists must also assess their own biases and attitudes toward Japanese Americans. Clinicians must be careful not to misinterpret culturally influenced responses to the treatment setting or interview as evidence of simple defense mechanisms. Reservations about being seen at a clinic, for example, should not be interpreted merely as signs of resistance. Rather, a culturally sensitive therapist would view this as a reasonable response for a member of a cultural group where having any psychological problems is perceived negatively and where past discrimination by the majority environment may have emphasized concerns about being perceived as different.

Gray and Cosgrove (1985) indicate that an ethnocentric clinician might also negatively misconstrue characteristics of a Japanese American family that are in actuality nonpathological. Avoidance of open praise or expectations that children should spend much of their free time studying might be viewed as emotionally harmful or punitive by a naive evaluator. In fact, such behaviors can be culturally congruent and valued.

In working with adolescents, therapists must also be aware that their stereotypes of Japanese Americans may influence their case conceptualization. Assessment of academic strengths and weaknesses and how these fit into decisions about goals for the future can play an important role in many adolescent cases. Many people believe that all Asian Americans are good in math and poor in verbal subjects. Sue and Frank (1973) found, however, that Japanese American male college students did not differ from Caucasian American subjects in mathematical ability and did not differ in their choice of occupations from other students in the physical or social sciences. Sata (1983) has also reported that Sansei are majoring in increasingly diverse disciplines. Consequently, a Japanese American adolescent who is failing math should not be seen as suffering from any greater academic failure than a Caucasian American peer. Nor should a failing grade in a social science be dismissed as less important because of assumptions that this is an area where one might expect such a student to have difficulties.

Therapists must maintain sensitivity to Japanese American culture when gathering information at the individual, family, and community levels. The following outline provides specific questions a therapist might explore within each of these levels, although it should be recognized that the answers to questions presented at any one level may draw on information across several levels.

Individual Assessment Issues. Issues to be explored at the individual level include the following:

• To what degree is ethnicity an issue for this child or adolescent? Issues of ethnicity will be different for a newly acculturated Japanese American child, for example, than for a fourth-generation Japanese American.

• How does the child feel about his or her own physical attractiveness and aptitude? Since Japanese Americans tend to be smaller in stature than their Caucasian American counterparts, they may feel they cannot do well in certain sports (such as basketball). They may also feel self-conscious or unsatisfied with their racial characteristics because they do not fit the Caucasian American standards for attractiveness. Some Japanese American adolescent girls, for example, use cellophane tape to create Western-looking double eyelids. If a client does this, it may be useful to explore her sense of personal attractiveness and ethnicity.

• How does the child or adolescent respond to persons with authority? Since Japanese American culture stresses obedience to authority, the client may defer to teachers and parents, as well as the therapist. A child who has been referred for poor school performance may "suffer" from a lack of communication rather than actual cognitive limitations. The child may be unclear about classwork instructions but feel it is rude to ask the teacher for clarification or assistance. At the other extreme, a therapist might encounter a Japanese American adolescent who rebels against all authority figures. In this case, the adolescent may be striking out against the pressure within the family to obey authority.

• If the client is an adolescent, how does he or she feel about issues related to dating and sexuality? The onset of dating and self-consciousness about appearance can raise one's awareness about being of a racial minority to new levels of intensity (Sata, 1983). At the same time, rebellion against parental authority and nonconformity to establish a unique identity can put the Japanese American adolescent into conflict with cultural values emphasizing conformity and deference to parents. Issues around sexuality are likely to intensify, and as noted previously, it may be difficult for the Japanese American family to respond to the adolescent's sexual issues.

Family Assessment Issues. Additional areas for exploration occur at the family level. For example:

• How much contact with the extended family is there? If there is close and constant contact with the extended family, the therapist should explore further the nature of this contact. Do the client's parents view the contact as a joy or as a burden? If a grandparent lives in the home, is that person the parent of the mother or the father? When significant extended family members are part of the household, it may be valuable to include them in the assessment and treatment process. Lack of contact with an extended family should also be explored. A child's family may, for example, experience isolation because they lack access to the extended family. Or they may have deliberately curtailed visits with the extended family because of familial conflicts.

• How much emphasis do the parents place on their child's achievement? If great emphasis is placed on achievement, the child may feel pressured to do well and may experience a disproportionate sense of failure if goals are not attained. Parental pressure to achieve might also create conflict within the family itself. For example, the child may want to participate in after-school sports, while the parents may see this as a frivolous use of time.

• What is the generational status for each parent and the child? If the parents are Nisei or older Sansei (born during World War II), it is important to know whether they were interned and, if so, at what age and for how long. A clinician should not expect the parents to discuss their internment at length, since this is a difficult topic for many former internees. However, most who were in camps will give brief factual information about their experiences. Further, the parents may themselves be of different generations and hence may differ in their philosophies of parenting and in their styles of interaction with the child.

• How has the family responded to changes in the generational family life cycle? If, for example, the parents are Sansei, in what ways are their family roles and attitudes about interracial dating similar to or different from those of their Nisei parents?

Community Assessment Issues. The community surrounding each Japanese American family should also be evaluated. For example, what is the ethnic/cultural composition of the child's current and past neighborhood and school? A Japanese American child who lives in a community with a sizable number of Japanese Americans will have a different sense of cultural identity than a child who lives in an all-White community. A child in a community where the majority of its members are non-Asian minorities will have yet another sense of cultural identity; for example, there are Japanese Americans who grew up in the predominantly Black community of Crenshaw, Los Angeles, and adopted the dialect and mannerisms of Black Americans. If the community includes other Asian Americans who are not Japanese, the therapist must also recognize that this may not necessarily be a positive factor. There have been many tensions, historically, between Japan, China, and Korea, and a similarity of racial characteristics with other Asian Americans does not ensure smooth intergroup interactions. A Japanese American boy who wants to date a Chinese American girl may encounter prejudice and rejection from her parents just as he might from the parents of a Caucasian American girl.

Selection of Assessment Techniques. Clinicians should also recognize that commonly used assessment techniques may have limited utility with Japanese American children and adolescents. Asian Americans frequently expect mental health professionals to be directive and action-oriented (Leong, 1986). This fits well with cultural expectations that emphasize deference to authority. As a result, ambiguous projective tests such as the Rorschach may be less useful than more structured behavioral assessments. Since many Japanese American parents are strongly committed to helping their children whenever possible, Kim (1985) suggests that explicit enlistment of their help in early assessment techniques is useful. Behavioral questions present a structured way in which parents can participate in their child's treatment.

Standardized objective tests may also have limited utility.

Little research has evaluated the degree to which particular objective measures are valid for Japanese Americans. The problem here is not one of language (as it is, for example, with Spanish-speaking children or recent Asian immigrants). The Sansei and Yonsei are native English speakers but have been raised with different sociocultural values than the majority Caucasian Americans who form the normative groups for most objective tests. A study by Saeki, Clark, and Azen (1985) illustrates the utility of examining the performance of Japanese American children in particular. These researchers compared the responses of Japanese, Japanese American, and Caucasian American children on a developmental test for sensory integration. They found that the Japanese American children did better than the Caucasian American children on the test, but not as well as the Japan-born children of equivalent age. The researchers suggest that because norms for this measure are based only on Caucasian American children, the test may actually be underselective of Japanese and Japanese American children with sensory integration difficulties.

Whenever possible, clinicians should also obtain cross-situational assessments of behavior for their Japanese American clients (Sue and Morishima, 1982). In a study by Ayabe (1971), Japanese American and Caucasian American college students did not differ in vocal strength (used here as an indicator of deference) when in the company of another student. In the presence of a professor, however, the Japanese American students spoke with less vocal strength than their Caucasian American peers. Perceived deference in one setting may be absent in other situations. Younger Sansei and Yonsei might show assertive behaviors outside the home but more deferent behaviors with parents. An adolescent who is outspoken or defiant at school may not behave similarly at home.

Finally, therapists should be aware of the way a Japanese American client responds to their evaluation results. Given that the Japanese American culture encourages deference to authority, a family may passively accept test results without asking for clarification. Diamond and Bond (1974) explored the possibility that Japanese American college students in Hawaii might be more likely to accept personality test interpretations than their

Caucasian American peers. Their results did not support this hypothesis. However, the limited scope of their study prohibits any generalization of the results to other Japanese American clients, suggesting that therapists should make every effort to elicit questions or concerns from Japanese American children and families when presenting evaluation results.

Intervention and Treatment

Although little has been written on methods of intervention and treatment with Japanese Americans, there is a growing literature on clinical work with Asian Americans as a larger group (see Leong, 1986, for a review). In part, this literature has been triggered by the data indicating underutilization of mental health services by Asian Americans and by additional data presented by Sue (1977) revealing that significantly more Asian Americans (over 50 percent) drop out of treatment after one session than Caucasian Americans (about 30 percent). These facts highlight the need for culturally sensitive treatments and interventions for Asian Americans. In the following sections, specific therapeutic issues in working with Japanese Americans are discussed in relation to (1) initiation of treatment, (2) therapist style, (3) culture specifics in treatment, and (4) advantages and disadvantages of selected treatment methods.

Initiation of Treatment. Most initial sessions with a child or adolescent include a parent. In this sense, initial contacts are often family sessions. Kim (1985) states that although most therapists realize the importance of maintaining flexibility in an initial family session, a flexible approach at this early stage of work is especially critical for Asian American families. Hsu and others (1985), for example, found that profiles of healthy families differed between Japanese American and Caucasian American families in Hawaii. The Japanese American families were rated as less direct than the Caucasian American families, less overtly affectionate, less revealing of private matters, and displaying greater incongruence between their stated and observed behaviors. Observers rated the Japanese American families as less competent and less "healthy" even though the research was conducted on nonclinical families! A therapist might similarly see "pathology" in a family when, in fact, what is really being observed is healthy, culturally influenced family functioning.

Henkin (1985) points to another danger: A therapist may try to change Japanese American clients into mainstream ideals (either as individuals or as a family) that are antithetical to the clients' cultural background. The following case presents a situation in which an evaluation of Japanese American cultural values would be useful before instituting a treatment strategy.

Ken, a 16-year-old Japanese American male, reported feeling depressed and fatigued. On further inquiry, Ken noted that his depression had increased at the same time that recent conflicts with his parents had arisen. Ken's parents, both Nisei who had been interned as adolescents, owned and operated a family grocery store that had been in the family for two generations. They hoped that Ken, the oldest son, would take over the store after they retired. Conflicts between Ken and his parents centered on his resistance to working in the store after school and on Saturdays. Whereas Ken's parents expected him to contribute his part to the family business, Ken resented having to spend his "free time" working for his parents. He pointed out that none of his Caucasian friends had such restrictions on their schedules. In fact, Ken stated, several of his peers made fun of the fact that he was "still tied to his parents' apron strings."

Ken noted that his mother and father just "didn't understand him." Rather than listen to him, they admonished him for his verbal outbursts of anger by telling him it was disrespectful to challenge their authority. Ken grew increasingly frustrated with his situation and began experiencing depressive feelings and fatigue as he internalized his frustration more and more, withdrawing from his parents and, eventually, his peers as well.

In this case, the therapist might be tempted to view Ken's rebellion as an example of his growing independence from the family and to focus treatment goals on facilitating Ken's separation from the family. Aoki (cited in Henkin, 1985), however, noted that whereas the Western goal of family therapy is to resolve family issues by encouraging family members to individuate and develop their independence, this goal may be inappropriate for Japanese American families. Because Japanese American families place a high value on cohesiveness and interdependence, it might not be appropriate to assume that Ken's separation from the family is desirable.

Much more is at stake in this case than whether or not Ken is to work at his parents' store. For example, the store represents a link with past family generations as well as with traditional Japanese ethics regarding work, responsibility, and obligation to the family. As a result, Ken is under considerable pressure to help his parents. This pressure may be compounded by the fact that Ken's parents were interned during the war. First, since they were about the same age as Ken were they were imprisoned behind barbed wire, they may view his need for free time as extravagant. In comparison with their experience as adolescents, Ken already has a great deal of freedom. Second, the internment experience may have caused Ken's parents to be extrasensitive to issues of financial stability and maintaining the family business. After seeing their own parents struggle with the losses of the internment, they may be especially intent on making plans for Ken to participate in the store.

Encouraging Ken to separate from his family could also be detrimental in other ways. Although some therapists might see his verbal outbursts as a healthy sign of self-assertion, Ken himself may have great ambivalence about losing control and challenging his parents. Clinicians need to be aware that adopting more Westernized styles of expression may cause discomfort even for third- and fourth-generation Japanese Americans. The fact that Ken's Caucasian peers compare his family against their own standards of family interaction and mock the cultural pressures he experiences complicates the situation. Ken is caught between saving face with his peers and saving face with his family. Hence, assessment would need to take into account the ramifications of self-assertion and independence in relation to both Ken's specific cultural/familial background and his interactions with the larger majority culture.

Because Japanese Americans tend to defer to authority figures and to view their emotional problems as physically based, they are likely to approach the therapist somewhat like a patient seeking concrete medical advice from a physician (Tsui and Schultz, 1985). Given such expectations, in initial sessions the therapist should establish a clear-cut structure for counseling and explain the therapy process itself (Henkin, 1985; Kim, 1985; Root, 1985). Without concrete explanations of what is to be expected, Asian American clients are less likely to return for services (Root, 1985). Hsu (1983) states that therapists should also avoid extensive diagnostic evaluations with Asian American clients and work toward tangible, problem-focused goals as soon as possible. Patience may be required of the therapist during these early sessions (Henkin, 1985). Japanese American clients may view self-disclosure as self-centered, losing control, and/or losing face in the presence of the therapist or other family members. Therapists, then, must recognize the need for early structure and goal setting as well as the need to avoid hasty diagnoses based on incomplete data. In dealing with these realities, a therapist might, early on, set immediate primary goals (some of which might incorporate enlisting the family's help in providing more information in certain areas) but allow for the formation of secondary goals as additional information emerges from the family work.

Related to assumptions that the therapist is an expert are expectations regarding age and sex. Respect for age is evident in Japanese American culture, and the following case example illustrates that younger therapists may be received with less confidence than older therapists.

The present author, while an intern at a major medical school in California, was treating a Sansei adolescent who was extremely depressed and anxious. After several meetings, the client's mother appeared in the waiting room after a session. The client introduced the therapist, at which point the mother's face dropped in disappointment. Her remark was simply "Oh, so young!"

The young, female therapist clearly did not meet the hopes and expectations of this concerned mother, despite the mother's stated preference for a Japanese American therapist. I responded by acknowledging the mother's concerns and then briefly describing my professional background and training. Once the mother heard that I was a "doctor," she visibly relaxed. Describing one's credentials to a client may seem egotistical. However, this case example demonstrates that it can serve a beneficial purpose in working with a Japanese American client.

Therapist Style. The way therapists present themselves can clearly influence the client's degree of comfort in sharing information. Most agree that an active, rather than a passive, therapist style works best with most Asian American clients (Yamamoto and Acosta, 1982). Henkin (1985) suggests, however, that therapists be aware that Western behaviors of intense eye contact, physical gestures, and direct questions may be seen as intrusive by Japanese American clients. At the same time, an overly aloof therapeutic style may be construed as a sign of lack of interest, as the following vignette illustrates:

A 16-year-old Japanese American adolescent girl was suicidal following the breakup of a relationship. The therapist adopted an analytically oriented, nondirective approach to the case and met with the family and the girl to discuss the current family structure. Unfortunately, the family did not feel they had established a trusting relationship with the therapist, nor did the therapist make an attempt to direct the interactions during the sessions. The net result was that the daughter felt awkward and embarrassed for having her family subjected to her therapy (which seemed a waste of time), and the family felt ineffectual in aiding their daughter. The therapist did not investigate the impact of the family session, and the client terminated treatment.

This termination might have been avoided if the therapist had adopted a more active role with the client and her family, explaining the goals of the family session and eliciting any concerns from the parents and their daughter. This would have provided a structure for the therapy and would have encouraged interaction between the clients and the therapist.

Suggestions have been made concerning the style of therapy that is most effective for Japanese American clients. Atkinson, Maruyama, and Matsui (1978) found that college-aged Japanese American students rated a counselor higher who used a logical, rational, and structured approach rather than an affective, reflective, ambiguous one. Henkin (1985) suggests that the therapist take on a nonthreatening, yet defined role with the Japanese American client that allows the client to ask questions. However, Japanese American clients may be hesitant to ask questions because the cultural dynamic of *enryo* may cause them to feel they should not assert their own viewpoint and challenge the therapist's authority. One solution is to elicit the client's questions as a specific task. Doing so enables clients to assist in the therapy by allowing them to ask questions in a culturally consonant way (that is, in a role of responding to an authority's request and also in a role of helping to alleviate the problem). This approach might be especially desirable in family therapy, since enlistment of the Japanese American family as a mobilizing force to augment individual work can be extremely useful.

The preceding suggestions concerning therapeutic style could be incorporated by any therapist who wishes to work effectively with Japanese Americans. However, questions have been raised about the degree to which Japanese American children and adolescents and their families can be treated effectively by non–Japanese American therapists. Research on the importance of therapist/client match in the therapeutic process for Japanese Americans is as yet unclear. Atkinson, Maruyama, and Matsui (1978) reported mixed results on this topic. One sample of Japanese American subjects in their study felt that racial similarity was highly significant in determining the credibility of a therapist, while a second sample did not indicate this preference. It is clearly desirable to have more trained Japanese American therapists who could be available to Japanese American clients. However, given that the Japanese American population is steadily declining, it is also important to train non–Japanese American therapists to be aware of the clinical issues raised here.

Culture Specifics in Treatment. Broader cultural issues, in addition to those related to therapeutic style, can affect one's treatment interventions with Japanese Americans. A lack of culturally sensitive services has been seen as contributing to the high dropout rate of Asian Americans from therapy. Unfortunately, the provision of culturally sensitive services is extremely complex. Clinicians working with a Japanese American child and family have a difficult task. On the one hand, they must be cognizant of Japanese American cultural differences, some of which are rooted in more general Asian American heritage and tradition. On the other hand, they must also be aware that current Japanese American parents and children are likely to be highly acculturated and "American" in many of their attitudes, values, and behaviors. Blind application of clinical style based only on a knowledge of Asian American families would be offensive to a fourth-generation Yonsei. At the same time, complete ignorance of the ways in which such a client may differ from Caucasian Americans may also jeopardize the effectiveness of an intervention. Recognizing this, the following serves more as a menu of issues that clinicians might consider in their work than as an exhaustive list of "how to's" to be followed dogmatically. Family therapy is used as a primary focus, since family work is often indicated in child and adolescent interventions.

First, treatment strategies must take into account two very important variables: (1) the structure of the Japanese American family and (2) the degree to which the particular family has become acculturated. Lack of appreciation for the family structure may impede therapy. Kim (1985) and Hsu (1983) note that it is safest to respect the family's vertical hierarchy (for example, addressing the father as the authority) at least initially, thus allowing the parents to save face until groundwork is laid to address the family in other ways. However, the issue of generational status must also be considered before implementing such a suggestion. If, for example, the parents are Sansei in their thirties with an egalitarian relationship, they may not adhere to the same vertical hierarchy that was once present in most Japanese American families. In this case, attempts to address a vertical hierarchy within the family could be offensive.

The clinician must also be alert to differences in acculturation that may exist among family members. For example, Japanese American children are likely to be more acculturated than their parents. Literature suggests that today's Japanese American adolescent may in many ways differ little from his or her Caucasian peers. McDermott and others (1984) found that Japanese American and Caucasian American adolescents in Hawaii did not differ in their family values. Interestingly, however, their parents differed significantly on several dimensions. Japanese American parents more strongly emphasized the need for important family decisions to include family discussion as a group and took a more cognitive attitude toward interactions. Caucasian American parents emphasized the importance of individual decisions and open expressions of affect in interactions. For the clinician, these findings indicate that one must be aware of the conflicts a Japanese American adolescent might face with parents concerning family values and styles of interaction. A case described by Sue and Morishima (1982, p. 141) illustrates how such issues might present themselves in therapy.

A Japanese American adolescent was brought in by his parents because he was constantly using drugs, had been arrested several times for shoplifting, and was associating with "the wrong crowd." He complained that his parents were too "Japanese-y" and did not understand him.

In this situation, the adolescent is clearly pointing to a barrier that exists between his parents and himself, a barrier that consists of both generational and value differences. Realistically, his parents may not be able to understand his world. At the same time, however, the adolescent is expressing another difficulty. The fact that his parents are "too Japanese-y" suggests that they may also be a source of embarrassment for him. Most adolescents are concerned about fitting in with their peers. Having parents who do not fit the majority stereotype of parents can cause added tensions in the family. The "Japanese-ness" of this client's parents may also have caused discomfort by serving as a constant reminder of his cultural heritage in a social world where he is trying to "be like" everyone else.

Another situation described by Sue and Morishima (1982, p. 142) illustrates similar issues.

An 18-year-old Japanese American student was upset over her family's reaction to her Caucasian American boyfriend. Her parents refused to meet him and on several occasions threatened to disown her. The reactions from her older brothers were more extreme. They threatened to beat up that "White bastard." Furthermore, the parents were disturbed by her low grades. Although she had done well in high school, her grades in college were now below average.

The student in this case is hurt by the animosity displayed by both her parents and her brothers. In the case of the parents, generational issues may be contributing to their rejection of the boyfriend. First, it is quite likely that they experienced strong social sanctions against dating Whites when they were growing up and were legally prevented from outmarrying. Second, if her parents were interned, they were imprisoned and dominated by Caucasian Americans during the war. Placed in this context, their threats of disownment become clearer. The student's brothers may be expressing a somewhat different reaction to the Caucasian boyfriend. As Sansei who grew up in the 1960s and 1970s, when ethnic pride and solidarity were highly valued, the brothers may see dating a Caucasian as evidence of "selling out" one's own ethnic group. Hence, even within a generational cohort, there may be value differences.

In both the cases discussed above, the differences between the parents' and the adolescent's cultural values and experiences are apparent. What is not described in these cases, but may also be a contributing factor, is the degree to which the adolescents' retention of Japanese American values can exacerbate the dilemma. For both adolescents, family upbringing that discourages open confrontation with (or even doubt of) a parent's opinion or behavior can make it especially difficult to express disagreement or disappointment openly.

Advantages and Disadvantages of Selected Treatment Methods. Research suggests that not all treatment methods will be equally effective with Japanese American children and adolescents. For family therapy, Kim (1985) believes that the strategic/behavioral framework may be most useful for Asian American families, since this approach focuses on active problem solving and structure. However, it is important to note that such approaches require the therapist to have a clear idea of the structure of the Japanese American family before intervening in that structure.

Miyoshi (1980) found a unique application of family therapy based on Boszormenyi-Nagy and Spark's (1973) theory of multigenerational dynamics. Adopting this framework, Miyoshi was interested in using family sessions as a way to encourage discourse between Nisei parents and their children. More specifically, sessions focused on discussing the internment experience. It was hoped that a discussion of this difficult topic would uncover the intergenerational burdens shared by both the Nisei and Sansei. Miyoshi conducted ten family therapy sessions with each of three Japanese American families and seven sessions with a fourth Japanese American family. Although she did not publish outcome data from her work, she did document the rich information that emerged from the family sessions. Clinicians who work with Japanese American families in which the impact of the internment appears especially central would benefit from reviewing Miyoshi's intervention technique.

Behavioral problems are likely to be presenting issues for younger Japanese American children who appear for services. As previously noted, behavioral, directed therapies have several advantages in work with Japanese American families. The following case exemplifies some of these advantages:

Mr. and Mrs. Y., both Sansei-generation Japanese Americans, contacted the clinic with concerns about their son Eric. Eric, 6 years old and the younger of two sons, was reported to be "unmanageable" at home. Both parents had postponed calling the clinic several times and admitted that they were somewhat embarrassed for "using up" the clinician's time with a problem they should have been able to correct themselves. Mrs. Y. was in particular distress over Eric's behavior and tearfully reported that she could not cope much longer with his tantrums and uncooperativeness. Mrs. Y. carried the majority of child-care responsibilities in addition to working part-time. Mr. Y. indicated that although he supported his wife's desire to work, he had been raised to see child care as a woman's role and felt ill equipped to help Mrs. Y. with Eric's tantrums. An intake interview with Eric revealed him to be a bright, outgoing child. Although he was cooperative with the clinician, he became increasingly disruptive and whiny when his parents entered the room.

Further assessment revealed that the Y.'s lived within 15 minutes of Mrs. Y.'s parents. Visits between the two families were frequent. Mrs. Y. had asked her mother for advice about Eric's behavior but found her unsupportive. In fact, Mrs. Y. noted that her mother blamed her for Eric's problems, suggesting that he would not be so difficult if his mother stayed at home full-time with the children. Mrs. Y.'s mother felt that family should always come first. Because Mrs. Y. worked, she was seen by her mother as compromising the family.

Mrs. Y.'s mother had also discouraged the Y.'s from contacting the clinic and had worried that friends might find out Eric was having problems. This, said Mrs. Y.'s mother, would reflect on the entire family. Consequently, by the time the Y.'s did show up for therapy, Mrs. Y. was anxious not only about whether she could get help with Eric but also about risking the family's reputation by seeking treatment.

A behavioral approach to treating Eric's tantrums was implemented. After a thorough behavioral assessment, the Y.'s were instructed in the use of reinforcements and contingencies to reduce the frequency of Eric's problem behaviors. Charts were used to monitor progress as the treatment progressed.

Like other forms of treatment, the behavioral therapy must be sensitive to the fact that many Japanese Americans are wary of seeking mental health services. The Y.'s, for example, have already expressed shame about seeking help. To enlist family confidence and alleviate feelings of shame, a clinician might label the Y.'s help-seeking as positive evidence of their parenting ability and concern for Eric's well-being, rather than as a sign of weakness.

A behavioral treatment is particularly useful in this case for several reasons. First, by asking Mr. and Mrs. Y. to identify the antecedents and consequences of Eric's behaviors and to give detailed descriptions of his tantrums, the clinician provided a clear structure within the interview itself. The clarity of these questions helped to ease the Y.s' discomfort and alleviated their sense of hopelessness about the problem. The clinician provided hope by assuming the role of an "expert" who could provide straightforward guidance on ways to handle Eric. At the same time, because the clinician's questions were ones that Mr. and Mrs. Y. could answer, they enabled the Y.'s to recognize that they knew more about Eric's problem than they had realized.

The behavioral approach also provided Mr. Y. with a way to become involved in the treatment without challenging his culturally influenced conceptions of sex roles. The clinician stressed that Mr. Y.'s observations and participation were critical in implementing a consistent behavioral program but did not suggest that he directly take on more child-care responsibilities or question the origins of his attitudes toward child care. Mr. Y., in fact, looked forward to active participation in the treatment and saw his involvement as an important way to help his wife and strengthen his family.

Mrs. Y. faced an especially difficult situation. As a Sansei, she had many of the same behaviors and attitudes as her Caucasian American peers. Like many women today, she found work outside the home important and gratifying. Her Nisei mother, however, constantly compared her to a more traditional Japanese standard of motherhood. Mrs. Y. felt close to her mother and did value the importance of family a great deal. This was evidenced, in part, by her decision to live near her parents. However, she also enjoyed working and felt guilty when her mother accused her of abandoning the children. A behavioral approach to Eric's problems could not alleviate the friction between Mrs. Y. and her mother. However, it did provide her with tools to feel more confident in handling her mother's criticisms and doubts. Whereas a nondirective or intrapsychic treatment might have seemed vague or nonproductive to Mrs. Y.'s mother, a behavioral treatment allowed Mrs. Y. to point to concrete interventions she was implementing to help her son as well as charts documenting Eric's progress.

Additional cultural variables may play a role in the application of behavioral techniques with a Japanese American family. Behavior modification treatment emphasizes the importance of observable and measurable behaviors. Much of the communication in a Japanese American family, however, may be nonverbal and not obvious to a Western therapist. Therefore, therapists using behavioral assessments and interventions may need to look for behaviors that are absent as well as those that are apparent in order to develop useful interventions. For example, they should be aware that Japanese Americans tend not to give overt praise or verbal feedback to their children. This may reflect an even more general hesitancy to provide verbal feedback. When comparing Japanese American and Caucasian American Hawaiian students engaged in a discussion task, Ogawa and Welden (1972) found that the Japanese American students engaged in significantly less verbal feedback than their Caucasian peers. Hence, simply instructing the Y.'s to verbally reinforce Eric's appropriate behaviors would ignore the cultural conflict inherent in such a request. As an alternative, a clinician might explore with the family other, perhaps nonverbal, ways in which approval is communicated.

Individual play therapy for Japanese American children has not been explored in the literature, and it is difficult to know what its potential effectiveness might be. Nonetheless, the following case description shows that play therapy can be an important form of treatment for Japanese American children.

Lisa, a 7-year-old fourth-generation Japanese American girl, was referred to the clinic by her school after becoming increasingly withdrawn and tearful. Lisa's teacher reported that she would not participate in class, did not play with other children in the classroom or at recess, and often asked to go home in the middle of the day. Her parents noted that Lisa frequently wanted to stay home to avoid school. They were worried by the fact that she had become increasingly withdrawn from them at home as well.

When Lisa was invited into the play therapy room, she appeared nervous and withdrawn. Although she did not speak to the therapist, she immediately went to a shelf lined with dolls, selected one with dark hair and one with blond hair, and staged a fierce battle between the two. The blond doll eventually knocked the dark-haired doll to the ground and exclaimed, "I win!" Additional dark-haired dolls then tried to "save" the defeated dark-haired doll but were unable to lift her from the floor.

Defeat of dark-haired dolls by blond dolls became a recurrent theme in Lisa's play. At times the battles were fought between light-colored animals and dark-colored animals. Whatever the characters, the light-colored character emerged the victor, and the efforts of other dark-colored characters to rescue the defeated would fail.

As therapy continued, Lisa eventually revealed that children at school made fun of her "tiny eyes" and black hair and did not pick her for their sports teams. Lisa's play in sessions indicated that she wished she were not Japanese and felt anger toward her parents, blaming them for her difference. In her eyes, if her parents were not Japanese, she would not be experiencing the ostracism she now faced. Since her parents were Japanese like herself, she did not feel they could rescue her from the "blond attackers."

In Lisa's case, play therapy proved an important vehicle for expressing a number of painful thoughts and feelings around ethnicity and peer relations that would be unlikely to emerge in family therapy or a behavioral treatment. In the safe context of play and fantasy, she could express her identity conflicts without directly challenging her parents or peers.

Although play therapy worked well for Lisa, other young Japanese American children may find the play situation somewhat confusing. If their families have encouraged them to respect and obey authority figures, they will want to comply with the therapist's requests. At the same time, if their families have also emphasized the importance of doing homework during free time and frowned on play as a frivolous activity, the therapist's invitation to play may be difficult to accept. (For these reasons, other projective techniques that are similar to schoolwork, such as telling and writing stories or drawing pictures, may be useful.) Similarly, it is important to explain clearly to the child's parents the function and goals of play therapy. Since Japanese American parents will likely be seeking concrete signs of progress in their child, they may see play therapy as fruitless and indulgent. Once again, however, the degree to which these hypotheses hold true will depend greatly on the particular Japanese American family being seen and their life experiences. For a Sansei couple who know about the principles underlying play therapy and who are highly acculturated, these issues may be less relevant.

Roleplaying can also present difficulties for the Japanese American child, as it requires a client to step out of a structured, prescribed role and to assume one that is ambiguous. Once again, the child may feel conflict between (1) pleasing an authority figure by complying with the therapist's request and (2) experiencing the request as culturally inappropriate or aberrant. This conflict can have countertherapeutic effects. Sue (1981) presents a case illustration in which roleplaying in the form of the Gestalt "empty chair" technique was used with an Asian American client and had an unintended negative consequence.

A student was in conflict with his parents about his career choice but could not openly express his conflict with them. After the therapist used the empty-chair technique to encourage him to express his anger toward his parents, the student became less actively involved in the therapy.

Several factors that are common in Japanese American culture could have contributed to the "failure" of this technique. The roleplay required the client to assert himself and his anger. However, he had been brought up to respect his parents and elders, not to talk back or confront them, and to keep negative emotions within. Simply to encourage behaving assertively is to ignore the network of associations a Japanese American adolescent might have around the meaning of assertive behavior.

Group therapy might provide a less individually focused, less intensive form of intervention with adolescents and might also serve to reduce shame about receiving services. However, Schlesinger (1981) has suggested that the implications of being a member of a group may be greater for a Japanese American client than for a Caucasian American client. Because group membership is taken very seriously in Japanese culture and co-operation within the group is strongly encouraged, a Japanese American client might be reluctant to become involved in the group process.

Finally, artwork may provide a useful form of intervention, given that the Japanese American child may have been raised in an environment where nonverbal communication is as important as verbal communication. If the child's work can be shared with the parents, this may also provide a way for the parents to gain an understanding of their child's issues without entering into a more confrontive verbal exchange. As a cautionary note, before incorporating artwork into the therapy, therapists should be aware of any preconceptions they may have of Asian Americans as artistic, quiet, and inarticulate. Certainly not all Japanese Americans fit this stereotype.

Summary and Conclusions

Assessment and treatment of Japanese American children and adolescents and their families present the clinician with challenging tasks. As this chapter has shown, Japanese Americans cannot be simplistically categorized into either Caucasian American or Japanese stereotypes. Variables such as generational status, composition of a child's ethnic community, level of acculturation, and the long-term impact, if any, of the internment on the family can influence the effectiveness of a therapist's efforts.

A major point in this chapter is that Japanese Americans, as well as other Asian Americans, underutilize mental health services. Many of the suggestions for therapeutic intervention may rarely, if ever, be implemented, since data indicate that Japanese American children appear for treatment infrequently. It is clear, however, that underutilization of services does not diminish the need for culturally sensitive interventions. The question becomes "What type of intervention would be most useful?" A "culturally sensitive" service is often defined as including the provision of (1) bilingual, bicultural, or culturally sensitive therapists, (2) parallel services in areas with large concentrations of ethnic communities, and (3) nonparallel services for ethnic minority clients (Sue and Zane, 1987). For Japanese Americans, however, these recommendations are inappropriate. Language is not a factor, since contemporary Japanese Americans are English-speaking; and their decreasing numbers, combined with the increasing geographical dispersal of Sansei and Yonsei, make the second and third suggestions difficult to implement.

Additionally, Uba (1982) notes that, given the diversity of individuals within any Asian American population, one cannot assume that culturally relevant services are automatically applicable to the same degree. Educating non–Japanese American therapists about the culture of Japanese Americans is important but insufficient, and any suggestions for the assessment and treatment of Japanese Americans must clearly be balanced with an understanding that each client, whether child, adolescent, or adult, brings to the therapeutic relationship a unique personal history of acculturation.

Interventions designed to enhance well-being need to be developed in recognition that the effects of discrimination may have diminished the positive mental health of Japanese Americans (Sue and Morishima, 1982). Future research is needed to illuminate the stresses experienced by Japanese American children and their families. In particular, as health psychology has begun to explore the interplay among stress, physical health, and psychological well-being, efforts should be made to explore the somatic complaints presented by Japanese Americans. Research and interventions sensitive to the increasing numbers of Japanese American children and adolescents from mixed marriages are another important area for future emphasis. Moritsugu, Foerster, and Morishima (1978) found that the Eurasians interviewed in their study (ages 17–21 years) reported experiences of alienation because of their mixed ancestry, despite providing positive self-descriptions. Research on the complex issues facing these children and the ways these issues might be integrated into assessment and intervention is needed.

Finally, attention should be paid to the international and political environment in which Japanese American children and adolescents find themselves. As tensions between the United States and Japan continue to be strained because of economic conditions, Japanese American children and their families may experience increased racism and discrimination. Prejudice against other Asian groups in the United States can also affect Japanese American families because many people fail to distinguish among the various Asian American ethnic groups. A recent *Wall Street Journal* report, for example, reported a 62 percent increase in anti-Asian incidents between 1984 and 1985 (Wong, 1986). Awareness of the larger sociopolitical climate surrounding Japanese Americans, and Asian Americans in general, will clearly be important for mental health professionals who work with this population.

References

Abramson, P. R., and Imai-Marquez, J. "The Japanese-American: A Cross-Cultural, Cross-Sectional Study of Sex Guilt." *Journal of Research in Personality*, 1982, *16*, 227–237.

Arkoff, A., and Weaver, H. "Body Image and Body Dissatisfaction in Japanese Americans." *Journal of Social Psychology*, 1966, *68*, 323–330.

Atkinson, D. R., Maruyama, M., and Matsui, S. "Effects of Counselor Race and Counseling Approach on Asian Americans' Perceptions of Counselor Credibility and Utility." *Journal of Counseling Psychology*, 1978, *25*, 76–83.

Ayabe, H. I. "Deference and Ethnic Differences in Voice Levels." *Journal of Social Psychology*, 1971, *85*, 181–185.

Boszormenyi-Nagy, I., and Spark, G. M. *Invisible Loyalties:*

Reciprocity in Intergenerational Family Therapy. New York: Harper & Row, 1973.

Cabezas, A. Y. "Disadvantaged Employment Status of Asian and Pacific Americans." Paper presented at a consultation by the U.S. Commission on Civil Rights—Clearinghouse Publication no. 64, 1979.

Caudill, W., and Frost, L. "A Comparison of Maternal Care and Infant Behavior in Japanese-American, American and Japanese Families." In U. Bronfenbrenner (ed.), *Influences on Development.* Hinsdale, Ill.: Dryden Press, 1972.

Connor, J. W. "Acculturation and Family Continuities in Three Generations of Japanese-Americans." *Journal of Marriage and the Family,* 1974, *36,* 159–165.

Danieli, Y. "Families of Survivors of the Nazi Holocaust: Some Short- and Long-Term Effects." In C. D. Spielberger, I. G. Sarason, and N. A. Milgram (eds.), *Stress and Anxiety.* Vol. 8. Washington, D.C.: Hemisphere, 1982.

Diamond, M. J., and Bond, M. H. "The Acceptance of 'Barnum' Personality Interpretations by Japanese, Japanese-American, and Caucasian American College Students." *Journal of Cross-Cultural Psychology,* 1974, *5,* 228–235.

Dubanoski, R. A., and Snyder, K. "Patterns of Child Abuse and Neglect in Japanese- and Samoan-Americans." *Child Abuse and Neglect,* 1980, *4,* 217–225.

Gardner, R., Robey, B., and Smith, P. "Asian Americans: Growth, Change, and Diversity." *Population Bulletin,* 1985, *40,* 1–43.

Gehrie, M. J. "Childhood and Community: On the Experience of Young Japanese-Americans in Chicago." *Ethos,* 1976, *4,* 353–383.

Gray, E., and Cosgrove, J. "Ethnocentric Perception of Child-rearing Practices in Protective Services." *Child Abuse and Neglect,* 1985, *9,* 389–396.

Hansen, A. A., and Mitson, B. E. *Voices Long Silent: An Oral Inquiry into the Japanese American Evacuation.* Fullerton: California State University Oral History Program, 1974.

Henkin, W. A. "Toward Counseling the Japanese in America: A Cross-Cultural Primer." *Journal of Counseling and Development,* 1985, *63,* 500–503.

Hsu, J. "Asian Family Interaction Patterns and Their Therapeutic Implications." *International Journal of Family Psychiatry*, 1983, *4*, 307–320.

Hsu, J., and others. "Family Interaction Patterns Among Japanese-American and Caucasian Families in Hawaii." *American Journal of Psychiatry*, 1985, *142*, 577–581.

Johnson, C. L. "Interdependence, Reciprocity, and Indebtedness: An Analysis of Japanese American Kinship Relations." *Journal of Marriage and the Family*, 1977, *39*, 351–363.

Kim, B.L.C. *The Asian Americans: Changing Patterns, Changing Needs.* Montclair, N.J.: Association of Korean Christian Scholars in North America, 1978.

Kim, S. C. "Family Therapy for Asian Americans: A Strategic-Structural Framework." *Psychotherapy*, 1985, *22*, 342–348.

Kitano, H.H.L. "Japanese-American Crime and Delinquency." *Journal of Psychology*, 1967, *66*, 253–263.

Kitano, H.H.L. "Japanese-American Mental Illness." In S. C. Plog and R. B. Edgerton (eds.), *Changing Perspectives in Mental Illness.* New York: Holt, Rinehart & Winston, 1969a.

Kitano, H.H.L. *Japanese Americans: The Evolution of a Subculture.* Englewood Cliffs, N.J.: Prentice-Hall, 1969b.

Kitano, H.H.L. "Mental Illness in Four Cultures." *Journal of Social Psychology*, 1970, *80*, 121–134.

Kitano, H.H.L. "Mental Health in the Japanese American Community." In E. E. Jones and S. J. Korchin (eds.), *Minority Mental Health.* New York: Praeger, 1982.

Kitano, H.H.L., and Kikumura, A. "The Japanese American Family." In C. H. Mindel and R. W. Habenstein (eds.), *Ethnic Families in America.* New York: Elsevier, 1976.

Kitano, H.H.L., Yeung, W. T., Chai, L., and Hatanaka, H. "Asian American Interracial Marriage." *Journal of Marriage and the Family*, 1984, *2*, 179–190.

Knoll, T. *Becoming Americans: Asian Sojourners, Immigrants, and Refugees in the Western United States.* Portland, Oreg.: Coast to Coast Books, 1982.

Leong, F.T.L. "Counseling and Psychotherapy with Asian Americans: A Review of the Literature." *Journal of Counseling Psychology*, 1986, *33*, 196–206.

McDermott, J. F., and others. "Cultural Variations in Family

Attitudes and Their Implications for Therapy." In S. Chess and A. Thomas (eds.), *Annual Progress in Child Psychiatry and Child Development.* New York: Brunner/Mazel, 1984.

Mass, A. I. "Psychological Effects of the Camps on Japanese Americans." In R. Daniels, S. C. Taylor, and H.H.L. Kitano (eds.), *From Relocation to Redress.* Salt Lake City: University of Utah Press, 1986.

Masuda, M., Matsumoto, G. M., and Meredith, G. M. "Ethnic Identity in Three Generations of Japanese Americans." *Journal of Social Psychology,* 1970, *81,* 199–207.

Miyoshi, N. "Identity Crisis of the Sansei and the American Concentration Camp." *Pacific Citizen,* Dec. 19–26, 1980, pp. 41–55.

Morales, A., Ferguson, Y., and Munford, P. R. "The Juvenile Justice System and Minorities." In G. J. Powell, J. Yamamoto, A. Romero, and A. Morales (eds.), *The Psychosocial Development of Minority Group Children.* New York: Brunner/Mazel, 1983.

Morishima, J. K. "The Evacuation: Impact on the Family." In S. Sue and N. N. Wagner (eds.), *Asian Americans: Psychological Perspectives.* Palo Alto, Calif.: Science and Behavior Books, 1973.

Moritsugu, J., Foerster, L., and Morishima, J. K. "Eurasians: A Pilot Study." Paper presented at convention of the Western Psychological Association, San Francisco, April 1978.

Nadler, A., Kav-Venaki, S., and Gleitman, B. "Transgenerational Effects of the Holocaust: Externalization of Aggression in Second Generation of Holocaust Survivors." *Journal of Consulting and Clinical Psychology,* 1985, *53,* 365–369.

Nagata, D. K. "Long-Term Effects of the Japanese Internment Camps: Impact on the Children of the Internees." Paper presented at second national convention of the Asian American Psychological Association, New York City, Aug. 1987.

Nakagawa, B., and Watanabe, R. *A Study of the Use of Drugs Among the Asian American Youth of Seattle.* Seattle: Demonstration Project of Asian Americans, 1973.

Nakane, C. *Japanese Society.* Berkeley: University of California Press, 1970.

Ogawa, D. M., and Welden, T. A. "Cross-Cultural Analysis of Feedback Behavior Within Japanese American and Caucasian American Small Groups." *Journal of Communication*, 1972, *22*, 189–195.

Okano, Y. *Japanese Americans and Mental Health.* Los Angeles: Coalition for Mental Health, 1977.

O'Reilly, J. P., Tokuno, K. A., and Ebata, A. T. "Cultural Differences Between Americans of Japanese and European Ancestry in Parental Valuing and Social Competence." *Journal of Comparative Family Studies*, 1986, *17*, 87–97.

Padilla, A. M., Wagatsuma, Y., and Lindholm, K. J. "Acculturation and Personality as Predictors of Stress in Japanese and Japanese Americans." *Journal of Social Psychology*, 1985, *125*, 295–305.

Prizzia, R., and Villanueva-King, O. *Central Oahu Community Mental Health Needs Assessment Survey. Part III: A Survey of the General Population.* Honolulu: Management Planning and Administration Consultants, 1977.

Root, M. P. "Guidelines for Facilitating Therapy with Asian American Clients." *Psychotherapy*, 1985, *22*, 349–356.

Saeki, K., Clark, F. A., and Azen, S. P. "Performance of Japanese and Japanese American Children on the Motor Accuracy–Revised and Design Copying Tests of the Southern California Sensory Integration Tests." *American Journal of Occupational Therapy*, 1985, *39*, 103–109.

Sata, L. S. "Mental Health Issues of Japanese-American Children." In G. J. Powell, J. Yamamoto, A. Romero, and A. Morales (eds.), *The Psychosocial Development of Minority Group Children.* New York: Brunner/Mazel, 1983.

Schlesinger, R. "Cross-Cultural Psychiatry: The Applicability of Western Anglo Psychiatry to Asian Americans of Chinese and Japanese Ethnicity." *Journal of Psychosocial Nursing and Mental Health Services*, 1981, *19*, 26–30.

Sue, D. W. *Counseling the Culturally Different: Theory and Practice.* New York: Wiley, 1981.

Sue, D. W., and Frank, A. C. "A Typological Approach to the Psychological Study of Chinese- and Japanese-American College Males." *Journal of Social Issues*, 1973, *29*, 129–148.

Sue, S. "Community Mental Health Services to Minority Groups: Some Optimism, Some Pessimism." *American Psychologist,* 1977, *32,* 616–624.

Sue, S., and McKinney, H. "Asian Americans in the Community Health Care System." *American Journal of Orthopsychiatry,* 1975, *45,* 111–118.

Sue, S., and Morishima, J. K. *The Mental Health of Asian Americans: Contemporary Issues in Identifying and Treating Mental Problems.* San Francisco: Jossey-Bass, 1982.

Sue, S., and Nakamura, C. Y. "An Integrative Model of Physiological and Social/Psychological Factors in Alcohol Consumption Among Chinese and Japanese Americans." *Journal of Drug Issues,* 1984, *14,* 349–364.

Sue, S., and Sue, D. W. "MMPI Comparisons Between Asian-American and Non-Asian Students Utilizing a Student Health Psychiatric Clinic." *Journal of Counseling Psychology,* 1974, *21,* 423–427.

Sue, S., and Zane, N. "The Role of Culture and Cultural Techniques in Psychotherapy: A Critique and Reformulation." *American Psychologist,* 1987, *42,* 37–45.

Tinker, J. N. "Intermarriage and Assimilation in a Plural Society: Japanese-Americans in the United States." *Marriage and Family Review,* 1982, *5,* 61–74.

Tsui, P., and Schultz, G. L. "Failure of Rapport: Why Psychotherapeutic Engagement Fails in the Treatment of Asian Clients." *American Journal of Orthopsychiatry,* 1985, *55,* 561–569.

Uba, L. "Meeting the Mental Health Needs of Asian-Americans: Mainstream or Segregated Services." *Professional Psychology,* 1982, *13,* 215–221.

U.S. Bureau of the Census. *General Population Characteristics.* Washington, D.C.: U.S. Bureau of the Census, 1983.

U.S. Commission on Civil Rights. *Success of Asian Americans: Fact or Fiction?* Clearinghouse Publication 64. Washington, D.C.: U.S. Government Printing Office, 1980.

Uomoto, J. M., and Gorsuch, R. L. "Japanese American Response to Psychological Disorder: Referral Patterns, Attitudes, and Subjective Norms." *American Journal of Community Psychology,* 1984, *12,* 537–550.

Wong, J. "Asia Bashing: Bias Against Orientals Increases with Rivalry of Nations' Economies." *Wall Street Journal,* Nov. 28, 1986, pp. 1, 12.

Yamamoto, J., and Acosta, F. X. "Treatment of Asian Americans and Hispanic Americans: Similarities and Differences." *Journal of the American Academy of Psychoanalysis,* 1982, *10,* 585–607.

Yamamoto, J., and Kubota, M. "The Japanese-American Family." In G. J. Powell, J. Yamamoto, A. Romero, and A. Morales (eds.), *The Psychosocial Development of Minority Group Children.* New York: Brunner/Mazel, 1983.

4

American Indian
Children and Adolescents

Teresa D. LaFromboise
Kathryn Graff Low

For centuries, American Indians have been uprooted, relocated, educated, and socialized in attempts to integrate them into the dominant culture and extinguish their tribal identity and tradition. Many demographic trends, such as the increasing urbanization of Indian families, tend to interfere with cultural practices and facilitate assimilation. The survival of American Indian tribal cultures and identity despite relocation, poverty, and disease attests to the strength and flexibility of the first Americans.

Over the last two decades, mental health services delivered to American Indians have expanded and contracted both in general availability and in range of care. These fluctuations have resulted from shifts in federal funding priorities, apart from careful consideration of questions concerning the essential components of psychological treatment. Often immediate need outstrips existing knowledge and resources for gathering epidemiological data, identifying salient help-seeking pathways, detecting assessment bias, or designing and evaluating appropriate interventions. It is time to assess the strengths of American Indians, their beliefs about mental health, and the existing knowledge about American Indian youth. Toward this end, this chapter selectively reviews the literature pertinent to assessment and treatment of American Indian children and adolescents. A series of clinical and research issues are posed as points of departure for further inquiry, the answers to which we believe will form the basis for competence in the delivery of psychological services to American Indian youth.

Demographic Data

The designator "American Indian" refers to all North American native people, including Indians, Alaska Natives, Aleuts, Eskimos, and Metis, or mixed bloods. For brevity, the terms *American Indian, Indian,* and *Native American* are used interchangeably throughout this chapter to denote these varied peoples from distinctive and diverse tribes. Bureaucratic ambiguity complicates the eligibility criteria for individuals of American Indian descent. Federal and state-managed treatment programs generally require one-quarter genealogically derived Indian blood for eligibility, rather than accepting tribally defined memberships or community consensus. However, private agencies and Indian community programs generally respect the right of tribes to define membership.

The American Indian population, once estimated at 10 million, has been reduced, through what some have called "cultural genocide," to a figure between 1.5 and 1.8 million. This population has doubled since the 1970 census and is currently characterized as mobile, urban, and young (U.S. Bureau of the Census, 1983). About 400,000 Indian people are under age 15 (U.S. Department of Health and Human Services, 1988). The median ages are 20 years for American Indians and 18 years for Alaska Natives, both significantly lower than the national average of 30 years (U.S. Congress, Office of Technology Assessment, 1986). Each of the 517 federally recognized native entities (196 in Alaska and 321 in the lower forty-eight states) and 36 state-recognized American Indian tribes maintains unique customs, traditions, social organizations, and ecological relationships. There are 200 distinct tribal languages still spoken today (Leap, 1981).

Rural poverty and federal reductions in tribal budgets

have forced reservation Indians into cities for employment, scattering families across the country and increasing the prevalence of intertribal and interethnic marriages (Broudy and May, 1983). In 1980, 24 percent of American Indians lived on reservations, 8 percent in the historically Indian areas of Oklahoma, 3 percent in Alaska Native villages, 2 percent on tribal trust lands, and 63 percent elsewhere in the United States (U.S. Bureau of the Census, 1983).

Frequent relocation, substandard living conditions, and chronic unemployment in both urban and reservation areas have taken their toll on Indian people. Malnutrition, an alcoholism rate 3.8 times as high as that of other ethnic groups, a rate of cirrhosis of the liver 4.5 times as high, a homicide rate 2.8 times as high, a suicide rate 2.3 times as high, and environmental contamination continue to have a significant impact on Indian life expectancy and prevalence of illness. The Indian mortality rate from motor vehicle accidents is about 5.5 times that of other races (Manson, Walker, and Kivlahan, 1987). The Indian infant mortality rate during the postnatal period (age 1 month to 1 year) is almost twice the national average. Indian life expectancy is a low 44 years. However, there is some glimmer of hope that health care progress has been made. A recent government report established that the infant mortality rate and the infectious disease death rate for American Indians have declined in recent years (U.S. Congress, Office of Technology Assessment, 1986).

American Indians report a median family income of $13,678 (U.S. Congress, Office of Technology Assessment, 1986), compared with $17,786 for Black families, and $29,152 for White families (U.S. Bureau of the Census, 1986). Median income for families on reservations is $9,942 and, for the 23 percent of Indian households headed by women, $9,320—both figures falling well below the U.S. poverty guidelines and approximating one third of the median income of White households. Average income varies from tribe to tribe. Notable are the absence of a large "middle class" and the substantially lower incomes on reservations. Unemployment on reservations ranges from 20 to 70 percent, with the highest rates concentrated in the Plains states (U.S. Senate Select Committee on Indian Affairs, 1985).

In light of this pervasive hardship, it is not surprising that Indians attain fewer years of formal education than members of other minority groups. For some, scholastic functioning is severely impaired, and lags in academic performance of one to two years in elementary school and two to four years in secondary school are not uncommon. Those 25 years or older average ten years of schooling, compared with a national average of twelve years (Development Associates, 1983). Academic performance is also hampered by neurosensory disorders, developmental disabilities, and other handicapping conditions that go undiagnosed and untreated (otitis media, or middle-ear disease, for example, a condition estimated to occur in over half of Indian children).

About one third of adult American Indians are classified as illiterate, and only one adult male in five has a high school education (Brod and McQuiston, 1983). Dropout rates in urban high schools are particularly high, sometimes reaching 85 percent. In reservation schools and in boarding schools, which together educate about 80 percent of Indian youth, approximately 50 percent drop out (Coladarci, 1983; Giles, 1985).

The dearth of college-educated American Indians (8 percent according to the U.S. Bureau of the Census [1984]) has a substantial impact on this population. At the graduate level, the underrepresentation of American Indians is even more dramatic. For example, of the 32,839 doctoral degrees awarded in 1987 nationwide, only 130 were to American Indians, and only 10 of those degrees were in psychology (Snyder, 1987). Without psychologists, social workers, psychiatrists, and researchers who are sensitive to the complexity of American Indian cultural values, tribal customs, family ecology, and communication styles, collaboration and service delivery with American Indians will continue to be ineffective. Thus, the low college enrollment of American Indians and the low priority placed on mental health professions by tribes perpetuate the underdevelopment of their current mental health service delivery system.

Epidemiological Studies

Much of the literature on American Indian and Alaska Native mental health emphasizes certain cultural factors that influence treatment: beliefs about causes of psychological disturbance and expectations about help seeking and help giving. Unfortunately, the empirical study of treatment decisions in therapy and methods of intervention has not kept pace with the recognition of their clinical importance. Many epidemiological studies, particularly those concerning American Indian children, have methodological difficulties because of the use of culturally biased instruments. Community tolerance makes deviance difficult to discern, and psychological disturbance is often camouflaged by alcoholism (Green, Sack, and Pambrun, 1981). In addition, conducting research in isolated Indian communities is difficult logistically and politically (LaFromboise and Plake, 1983).

For the reasons noted above, only three communitywide psychiatric epidemiological studies have been conducted among American Indians and Alaska Natives. Each of these studies reports alarmingly high rates of psychological dysfunction according to diagnostic criteria refined on the general population (Roy, Chaudhuri, and Irvine, 1970). Shore, Kinzie, Hampson, and Pattison (1973) reported that 57 percent of their sample were definitely disturbed and another 15 percent were probably disturbed. Sampath (1974) found that 37 percent of a sample of Eskimo adults met *DSM-III* criteria for psychological disorders.

Little research has focused systematically on the psychological development of Indian children and adolescents, but some studies have estimated the prevalence of psychological disorders among them. In 1967, Ablon, Metcalf, and Miller estimated that 10–20 percent of Indian youth needed psychiatric help. In 1972, Wallace found that up to 25 percent of Indian children displayed psychological problems. Green, Sack, and Pambrun (1981) more recently noted problems of abuse, neglect, excessive foster care placements, school delinquency, and suicide. Studies of substance abuse and suicide show that adolescent depression, feelings of meaninglessness, alienation, self-estrangement, and withdrawal are recurring problems on many reservations throughout the country (Berlin, 1982). Boyce and Boyce (1983) found, for both male and female Indian youth, a trend toward higher numbers of clinic visits among those whose families were poorly matched with the surrounding community with respect to cultural identity. Unfortunately, although juvenile psychopathology may be on the rise, children, who make up 32 percent of the Indian population, receive only about 10 percent of the mental health care administered to that population (McShane and Plas, 1982; Neligh, 1985).

Child abuse and neglect appear to be increasing among Indians (Ishisaka, 1978; Robbins, 1982). In larger Indian populations, up to 35 percent of children are placed in foster care or boarding schools (Unger, 1977). Of those placed in boarding schools because of inadequate familial support or significant academic deficits and behavioral problems, 75 percent suffer school-related social/emotional problems (Kleinfeld and Bloom, 1977).

As Indian youth enter school, they often feel stranded between two cultures. Many of them speak an entirely different first language, practice an entirely different religion, and hold different cultural values than the dominant culture, and yet they are expected to perform successfully according to conventional Anglo educational criteria. They encounter their parents' often hopeless attitudes resulting from overwhelming impoverishment and discrimination. They are also increasingly reminded of economic, experiential, and social discrepancies that exist between Indian and Anglo cultures.

A fundamental problem for Indian youth continues to be the high incidence of alcohol and drug abuse. Alcohol abuse alone has critical consequences for young children in the form of fetal alcohol syndrome, which can lead to mental and psychosocial retardation (Boyce and others, 1986; May, 1982). Indian youth come into contact with both legal and illegal drugs at an early age. They continue to sustain utilization rates for alcohol up to three times that of adolescents in the population at large and for marijuana and amphetamines twice that of their White counterparts. Substance abuse is a widely modeled means of coping with depression, anxiety, hostility, feelings of powerlessness, and stress reactions among Indian youth (Bobo, 1985; Oetting and others, 1983). For adolescents, this coping mechanism exacerbates, rather than solves, the problems that contribute to educational underachievement, teen pregnancy, self-destructive behavior patterns, and high delinquency and arrest rates.

The growing literature on Indian youth suicide and accidental deaths attests to their special place among mental health concerns. Dizmang, Watson, May, and Bopp (1974) cited rapid social change, frequent changes in living situations, and conflicts experienced with different caretakers as significant factors contributing to the extremely high suicide rate—three times the rate in the general population—among Indian children and youth. Indian youth experience traumatic loss of family and friends at a rate much higher than the general population because of accidental and premature deaths and long separations from family for medical treatment or educational and employment opportunities (Long, 1983). Indian adolescents who have been adopted into Anglo families are twice as likely to commit suicide during their teen years as Indian adolescents raised in their own families (Berlin, 1978). Those who come from tribes classified as traditional (maintaining the old ways) are less likely to commit suicide than youth from transitional (neither highly traditional nor highly modern) or acculturated tribes (May, 1987).

American Indian Families: Strengths and Stresses

Complex and richly diverse, American Indian family life is difficult to describe because the roles of specific family members and the structure of extended families vary across tribes and among families within tribes. Nonetheless, obvious contrasts emerge when American Indian families are compared with Anglo families.

Traditionally, Indian people live in relational networks that serve to support and nurture strong bonds of mutual assistance and affection. Many tribes still engage in a traditional system of collective interdependence, with family members responsible not only to one another but also to the clan and tribe to which they belong. The Lakota Sioux use the term *tiospaye* to describe a traditional, community way of life facilitated by well-functioning extended families, in which an individual's well-being remains the responsibility of the extended family (Red Horse, Lewis, Feit, and Decker, 1978). When problems arise among Indian youth, they become problems of the community as well. The family, kin, and friends join together to observe the youth's behavior, draw the youth out of isolation, and integrate that person back into the activities of the group.

Relationships between family members and the community can be quite complex. The amount of social and governing control exhibited by women or men depends on the tribe. In the traditional matriarchal Navajo family, for example, an older woman might reside with her husband, her unmarried children, her married daughter, and the daughter's husband and children (Ryan, 1980).

Generally, in patriarchal tribes, a major role of the male as head of the family is to make important decisions. Women in these tribes influence family functioning as the central "core" of the family, maintaining primary responsibility for the welfare of the children. Uncles and aunts are important teachers: They share wisdom, impart values, often serve as role models, and reinforce tribal tradition. Grandmothers and aunts often supply child care. In some tribes, child care is shared by the men. Mescalero Apache men, for example, take responsibility for children when not working away from the family (Ryan, 1980). Grandparents and other elders are particularly important in that they are the safekeepers of tribal stories and songs and often spend time with children sharing their "oral tradition."

Traditionally speaking, tribal spirituality is the same as tribal life; the two are not deliberately separated (Hungry Wolf and Hungry Wolf, 1987). In children, early introduction to the spiritual life of the tribe fosters a loving respect for nature as well as independence and self-discipline.

Indian child-rearing practices are largely shaped by Indian world views, which regard children as beloved gifts (Hill Witt, 1979). Time spent caring for, admiring, and playing with Indian children is cherished (Morey and Gilliam, 1974). Early childhood is often marked by a variety of celebrations that honor an infant's developmental milestones, such as the first smile, first laugh, first steps, or first attempts at using language. Although American Indian families celebrate these developments, they feel little pressure over the timing of such events. Their beliefs involve acceptance of a child's own readiness and restraint from pressuring a child to perform (Everett, Proctor, and Cartmell, 1983; Dell, 1980). Historically, children were seldom physically punished in Indian households. After misbehaving, a child might quickly experience disapproving words, "tsk-tsk" sounds from the adults, or being ignored.

Communication patterns in Indian families differ from tribe to tribe. In general, these patterns might be characterized as hierarchal and diffuse. For example, information about a youth's misbehavior might be passed from the mother to her parents and sisters or from the mother or father to an aunt or uncle who has been designated as responsible for guiding the youth's character development. Restitution for the wrongdoing on the part of the youth may involve an apology to each of the family members who worry about the youth or are embarrassed by the youth's misbehavior. This indirect line of communication serves to protect the bonds between parents and youth and reinforces extended family involvement in maintaining standards of behavior. Similarly, when a youth is worthy of praise for a significant accomplishment, one of the family members might share this information with others in the community through a person known as the "camp crier." One role of the "camp crier" is to convey good news about members of the community while maintaining each family's humility.

Because autonomy is highly valued among American Indians, children are expected to make their own decisions and operate semi-independently at an early age. In this child-rearing style, family members allow children choices and the freedom to experience the natural consequences of those choices. The impact of a child's behavior on others is also emphasized. This seemingly diffuse approach to child rearing has often been labeled as permissive or negligent by social service providers because it appears to them that Indian parents exercise minimal observable control over their children (Gray and Cosgrove, 1985).

An adequate historical coverage of the voluntary migration patterns of American Indian families, their forced dispossession of traditional homelands, and governmental sponsorship of relocation efforts to urbanize and acculturate Indians is beyond the scope of this chapter. Excellent treatment of this subject is contained in Fixico (1986), Jacobs (1985), Kerri (1976), and Sandefur (1986).

In recent years, increased movement to urban areas has complicated Indian extended family functioning. Many Indians who have relocated to cities from reservations and other traditional Indian areas have felt isolated from their families and other Indian social support networks. To combat this sense of alienation, Indian people in urban environments often seek support from other Indians, neighbors, and non–family members and, over time, reconstitute their extended family network. Unfortunately, some contemporary Indian families are less able to establish social support networks and, without the benefit of extended family life, may experience greater stress in daily living than their more traditional relatives. Boyce and Boyce (1983) argue that cultural "fit" between the family and the surrounding community may be a more critical determinant of health and illness than isolated measures of individuals' levels of acculturation.

Indian youth from extended family networks in either reservations or urban areas face special problems. Family responsibilities and expectations become problematic at times for all youth. Because tribal spirituality remains paramount among Indian people, families encourage and expect their children and adolescents to participate in various ceremonies. Unfortunately, their participation in these ceremonies sometimes violates attendance policies of Anglo-operated schools and work sites. Students living away from home in boarding schools or universities often want to return home from great distances in order to participate in important family activities and ceremonies. Negative consequences often ensue for young people who opt to attend tribal ceremonies during school or work hours.

The high premium placed on individual achievement and success in academic institutions often causes conflict for Indian students and their families. For instance, Indian university students receiving scholarships may feel they should share their financial awards with family members even though financial aid packages are designed to fund subsistence support for students. Furthermore, American Indian students quickly discover that the academic success for which they receive praise on campus may yield further estrangement from their own people. Sometimes the community will actively discourage ambitions that involve leaving the reservation or the family (Lefley, 1975). Failing to meet community expectations can create dissent and generate guilt over social responsibility and noncompliance.

Sociocultural Issues in Assessment

The psychological assessment of American Indian children and adolescents presents a perplexing array of considerations. This section highlights some assessment issues one must consider in working with Indian youth: the testing situation, the use of standardized assessment instruments, and diagnostic procedures for the three psychological interventions presented in the intervention and treatment section that follows in this chapter.

In the testing situation, a person seeking information in intake interviews and standardized assessment situations must consider the testing environment; the biases, questioning style, and physical features of the test administrator; the biases inherent in the diagnostic instrument; and sociocultural factors that may affect the youth's perceptions of the assessment event and consequent performance.

It is crucial that interpretations of assessment results take into account environmental factors that may facilitate or hinder the youth's response tendencies. These include the social organization that the test administrator represents, physical features and location of the classroom or testing room, and the presence or absence of contextually relevant materials (for example, pictorial stimuli of children with pale faces). The clinician must also be aware of his or her personal biases in noting, scoring, and interpreting responses to test items.

Hynd and Garcia (1979) summarize behaviors of Ameri-

can Indian children during diagnostic interviews that may negatively affect assessment outcome: nonassertive, nonspontaneous,
and soft-spoken verbal interaction; limited eye contact; discomfort and decreased performance on timed tasks; reluctance to
offer self-disclosures; and selective performance of only those
skills that contribute to the betterment of the group. In addition,
because many tribal cultures emphasize perfection, American Indian children may be apprehensive about creating a block design
or enacting some other task without long periods of observation
or previously established competence in performing the task.

Use of standardized tests with minority children is, of
course, controversial. Most assessment instruments have built-in
biases; in fact, some argue that there is no such thing as a culturally unbiased instrument. Tests are designed and validated
according to middle-class values and life-styles and thus discrim-
inate against other socioeconomic and nondominant cultural
groups (Hynd and Garcia, 1979). Primarily, the biases involve
the assumptions that children are fluent in English and that
they have had a high degree of exposure to Anglo culture.

Test instructions assume a minimum vocabulary. They
often use temporal concepts and terms that may be alien to Indian world views. In addition, many tribal languages are vastly
different from English in vocabulary and structure. Even when
there is semantic equivalence, "language evokes a specific culture frame, with selective demand characteristics for the assessment of one's own behavior or the projection of personality
variables" (Lefley, 1975, p. 36).

Special considerations apply as well at the stage of making a psychological diagnosis. In his review of methodological
limitations of Indian children's mental health assessment, Beiser
(1981) recommends a multiaxial model for conducting evaluations that takes into account not only mental status and academic potential but additional information about the youth's
strengths, age-appropriateness of the youth's behavior, the
youth's social environment, and the youth's culture.

For example, a service provider considering social cognitive interventions might first conduct a functional analysis of
the cognitive, behavioral, and social elements of disturbance

associated with the target problem so as not to overlook essential cultural information. Consideration is given to both external (social, environmental) and internal (cognitive, emotional) antecedents and consequences (Bandura, 1986). Attention is paid particularly to the youth's personal and cultural schemata, or beliefs about self and relationships with others, that may contribute to the onset and maintenance of the problem behavior. This analysis relies on the ability of the service provider to establish trust and credibility early in treatment. Another professional or an extended family member may be able to assist in interpreting cultural cognitions and designing culturally appropriate reinforcement regimens.

A service provider considering family systems therapies would search for information about how the presenting problem affects the identified client and other extended family members as individuals and as a social unit. Information about how families might be mobilized to support the client in dealing with problems can be gathered during network analysis (Attneave, 1969; Red Horse, 1982). Network analysis includes an assessment of the cultural fit between the family and the surrounding community regardless of the family's absolute degree of acculturation.

A service provider considering Indian traditional methods can be aided by recent advances in research on indigenous concepts of mental well-being and the development of measurement scales specific to American Indian cultures. Mohatt and Blue (1982) used these methods to develop a scale to rate *tio-spaye*, or degree of traditionality, among members of the Lakota Sioux. Manson, Shore, and Bloom (1985) have pioneered the use of culturally adjusted psychiatric diagnostic measures among diverse American Indian groups and, in that process, delineated patterns of depressive symptoms and clinical presentation among the Hopi. Preliminary analysis of pretest data from a national study of Indian freshmen's adjustment to academic life, conducted by the Center for American Indian and Alaska Native Mental Health Research, has uncovered tribally distinct factor structures on the Center for Epidemiologic Studies Depression Scale (CES-D; Radloff, 1977), a commonly used self-report scale to measure depression (J. Jordan, personal communication, Sept. 17, 1987). These recent advances in assessment provide useful alternatives to conventional diagnostic procedures and allow the clinician to make data-based decisions in the selection of traditional treatment.

Intervention and Treatment

American Indian youth may consider mental illness a justifiable outcome of human weakness or of a tendency to avoid the discipline necessary to maintain traditional cultural values. Indian people value social responsibility, honesty, independence, reciprocity, kindness, and self-control over the cultivation of social skills (Plas and Bellet, 1983; Trimble, 1981). Several qualities important to Anglo culture, such as individualism and competitiveness, may be actively discouraged by tribes. The Coyote stories, for example, carried from one generation to the next, warn of the danger associated with excessively individualistic and manipulative behavior.

Tribal diversity makes it difficult to generalize about therapeutic issues. It is clear that Indian youth may have different values and priorities than other youth. Does it follow that American Indian youth considering counseling or being referred for treatment have different needs and expectations than clients from the dominant culture? Recent research lends empirical support to the importance of culture in the application of counseling interventions as well as assessment procedures with school-age Indian youth.

A study of perceived problems and sources of help among American Indian high school students by Dauphinais, LaFromboise, and Rowe (1980) found that, compared with Anglo youth, Indian youth preferred to talk with friends and parents when they had problems rather than with school counselors or other support personnel. Their problems included concerns about the future, depression, apathy, decisions that needed to be made, ways of maintaining good grades, class scheduling problems, and whether to stay in school. Indian youth generally sought formal help only when they had been referred to psychological services by school officials or tribal judges.

Studies of Indian students' assessments of positive counselor attributes have rendered conflicting findings on the importance attached to counselor race. Three studies found a strong preference for an Indian person (Dauphinais, Dauphinais, and Rowe, 1981; Haviland, Horswill, O'Connell, and Dynneson, 1983; Littrell and Littrell, 1982); yet, other investigations (LaFromboise and Dixon, 1981; LaFromboise, Dauphinais, and Rowe, 1980) did not confirm these results. These conflicting findings may be attributed to methodological differences among the studies. Preferences for same-sex counselors among Indian high school students have been supported (Haviland, Horswill, O'Connell, and Dynneson, 1983; Littrell and Littrell, 1982).

Trustworthiness is obviously important in every counseling relationship, regardless of the client's race or cultural background. This counselor attribute was even more crucial for Indian clients, who have learned from their past that authorities purporting to give help may have ulterior motives.

In general, Indian youth are looking for someone who understands the practical aspects of their culture and can give them sound advice about their lives, not someone who reflects and restates their feelings for the purpose of analysis (Dauphinais, Dauphinais, and Rowe, 1981). In fact, a recent study by LaFromboise, Davis, and Rowe (1985) indicates that, in many cases, conventional psychological training is not necessary to enable one to be a good counselor with Indian adolescents.

Compared with the research on preferred attributes of helpers, little empirical evidence exists on the comparative efficacy of psychological interventions with American Indian youth. The three therapeutic approaches outlined below—social cognitive interventions, traditional Indian interventions, and systems therapy—are by no means the only interventions available to service providers working with American Indians. Although there are major differences among these psychological treatment approaches, they have one important commonality: They incorporate the Indian youth's environment or social context into treatment and therefore better accommodate Indian cultural practices (Attneave, 1982).

Social cognitive interventions have been considered less culturally biased than other theoretical approaches because they recognize the impact of culture on personal and environmental

variables and allow each culture to define its own appropriate
behaviors or targets for intervention (LaFromboise and Rowe,
1983). This is particularly important in light of tribal differences. Because social cognitive interventions include the examination of belief systems associated with target behaviors, they
have heuristic appeal for accommodating cultural values and expectations (LaFromboise and BigFoot, 1988). A counselor
working with an American Indian population is well advised to
research the specific cultural practices and traditions of the
tribes represented in his or her clientele. Generalizing about Indian cultural practices or making assumptions about tribe-
specific conventions such as family structure may be insulting
to an Indian client and damaging to the therapeutic process
(Attneave, 1982).

External stimuli and reinforcers in an American Indian
social environment may differ dramatically from stimuli and
reinforcement in the dominant culture. Consequently, a therapist
working with American Indian clients must be sensitive to the
important philosophical differences between traditional cultures
and the dominant culture. Dell (1980) describes an intervention
for families and children based on Hopi world views that illustrates the importance of understanding Indian culture before
designing an intervention or attempting to analyze stimuli and
reinforcers.

Essentially, the Hopi feel that repetitive "bad" behaviors
have a cumulative effect and that accrual of these behaviors
leads to eventual change (Dell, 1980). A Hopi parent might
therefore welcome the repetition of negative behavior as a sign
of imminent change. A therapist unaware of Hopi philosophy
might point out that the parents appear to be reinforcing poor
behavior with their continual optimism and refusal to intervene.
An intervention designed to eliminate these reinforcing behaviors would strike at the underpinnings of Hopi philosophy. Tail-
oring an intervention to the particular tribe while reinforcing
the importance of Hopi optimism regarding outcome reduces
the client's justified concern that psychological interventions
might dilute culture-specific behaviors and norms and allows the
therapist to enlist tribal belief and tradition as resources.

In addition to individual therapy, social cognitive group

interventions have been used successfully in the areas of parenting (BigFoot, 1987), assertiveness and other professional skills (LaFromboise, 1988; LaFromboise and Rowe, 1983), and substance abuse (Schinke and others, 1985). Group skills training may be particularly effective because it reduces the emphasis on individual disclosure, which is difficult for some Indians, and introduces collective responsibility. Because a collective approach is characteristic of some Indian tribes and families, a group format may draw on an already familiar and powerful cultural ethic.

In contrast to the disease model of psychopathology, the theory behind cognitive therapies holds that most psychological problems are learned within the social milieu and maintained through cognitive reinforcement (Meichenbaum, 1977). When analyzing "faulty" or irrational cognitions, a therapist working with American Indian clients must be highly sensitive to the fact that self-deprecating beliefs may reflect an internalization of the dominant culture's attitude toward ethnic minorities. Likewise, beliefs that are irrational by the standards of the dominant culture may be perfectly reasonable in light of American Indian history. Faith in a medicine man, tribal prophecies, or tribal traditions may seem irrational in the dominant culture but may have substantial healing power in therapy with Indians. An American Indian youth who has broken a cultural taboo may experience anxiety that a therapist in the dominant culture would label "catastrophic." Yet, given the power of some Indian beliefs, the youth's fear of retribution or spiritual consequences may be well founded. A therapist must assess the rationality of beliefs in the context of the culture. Once a therapist has identified dysfunctional thoughts in cultural context, treatment focuses on the current determinants of behavior (as distinct from past or unconscious factors) and involves the analysis of components of the behavior or beliefs and the modification of these components in accordance with specific subgoals.

It is important that the therapist balance the need for successfully establishing trust and the need for effecting change. Some Indian clients may expect immediate results and will be frustrated by a slow rate of change. In addition, they may be quite reticent, expecting the therapist to supply the therapeutic answers. Asking Indian clients to keep behavior logs or to solicit help from the extended family may actively engage them in therapy earlier and allow some immediate insight or feedback on the nature of the problem.

The following case illustrates the use of a social cognitive intervention.

Mark, a 16-year-old Indian male of average intelligence, has been "acting out" for more than a year. Often truant, Mark has fallen behind in his academic work. He uses drugs and alcohol, has had several violent encounters with fellow students, and has been in minor trouble with local authorities. Mark has lived with his maternal aunt and uncle on the reservation for the last ten years. His mother is a chronic alcoholic, and Mark rarely sees her. The identity of Mark's father is unknown. Recently, Mark's uncle lost his job and began to disappear for days on end. Mark has been referred by a school counselor, who has become increasingly concerned about his apparent depression.

Clearly, an initial goal in therapy with Mark would be to establish the therapist's credibility and trustworthiness. A variety of techniques are available, but strategies for engaging Mark in therapy may depend on tribal and family tradition. Conferences with the family and enlistment of the support of extended family members are crucial. In particular, relatives may help ensure that Mark attends therapy sessions. In addition, tribal elders or other adults with whom Mark interacts might be consulted. The power of the extended family or tribe should not be underestimated.

Early in therapy, American Indian clients may feel more comfortable if the therapist practices some self-disclosure and indicates a desire for reciprocity (LaFromboise, 1985). Mark should not be pushed to make disclosures or assume a familiarity that he does not feel. Considerable time could be spent developing a definition of the problem from Mark's personal and cultural point of view. Asking Mark to help define the problem and provide input for establishing treatment goals may increase comfort and trust during the early stages of therapy.

The therapeutic problem, when defined through cognitive and behavioral assessment techniques, would involve exploring Mark's thoughts about himself and the cues and reinforcements for his negative behavior. His substance abuse may be a way of coping with peer and family pressure, or it may be the only way he has learned to make himself "feel good." In addition, Mark may be struggling with identity issues, involving both his paternity and his need to function adequately in Anglo and Indian cultures. His inability to function in either environment may be painful enough to prompt his angry behavior.

The counselor's goal in therapy would be to influence Mark to change his irrational thoughts, internal dialogue, and negative self-assessments by means of self-monitoring, discrimination training, behavior change, and social validation. Typical intervention strategies might include identifying the origin of his negative beliefs about himself (particularly if they are internalized from the dominant culture), exploring the effects of negative stereotypes about Indian drinking patterns, recording his irrational thoughts to help him discover self-statements that contradict these negative cognitions, verbal persuasion, modeling of positive thoughts and appropriate drinking behavior from tribal leaders, and specific techniques such as problem solving and increasing pleasant activities.

Because school is a problematic environment, a specific subgoal of therapy might involve rehearsal of school situations, starting with those in which Mark is quite comfortable (for example, talking with a friend), in order to develop his coping skills. With rehearsal of ever more stressful scenarios, Mark's confidence will increase, ultimately improving his performance. Through consultation with Mark's teachers, methods of classroom participation might be modified to include cooperative learning activities that structure small-group activities and presentations rather than individual presentations to the entire class (Cohen, 1983).

In general, cognitive behavior therapy should not replace traditional Indian behaviors or therapeutic processes but should expand the adolescent's repertoire of coping options. For Mark, participation in social gatherings such as basketball tournaments, rodeos, powwows, feasts, and giveaways would be an important first step in helping him reaffirm his Indian identity. Gradually, we would hope to see an increase in Mark's self-esteem, the confirmation of personal identity and the emergence of a stronger Indian identity, improved academic performance, and comfortable and effective interactions in diverse and multicultural contexts.

Therapies based on systems theory effectively integrate ongoing strengths inherent in Indian extended family networking. Systems theory includes a variety of specific therapeutic interventions, including transactional analysis, family therapy, and group therapy. These interventions share the assumption that the individual and the environment have continuous reciprocal interactions, that a client is one portion of a dynamic and interrelated whole. Systems theory argues that the most helpful therapeutic interventions are those that enhance an individual's interaction with others or with the environment and therefore ensure lasting changes outside the context of the therapeutic relationship (Ivey, Ivey, and Simek-Downing, 1987). This approach takes advantage of the potentially supportive extended family in American Indian life while seeing that family members become aware of their own maladaptive patterns that may contribute to an individual's dysfunction.

The extended family, rather than conventional service delivery agencies, has remained the forum for problem solving and support in Indian communities, and most traditional interventions involve the extended family to ensure success. A therapist who persists in focusing primarily on an Indian youth's relationships within the nuclear family may be missing important contributions from more distant family members.

Shangreaux, Pleskac, and Freeman (1987) have developed an excellent systems intervention program for Indian families. Aspects of systems interventions that are particularly important for Indian families are summarized below.

Defining the family may be a difficult task for some Indian families, and the therapist must make sure that the client has salient family members included in therapy. Asking Indian youth to draw a genogram, draw a portrait of the family, or tell a story about their family may elicit important information about family function. Generally, family members who have a reasonable amount of contact with the youth (for example, living in the same household) should be included in systems analysis. Engaging the family in therapy may be difficult and may require the support of the tribe or Indian community, persistent requests by the therapist or referring agency, or frequent visits to the home to establish trust and rapport before beginning treatment.

Shangreaux, Pleskac, and Freeman (1987) suggest specific techniques for engaging a family in therapy. These include exercising patience, using self-disclosure to establish trust, allowing time for relationship building using humor and small talk, and establishing credibility through genuine concern and caring. Active listening techniques that focus on the client and family, work with the extended family, and asking community members to lend support by accompanying the family on initial visits are also recommended.

Once key family members are attending therapy, they should be asked to define the family and its structure, addressing such issues as hierarchy, triangulation, and alliances. The therapist must keep in mind that extended family interchanges and interdependence are encouraged in many Indian families, in contrast to the independence valued by Anglo families. The therapist who labels Indian families "enmeshed" often mistakes interdependence for inadequate boundaries. Further, therapists should be sensitive to problems in defining family and alliances. In particular, intergenerational conflicts around traditional practices, inappropriate family expectations (for example, that students should miss school to attend tribal events), and dependence issues may be problematic. Shangreaux, Pleskac, and Freeman (1987) suggest family sculpting as a useful tool for clarifying relationships within the family and for demonstrating a variety of possible relationships in Indian families. Drawing, storytelling, or using family models may elicit information about structure and alliances without being threatening.

Family roles, often crucial in systems therapy, may be quite different in Indian families. The role of aunts and uncles in the guidance of Indian youth has been noted above. The youth may feel as if he or she had several "parents" in the forms of grandparents, aunts, uncles, and cousins and may use all of these as role models. The systems therapist working with an Indian family must explore the degree to which the family utilizes extended family roles and the nature of these roles.

Family values, as well, may reflect the values of American Indian culture. Reverence for elders, emphasis on interdependence and community, and the ethic of sharing are all values typical of traditional Indian culture. The therapist who insists on promoting Anglo values in therapy is likely to meet substantial resistance and may not be acting in the best interest of the client. Instead, an intervention that focuses on increasing the cooperation, connectedness, and patience of the child may be a more culturally consonant approach.

Techniques that may be particularly effective with American Indian families in early sessions include employing ecomaps and genograms, assessing level of acculturation, having various family members monitor family function, and asking the family to share a story that represents the family history (Shangreaux, Pleskac, and Freeman, 1987).

In the case of Mark, a therapist conducting a systems intervention might want to assemble Mark's extended family in hopes of defining and solving his specific problems and eliciting the cooperation and support of family members. In addition, the therapist might explore ways in which the family contributes to or reinforces Mark's current maladaptive behavior. Particularly helpful may be the Indian belief that the behavior of any single family member reflects on the entire family or clan and is therefore the concern and responsibility of all family members. In addition, other significant community members may be helpful resources for Mark, assisting in monitoring, supporting, and rewarding positive behavior.

Group therapy involving a peer group or, in Mark's case, a group of alcohol abusers might also be effective (Kahn, Lewis, and Galvez, 1974). Social skills training interventions for alcohol abuse have been relatively successful with American Indian youth because they de-emphasize the individual and instead focus on the harm that substance abuse has brought to Indian people (Bobo, 1985).

Several traditional interventions may be used effectively in the treatment of Indian youth, particularly those who have been raised in more traditional Indian ways. Any of these could be incorporated into Mark's treatment. A counselor's decision to collaborate with a traditional healer usually begins with an assessment of the client's desire for ceremonial healing. These ceremonies are conducted either before or in conjunction with therapy.

"Sweat lodge" ceremonies are frequently conducted among American Indian groups for purification and prevention purposes. Participation in the sweat lodge consists in preparatory fasting, prayer, and offerings throughout serial purification sessions referred to as "rounds." The ceremony lasts several hours while participants make offerings for health and balance in life (Manson, Walker, and Kivlahan, 1987).

Manson, Walker, and Kivlahan (1987) suggest two other American Indian treatment strategies based on traditional healing practices: the "four circles" and the "talking circle." The four-circles intervention involves the symbolic organization of the important relationships in one's life: The centermost of four concentric circles represents the Creator, the second circle symbolizes the relationships with a partner or spouse, the third represents the extended or immediate family, and the fourth signifies tribal members. Four circles is a symbolic search for balance in relationships and is a useful tool for clarifying and assigning priorities to allegiances and social responsibility.

The "talking circle" intervention resembles conventional group therapy. The participants form a circle and remain in the circle until the ceremony is complete. Sweet grass is burned to produce purifying smoke and provide direction for the group conversation. The leader begins by sharing feelings or thoughts about the group. Each participant is free to speak, and no one is allowed to interrupt. Often, a sacred object is circulated, and the ceremony ends with a joining of hands in prayer.

These traditional practices might be particularly effective in a case like Mark's, in which an adolescent is struggling to assert his tribal identity and feelings of self-worth. A traditional intervention like the "talking circle" would reaffirm Mark's Indian identity and acceptance by the group. It could also offer him the opportunity to share his frustrations and concerns with supportive community members. In turn, older participants in the talking circle could model behaviors or make suggestions that might help Mark cope with diverse cultural demands and enhance his self-esteem. Finally, the fact that a number of community members would engage in this level of support could enhance his estimate of self-worth. This combination of traditional healing and contemporary psychotherapy can solidify social support, facilitate communication with and cooperation from the community, and offer opportunity for purification.

All the techniques described above can be adapted in a multimodal intervention and used effectively with American Indian youth. The case of Carol illustrates this blended approach.

A group of adolescents, mostly males, had gathered in a remote area of the reservation for a drinking party. After the late-night affair, Carol, a 13-year-old member of the group, was raped by a distant cousin. She reported the incident to her parents. They felt, however, that she had "brought the problem on herself" and refused to take any action. Carol was referred to therapy by school authorities because of noticeable weight loss and symptoms of depression.

An approach that combines a variety of intervention techniques might help Carol. Therapy could explore her negative thoughts, particularly those relating to having been "violated" and to feeling dirty. The tribe's attitude toward early sexual activity and possible strong taboos against incest and forced copulation might be revealed as the cause of Carol's depression. The therapist might also incorporate behavioral techniques to relieve depression and improve Carol's eating habits. Such techniques might include increasing Carol's physical activity, monitoring her diet, and constructing a system of rewards for weight gain and positive interaction with others.

Meanwhile, traditional interventions such as a sweat-lodge ceremony or a talking-circle ceremony might be particularly effective in Carol's case. The sweat-lodge ritual could help relieve Carol's feelings of "dirtiness" or guilt through purification. The talking-circle ceremony would provide the opportunity for Carol to obtain support and reinforcement and give her a safe forum in which to express anger and pain. Systems therapy could focus on family interaction and provide an understanding of the parents' reaction to Carol's rape.

Defining the family is an important task. Carol's mother and father may not have been her primary caretakers. Other adults may have been equally supportive or influential in Carol's life. For whatever reason, Carol's family may be resistant to traditional interventions or to conventional therapeutic techniques. Nonetheless, assembling even part of the family is beneficial. Parent/child interaction, family roles, the impact of the rape, and individual family members' attitudes should all be explored.

Summary and Conclusions

Although advances have been made toward understanding and addressing the problems facing Indian youth today, extensive work still needs to be done to offset the impact of pervasive poverty, underachievement, and poorly coordinated educational and social services.

Despite past governmental policies of relocation, Indian cultural beliefs and practices prevail. American Indians not only assert that children are their most vital natural resource, they daily acknowledge the importance of children through child-rearing practices. Indians realize that the pressures for acculturation will not soon diminish and that they must continue to work diligently for personal strength through traditionality. Even though Indians are moving to urban areas in increasing numbers, they maintain clan and extended family structures through frequent home visits and reconstitution of networks with other Indians. Unfortunately, this family structure and method of functioning can be misunderstood by professional helpers who fail to see the value of extensive support systems in protecting against stress.

Some progress has been made in the refinement of psychological interventions for American Indians. The cultural adaptation of psychological interventions must be accompanied by empirical validation of modified treatment procedures. Further progress toward identifying effective areas of influence with Indian youth depends on definitions of psychological dysfunction that take into account local beliefs about mental health and mental illness.

Several directions for future epidemiological research have already been set forth (Manson, 1982; Manson and Trimble, 1982). Research considerations of particular relevance to American Indian youth include the need to better understand critical antecedents of academic apathy, the need to distinguish among stages of inter- and intracultural Indian identity development, the need to determine tribe-specific traditional beliefs associated with self-esteem enhancement as well as self-destruction, and the need to delineate more tribe-specific behavioral manifestations of depression, anxiety, and anger.

It is time to reverse the emphasis on pathology in research and treatment with American Indians. Social cognitive interventions, systems approaches, and American Indian traditional healing methods are recommended because of their ability to focus on Indian cultural attributes and strengths. We propose that Indian traditional beliefs and healing practices be incorporated into conventional treatment designs whenever they are desired by the client and deemed appropriate by the community. Social cognitive interventions, in particular, lend themselves to application in educational settings with American Indian youth.

Research has shown that clinical treatment need not involve professionally trained caregivers to be effective with Indian youth (LaFromboise, Davis, and Rowe, 1985). In fact, it has been suggested that the natural skills of Indian helpers may be obviated by conventional clinical training experiences that impart Rogerian interviewing skills (Dauphinais, Dauphinais, and Rowe, 1981). Ways of legitimizing the work of Indian community advisers and strategies for incorporating their helping style into individual and family therapy should be explored. Increased collaboration between service providers and traditional healers is both exciting and challenging. American Indians should be encouraged to help fill the desperate need for community leaders in the mental health arena.

Mental health professionals can help Indian youth acquire the life skills and perspectives necessary for optimal development. To do so, the Indian community must become the locus of intervention, and the relationships among Indian youth, their families, their schools, their communities, and the larger society must be clearly defined.

References

Ablon, J., Metcalf, A., and Miller, D. *An Overview of Mental Health Problems of Indian Children.* Report to the Joint Commission on the Mental Health of Children. Washington, D.C.: U.S. Government Printing Office, 1967.

Attneave, C. L. "Therapy in Tribal Settings and Urban Network Intervention." *Family Process,* 1969, *8,* 192–210.

Attneave, C. L. "American Indians and Alaska Native Families: Emigrants in Their Own Homeland." In M. McGoldrick, J. K. Pearce, and J. Giordano (eds.), *Ethnicity and Family Therapy.* New York: Guilford Press, 1982.

Bandura, A. *Social Foundations of Thought and Action: A Social Cognitive Theory.* Englewood Cliffs, N.J.: Prentice-Hall, 1986.

Beiser, M. "Mental Health of American Indian and Alaska Native Children: Some Epidemiological Perspectives." *White Cloud Journal,* 1981, *2,* 37–47.

Berlin, I. N. "Anglo Adoptions of Native Americans: Repercussions in Adolescence." *Journal of the American Academy of Child and Adolescent Psychiatry,* 1978, *17,* 387–388.

Berlin, I. N. "Prevention of Emotional Problems Among Native-American Children: Overview of Developmental Issues." *Journal of Preventive Psychiatry,* 1982, *1,* 319–330.

BigFoot, D. "Parent Training for American Indian Families." Unpublished doctoral prospectus, University of Oklahoma, Norman, 1987.

Bobo, J. K. "Preventing Drug Abuse Among American Indian Adolescents." In L. D. Gilchrist and S. P. Schinke (eds.), *Preventing Social and Health Problems Through Life Skills Training*. Seattle: School of Social Work, University of Washington, 1985.

Boyce, W. T., and Boyce, J. C. "Acculturation and Changes in Health Among Navajo School Students." *Social Sciences and Medicine*, 1983, *17*, 219–226.

Boyce, W. T., and others. "Social and Cultural Factors in Pregnancy Complications Among Navajo Women." *American Journal of Epidemiology*, 1986, *124*, 242–253.

Brod, R. L., and McQuiston, J. M. "American Indian Adult Education and Literacy: The First National Survey." *Journal of American Indian Education*, 1983, *1*, 1–16.

Broudy, D. W., and May, P. A. "Demographic and Epidemiological Transition Among the Navajo Indians." *Social Biology*, 1983, *30*, 12–19.

Cohen, E. G. "Talking and Working Together: Status, Interaction and Learning." In P. Peterson, L. C. Wilkinson, and M. Hallinon (eds.), *The Social Context of Instruction: Group Organization and Group Processes*. Orlando, Fla.: Academic Press, 1983.

Coladarci, T. "High School Dropout Among Native Americans." *Journal of American Indian Education*, 1983, *23*, 15–23.

Dauphinais, P., Dauphinais, L., and Rowe, W. "Effects of Race and Communication Style on Indian Perceptions of Counselor Effectiveness." *Counselor Education and Supervision*, 1981, *21*, 72–80.

Dauphinais, P., LaFromboise, T. D., and Rowe, W. "Perceived Problems and Sources of Help for American Indian Students." *Counselor Education and Supervision*, 1980, *20*, 37–44.

Dell, P. F. "The Hopi Family Therapist and the Aristotelian Parents." *Journal of Marital and Family Therapy*, 1980, *6*, 123–130.

Development Associates (ed.). *The Evaluation of the Impact of the Part A Entitlement Program Funded Under Title IV of the Indian Education Act*. Contract No. 380-80-0862. Washington, D.C.: U.S. Department of Education, 1983.

Dizmang, L. H., Watson, J., May, P. A., and Bopp, I. "Adolescent Suicide at an Indian Reservation." *American Journal of Orthopsychiatry*, 1974, *44*, 43–49.

Everett, F., Proctor, N., and Cartmell, B. "Providing Psychological Services to American Indian Children and Families." *Professional Psychology: Research and Practice*, 1983, *14*, 588–603.

Fixico, D. *Termination and Relocations: Federal Indian Policy, 1945–1960.* Albuquerque: University of New Mexico Press, 1986.

Giles, K. N. *Indian High School Dropouts: A Perspective.* Milwaukee, Wis.: Midwest National Origin Desegregation Assistance Center, 1985.

Gray, E., and Cosgrove, J. "Ethnocentric Perception of Child-rearing Practices in Protective Services." *Child Abuse and Neglect*, 1985, *9*, 389–396.

Green, B. E., Sack, W. H., and Pambrun, A. "A Review of Child Psychiatric Epidemiology with Special Reference to American Indian and Alaska Native Children." *White Cloud Journal*, 1981, *2*, 22–36.

Haviland, M. G., Horswill, R. K., O'Connell, J. J., and Dynneson, V. V. "Native American College Students' Preference for Counselor Race and Sex and the Likelihood of Their Use of a Counseling Center." *Journal of Counseling Psychology*, 1983, *30*, 267–270.

Hill Witt, S. "Pressure Points in Growing Up Indian." Paper presented at 87th annual meeting of the American Psychological Association, New York City, Aug. 1979.

Hungry Wolf, A., and Hungry Wolf, B. *Children of the Sun.* New York: Morrow, 1987.

Hynd, G. W., and Garcia, W. I. "Intellectual Assessment of the Native American Student." *School Psychology Digest*, 1979, *8*, 446–454.

Ishisaka, H. "American Indians and Foster Care: Cultural Factors and Separation." *Child Welfare*, 1978, *57*, 299–388.

Ivey, A. E., Ivey, M. B., and Simek-Downing, L. *Counseling and Psychotherapy: Integrating Skills, Theory and Practice.* (2nd ed.) Englewood Cliffs, N.J.: Prentice-Hall, 1987.

Jacobs, W. R. *Dispossessing the American Indian.* (2nd ed.) Norman: University of Oklahoma Press, 1985.

Kahn, M. W., Lewis, J., and Galvez, E. "An Evaluation Study of Group Therapy Procedure with Reservation Adolescent Indians." *Psychotherapy: Theory, Research and Practice,* 1974, *11,* 239–242.

Kerri, J. N. "Push and Pull Factor: Reason for Migration as a Factor in American-Indian Urban Adjustment." *Human Organization,* 1976, *35,* 215–220.

Kleinfeld, J., and Bloom, J. "Boarding Schools: Effects on the Mental Health of Eskimo Adolescents." *American Journal of Psychiatry,* 1977, *134,* 411–417.

LaFromboise, T. D. "Effects of Race and Communication Style on American Indian Perceptions of Counselor Impact." Invited symposium presented at meeting of the American Educational Research Association, Chicago, Apr. 1985.

LaFromboise, T. D. *Circles of Women: Professionalization Training for American Indian Women.* Newton, Mass.: Women's Educational Equity Act, 1988.

LaFromboise, T. D., and BigFoot, D. "Cultural and Cognitive Considerations in the Prevention of American Indian Adolescent Suicide." *Journal of Adolescence,* 1988, *11,* 139–153.

LaFromboise, T. D., Dauphinais, P., and Rowe, W. "Indian Students' Perceptions of Positive Helper Attributes." *Journal of American Indian Education,* 1980, *19,* 11–16.

LaFromboise, T. D., Davis, B., and Rowe, W. "Verbal Response Patterns of Effective American Indian Helpers." Paper presented at annual meeting of the American Psychological Association, Los Angeles, Aug. 1985.

LaFromboise, T. D., and Dixon, D. "American Indian Perceptions of Trustworthiness in a Counseling Interview." *Journal of Counseling Psychology,* 1981, *28,* 135–139.

LaFromboise, T. D., and Plake, B. "Toward Meeting the Educational Research Needs of American Indians." *Harvard Educational Review,* 1983, *53,* 45–51.

LaFromboise, T. D., and Rowe, W. "Skills Training for Bicultural Competence: Rationale and Application." *Journal of Counseling Psychology,* 1983, *30,* 589–595.

Leap, W. L. "American Indian Language Maintenance." *Annual Review of Anthropology,* 1981, *10,* 271–280.

Lefley, H. P. "Differential Self-Concept in American Indian Children as a Function of Language and Examiner." *Journal of Personality and Social Psychology,* 1975, *31,* 36–41.

Littrell, J. M., and Littrell, M. A. "American Indian and Caucasian Students' Preferences for Counselors: Effects of Counselor Dress and Sex." *Journal of Counseling Psychology,* 1982, *29,* 48–57.

Long, K. "The Experience of Repeated and Traumatic Loss Among Crow Indian Children: Response Patterns and Intervention Strategies." *American Journal of Orthopsychiatry,* 1983, *52,* 116–126.

McShane, D. A., and Plas, J. M. "Wechsler Scale Performance Patterns of American Indian Children." *Psychology in the Schools,* 1982, *19,* 8–17.

Manson, S. M. (ed.). *New Directions in Prevention Among American Indian and Alaska Native Communities.* Portland: Oregon Health Sciences University, 1982.

Manson, S. M., Shore, J. H., and Bloom, J. D. "The Depressive Experience in American Indian Communities: A Challenge for Psychiatric Theory and Diagnosis." In A. Kleinman and B. Good (eds.), *Culture and Depression.* Berkeley: University of California Press, 1985.

Manson, S. M., and Trimble, J. E. "American Indian and Alaska Native Communities: Past Efforts, Future Inquiries." In L. R. Snowden (ed.), *Reaching the Underserved: Mental Health Needs of Neglected Populations.* Newbury Park, Calif.: Sage, 1982.

Manson, S. M., Walker, R. D., and Kivlahan, D. R. "Psychiatric Assessment and Treatment of American Indians and Alaska Natives." *Hospital and Community Psychiatry,* 1987, *38,* 165–173.

May, P. "Substance Abuse and American Indians: Prevalence and Susceptibility." *International Journal of the Addictions,* 1982, *17,* 1185–1209.

May, P. "Suicide and Self-Destruction Among American Indian

Youths." *American Indian and Alaska Native Mental Health Research,* 1987, *1,* 52–69.

Meichenbaum, D. H. (ed.). *Cognitive Behavior Modification: An Integrative Approach.* New York: Plenum, 1977.

Mohatt, G., and Blue, A. W. "Primary Prevention as It Relates to Traditionality and Empirical Measures of Social Deviance." In S. M. Manson (ed.), *New Directions in Prevention Among American Indian and Alaska Native Communities.* Portland: Oregon Health Sciences University, 1982.

Morey, S. M., and Gilliam, O. J. (eds.). *Respect for Life: The Traditional Upbringing of American Indian Children.* New York: Myrin Institute, 1974.

Neligh, G. "Major Mental Disorders and Behavior Among American Indians and Alaska Natives." Presentation at the Conference on Health and Behavior: A Research Agenda for American Indians and Alaska Natives, Government Camp, Oreg., Apr. 1985.

Oetting, E. R., and others. *Drug Use Among Native American Youth: Summary of Findings (1975–81).* Fort Collins, Colo.: Western Behavioral Studies, 1983.

Plas, J. M., and Bellet, W. "Assessment of the Value-Attitude Orientations of American Indian Children." *Journal of School Psychology,* 1983, *21,* 57–64.

Radloff, L. S. "The CES-D Scale: A Self-Report Depression Scale for Research in the General Population." *Applied Psychology Measurement,* 1977, *1,* 385–401.

Red Horse, J. "American Indian Community Mental Health: A Primary Prevention Strategy." In S. M. Manson (ed.), *New Directions in Prevention Among American Indian and Alaska Native Communities.* Portland: Oregon Health Sciences University, 1982.

Red Horse, J., Lewis, R. G., Feit, M., and Decker, J. "Family Behavior of Urban American Indians." *Social Casework,* 1978, *59,* 67–72.

Robbins, M. "Project *Nak-nu-we-sha:* A Preventive Intervention in Child Abuse and Neglect Among a Pacific Northwest Indian Community." In S. M. Manson (ed.), *New Directions in*

Prevention Among American Indian and Alaska Native Communities. Portland: Oregon Health Sciences University, 1982.

Roy, C., Chaudhuri, A., and Irvine, O. "The Prevalence of Mental Disorders Among Sasketchewan Indians." *Journal of Cross-Cultural Psychology,* 1970, *1,* 383–392.

Ryan, R. A. "Strengths of the American Indian Family: State of the Art." In F. Hoffman (ed.), *The American Indian Family: Strengths and Stresses.* Isleta, N.Mex.: American Indian Social Research and Development Associates, 1980.

Sampath, H. M. "Prevalence of Psychiatric Disorders in a Southern Baffin Island Eskimo Settlement." *Canadian Psychiatric Association Journal,* 1974, *19,* 363–367.

Sandefur, G. D. "American Migration and Economic Opportunities." *International Migration Review,* 1986, *20,* 55–68.

Schinke, S. P., and others. "Preventing Substance Abuse with American Indian Youth." *Social Casework,* 1985, *66,* 213–217.

Shangreaux, V., Pleskac, D., and Freeman, W. *Strengthening Native American Families: A Family Systems Model Curriculum.* Lincoln, Nebr.: Lincoln Indian Center, 1987.

Shore, J. H., Kinzie, J. D., Hampson, D., and Pattison, E. M. "Psychiatric Epidemiology of an Indian Village." *Psychiatry,* 1973, *36,* 70–81.

Snyder, T. D. (ed.). *Digest of Education Statistics, 1987.* Washington, D.C.: Center for Education Statistics, 1987.

Trimble, J. E. "Value Differentials and Their Importance in Counseling American Indians." In P. Pedersen, J. Draguns, W. Lonner, and J. Trimble (eds.), *Counseling Across Cultures.* Honolulu: University Press of Hawaii, 1981.

Unger, S. *The Destruction of American Indian Families.* New York: Association on American Indian Affairs, 1977.

U.S. Bureau of the Census. *1980 Census of Population: Characteristics of the Population.* U.S. Summary, PC 80-1-B1. Washington, D.C.: U.S. Department of Commerce, 1983.

U.S. Bureau of the Census. *A Statistical Profile of the American Indian Population: 1980 Census.* Washington, D.C.: U.S. Government Printing Office, 1984.

U.S. Bureau of the Census. *Money Income and Poverty Status of Families and Persons in the United States, 1985.* Current Population Reports, Series P-60, No. 154. Washington, D.C.: U.S. Government Printing Office, 1986.

U.S. Congress, Office of Technology Assessment. *Indian Health Care.* OTA-H-290. Washington, D.C.: U.S. Government Printing Office, 1986.

U.S. Department of Health and Human Services. *Indian Health Service Chart Series Book.* O-218-547. Washington, D.C.: U.S. Government Printing Office, 1988.

U.S. Senate Select Committee on Indian Affairs. *Indian Juvenile Alcoholism and Eligibility for BIA Schools.* Senate Hearing 99-286. Washington, D.C.: U.S. Government Printing Office, 1985.

Wallace, H. M. "The Health of American Indian Children." *Health Service Report,* 1972, *87,* 867–876.

5

Black American Children

LaRue Allen
Shayda Majidi-Ahi

This chapter will focus on issues in the definition, assessment, treatment, and prevention of psychological problems in Black American children, members of the country's second-largest racial group. The age range under consideration, 5 to 12, has been called middle childhood, elementary school age, and latency age. These children and their families are descended largely from slaves who were brought to the United States from the sub-Saharan, middle West African coast, where relationships, political and economic as well as social, were based on patterns of kinship. In these societies, individuals were defined in part by their ecological context (Comer, 1985)—for example, their tribal affiliation, family membership, and geographical region—in preference to criteria based on individual characteristics. In this chapter too, we have adopted the position that the functioning of Black children is best understood when viewed as the product of an interaction between children and their various ecological niches, such as school, home, or church (Bronfenbrenner, 1979; Rickel and Allen, 1987).

Theoretical Orientation

This chapter reflects the belief, expressed also by Comer (1985) in his introduction to a special issue of the *Journal of the American Academy of Child Psychiatry* on Black children

148

and child psychiatry, that the one-to-one clinical, or medical, model does not encourage the examination of strengths, but emphasizes instead the cataloguing of deficits. Given that most Black children and their families adjust well despite poverty and racial discrimination (Hill, 1972), examination of the pathways to adaptive behavior may be even more informative than the study of the determinants of maladaptive behavior. Accordingly, we have adopted a social-ecological approach in discussing Black children, and we assume that promoting competence is no less important than treating maladjustment.

The social-ecological approach can be briefly described as an effort to understand the impact of person/environment interaction on development (Lewin, 1951). Bronfenbrenner (1979) offered a comprehensive ecological framework for understanding the developing child in context, incorporating four concentric systems that encompass the youth. *Microsystems* are those systems that have direct contact with and immediate daily effects on the child (for example, family, peers, school, neighborhood). *Mesosystems* involve the relationships between and among the microsystems (for example, the interaction between family and school and the impact of that interaction on the child). *Exosystems* are settings which do not have immediate contact with the child but in which decisions are made that directly influence the child or the child's microsystems (for example, mental health agencies, school boards, parents' employers). Finally, the *macrosystem* represents the values and mores of the institutions of society. Pervasive macrosystem values such as discrimination against Blacks have both direct and indirect effects on the child. Such values can influence decisions made at all other levels of the ecological environment—at the exosystem level (schools in Black neighborhoods may not get a fair share of the school budget resources), the mesosystem level (Black parents and White teachers may fail to collaborate to remediate children's learning problems because of mutual mistrust stemming from years of exposure to racial stereotypes), and the microsystem level (the Black child who travels to a library in another part of the city may find that the extra resources available there are offered to him only grudgingly).

Demographic Data

In the United States, the Black population is increasing in size relative to the White population. The population of Black Americans was 29,306,000 (11.5 percent of the total population) in 1986 (U.S. Bureau of the Census, 1987). Since 1900, the proportion of Blacks has been in the 10–12 percent range. By the year 2000, their proportion in the population is expected to increase to 13.3 percent, or a total of over 35 million.

Although Black Americans are increasing in numbers, they continue to have a shorter life expectancy (69.6 years) than White Americans (75.2 years). This disparity continues to exist despite technological advances that have increased Whites' life expectancy to an all-time high. In 1986 the median age of the Black population was 26.9 years, compared with 32.7 years for the White group, a difference largely attributable to the differing life expectancies. In 1985 children aged 5 to 14 represented 18.5 percent of all Blacks, while 13.8 percent of the White population were in that age group. By the year 2000, it is projected that 32 percent of Blacks will be under 18 years old, compared with 24 percent of Whites (U.S. Bureau of the Census, 1986a).

From 1910, when 90 percent of all Blacks lived on farms in the South, through 1970, Blacks migrated from the South to the North and West. Between 1970 and 1980 the Black population in the South declined from 60 to 57.8 percent of the total Black population in the United States. Blacks formed the highest proportion of the total population in the South (18.4 percent), the lowest in the West (5.1 percent), and intermediate proportions in the North Central (9.0 percent) and northeastern (9.6 percent) regions of the country (U.S. Bureau of the Census, 1983).

The Black population is characterized by higher levels of poverty than among Whites. In 1986 the median income for Black families was $17,604, or 57 percent of White family income (U.S. Bureau of the Census, 1987). In high income categories, Blacks are underrepresented. Twenty-nine percent earn $25,000 or more, while over 50 percent of White families do.

At the lowest income levels, Blacks are overrepresented, with 30.9 percent of families living in poverty in 1984, compared with 9.1 percent of White families. Both race and poverty are risk factors for the development of psychological problems (Rickel and Allen, 1987). It is therefore important to note that nearly one in every two Black children in the United States is poor, compared with one in five for children as a whole (U.S. Bureau of the Census, 1986a). Among Blacks, 42.7 percent of children under 18 lived in a female-headed household in 1986, compared with 18.5 percent of White children. And 67.1 percent of Black female-headed households with children living at home were poor (U.S. Bureau of the Census, 1987). In 1985, levels of educational attainment were unequal for Blacks and Whites. For Blacks aged 25 and older, 40.2 percent had not attained a high school diploma, in contrast to 24.5 percent for Whites aged 25 and older. At the college level, 11.1 percent of Blacks had completed four years, while the comparable figure for Whites was 20 percent (U.S. Bureau of the Census, 1986a).

Epidemiological Data

Determining the scope of the problem—the number of Black children who need, or are likely to become needy of, assessment and/or intervention—is not a simple matter. Estimating the prevalence of psychological disorders among groups of children is an inexact science at best. Transient, developmentally appropriate change in behavior may be difficult to distinguish from clinical disorders that should be treated. Compounding the problem is the fact that demographic variables such as race have rarely been evaluated in the few epidemiological studies done. Although the problem in classifying disorders has been acknowledged in the literature, to date there has been no scientifically sound resolution (Gould, Wunsch-Hitzig, and Dohrenwend, 1981).

Behavioral and Academic Problems. A significant percentage of referrals for school-age Black children are for academic and behavioral problems, particularly hyperactivity. In a survey of over 200 Black school counselors and psychologists, poor academic achievement was the most frequently cited problem, followed closely by learning problems and excessive aggression (Gary, Beatty, and West, 1982).

Low levels of agreement among teachers, parents, and clinicians when rating the same child's behavior make diagnoses highly dependent on the source of data and the setting in which the data are collected. Parents and teachers appear to identify different children as maladjusted. Rutter, Tizard, and Whitmore (1970) found that reports of parents and teachers overlapped only 7 percent. The disparity between teacher and parent ratings of maladjustment correlates negatively with social class, agreement between ratings increasing with higher social class (Glidewell and Swallow, 1968, cited in Gould, Wunsch-Hitzig, and Dohrenwend, 1981).

Even when the focus is on adaptive rather than maladaptive behavior, the rating disparity persists. For example, Wall and Paradise (1981) compared mother and teacher reports on two scales of the Adaptive Behavior Inventory for Children, of the System of Multicultural and Pluralistic Assessment (SOMPA). Agreement for ratings of the behavior of Black boys and girls from lower-middle-income families averaged from 30 to 49 percent. Mothers consistently gave ratings that would indicate more competent functioning. Thus, the children most at risk, such as those from lower socioeconomic groups, are most likely to have teachers who refer them for help with problem behavior that their parents do not identify. This potential for conflict rather than collaboration in the interaction of these two microsystems (parent/teacher mesosystem) constitutes an additional risk factor.

Emotional Problems. Over the years, several panels of experts have assessed the prevalence of emotional problems in children (U.S. Congress, Office of Technology Assessment, 1986). The Joint Commission on Mental Health of Children (1968) adopted a broad definition of emotional disorder and estimated that 13.6 percent of children from birth to 18 met its criteria. The Task Panel on Infants, Children, and Adolescents of the President's Commission on Mental Health (1978) estimated that 15 percent of children aged 3 to 15 have mental problems that impair their functioning.

More recent epidemiological studies in the United States (for example, Gould, Wunsch-Hitzig, and Dohrenwend, 1981; Links, 1983) have concluded that 7.5 million children—12 percent of the population under age 18—need mental health intervention. This estimate does not distinguish the proportions of severe and mild disturbance. Nor did this, or the two national studies, assess racial differences.

Because the social ecology of Black children as a group includes risk factors such as poverty and racial oppression, it is reasonable to predict that Black children will be overrepresented among children with psychological problems (Comer, 1985; Rickel and Allen, 1987). In fact, a Manhattan study reported that proportionately twice as many Black as White children showed "psychiatric impairment" (Langner, Gersten, and Eisenberg, 1974). In a review of thirty-five studies of the epidemiology of childhood psychopathology, Gould, Wunsch-Hitzig, and Dohrenwend (1981) found that studies in poor, Black, urban communities reported the highest rates of disorder. Vincenzi's (1987) study of Black urban sixth-graders found that at least 36 percent of the children at one school were at least mildly depressed as evidenced by scores on the Child Depression Inventory. At a second school, with three times the number of Aid to Families with Dependent Children recipients, the depression rate was double that in the first school.

What little data are available do not, however, uniformly endorse the idea that disorder rates among Black children are higher than among Whites. In a midwestern study of personality differences among 433 Black and 897 White schoolchildren (Gillum, Gomez-Marin, and Prineas, 1984), Black parents rated their sons' levels of aggression, somatization, and sleep disturbance higher than White parents. Black girls were rated higher on sleep disturbance than White girls. The Missouri Children's Picture Series, a personality inventory for children, showed Black boys significantly higher than White boys on aggression and somatization and significantly lower on masculinity and maturity. Differences between Black and White girls, however, were not significant. In the same vein, Achenbach and Edelbrock (1981) found, in their normative sample for the Child Be-

havior Checklist, that of 119 items analyzed for demographic
differences, only five showed significant race effects, and all
these effect sizes were quite small.

Cultural and Familial Factors

In order to work effectively with Black children, clinicians must be sensitive to the ecological context in which their
clients exist. There is no single entity called "the Black family."
Black families vary in their family backgrounds, their economic
and social standing, their values, and the degree to which they
are acculturated to the norms and values of mainstream America. There are, however, commonalities derived from the macrosystem devaluation of Black people.

The present status of Blacks has been shaped by a 300-
year history that began with slavery, was succeeded by racism
and oppression, and continues to be a story of persistent social
and economic discrimination. Despite these obstacles, Blacks in
America have shown what Billingsley (1968) called "an amazing
ability to survive in the face of impossible conditions." A theoretical orientation called the "cultural variant" approach, proposed by Billingsley (1968) and others, acknowledges the differing histories and current ecological contexts of Black and White
families. When differences in family norms and behavior are encountered, it is not automatically assumed that Black family
patterns are indicative of pathology in the Black family. This
orientation contrasts with Moynihan's (1965) earlier "cultural
deviant" perspective, which assumed that any differences between Black and White families were attributable to the inferiority of Blacks.

The differences in ecological relations between Black and
mainstream groups generate implications for treatment and for
prevention. Research on how Black families cope has pointed to
elaborate arrangements that allow kin and friends to share resources, housing, and household tasks. Stack (1974) suggests
that economic factors reduce the chances that lower-class Black

people can establish nuclear families, making extended families a plausible alternative for achieving family stability. Hill (1972), writing of Black family strengths that most researchers ignore, cites the flexibility of roles between males and females and the presence of the extended family network as an important survival resource. A clinician who can acknowledge these microsystem differences will be better able to plan contextually sensitive interventions that capitalize on available resources.

McAdoo (1977) points to potential class differences in resources that further complicate the picture. For middle-class Blacks, the costs of remaining involved in the kinship network may be too high. She describes a typical scenario in which older children in a family leave school and go to work so that the youngest child can get an education. The family pools its efforts so that at least one member can rise above the poverty level. The upwardly mobile child, often a female, is expected to help her family as she was helped. Consequently, her resources—emotional, financial, and physical—cannot be devoted solely to her career. Thus, the beneficiary of the family sacrifice faces a dilemma: She can continue to participate in the resource exchange network with its obligation to give as needed, or she can isolate herself from her family of origin and concentrate on her own nuclear family and her career. This may account for the "alienation and antagonism that exist between working-class and middle-class Blacks" (McAdoo, 1977, p. 78).

Differences in child-rearing practices between Black families and the dominant culture constitute, for the child, an additional microsystem factor that contributes to a different social reality for Blacks. Early studies found significant differences between Black and White practices, including more permissiveness in feeding and weaning, greater restrictiveness in toilet training, and greater reliance on physical punishment among Blacks (Davis and Havighurst, 1946). To some extent, these differences reflected social-class rather than racial differences (Bronfenbrenner, 1965). Evidence of this can be seen in the convergence of Black and White child-rearing behaviors as the economic position of Blacks has improved. The extent of this convergence seems, however, to have an upper limit well before the point at which Blacks' and Whites' behaviors would be identical. Black parents are more likely to socialize children without strict differences determined by the sex of the child, to share child care and decision making about child rearing, and to consider a child's competence in interpersonal relationships more important than competence in dealing with the physical environment (Lewis, 1975). Highly significant differences between the races on all dimensions of Moos's (1974) Family Environment Scale have been found in a large midwestern sample (Gillum, Gomez-Marin, and Prineas, 1984). For both male and female children, Black families showed less openly expressed conflict, more achievement orientation and moral-religious emphasis, and more organization and control than White families.

The impact of these differences on child behavior and personality development, as well as implications for child clinicians, is not yet clear. Some implications can, however, be drawn from research on sex-role socialization and on the development of the self-concept. The first implication comes from the absence of strict sex-role distinctions when Black parents socialize children. Girls are encouraged to be aggressive and assertive; boys are encouraged to express emotion and be nurturant (Lewis, 1975). A clinician who was not aware of these possibilities might draw erroneous conclusions about the sex-role-appropriateness of Black clients' behavior.

The quality of the self-concept is another socialization outcome that has generated research interest. Before the late 1960s, social science disseminated the notion that Black parents' child-rearing practices led to negative self-concepts in their offspring. This belief changed as the prevailing theory on Black families changed from "cultural deviant" to "cultural variant." That change, along with the increase in racial pride that began for Blacks with political activities in the late 1960s, led to new research that challenged the notion of negative self-concept. The work of McCarthy and Yancy (1971), among others (for example, Hines and Berg-Cross, 1981; Hraba and Grant, 1970; Powell and Fuller, 1972; Rosenberg and Simmons, 1971; Soares and Soares, 1969), has shown higher self-concepts in Black than

in White children. Powell's (1985) research with 4,088 Black
and White children in three northern and southern cities re-
minds us of the importance of ecological context in determining
individual differences. Powell found that Black children in segregated southern schools scored higher than any other group
and attributes this, in part, to the cohesiveness that can develop
in homogeneous Black communities as a defense against a hostile outside world. Clearly, earlier assumptions that Blacks must
have low self-esteem because of the negative evaluative feedback
they receive from all levels of their ecological system are not
correct. If Blacks' self-esteem is determined by factors different
from those that support Whites' self-esteem, then the meaning
of self-esteem for Blacks is quite likely different from that for
Whites (Gray-Little and Appelbaum, 1979). Further, relations
between esteem and factors such as depression, typically found
in White samples, may or may not be valid among Blacks. Only
empirical data can resolve this issue.

A final socialization issue, which exemplifies all that is
distinct about the Black experience in America, is teaching children how to cope with racism. Pierce (1974), a Black psychiatrist, describes Blacks' everyday experiences as riddled with
multiple encounters with racism, creating a stressful environment filled with subtle to blatant incidents. The need to combat
racism leads Black parents to emphasize the development of
achievement motivation, self-confidence, and high self-esteem
in their children (Peters, 1981).

Sociocultural Issues in Assessment

The views of ethnic minorities on the definition, etiology,
and appropriate treatment of mental illness differ from those of
Western mental health professionals (Flaskerud, 1984). Members
of six ethnic groups differed significantly from mental health
professionals both in labeling behaviors as mental illness and in
types of behavior management recommended. Minorities' views
of maladaptive behavior were broader than those of mental
health professionals, including spiritual, moral, somatic, psychological, and metaphysical components. Suggestions for man-

agement of disordered behavior included social, spiritual, economic, vocational, recreational, personal, physical, and psychological assistance, while professionals relied on traditional psychotherapeutic and psychopharmacological approaches (Flaskerud, 1984). These findings give some clues to the differing value that Black clients may place on various microsystem relationships. The well-prepared service provider needs to be familiar with the resources that could be made available to the client and family— from traditional churches and social service groups to social clubs, aid societies, and athletic leagues (Spurlock, 1985)—and the degree to which they enhance the fit between Black clients and mental health interventions (Sue, 1977).

Assessment of symptom patterns and problem behaviors in Black children is complicated by the much-documented fact that racial and class biases influence diagnostic judgments, as well as by the lack of a reliable classification system for describing disorders. Hollingshead and Redlich's (1958) seminal work on class structure and mental illness showed that psychological disorder was rarer among members of the most affluent class and twice the expected rate for members of the lowest social class. Hollingshead and Redlich also found that class influenced the diagnoses given to patients, more severe diagnoses being given to the lower classes.

Traditional individually focused therapies *can,* under the right circumstances, be as effective with Black children and their parents as with any other group (Spurlock, 1985). But most therapeutic interventions, should they be made available, are most likely to be conducted by a White, middle-class therapist. The historical difficulties between races make it extremely difficult, if not impossible, for most Black clients to trust a White, or even a Black middle-class, therapist. Jones and Seagull (1977) found that Black clients defended themselves by either using lack of verbal clarity or uttering largely meaningless phrases and telling the therapist what they believed he wanted to hear.

On the therapist's part, there may be a tendency either to deny that race is an issue in the interaction or to overcompensate by attributing all the client's problems to cultural and racial conflict. The effective therapist must be able to sift through presented behavior, considering the many alternative explanations for it and generating causal hypotheses consistent with the client's presentation of self and with the therapist's knowledge of the ecology of the client's life. Therapists need to know, for example, that lower-income Black people do not nod or say "Uh-huh" to indicate that they have heard something being said to them. Without this knowledge, a Black child who sits silently while being given directions may be called "sullen" or "uncommunicative" when, for his reference group, the child is interacting normatively.

An area that has received much attention is the examination of the validity and reliability of standard psychological tests as diagnostic tools for Black children. A full discussion of the controversy surrounding this issue is well beyond the scope of this chapter. But it is important to sketch the main points here and lay out some of the implications for interventions with Black children. It is important, also, to try to distinguish ethnic group differences from differences due to social class. The often-reported 15-point difference in IQ in favor of Whites over Blacks is reduced to 5 points when social class becomes more similar for the two groups (Nichols and Anderson, 1973). This finding does not, however, vitiate the need to discover whether these tests are differentially valid across sociodemographic subgroups. Identical test scores may have vastly different meanings if the tests were not measuring the same abilities or characteristics across groups.

The major argument against the use of psychological tests, particularly intelligence tests, with Black children is that these tests tend to be standardized on White, middle-class children and are insensitive to cultural differences (Flaugher, 1978; Sattler, 1988). Another charge is that tests that measure performance against national norms are inappropriate for use with Black children. The countercharge is that the use of pluralistic rather than a single set of norms can lead to invidious comparisons between subgroups of children (Sattler, 1988).

In evaluating the validity of either position, one must consider the purpose for administering the test and the qualifications of the tester. Use of national norms can provide information about *relative* performance among children but cannot be said to be a source of information about the *absolute* abilities of any child. The examiner can also reduce the negative impact that the lack of test-taking skills may have on a child's performance through rehearsal, explanation of tasks, and careful attention to establishing rapport before testing begins. An examiner from a different racial group than the child must be sensitive to the possibility that this difference makes the child wary and mistrustful of the situation, thus threatening the validity of test results. For many Black children, mistrust of the White population and White institutions is the acceptable normative behavior. Consequently, multiple reassurances of confidentiality from a White examiner may have little effect on the Black child's feelings of suspicion and mistrust. Further, speaking about certain topics outside the home, such as "family business," is most certainly a violation of family rules.

Children from different ethnic and social-class groups are motivated by different sets of reinforcers. Zigler and his colleagues found that rapport with the examiner was strongly related to academic performance for Black students but not for Whites (Zigler and Butterfield, 1968; Zigler, Abelson, and Seitz, 1973). Given this finding, it is particularly important for the therapist to attend to the relationship with the child in order to generate valid and reliable data.

Another factor that may undermine a positive relationship is the therapist's own feelings about interacting with Black children. Smith (1981) describes a White counselor who states that he is tired of having to prove himself to every new Black client. White therapists who consider themselves "liberal" are sometimes aghast that Black clients do not trust them. One way to address these feelings of frustration is to meet regularly with colleagues to discuss ways to foster positive cross-racial interactions. Once it can be acknowledged that *no one* has a simple formula, it should be easier for all to admit their uncertainty and fear.

Intervention

In working with the behavioral and emotional problems of Black children, the mental health interventionist must be cognizant of individual as well as ecological approaches to prevention and treatment. Since behavior is embedded within multiple systems that affect behavior both directly and indirectly (Bronfenbrenner, 1979), and since transactions in a child's relationships are bidirectional and reciprocal (Bell and Harper, 1977), interventions should focus simultaneously on children's individual behavior and on dysfunctional microsystem or mesosystem relationships. In addition, cultural dimensions of the Black family will influence the individual's interpretation of and response to these interventions.

Given the bias in the mental health profession toward assigning Black clients to behavioral rather than insight-oriented therapies, relatively small numbers of Black parents and their children are referred for individual treatment. When they are referred, Blacks are more likely than Whites to drop out of treatment. By one report, 52.1 percent of Blacks dropped out, compared with 29.8 percent of Whites (Sue, 1977). These statistics underscore the importance of adapting interventions to the culturally determined preferences and expectations of the client.

One issue over which Black clients and their middle-class therapists often clash is the interpretation of time. Wilkinson and Spurlock (1986) found that clients at a mental health center were consistently fifteen to thirty minutes late, despite clinicians' efforts to interpret the "resistance" and get clients to change their behavior. The concept of time varies in meaning from one culture to another, however, and so one might handle the client's lateness differently. One might confront the issue with the client and negotiate some boundaries around the behavior that are mutually agreeable. In addition, alternative explanations for the lateness must be considered. Some clients may desire a shorter session and thus have no motivation to arrive on time. Others may want the whole session but be accustomed to arriving late for appointments. This behavior may have been shaped by cultural differences in attitudes toward time, as well as years of experience being kept waiting indefinitely in a health clinic despite having had "an appointment" for a particular time. For child clinicians, whose clients are dependent on adults to get them to their sessions, it is especially important at least to confront the lateness issue. Even though the child may not be able to effect a change in her parents' behavior, the existence of the time boundary should be acknowledged. Among middle-class Black clients who have become more acculturated to mainstream American values, lateness is more likely to be a manifestation of resistance and should be confronted as such by the clinician.

A second area of conflict and misunderstanding derives from differences in communication style. Blacks often converse among themselves while engaging in another activity. It is understood within the group that one can participate in the conversation without needing to maintain constant eye contact. However, among clinicians, avoidance of eye contact is an important criterion of relatedness. Consequently, clinicians who work with Black children must consider other indexes of social relatedness before concluding that a Black child has problems in social development because of "poor" eye contact.

In addition to eye contact, Blacks are less likely to verbally reinforce one another in conversation. This means that a therapist might find herself explaining the purpose of an interview and the procedures and objectives for the next few sessions without getting any observable sign that the client has received or understood this information. In this situation, it is important to be attuned to body language, a dimension of communication generally considered more developed among Blacks than Whites (Smith, 1981).

Premature termination, often due to miscommunication and misunderstanding, is such a pervasive problem in reaching Black and other minority clients that programs have been designed to orient these clients to the therapeutic process (Acosta, Evans, Yamamoto, and Wilcox, 1980). Acosta and associates developed a multifaceted orientation program to prepare clients for psychotherapy. Their slide/cassette program uses twenty-four actors to represent a cross-section of ethnic backgrounds, age, and gender. Pilot testing of the program showed that clients' knowledge about the therapy process increased after exposure to the orientation program. This and other orientation curricula should be tested with children and their families to determine the most effective means of helping clients and therapists adapt to each other.

Clients often come to the mental health system because of a crisis:

Mrs. J., a working mother, had exhausted herself and her resources trying to improve the behavior of her son Mike, age 12. After Mike was suspended from school, Mrs. J., concerned that he would be unsupervised during the day and on the streets, requested help from the mental health clinic. A social worker from the clinic visited the home to meet with all family members and discuss the situation. The social worker enabled them to express their frustrations with Mike and with the whole situation. Together, they worked out a plan to defuse the situation and to get family members linked to the resources they needed to resolve the crisis. For example, a community-based mediation and dispute resolution service was called on to assist the family in negotiating the child's return to the classroom.

Families who continue follow-up work at the community mental health center or who accept referrals to other sources of mental health assistance might be offered a range of individual therapies, group therapy, or family therapy. The range of individual therapies that might be offered includes psychodynamic, cognitive, and behavioral approaches.

Psychodynamic Therapy. An assumption of psychodynamic therapy is that a client's symptoms or behaviors are not his or her "real" problem. Rather, it is assumed that these behaviors are surface manifestations of underlying problems that are buried so deeply in the client's psyche that he or she is unaware of what the underlying issues are (Achenbach, 1982). The primary goal of therapy is to help the child to achieve insight—to uncover underlying conflicts and deal with them directly. In showing a child the relationship between present and past feelings, the therapist interprets the child's utterances and play. To do this with any child, the therapist must learn the child's language and communicate warmth and acceptance. For work with Black children, understanding the child's communications may be complicated by class and racial differences between therapist and child that limit the therapist's familiarity with the child's social reality.

Despite early reports in the literature that poor and/or Black children and their families are not capable of insight, clinicians have documented the successful use of insight therapies with Black clients (for example, Meers, 1970).

A 6-year-old boy, Bobby, born of a Black father and White mother, was referred for a psychiatric evaluation by the Department of Social Services for suspected sexual abuse. Bobby, his mother, his 15-year-old stepbrother, his 4-year-old sister, and his maternal grandmother lived in a two-bedroom apartment in an urban housing project. The referral was initiated by the school when Bobby was observed to be engaging in continuous masturbation, to be easily startled while napping, and to be enuretic. It was also reported that the child used sexually graphic language.

For a 6-year-old who was not fully able to express himself and resolve issues verbally, play therapy and drawings as communication media were useful for the expression of uncomfortable thoughts and feelings. After nine months of intensive play therapy, Bobby disclosed the nature of the sexual abuse through a drawing of himself in his bed with a huge, muscular man "peeing" on him. This huge man was not identified at the time. In play depicting family events, however, the child expressed a lot of anger and fear toward his stepbrother, who was eventually identified as the abuser.

Through play therapy, the therapist was able to introduce alternative ways of being and acting in situations similar to those that Bobby experienced. This exploration was designed to allow a corrective experience to take place that would facilitate the psychodynamic resolution of his feelings of hopelessness and hatred toward himself for "causing" the abuse and toward his mother for not protecting him. A turning point in the establishment of the therapeutic relationship occurred when the therapist expressed interest in Bobby's rapping, allowing him to teach her rap music—a language that became an integral part of their interactions and their efforts to communicate.

In many ways such an approach is similar to what would be done with a child from any other racial group. The therapist in this case, however, had to continually question her understanding of Bobby's communications. That questioning alone will increase the sensitive therapist's chances of detecting subtle differences in meaning.

Behavioral Approaches. Behavioral approaches assume that maladaptive behaviors are learned because they have been reinforced in the child's social environment, and thus these approaches are more sensitive to ecological variables than psychodynamic therapy is (Bandura, 1977). The first task for the behavior therapist is to determine how often the undesired behaviors occur and in what settings. Then an intervention plan is designed and implemented. In operant conditioning, the most commonly applied behavioral model, adaptive behaviors are explicitly rewarded, while maladaptive behaviors are explicitly not rewarded or are extinguished.

Eight-year-old Sandra became enuretic after her mother's boyfriend moved into their apartment, leading her to feel neglected by her mother. Sandra was observed by her teachers to be suddenly quite needy and dependent. This observation resulted in a referral for psychological services provided by a school consultation team that was associated with a local community mental health center.

The consultation team implemented a behavioral program to reduce the frequency of bedwetting. Sandra and her therapist developed a chart for recording the frequency of bedwetting on a weekly basis. Whenever the child was able to stay dry for two consecutive nights, she would get a star. On collecting four stars, she was rewarded with a special outing with her mother to the local children's museum or a nearby shopping mall. At the same time, whenever she wet her bed, she had to get up, change her sheets, and take a shower. This plan was carefully monitored by the mother, who communicated the information to the consultation team. By the end of the second month, this intervention had reduced the bedwetting to fewer than three incidents a month.

In behavioral interventions, the assistance of a parent is often required. When interacting with parents, therapists approach the work with Black families in a collaborative mode. Black families, more than White families, are likely to judge a person's competence by his or her warmth and interpersonal skill, rather than simply on the basis of instrumental competence. One must convey competence as a caring person before attempting to document competence as a behaviorist. By collaborating with the family, one also increases the chance that the program is truly addressing the conditions that one wants to address.

Cognitive Therapy. Cognitive therapy, based on research findings that disturbed children have different thought processes than other children (Luria, 1961), has been used to help children with behavioral, emotional, social, and learning problems. For example, cognitively based social skills training has been used in the Detroit public schools to teach high-risk children how to interact in an assertive yet nonaggressive manner in their social environment. Each child received a program tailored to his behavior problem, with intervention focused on substituting acceptable behaviors for the maladaptive ones that had prompted referral (Rickel and Allen, 1987).

Cognitive interventions are also useful as an adjunct to or component of other types of interventions, as the following case illustrates.

A group of fifth-grade girls, all Black, were identified by their teacher as having severe behavior problems in class and exhibiting "gang behavior" in their bullying of other children in the class. In extensive individual interviews, threats to their safety, and the threat of sexual abuse in particular, were identified as common concerns. Activity-oriented group therapy was chosen as the intervention for these girls.

One phase of the group intervention involved a workshop geared toward education about sexual abuse, in which the therapists defined abuse and provided concrete cognitive information about dimensions of abuse. The group then roleplayed the situation of a young girl approached by a man who intends to abuse her. This was followed by a discussion of problem-solving strategies. This exercise helped the girls to adopt a cognitive problem-solving style for this situation and enabled them to actively participate in developing effective coping behaviors and roleplaying various alternatives.

The objective of the social skills training workshop was to provide these girls with the cognitive skills necessary to problem-solve in frightening situations such as threatened sexual abuse. The cognitive intervention focused on the development of assertiveness, supportive behaviors toward peers, and skills for communicating feelings and facts that may be difficult to talk about. The purpose was also to empower these girls with a sense of competence that would generalize from the roleplay environment to the other settings in which they frequently found themselves.

In work with Black clients, therapists will frequently encounter cognitions that are disturbing to them—cognitions about sexual abuse and other signs of very stressful lives. Therapists must guard against overidentifying with clients, as this renders them less capable of objectively helping clients to master difficult situations.

Microsystem Interventions. Because ecological relationships are so important in a child's life, therapy using the peer group or family group as the unit of intervention should be used more commonly. Group therapy is recommended when children might benefit from exposure to peers. Each child can serve as a model for peers and can also see others model behaviors that the child is trying to learn. Group therapy is often recommended for children with problems in relating to their peers. What actually happens in group therapy depends on the developmental level of group members. The youngest elementary-school-aged children might be involved in an activity group, using crafts or group play as a vehicle for verbal exchange and for generating material that the group leader or group members might interpret or comment on (Schamess, 1976).

Danny, age 7, was seen in twice-weekly activity group therapy aimed at helping him to develop impulse control. Danny actively avoided any direct attempts to discuss his behavior problem, actually averting his head or covering his ears on many occasions. He listened intently, however, when the therapist discussed behavior control with other children in the group. As long as the therapist did not attempt to make eye contact with him or to involve him in such discussions directly, he remained involved. Danny was especially interested in what the therapist had to say about needing to fight back when you get picked on in your neighborhood but needing to turn the other cheek on the school playground or else get into big trouble.

The group therapist needs to know what is usual when Black children interact with one another. For instance, trading insults about each other's families is a game commonly played in low-income neighborhoods. A novice to "playing the dozens" might fear that physical conflict is imminent and inappropriately intervene. Checking with group members about the meaning of words and actions will give a therapist more credibility with a group than trying to bluff one's way through.

Another microsystem intervention, family therapy, is particularly important to consider for Black families, given the importance of the extended family in the Black community. For family therapists, problems lie not in the individual child client but, rather, in disturbed family relationships (French, 1977). A child's delinquency at school, for example, might be seen as a form of acting out to deflect parental attention from a troubled marriage, thus delaying a feared parental separation or divorce. Some family therapists consider the family system the locus of intervention; others consider family therapy a chance to augment individual work with an examination of family dynamics to determine how they affect the "target patient."

Clinicians who work with Black families need to ask questions about people who may live with the child, such as a mother's boyfriend, or who live outside the home but are an integral part of the child's life, such as an aunt who regularly provides after-school care (Hines and Boyd-Franklin, 1982). The presence of such individuals might not be detected using the usual intake forms. To establish credibility with the family, the family therapist needs to be flexible enough to abandon the therapist's usual job description and explore the impact of the family's environment on its functioning. Clinicians must be ready to address problems posed by systems external to the family—social, political, economic, religious, physical, and other—while also helping the family improve its interactions with these systems (Harris and Balgopal, 1980).

Prevention Approaches. Epidemiological studies have revealed that as many as a third of all schoolchildren experience adjustment problems. Early school problems frequently persist, intensifying over time and becoming more severe mental health problems at later ages (Cowen and others, 1976). At the same time, traditional psychotherapy is not available to all who need it (Albee, 1970), is even less available to members of minority groups, and, when available, may not be attuned to the context and needs of many members of ethnic minority groups (Sue, 1977).

Faced with this set of facts, many clinicians have joined other mental health professionals in developing interventions that will decrease the need for therapy by reducing the number of children who develop problems. Development of such programs would lessen the need for more expensive, time-consuming interventions that require the commitment of highly trained professionals, such as individual psychotherapy (Rickel and Allen, 1987).

Primary prevention programs have been designed to reduce the incidence (number of new cases) of nearly every category of diagnosable mental illness and have targeted children, parents, families, classrooms, and schools. Secondary prevention programs are designed to reduce the severity and duration of problems through early detection and intervention. Both primary and secondary prevention programs have occurred in a variety of settings, including hospitals (Minde, Shosenberg, and Marton, 1982), homes (Tableman, 1982), and schools (Rickel, 1977). Schools are particularly important sites for the delivery of prevention services because the vast majority of children in the elementary school years spend a good many of their waking hours there. Given the reluctance of many families to visit a place labeled "mental health center," the schools are a potential vehicle for reaching hard-to-serve groups and delivering services that reach more children than could be served even in group therapy within the same time frame.

The Yale–New Haven Primary Prevention Program (Comer, 1985) is based in a school that serves a kindergarten through fourth-grade population which is 99 percent Black; over half the families receive Aid to Families with Dependent Children (AFDC). The program's design is based on an ecological model and "focuses on creating a desirable climate or social environment in schools through application of mental health principles in a way that effects a coordinated management, curriculum, and staff development program" (Comer, 1985, p. 155). The mental health team—a psychiatrist, a psychologist, a social worker, and a psychologically oriented teacher—does not focus on children or families as "patients." Rather, the team addresses the organization and management of all aspects of the school environment, as well as intra- and interpersonal issues involving pupils and/or staff.

Since the program began in 1969, it has had a measurable impact. The school moved from serious attendance problems in 1969 to a place in the top five schools in attendance in the city from 1976 on. On four occasions, the school was first in attendance for the entire city. Children who had gone through the intervention program over three years earlier scored significantly better than matched controls on all nine subtests of the Iowa Test of Basic Skills. Further, intervention-group children scored higher on a measure of school competence and had significantly higher grades in math and higher overall grade-point averages (Comer, 1985).

Another type of primary prevention program that is sensitive to the importance of ecological and cultural factors is the family support program. The Yale Child Welfare Research Program (Seitz, Rosenbaum, and Apfel, 1985) is one example of such a program and is distinguished by its emphasis on outcome research. The interventions are delivered by an interdisciplinary team that works to enhance parents' ability to deal with their children as well as with their own lives. The target population, impoverished and predominantly Black, received an array of services over a two-and-a-half-year period. A ten-year follow-up of program families and their equivalent controls showed that the program had positive and enduring effects. For example, intervention-group mothers were more likely than control-group mothers to be financially self-sufficient, had completed more years of school, and had had fewer children. Their children had better school attendance records, had better school and social adjustment, and required fewer costly social services.

An appreciable decrease in the prevalence of mental illness among Black children would occur if primary prevention programs were fully implemented in appropriate community settings (Washington and Wilson, 1986). Yet, even under the best of circumstances, there would still be children in need of services. Hence, the clinician who wants to promote the development of mental health among Black children should be well versed in both individual and ecological approaches to treatment and intervention. Complex problems often require complex solutions, such as the integration of theories on individual, family, classroom, and community determinants of adaptive and maladaptive behaviors in Black children.

Conclusions and Recommendations

Intervention needs of Black children and their families can be better served under two conditions. First, more Blacks should be encouraged and actively recruited for training as mental health professionals. For some clients, having a therapist of the same race is important for the success of treatment. In 1982 only 2 percent of American psychiatrists were Black. Additionally, fewer than 10 percent were child psychiatrists, despite the fact that children constitute about 40 percent of the clientele in community mental health centers (Washington and Wilson, 1986). Blacks make up less than 1 percent of the psychologists in this country but are somewhat better represented in the professions of counseling and social work, for example. About 9 percent of master's-level social workers are Black. In psychiatric nursing, Blacks make up about 4 percent of the total number (Washington and Wilson, 1986).

A second factor that needs to be addressed in order to better serve the mental health needs of Black children is the training of mental health professionals, regardless of race or ethnicity. Most clinicians do not receive adequate training that increases their ability to understand how economic status, education, health care, housing, racism, and other ecological factors affect the functioning of the child and the child's social network (Comer and Hill, 1985). The need is great for course work that integrates cultural pluralist views into graduate theory and practicum work, rather than making discussion of such issues an "extra" that overburdened students have to try to squeeze into their schedules. Practicum courses must provide opportunities to work with Black clients, with field- or university-based supervision from Black clinicians and faculty members. Graduate programs must also include a critical mass of Black graduate students in training programs, so that students can learn from one another and so that the pain of "tokenism" is not visited upon yet another generation of Black achievers.

As we have suggested throughout this chapter, the state of knowledge of issues central to promoting mental health in Black and other children is in its infancy, at best. The entire mental health field would benefit from well-funded, careful research to produce reliable differential diagnostic procedures. To gauge the effectiveness of treatments and preventive interventions, we need better baseline data on the incidence and prevalence of psychological disorders in children, with particular emphasis on how rates vary for different sociodemographic groups. Finally, the effectiveness of therapies and preventive interventions must be more carefully evaluated, more often, so that the scarce resources available to meet the tremendous need can be used most effectively.

References

Achenbach, T. *Developmental Psychopathology.* (2nd ed.) New York: Wiley, 1982.

Achenbach, T., and Edelbrock, C. "Behavioral Problems and Competencies Reported by Parents of Normal and Disturbed Children Aged Four Through Sixteen." *Monographs of the Society for Research in Child Development,* 1981, *46* (1), Serial No. 188.

Acosta, F. X., Evans, L. A., Yamamoto, J., and Wilcox, S. "Helping Minority and Low-Income Psychotherapy Patients 'Tell It Like It Is.'" *Journal of Biocommunication,* 1980, *7,* 13–19.

Albee, G. W. "The Uncertain Future of Clinical Psychology." *American Psychologist,* 1970, *25,* 1071–1080.

Bandura, A. *Social Learning Theory.* Englewood Cliffs, N.J.: Prentice-Hall, 1977.

Bell, R. Q., and Harper, L. U. *Child Effects on Adults.* Hillsdale, N.J.: Erlbaum, 1977.

Billingsley, A. *Black Families in White America.* Englewood Cliffs, N.J.: Prentice-Hall, 1968.

Bronfenbrenner, U. "Socialization and Social Class Through Time and Space." In H. Proshansky (ed.), *Basic Studies in Social Psychology.* New York: Holt, Rinehart & Winston, 1965.

Bronfenbrenner, U. *The Ecology of Human Development.* Cambridge, Mass.: Harvard University Press, 1979.

Comer, J. "The Yale–New Haven Primary Prevention Project: A Follow-up." *Journal of the American Academy of Child Psychiatry,* 1985, *24,* 154–160.

Comer, J., and Hill, H. "Social Policy and the Mental Health of Black Children." *Journal of the American Academy of Child Psychiatry,* 1985, *24* (2), 175–181.

Cowen, E. L., and others. "Long-Term Follow-up of Early Detected Vulnerable Children." *Journal of Consulting and Clinical Psychology,* 1976, *44,* 775–786.

Davis, A., and Havighurst, R. "Social Class and Color Differences in Child Rearing." *American Sociological Review,* 1946, *11,* 698–710.

Elder, G. "Household, Kinship, and the Life Course: Perspectives on Black Families and Children." In M. B. Spencer, G. K. Brookins, and W. Allen (eds.), *Beginnings: The Social and Affective Development of Black Children.* Hillsdale, N.J.: Erlbaum, 1985.

Flaskerud, J. "A Comparison of Perceptions of Problematic Behavior by Six Minority Groups and Mental Health Professionals." *Nursing Research,* 1984, *33,* 190–228.

Flaugher, R. L. "The Many Definitions of Test Bias." *American Psychologist,* 1978, *33,* 671–679.

French, A. P. *Disturbed Children and Their Families: Innovations in Evaluation and Treatment.* New York: Human Sciences Press, 1977.

Gary, L., Beatty, L., and West, J. *The Delivery of Mental Health Services to Black Children.* Final report. Washington, D.C.: Mental Health Research and Development Center, Institute for Urban Affairs and Research, Howard University, 1982.

Gillum, R., Gomez-Marin, O., and Prineas, R. "Racial Differences in Personality, Behavior, and Family Environment in Minneapolis School Children." *Journal of the National Medical Association,* 1984, *76,* 1097–1105.

Gould, M., Wunsch-Hitzig, R., and Dohrenwend, B. S. "Estimating the Prevalence of Childhood Psychopathology." *Journal of the American Academy of Child Psychiatry,* 1981, *20,* 462–476.

Gray-Little, B., and Appelbaum, M. "Instrumentality Effects in the Assessment of Racial Differences in Self-Esteem." *Journal of Personality and Social Psychology,* 1979, *37,* 1221–1229.

Harris, O., and Balgopal, P. "Intervening with the Black Family." In C. Janzen and O. Harris (eds.), *Family Treatment in Social Work.* Itasca, Ill.: Peacock, 1980.

Hill, R. *The Strengths of Black Families.* New York: Emerson Hall, 1972.

Hines, P. M., and Berg-Cross, L. "Racial Differences in Global Self-Esteem." *Journal of Social Psychology,* 1981, *113,* 271–281.

Hines, P. M., and Boyd-Franklin, N. "Black Families." In M.

McGoldrick, J. K. Pearce, and J. Giordano (eds.), *Ethnicity and Family Therapy.* New York: Guilford Press, 1982.

Hollingshead, A. B., and Redlich, F. C. *Social Class and Mental Illness.* New York: Wiley, 1958.

Hraba, J., and Grant, G. "Black Is Beautiful: A Reexamination of Racial Preference and Identification." *Journal of Personality and Social Psychology,* 1970, *16,* 398–402.

Joint Commission on Mental Health of Children. *Crisis in Child Mental Health: Challenge for the 1970s.* New York: Harper & Row, 1968.

Jones, A., and Seagull, A. "Dimensions of the Relationship Between the Black Client and the White Therapist." *American Psychologist,* 1977, *32,* 850–856.

Langner, T., Gersten, J., and Eisenberg, J. "Approaches to Measurement and Definition in the Epidemiology of Behavior Disorders." *International Journal of Health Services,* 1974, *4,* 483–501.

Lewin, K. *Field Theory in Social Science: Selected Theoretical Papers.* New York: Harper & Row, 1951.

Lewis, D. "The Black Family: Socialization and Sex Roles." *Phylon,* 1975, *36,* 221–237.

Links, P. "Community Survey of the Prevalence of Childhood Psychiatric Disorders: A Review." *Child Development,* 1983, *54,* 531–548.

Luria, A. R. *The Role of Speech in the Regulation of Normal and Abnormal Behavior.* New York: Liveright, 1961.

McAdoo, H. "Family Therapy in the Black Community." *American Journal of Orthopsychiatry,* 1977, *47,* 75–79.

McCarthy, J., and Yancy, W. "Uncle Tom and Mr. Charlie: Metaphysical Pathos in the Study of Racism and Personal Disorganization." *American Journal of Sociology,* 1971, *76,* 648–672.

Meers, D. "Contributions of a Ghetto Culture to Symptom Formation: Psychoanalytic Studies of Ego Anomalies in Childhood." *Psychoanalytic Study of the Child,* 1970, *25,* 209–230.

Minde, K. K., Shosenberg, N. E., and Marton, P. "The Effects of Self-Help Groups in a Premature Nursery on Maternal Autonomy and Caretaking Style 1 Year Later." In L. A. Bond and

J. M. Joffe (eds.), *Facilitating Infant and Early Childhood Development.* Hanover, N.H.: University Press of New England, 1982.

Moos, R. *Family Environment Scale Manual.* Palo Alto, Calif.: Consulting Psychologists Press, 1974.

Moynihan, D. P. *The Negro Family: A Case for National Action.* Washington, D.C.: U.S. Government Printing Office, 1965.

Nichols, P., and Anderson, E. "Intellectual Performance, Race, and Socioeconomic Status." *Social Biology,* 1973, *20,* 367–374.

Peters, M. "Parenting in Black Families with Young Children." In H. McAdoo (ed.), *Black Families.* Newbury Park, Calif.: Sage, 1981.

Pierce, C. M. "Psychiatric Problems of the Black Minority." In G. Caplan (ed.), *American Handbook of Psychiatry.* Vol. 2: *Child and Adolescent Psychiatry, Sociocultural and Community Psychiatry.* (2nd ed.) New York: Basic Books, 1974.

Powell, G. J. "Self-Concepts Among Afro-American Students in Racially Isolated Minority Schools: Some Regional Differences." *Journal of the American Academy of Child Psychiatry,* 1985, *24,* 142–149.

Powell, G. J., and Fuller, M. "The Variables for Positive Self-Concept Among Young Southern Black Adolescents." *Journal of the National Medical Association,* 1972, *43,* 72–79.

President's Commission on Mental Health. *Report to the President.* Washington, D.C.: U.S. Government Printing Office, 1978.

Rickel, A. "Screening and Remediation of Preschool Children from Low-Income Families." *Perceptual and Motor Skills,* 1977, *45,* 757–758.

Rickel, A., and Allen, L. "Preventing Maladjustment from Infancy Through Adolescence." In A. E. Kazdin (ed.), *Developmental Clinical Psychology and Psychiatry,* no. 11. Newbury Park, Calif.: Sage, 1987.

Rosenberg, M., and Simmons, R. *Black and White Self-Esteem: The Urban School Child.* Washington, D.C.: American Sociological Association, 1971.

Rutter, M., Tizard, J., and Whitmore, K. *Education, Health and Behaviour.* London: Longmans, 1970.

Sattler, J. M. *Assessment of Children.* (3rd ed.) San Diego, Calif.: Jerome M. Sattler, 1988.

Schamess, G. "Group Treatment Modalities for Latency-Age Children." *International Journal of Group Psychotherapy,* 1976, *26,* 455–473.

Seitz, V., Rosenbaum, L., and Apfel, N. "Effects of Family Support Intervention: A Ten-Year Follow-up." *Child Development,* 1985, *56,* 376–391.

Smith, E. "Cultural and Historical Perspectives in Counseling Blacks." In D. W. Sue, *Counseling the Culturally Different: Theory and Practice.* New York: Wiley, 1981.

Soares, A. T., and Soares, L. M. "Self-Perception of Culturally Disadvantaged Children." *American Educational Research Journal,* 1969, *6,* 31–45.

Spurlock, J. "Assessment and Therapeutic Interventions of Black Children." *Journal of the American Academy of Child Psychiatry,* 1985, *24,* 168–174.

Stack, C. *All Our Kin: Strategies for Survival in a Black Community.* New York: Harper & Row, 1974.

Sue, S. "Community Mental Health Services to Minority Groups: Some Optimism, Some Pessimism." *American Psychologist,* 1977, *32,* 616–624.

Tableman, B. "Infant Mental Health: A New Frontier." *Infant Mental Health Journal,* 1982, *3,* 72–76.

U.S. Bureau of the Census. *General Population Characteristics, United States Summary, 1980 Census of Population.* Washington, D.C.: U.S. Department of Commerce, 1983.

U.S. Bureau of the Census. *Statistical Abstract of the United States, 1987.* (107th ed.) Washington, D.C.: U.S. Government Printing Office, 1986a.

U.S. Bureau of the Census. *We, the Black Americans.* Washington, D.C.: U.S. Department of Commerce, 1986b.

U.S. Bureau of the Census. *Statistical Abstract of the United States, 1988.* (108th ed.) Washington, D.C.: U.S. Department of Commerce, 1987.

U.S. Congress, Office of Technology Assessment. *Children's*

Mental Health: Problems and Services—a Background Paper. Washington, D.C.: U.S. Government Printing Office, 1986.

Vincenzi, H. "Depression and Reading Ability in Sixth-Grade Children." *Journal of School Psychology,* 1987, *25,* 155–160.

Wall, S. M., and Paradise, L. V. "A Comparison of Parent and Teacher Reports of Selected Adaptive Behaviors of Children." *Journal of School Psychology,* 1981, *19,* 73–77.

Washington, A., and Wilson, S. "Providing Mental Health Services to Black Children and Youth." In L. Beatty (ed.), *Readings on Black Children and Youth.* Washington, D.C.: Mental Health Research and Development Center, Institute for Urban Affairs and Research, Howard University, 1986.

Wilkinson, C., and Spurlock, J. "The Mental Health of Black Americans: Psychiatric Diagnosis and Treatment." In C. Wilkinson (ed.), *Ethnic Psychiatry.* New York: Plenum, 1986.

Zigler, E., Abelson, W., and Seitz, V. "Motivational Factors in the Performance of Economically Disadvantaged Children on the Peabody Picture Vocabulary Test." *Child Development,* 1973, *44,* 294–303.

Zigler, E., and Butterfield, E. "Motivational Aspects of Changes in IQ Test Performance of Culturally Deprived Nursery School Children." *Child Development,* 1968, *39,* 1–14.

6

Black American Adolescents

Jewelle Taylor Gibbs

Black adolescents are one of the most vulnerable and victimized groups in contemporary American society. They have been mislabeled and miseducated by the schools, mishandled by the juvenile justice system, mistreated by mental health agencies, and neglected by the social welfare bureaucracy until very recently. Their plight has been minimized by health care professionals and ignored by policy makers, so that they have been labeled as an "endangered species" (Gibbs, 1984, 1988b) and members of a growing "underclass" (Glasgow, 1981; Wilson, 1987).

As a result of generations of discrimination and deprivation, Black adolescents have developed high rates of psychological and behavioral disorders, as well as certain problematic psychosocial behaviors. However, in spite of the high incidence of these problem behaviors, many Black youth have also managed to become competent, well-functioning young adults.

This chapter presents an overview of the psychological and psychosocial problems of Black adolescents, discusses issues of assessment and diagnosis, and describes intervention strategies that are appropriate and effective for this group. Whereas Chapter Five provided information on Black children up through age 12, this chapter will focus on adolescents and youth in the 13–21-year age group—roughly the school years from junior high school through college. Additionally, the discussion will fo-

179

cus primarily on non-Hispanic Black youth who are identified as Afro-American rather than West Indian in their ethnic heritage, since the former group constitutes the great majority of Black Americans.

The mental health problems and needs of these youth are discussed in the context of historical, social, economic, and political factors that have shaped their experiences in American society, and the cultural values and adaptive behaviors that many Blacks have developed in response to these experiences are described.

The overarching conceptual framework of the chapter is a combination of two major perspectives: an ego-psychology perspective on adolescent development (Erikson, 1950, 1959) and an ecological perspective on the social environment in which this development occurs (Bronfenbrenner, 1979). Only through some comprehension of the complex socioeconomic and political forces impinging on Black youth and their families is it possible to understand their adaptive and maladaptive behaviors. Accordingly, I propose that assessment and treatment of the psychological, behavioral, and psychosocial problems of Black youth should be carried out with particular attention to the interaction of intrapsychic, interpersonal, familial, cultural, and environmental factors, all of which have a significant impact on adolescent development, adaptation, and dysfunction.

Demographic Data

In 1983 there were 5,463,000 Black youth in the age range 10–19 years, 2,831,000 of them in the 15–19-year bracket, and another 2,961,000 in the 20–24-year range (U.S. Bureau of the Census, 1986). The numbers of males and females are about equal. Since children and youth constitute nearly half of the total Black population, the median age for Blacks is 26.9 years, compared with a White median age of 32.7 (U.S. Bureau of the Census, 1987). The youthfulness of this population has important implications for mental health policies, programs, and services targeted to the Black community.

In 1986 nearly half (42.7 percent) of all Black youth

under 18 lived in families below the poverty line, while over two-thirds (67.1 percent) of those in female-headed households were poor (U.S. Bureau of the Census, 1987). Two of every five Black children live in female-headed families, which are five times as likely to be welfare-dependent as two-parent families. Over half of Black youth live in two-parent families; however, Black youth have higher rates than White youth of out-of-home placements in foster homes and institutions (Children's Defense Fund, 1987).

The median income of Black families in 1986 was $17,604, 57 percent of the White family income of $30,809 (U.S. Bureau of the Census, 1987). However, there was a striking disparity between the median income of intact families with two parents employed ($26,583) and female-headed families ($9,300). Thus, middle-class status for most Black youth is related to having two employed parents and a stable economy. Unemployment among Black males is 2.5 times that among White males; among Black females, 2 times that of White females. In July 1988 the unemployment rate for Black teenagers aged 16–19 was 31.1 percent, twice the rate for White teenagers.

The median educational level completed for all Blacks aged 25 and older was 12.3 years in 1985. The proportion of Blacks completing four years of high school or more increased from 20.1 percent in 1960 to 59.8 percent in 1985. High school dropout rates for 16–19-year-olds declined from 22.0 percent in 1970 to 12.4 percent in 1983 (U.S. Bureau of the Census, 1986).

Finally, Black youth were more likely than White youth to live in deteriorating central-city neighborhoods, in substandard housing with poor sanitation, located in urban areas with depressed economies, where they have much less access to adequate health and mental health facilities (Kasarda, 1985; Schorr, 1986; Children's Defense Fund, 1986a). As several researchers have pointed out, these social and economic characteristics of inner-city neighborhoods generate chronic levels of stress for Black youth and their families (Comer and Hill, 1985; Myers and King, 1980; Wilson, 1987). Thus, an understanding of these ecological realities is essential for clinicians who deliver mental health services to black youth.

Historical, Social, and Political Influences

The current status of Blacks in the United States can be directly attributed to four major historical and social factors: slavery, segregation and discrimination, poverty, and urbanization (Franklin, 1967; Omi and Winant, 1986; Wilson, 1987). Moreover, these factors significantly weakened the functioning of the Black family and major institutions of the Black community, thus indirectly creating a hospitable environment for the development of social, psychological, and behavioral problems among Black youth.

The effects of nearly 250 years of slavery on the Black family have been widely debated, but there is general agreement that slavery had a deleterious impact on the structure and functioning of the family as a unit, particularly on the role of the Black male as the head of the household (Frazier, 1966). The racial caste system, introduced by slavery, defined Blacks as inferior and subordinate to Whites. This caste system has been reinforced by the educational and economic disparities between Blacks and Whites, which have persisted since slavery was abolished in 1863 (Omi and Winant, 1986).

Even after legal segregation was eliminated by a series of Supreme Court decisions, culminating in the landmark school desegregation decision in 1954, discriminatory practices were still pervasive and pernicious, depriving Blacks of equal access to schools, jobs, housing, health care, political participation, recreation, and public facilities (Franklin, 1967; Omi and Winant, 1986). By enforcing the status of second-class citizenship for Blacks, the dominant society created a "separate and unequal" society that developed its own institutions, subcultural values, and behavioral norms, forcing Black parents to develop child-rearing strategies that would enable them to promote healthy development in their children in spite of their minority status (Cross, 1984; Peters, 1981; Spencer, 1982).

A third factor that has significantly influenced the status of Black families is persistent poverty and low socioeconomic status. Black families are still three times as likely to be poor as White families. Poverty obviously has multiple adverse effects on Black youth, placing them at greater risk for a range of health and mental health problems, conduct disorders, and psychosocial problems (Children's Defense Fund, 1987; Kovar, 1982).

Fourth, the mass migration of Blacks between World Wars I and II from the rural South to northern industrial centers transformed the Black population from a predominantly rural agrarian group to an urban working class. Although this rapid urbanization brought many benefits, including opportunities for educational and occupational mobility, it also resulted in the development of huge ghettos in most urban areas, concentration of Black males in a few industries, and social and cultural isolation from the dominant society (Clark, 1965; Franklin, 1967). These negative outcomes of urbanization laid the foundation for development of the so-called underclass two decades later (Glasgow, 1981; Wilson, 1987).

More recent social forces shaping the experience of Black youth and their families have included three major socioeconomic and political developments—the civil rights movement, the affirmative action legislation and backlash, and the radical structural and technological changes in the American economy. The civil rights movement, which began with the Montgomery, Alabama, bus boycott in 1955 and ended with the passage of two major civil rights bills in 1964 and 1965, signaled a new era of militancy among Blacks to obtain their full rights as citizens. Participation by thousands of college youth in the movement provided positive role models and raised the expectations and aspirations of millions of Black youth (Chambers, 1968).

After the successful passage of civil rights legislation, direct-action strategies were replaced in the early 1970s by legislative and administrative programs of affirmative action to promote equal opportunity in education and employment. However, these efforts were only moderately successful before a widespread backlash developed among Whites who perceived these efforts as "reverse racism" and as an organized effort to deprive them of their privileged status (Omi and Winant, 1986). Reinforcement of this backlash since 1980 by a conservative political administration has had a particularly negative impact on Black youth, as their gains in employment rates and college enrollment rates achieved by the mid 1970s were virtually wiped out by the mid 1980s.

Finally, the post–World War II structural and technological changes in the economy from a predominantly industrial and agricultural base to a high-technology and service base have had devastating effects on the Black community. Northern industrial cities with large Black populations have suffered economic decline, while the suburbs and the Sunbelt cities have expanded their white-collar economies. The lack of fit between a largely unskilled Black labor supply and the demands of a highly technical job market has resulted in high rates of unemployment, high rates of poverty, and high rates of family dysfunction, contributing to high levels of stress for Black youth and their families (Comer and Hill, 1985; Edelman, 1987; Wilson, 1987).

Cultural Attitudes, Values, and Norms of Black Families

The literature has identified four major values of Black families, all of which can be understood as adaptive responses to their historical and social experiences in American society. These values concern the importance of religion and the church, the importance of the extended family and kinship networks, the importance of flexible family roles, and the importance of education (Allen, 1978; Billingsley, 1968; Leigh and Green, 1982; McAdoo, 1981; Staples, 1981).

Role of Religion. In the Black community, the church is often the central focus of social and civic activity. Most Blacks are Protestants, and many participate in Fundamentalist denominations (for example, Baptists, Methodists, Church of God), which stress asceticism, tithing, and piety. In recent years the Black Muslims have made inroads in urban inner-city communities, while more liberal denominations have attracted upwardly mobile and professional Blacks. Even if Black families are not currently involved in a particular church, their religious heritage will shape their beliefs and values, their views on marital relationships and divorce, abortion, adoption, child-rearing practices, and so on. Awareness of the client's religious background will increase the clinician's understanding of attitudes and values that may affect treatment decisions. In addition, clinicians should identify the local Black ministers and view them as resources in helping clients to cope with problems.

Role of Family. Blacks value their family ties and tend to maintain contact with a large network of relatives and fictive kin, a pattern especially functional for low-income Black families, who exchange resources, services, and emotional support. Knowledge of this pattern is valuable for the clinician, who can often mobilize relatives to offer support to a troubled adolescent (McAdoo, 1981; Stack, 1974; Aschenbrenner, 1975). It is not unusual for parents to send adolescents to live with other relatives in order to change their environment or to defuse a conflictual family situation.

Roles Within Families. Flexibility in family roles has always been an important aspect of Black family functioning, since most Black women have had to work in order to maintain an adequate standard of living for their families (McAdoo, 1981). Thus, parents have divided their responsibilities less in accord with traditional gender-based roles and more by household task. Traditional child-rearing patterns also foster early independence in male and female children as well as less differentiation in roles and family tasks (Peters, 1981). Although these patterns vary according to socioeconomic level and rural/urban residence, recent empirical studies generally support the descriptive accounts of greater role flexibility and less gender-specific role functioning in Black families (Staples and Mirande, 1980). These findings have obvious implications for the assessment of Black families, as well as the interpretation of gender-related behaviors in male and female adolescents.

Role of Education. Black families have historically valued hard work, education, and social mobility (Billingsley, 1968; Bowman and Howard, 1985; Frazier, 1966; Gurin and Epps, 1975). These values prompted the mass migrations from the rural agrarian South to the urban industrial North, which offered greater educational and economic opportunities to Blacks. In spite of widespread discrimination and poverty, many Black families have sacrificed to send their children to college and prepare them for professional careers, often serving the Black community. Unfortunately, this impetus for higher education has slowed down in recent years for several reasons, including the social isolation of poor, inner-city Blacks, who lack middle-class role models; the changing nature of the economy; and the government's declining commitment to affirmative action (Omi and Winant, 1986; Wilson, 1987). These social changes have created a widening gap between middle-class Blacks, who are able to take advantage of educational opportunities, and poor Blacks, who are not even aware of these opportunities.

Mental Health Issues for Black Adolescents

There are no large-scale epidemiological surveys of Black adolescent mental health problems, but there have been a few community surveys and clinical studies that provide estimates of the incidence of psychological and behavioral disorders in this population group.

The incidence of depression among Black youth has been investigated by several researchers in a variety of school and community samples (Kaplan, Landa, Weinhold, and Shenker, 1984; Schoenbach and others, 1983; Gibbs, 1986a). In these nonclinical samples, rates of mild to moderate depression have ranged from 20 to 40 percent, while rates of severe depression have ranged from 5 to 15 percent. Higher rates of depression have generally been found among males and low-income Black adolescents in these studies.

Eating disorders such as anorexia nervosa or bulimia are very rare among Black youth, with only sixteen cases (two of them in males) reported in the clinical literature through 1985 (Pumariega, Edwards, and Mitchell, 1984; Robinson and Andersen, 1985). The primary diagnosis of these cases was anorexia nervosa, but several were described as "atypical" in their psychodynamics. Certain patterns characterized these cases, such as parental conflict and/or separation, conflicts around sexuality, underlying depression, and problems with autonomy.

Although the prevalence of conduct disorders among Black adolescents is not known, it can be safely said that this group has a disproportionately high rate of conduct problems in school settings. Black teens are suspended or expelled more often than Whites for fighting, extortion of money, verbal or physical abuse of teachers, vandalism, and truancy in junior high and high schools (Children's Defense Fund, 1985).

Psychiatric hospitalization rates of Black youth have traditionally been two to three times the rates for White youth (Myers, forthcoming). In a large-scale survey of public and private psychiatric facilities, Milazzo-Sayre, Benson, Rosenstein, and Manderscheid (1986) found that although the rate of hospitalization had declined for all youth, it was still higher among non-Whites, particularly Black males. Blacks were more likely than Whites to receive more severe diagnoses such as affective disorders, schizophrenia, and personality disorders. Black males in public psychiatric institutions were six times as likely as White males to obtain a diagnosis of schizophrenia or other severe disorder.

Finally, suicide is increasing among Black adolescents and is now the third leading cause of death for Black youth in the 15–24 age group. Between 1960 and 1984, the suicide rate for Black males in this age range nearly tripled, from 4.1 to 11.2 per 100,000, while the rate for Black females nearly doubled, from 1.3 to 2.4 per 100,000 (U.S. Department of Health and Human Services, 1986). Although suicide rates are much lower than homicide rates for Black youth, they may be underestimated, and many "undetermined deaths" may be misclassified as accidents because of the strong prohibition against suicide in the Black community (Warshauer and Monk, 1978; Shaffer and Fisher, 1981). Moreover, the symptoms of suicidal behavior in Black youth are often masked by acting-out and high-risk behaviors, making it more difficult for clinicians to assess suicidal intent. Consequently, it is essential for clinicians to recognize "depressive equivalents" and high-risk behaviors as potential clues to suicidal behavior in Black youth and to conduct a suicide assessment whenever these symptoms are chronic or severe (Gibbs, 1988a).

Studies of the utilization of mental health facilities by Black college students find that they seek treatment for the same range of late-adolescent problems as their White peers, including anxiety, depression, psychosomatic symptoms, interpersonal conflicts, sexual problems, and identity conflicts (Davis and Swartz, 1972; Gibbs, 1975). In addition, they are more likely than White students to express feelings of alienation, acculturation conflicts, academic anxieties, and feelings of victimization.

Psychosocial problems of Black youth are reflected in the statistics on social indicators, those conditions that cause social or legal difficulties for the youth and usually have adverse consequences for the family and community, such as dropping out of school, juvenile delinquency, substance abuse, and unwed teenage pregnancy and parenthood. Although the causal sequence is not clear, many of these youth experience anxiety, depression, and other emotional distress in connection with these problems.

School Dropout Rates. In spite of the overall improvement in school dropout rates among Black youth since 1960, the rates in many urban areas currently range from 40 to 60 percent, and some students leave school as early as seventh grade (Reed, 1988). Moreover, in 1980 nearly one fourth of all 18–21-year-old Black youth neither had completed nor were currently enrolled in high school (U.S. Bureau of the Census, 1981). Further, several surveys have found high rates of functional illiteracy, particularly among Black male adolescents (College Entrance Examination Board, 1985; Reed, 1988). Handicapped by educational deficiencies and lack of vocational training, inner-city Black youth have high unemployment rates and few opportunities for legitimate income.

Juvenile Delinquency. Official delinquency rates indicate that Black youth are more likely to be arrested than White youth for status offenses and index offenses. In 1960 Black youth accounted for 19.6 percent of all juvenile arrests, and that had increased to 23.2 percent in 1985. They were also more likely to be arrested for serious felony offenses than any other race/sex category. Although Black youth were more likely than White youth to be arrested, convicted, and incarcerated for the same category of offenses, a recent study concluded that there are no significant differences between Black and White youth in their rates of self-reported delinquency (Krisberg and others, 1986).

Black juvenile delinquents also have higher rates (than White juvenile delinquents) of depression and of psychological and neurological symptoms, which are often undetected and undiagnosed (Dembo, 1988; Gibbs, 1982; Lewis and Balla, 1976). As Dembo (1988) points out, the juvenile justice system is increasingly the channel for "handling" Black youth with behavioral disorders, while White youth with similar behaviors are more likely to be referred for treatment in the mental health system. The system of entry will obviously determine the nature and quality of the services offered, the assessment and diagnosis of the problem behaviors, and the effectiveness of the intervention used.

Substance Abuse. Community surveys of drug and alcohol use have consistently shown that Black youth have lower rates of alcohol use than Whites and equal rates of marijuana use (National Institute of Drug Abuse, 1979; Dembo, 1988). However, rates of cocaine and heroin use are generally reported to be higher among older Black youth than among Whites (Brunswick, 1979). In large samples of junior high and high school students in New York and California, Black teenagers reported lower rates of alcohol and drug use (Gibbs, 1985a; Kandel and others, 1977; Skager, 1986). An important limitation of these school-based surveys is that school dropouts are not included, probably resulting in an underestimation of drug use in this age cohort, since dropouts are more likely to be involved in deviant activities.

Drug use for many low-income Black youth is particularly problematic because it is often linked to a larger life-style that includes delinquency and selling drugs (Brunswick and Messeri, 1986). Consequently, when these youth are referred for treatment, they are usually involuntary clients with multiple social, behavioral, and psychological problems, including low self-esteem, impulsivity, high levels of anger and hostility, psychosomatic symptoms, depression, and suicidal behaviors (Beschner and Friedman, 1986; Halikas, Darvish, and Rimmer, 1976; Lee, 1983).

Currently, young Black intravenous drug users who use unsterilized needles face the threat of infection with the AIDS (acquired immunodeficiency syndrome) virus. In late 1987, 35 percent of blacks in whom AIDS was diagnosed had contracted it through intravenous drug use; 25 percent of these patients were under 30 years of age ("Human Immunodeficiency Virus Infection," 1987). As of May 1988, non-Hispanic Black youth constituted 50 percent of the 1,212 persons under age 20 identified as having AIDS in the United States; 88 (14.6 percent) of these 601 youth were adolescents between 13 and 19 ("AIDS: A Complex New Threat," 1988). AIDS patients need counseling as well as long-term medical care to cope with their increasing disability and invariably fatal disease. Yet, at this point, there are inadequate services for counseling Black youth, their families, and their sexual partners about the chronic course of the disease, the behavioral changes necessary, and the prolonged grieving process (Honey, 1988; Mays and Cochran, 1987).

Teenage Pregnancy and Parenthood. Teen pregnancy is a major psychosocial problem for Black teenagers, particularly because it is often followed by a number of negative social and psychological sequelae (Children's Defense Fund, 1986b; Chilman, 1983). In 1983 the birthrate for unmarried Black females aged 15–19 was 86.4 per 1,000, compared with 18.5 per 1,000 for comparable White females. Nearly 10 percent of all Black teenage females (aged 10–19) gave birth, compared with nearly 2 percent of all White teenage females (aged 10–19). Although White females had much higher abortion rates than Blacks, the outcomes for White teenagers were far more favorable. Black teenage mothers had high rates of school dropout, welfare dependency, and unemployment (Children's Defense Fund, 1986b). They were also more likely than girls who delayed their first pregnancy to experience health problems, psychological problems, and family problems (Chilman, 1983; Furstenberg, Lincoln, and Menken, 1981). Several studies have indicated that these teen mothers need a range of comprehensive health, mental health, and educational/vocational services (Colletta, Hadler, and Gregg, 1981; Field, Widmayer, Stinger, and Ignatoff, 1980).

One of the major issues in counseling this group is that their own adolescent developmental needs are frequently in conflict with the needs of their infants and children.

It is interesting to note that statistics on the psychosocial problems of Black youth are much more accessible than statistics on their psychological problems. This may reflect an actual difference between Black and White youth in their patterns of response to anxiety and stress, or it may reflect differential treatment and bias in their patterns of referral for evaluation—that is, Black youth are more likely to be referred through the social welfare and juvenile justice systems and White youth through the mental health system (Dembo, 1988; Lewis and Balla, 1976; Myers and King, 1980).

Sociocultural Issues in Assessment

The assessment of Black youth will be discussed from three vantage points: theoretical perspectives, sociocultural issues, and levels of assessment.

First, two theoretical perspectives that are useful in understanding the mental health issues of Black youth are the ego-oriented developmental theory of Erik Erikson (1950, 1959) and the ecological theory of Urie Bronfenbrenner (1979), as described in Chapter One. Both these theories might predict differential outcomes for non-White and low-income youth, particularly since they are more likely than White and higher-income youth to experience socioeconomic deprivation, prejudice and discrimination, and restricted access to educational and vocational opportunities in American society. Hence, Erikson (1959) suggests that teens growing up in these "disadvantaged" or minority families could develop "negative" identities and thus be "at risk" for dysfunctional or maladaptive behaviors.

Second, sociocultural factors must be considered in the assessment of all Black adolescents, particularly those from socially segregated and economically disadvantaged families. A growing literature documents differences between Blacks and Whites in definitions of mental health and mental disorders, symptomatology, distribution of psychiatric disorders, help-seeking behaviors, and response to treatment (Gardner, 1971; Griffith and Jones, 1978; Jones and Korchin, 1982; Neighbors, 1985; Ridley, 1984; Hall and Tucker, 1985).

Third, the four levels of assessment necessary to obtain a comprehensive picture of the Black adolescent are (1) individual, (2) family, (3) school, and (4) community. These four levels of assessment are consistent with the dual individual and ecological theoretical perspective.

Individual Assessment

Erikson's (1959) view that Black adolescents may have greater difficulty in forming a positive identity because of negative societal feedback has been challenged by Chestang (1984). Chestang distinguishes between "personal identity" and "racial identity" for Black youth, who have shown in a number of studies that they are able to separate their personal self-evaluations from the social evaluation of their racial identity (Cross, 1984; Foster and Perry, 1982; Spencer, 1982). Since the process of identity formation is intimately connected to the development of a self-concept and a sense of competence, management of sexual and aggressive feelings, establishment of autonomy from parental control, and educational aspirations, the clinician should evaluate these areas of adjustment in Black adolescents.

Attitudes Toward Self. Black children and adolescents develop their self-concept and self-esteem from the reflected appraisals of parents, relatives, and peers in their own ethnic communities (Spencer, 1982). Before the 1970s, many clinical and empirical studies found that Black youth had negative self-concepts and low self-esteem (Clark and Clark, 1940; Goodman, 1964). However, more recent studies of nonclinical samples of Black youth have consistently found that their self-concepts and self-esteem are as positive as or more positive than those among comparable samples of Whites (Gibbs, 1985a; Powell, 1985; Rosenberg and Simmons, 1971; Smith, 1982; Taylor, 1976). Contrary to predictions, Blacks in segregated school settings frequently express higher levels of self-esteem than Blacks in integrated settings (Nobles, 1973; Powell, 1985).

Clinicians are more likely to find evidence of negative self-concepts and low self-esteem among Black youth referred for behavioral or psychological problems. These youth may develop negative feelings about themselves because of their physical appearance, their atypical family structures, their lack of competence in culturally valued skills, or their feelings of racial victimization (Franklin, 1982; Grier and Cobbs, 1968; Mayo, 1974). In assessing a Black adolescent's self-concept or self-esteem, the clinician should be cognizant of the significant sources of esteem for these youth, parental and peer reinforcement, and environmental factors. For example, studies find that athletic ability is a major source of esteem for Black male adolescents, while physical attractiveness and social skills are very important assets for Black females (Cauce, 1986; Mancini, 1980). Other abilities valued by both sexes are verbal skills (for example, "rapping"), assertiveness, and fashionable dressing (for example, "styling") (Jenkins, 1982; Ladner, 1971; Mancini, 1980; Schulz, 1969).

Intellectual achievement is valued in some settings, while in other settings it is demeaned. High-achieving students in predominantly Black high schools are often ridiculed as "brainiacs" and accused of acting "like White folks." Boys who are physically small and girls who are precociously mature may become the targets of sarcasm and humor, sometimes developing overcompensatory behaviors as a result. Social distinctions may be made on the basis of skin color or socioeconomic status, which can have damaging effects on the adolescent's self-concept and self-esteem, particularly for Black females (Foster and Perry, 1982; Heiss and Owens, 1976). Thus, an assessment of Black adolescent self-esteem must take into account the adolescent's *subjective* evaluation of assets and liabilities, the reflected appraisal of parents, peers, and significant others in the social environment, and whether the environment is a consonant or dissonant context—that is, whether the adolescent is in a majority or minority social context (Rosenberg, 1979).

Affect. Black adolescents are characteristically described as expressive, lively, and extraverted (Gibbs, 1985a; Ladner, 1971; Mancini, 1980). Yet, in treatment situations they often appear angry and hostile or sullen and withdrawn (Franklin, 1982; Ridley, 1984). Angry, hostile teenagers may express a great deal of negative affect and appear to be physically intimidating, especially older youth who are referred for delinquent behaviors and substance abuse. Outwardly uncommunicative and uncooperative, these youth have an unresponsive demeanor that often masks underlying depression over family problems, school failure, interpersonal rejection, or self-destructive behaviors (Franklin, 1982; Gibbs, 1981).

Speech and Language. Black adolescents tend to have good verbal skills, but those reared in Black neighborhoods often speak a variety of "Black English" that may be unfamiliar to non-Black clinicians (Kernan, 1971; Kochman, 1972; Labov, 1972). Since many are able to switch back and forth between "Black English" and standard English, the clinician can usually communicate effectively by responding with flexibility and a willingness to clarify unfamiliar terms. Clinicians should also be aware that language serves many symbolic functions for Black youth, who use it as a means of artistic expression (for example, "rapping") as well as a means of verbal assault (for example, "playing the dozens") (Hannerz, 1969; Kochman, 1972; Labov, 1972; Mancini, 1980). Language can also be a source of conflict in schools and in the workplace, placing Black youth at a competitive disadvantage in both settings (Ogbu, 1985).

Interpersonal Relations. The quality and intensity of relationships among Black adolescents must be evaluated in the context of their social and cultural environment. Same-sex peer groups have very close bonds with strong pressures to conform to group norms, particularly in situations where the peer group or gang also serves the functions of social identity and mutual protection (Mancini, 1980; Schulz, 1969). In areas with many single-parent families and few community resources, peer-group bonds among females function as social support networks (Belle, 1982; Ladner, 1971; Stack, 1974). However, these intense bonds can also cause intense rivalries and conflicts, reduce individual autonomy, and foster involvement in antisocial or self-destructive activities. For example, studies have found that high involvement of low-income Black teenagers in certain types of peer networks was related to low academic achievement and premarital sexual activity (Felner, Aber, Primavera, and Cauce, 1985). Moreover, the inner-city Black adolescent who is not a member of a cohesive peer group or gang is often excluded from activities, labeled negatively, or even physically harassed (Schulz, 1969; Viadero, 1988).

Sexuality. Both the expression of sexuality and sexual relationships are major issues for Black adolescents. Black adolescents tend to initiate sexual activity about one year earlier, on the average, than White adolescents and are less well informed about contraception, less positive about its use, and less effective about using it (Chilman, 1983; Children's Defense Fund, 1986b; Gibbs, 1986b). Consequently, Black teenage females have higher rates of unintended pregnancy and higher birthrates than White females (Chilman, 1983). Attempts to cope with teenage parenthood often result in psychological problems for both males and females, including depression, anxiety, anger, psychosomatic symptoms, and feelings of helplessness (Chilman, 1983; Colletta, Hadler, and Gregg, 1981; Hendricks, 1980; Robinson, 1988). Since Black teenage females are often referred for issues of sexuality, pregnancy, and parenting, clinicians should be familiar with their cultural attitudes about premarital sexual activity, contraception, childbearing, and child rearing and should be sensitive to the values they attach to these behaviors and the meaning of these behaviors in their lives (Dougherty, 1978; Ladner, 1971; Stack, 1974).

Anxiety and Patterns of Defense. It is important to assess the level of anxiety, the ways it is expressed, and the situations in which it is most likely to occur. Anxiety may be triggered for Black youth by academic problems, family conflict, community violence, interpersonal/sexual relationships, or employment/career issues, and so it is important for the clinician to assess the impact of all these factors on the adolescent client. High levels of anxiety may not be evident in Black adolescents under direct observation, partly because culturally acceptable child-rearing patterns, particularly in low-income Black families, often reinforce the externalization of anxiety in Black youth (Franklin, 1982; Myers and King, 1980; Schulz, 1969). Thus, anxiety may be denied, projected, or displaced. Hyperactivity, acting out, and aggression in younger adolescents may be a clue to anxiety, while delinquent activity, substance abuse, and sexual promiscuity may be responses to underlying anxiety or depression in older adolescents (Franklin, 1982; Gibbs, 1982). Some clinical studies of Black college students suggest that they may have fairly high rates of somatic symptoms, and so clinicians should be alert to signs of physical distress and psychosomatic complaints as possible evidence of anxiety (Davis and Swartz, 1972; Gibbs, 1974).

Coping and Adaptive Behaviors. Black adolescents have developed a number of coping skills and adaptive behaviors to compensate for their marginal minority status in this society. Many young Black males, having learned that athletic ability is one route to mobility, develop skills in a competitive sport (especially basketball, baseball, and track) that requires discipline, physical coordination, and motivation. Reinforced for social and interpersonal skills, young Black females may become sexually active, often an unintentional route to premature parenthood that may foreclose their educational and career opportunities (Gibbs, 1986b; Ladner, 1971; Stack, 1974). In response to the uncertainties of their environment, many inner-city Black youth have developed a patterned set of behaviors known as "playing it cool" or "getting over." Researchers have identified a number of coping styles that have enabled these youth to adapt to the realities of ghetto life and yet may be maladaptive for success in mainstream society (Mancini, 1980; Myers and King, 1980; Schulz, 1969). Nonetheless, Black adolescents have consistently demonstrated much resilience, creativity, and persistence in the face of economic deprivation, social disorganization, and limited community resources, all of which reduce their opportunities and restrict their mobility.

The Family System

An assessment of the family environment of the Black adolescent should focus on the structure and roles of the family, socioeconomic status and living arrangements, degree of integration/acculturation, support system, communication patterns, and help-seeking patterns (Foley, 1975; Hines and Boyd-Franklin, 1982; Gwyn and Kilpatrick, 1981).

Family Structure and Roles. It will be helpful to the clinician to know whether the adolescent lives in an intact nuclear family, a single-parent family with or without other adults in the household, or an extended family. Family structure not only helps to shape the psychosocial identity and social experiences of adolescents but also may place constraints on the development of their social roles. For example, teenagers in single-parent families are often given more household and child-care responsibilities than those in two-parent families, with possible detrimental effects on their health and school achievement. Teenagers living in extended families with several adult caretakers (for example, mothers, grandmothers, aunts) may experience conflicts over discipline and autonomy because of unclear lines of parental authority. In a study of Black adolescents' perceptions of family climate, Dancy and Handal (1984) found that those teenagers who perceived high levels of conflict in their families reported more psychological symptoms than those who perceived low levels of conflict.

Socioeconomic Status and Living Arrangements. Occupational status and income of the parent(s) are important indicators of the adolescent's socioeconomic status, material resources, and life-style. Living arrangements should also be investigated to determine the size of the household, sleeping arrangements, and household responsibilities of the adolescent. Many low-income Black youth live in crowded households with very little privacy, inadequate sleeping and study facilities, and exposure to negative role models, all of which may endanger their health and mental health.

Degree of Integration/Acculturation. The extent to which the family is integrated into the mainstream culture and has assimilated its values and norms is also relevant to treatment of Black youth. Adolescents with varying levels of exposure to integrated schools and neighborhoods may present different patterns of symptomatology, problem behaviors, and adaptation to the community (Gibbs, 1974, 1986a; Powell, 1985).

Social Support System. The clinician should assess the wider kinship network and social support network of the adolescent's family. As noted earlier, church affiliation is an important source of social support for many Black families. Further, many Black families are involved in neighborhood associations, civic organizations, and fraternal lodges, which can be valuable sources of support. Urban Black families also sometimes send troubled teenagers to live temporarily with relatives in more rural areas, so that northern/southern family ties are continually reinforced through mutual assistance (McAdoo, 1981; Stack, 1974).

Communication Patterns. Interaction in Black families also varies by socioeconomic status and level of acculturation. In low-income families, there is some ethnographic evidence that parent/child communication tends to be authoritarian, critical, unidirectional, and confrontational (Bartz and Levine, 1978; Cahill, 1966; Peters, 1981). Black parents and siblings sometimes engage in mutual teasing, sarcasm, and denigrating comments (Ladner, 1971; Schulz, 1969). Overt expressions of affection, nurturance, support, and praise are not frequent in these families, and self-deprecating humor may be used as a protective mechanism to preserve one's self-esteem. Patterns of communication in middle-class families are more likely to be bidirectional, authoritative, and mutually supportive than in low-income families (Bartz and Levine, 1978; Durrett, O'Bryant, and Pennebaker, 1975; Peters, 1981).

Help-Seeking Patterns. Black families generally do not voluntarily seek psychiatric treatment for the emotional or behavioral problems of their children, who are more likely to be referred by the school, the juvenile court, or the social welfare system (Franklin, 1982; Myers and King, 1980). Although this varies by socioeconomic status and level of acculturation, Black families are more likely to seek counseling initially from family doctors, ministers, and friends or relatives than from mental health professionals (Neighbors, 1985). Thus, by the time Black youth are referred for treatment, their symptoms may be more severe and the intervention required may be more intensive.

School Assessment

The school as an instrument of education and socialization has long been a source of conflict and controversy for Black youth. That these youth are frequently referred for school-related academic or behavioral problems is not surprising, but the clinician's task is to disentangle the client's presenting problems from factors in the school environment that may have substantially contributed to or exacerbated them.

School Environment. The milieu of the school may be a safe, orderly setting that facilitates learning and personal growth or it may be a violent, chaotic setting that intimidates students and teachers and undermines both learning and social development. Black students may respond to these latter school environments with apathy and alienation, anger and hostility, fear and anxiety, or acting out and identification with the antisocial elements in the school.

Educational Program. Black students are overrepresented in special educational programs and nonacademic tracks. Frequently mislabeled in elementary school, many Black adolescents either drop out or are "pushed out" of high school after experiencing years of academic failure or low achievement, low teacher expectations, high rates of suspension, and chaotic school environments (Committee for Economic Development, 1987; Reed, 1988; Rivers and others, 1975). Clinicians who suspect that students are performing below their abilities should use a culturally sensitive measure, such as the System of Multicultural and Pluralistic Assessment (SOMPA) battery, to assess their ability levels (Mercer, 1975; Samuda, 1975; Snowden and Todman, 1982). Should the clinician discover a discrepancy between the client's potential ability and the educational program, a recommendation for a more appropriate academic placement could be the most effective intervention.

Peer Relationships. Attitudes and behaviors of peers are very influential in shaping the school experiences of Black adolescents (Cauce, Felner, and Primavera, 1982; Gibbs, 1985a; Ogbu, 1985). Where the prevailing norms are anti-intellectual and college is not viewed as a realistic option, Black teenagers have an especially difficult time if they are viewed as high achievers (Hare, 1988). Similarly, in many inner-city neighborhoods there are permissive attitudes toward early involvement in sexual activity and experimentation with drugs (Brown, 1985; Hare, 1988; Ladner, 1971). When students resist pressures to conform to these norms, they may be socially isolated and ridiculed. In these situations, clinicians should evaluate the students' psychological distress and ability to cope with the peer pressures, as well as the environmental supports or modifications necessary to reinforce their proactive behaviors.

Community Assessment

When Black children reach adolescence and venture out beyond their immediate social environment, they may have their first experience with racial discrimination. If they enter an integrated high school, seek a part-time job, or participate in community youth groups or athletic teams, Black teenagers begin to sense racism and barriers to their opportunities and aspirations (Hare, 1988). Further, early exposure to unemployment, drugs, and illegal activities in inner-city communities often fosters cynicism, anger, and antisocial attitudes in these youth (Gibbs, 1984, 1988b; Glasgow, 1981; Schulz, 1969; Wilson, 1987). In response to these environmental realities, Black youth often develop a sense of social isolation and hopelessness about their life chances, which increases their vulnerability to involvement in self-destructive activities such as drug abuse, unwed teenage pregnancy, suicide, and homicide (Gibbs, 1984, 1988; Hare, 1988).

Clinicians who evaluate youth referred for antisocial or self-destructive behavior need to assess their underlying feelings of alienation, depression, and rage in order to recommend appropriate treatment interventions (Franklin, 1982; Grier and Cobbs, 1968).

Intervention and Treatment

In this section four modalities of treatment for Black adolescents will be examined: individual, family, group, and crisis intervention.

Individual Treatment

Short-term ego-oriented psychotherapy is the model of individual treatment recommended for Black adolescents with nonpsychotic disorders, who are usually seen in outpatient settings. As described by Norman (1980), this approach is appropriate for this group because it focuses on problem solving, strengthens coping skills, and is time-limited. This approach is also useful for a wide range of adolescent problems, ranging from anxiety and depression to identity conflicts and acting-out behaviors.

Entry into Treatment. Starting with the initial contact with the therapist, the Black adolescent will be judging the therapist's affect and behaviors while he or she is also being evaluated. It is therefore important for the therapist to project warmth, genuineness, and positive regard for the client, being especially attentive to cues that the client is testing the therapist for signs of prejudice, feelings of superiority, disapproval, and rejection (Gibbs, 1985c; Ridley, 1984). Therapists should be aware that Black youth are sensitive to how they are addressed (avoid being overfamiliar or patronizing), how they are engaged in conversation (avoid using ethnic slang or an overly simple vocabulary), how your office is furnished (they appreciate attractive decor even if they live in projects), how you are dressed (they believe that clothes reflect social status), and how respectful you are toward them (do not keep them waiting interminably and do not answer a string of phone calls during their sessions) (Franklin, 1982). Clients will be more favorably disposed toward clinicians who demonstrate interpersonal competence rather than instrumental competence in the first sessions (Gibbs, 1985a). Black adolescents may initially approach treatment with a great deal of misapprehension, suspicion, and anxiety due to lack of knowledge or prior treatment experience. The therapist can minimize the client's anxiety by spending a few minutes at the beginning of the first session in informal conversation, followed by a brief description of the treatment process through a "role induction" technique (Frank and others, 1978) or a patient-orientation program (Acosta, Yamamoto, and Evans, 1982). The goal is to demystify the therapeutic process for these clients and to be certain that they fully understand the "talking cure" before treatment proceeds.

Like all adolescents, Black youth are rarely psychologically sophisticated and generally have trouble distancing themselves from their own behaviors—that is, their observing egos are much less developed than their experiencing egos. They also tend to be less comfortable with self-disclosure than White adolescents, partly reflecting the Black cultural pattern of masking their true feelings and concerns from Whites and authority figures (Jenkins, 1982; Pinderhughes, 1973; Ridley, 1984). Moreover, Black adolescents often have a history of conflict with authority figures, and so they may appear unusually resistant, sullen, or hostile in the early sessions, especially since most of them have been referred by schools or social agencies.

To overcome this initial resistance and to establish rapport, the clinician needs to be fairly active, outgoing, directive, and open, encouraging adolescents to discuss their anger and ambivalent feelings about being referred for treatment, their fears about being labeled "crazy" by their peers, and their reluctance to reveal their true feelings and concerns to a stranger. By showing sensitivity to these issues and understanding of their cultural context, therapists can reassure the clients that their concerns about treatment are fairly common among teenagers. At this point the therapist should reiterate the role of confidentiality in treatment and its specific limitations with minors and in involuntary cases, so that clients can clarify any concerns about freely discussing their problems. The following case provides an example of these issues in the initial phase of treatment.

Wanda, a 14-year-old Black female, was referred by her junior high school counselor because of frequent somatic symptoms, immature behaviors, and problems in getting along with peers. During her first session, Wanda seemed very anxious and fearful and responded very reluctantly when asked about her concerns. At the beginning of the second session, she blurted out that she didn't want to be "sent away to a special school." The therapist learned that Wanda's older brother had been abruptly institutionalized several years earlier for mental retardation when her mother remarried. Whenever her stepfather became angry with her, he would threaten to send her to join her brother. In order to please her very strict parents, Wanda had become excessively compliant at home, but she had frequent nightmares and physical symptoms. At school she was unable to contain her anxiety, and so she frequently did inappropriate things to get attention from her teachers and peers. After the therapist clarified the referral and explained her role and her interest in helping Wanda, the teenager was able to feel more comfortable, to express her fears about being abandoned by her parents, and to set some short-term goals for improving her communication with her parents and reducing the frequency of her impulsive and inappropriate behaviors in the school setting.

Establishing the Working Alliance. To establish a working alliance with the Black adolescent, the clinician should proceed cautiously and expect repeated "testing" behaviors, which may include wearing hats and sunglasses in sessions (for males), refusing to remove heavy coats and jackets, using obscene or provocative language, coming late for appointments, terminating the session prematurely, being unresponsive, and acting hostile and rebellious. These behaviors will quickly diminish and usually disappear as the teenager becomes more comfortable in the relationship.

During this phase of treatment, the adolescent will expend a great deal of energy in challenging the therapist's authority and ability to maintain control of the sessions (see Franklin, 1982). The therapist must avoid being drawn into a power struggle with the client and, at the same time, must establish structure and set firm limits for the sessions. Male adolescent clients may try to intimidate the therapist with aggressive behaviors and sarcastic, street-style verbal responses, while adolescent females may act in a seductive or sullen manner. Franklin (1982) has described three types of urban Black adolescent clients as "reluctant talkers," who are difficult to engage in conversation, "babblers," who control sessions by compulsively talking about superficial issues, and "impressors," who brag about antisocial activities in an attempt to shock the therapist. Therapists should recognize some of these behaviors as manipulative but should avoid premature interpretations, which will threaten the adolescent's fragile self-esteem and weak defense mechanisms.

Therapists should understand that many Black adolescents have adopted a demeanor of "being cool" and a repertoire of street-smart behaviors in order to survive in an environment that is stressful, frequently chaotic, and unpredictable. To facilitate rapport in the treatment relationship, clinicians should be familiar with the inner-city adolescent culture, with some of the slang, and with some of the characteristic behaviors. This does not imply that clinicians should use the language or engage in the behaviors; that would be condescending or patronizing to the client. Clinicians can also inquire about unfamiliar language or behaviors to find out whether these patterns are cultural or idiosyncratic in origin.

Humor is an important tool in forming a working alliance with the Black adolescent. Black culture has a highly developed oral tradition in which humor has always played a prominent role, as exemplified in many contemporary soul/rock songs, "rapping," and routines of Black comedians (Kochman, 1972; Labov, 1972). Humor can be employed to foster insight in a client who might not be responsive to dynamic interpretations of his underlying conflict but who can see the irony of his self-defeating behaviors.

The following case provides an example of therapeutic strategies to facilitate a working alliance with a Black adolescent.

John, a 16-year-old high school sophomore, was referred by his probation officer for excessive truancy, failing grades, and constant conflict with his mother. Born out of wedlock to a teenage mother, John had a two-year history of minor delinquency and was suspected of drug use. He had begun to act out shortly after the death of his grandmother, who had reared him while his mother worked in a nearby city. John was initially hostile and rude to the therapist, clearly communicating that he was there against his will and did not intend to cooperate. In addition to coming late, he hummed popular songs, leafed through magazines, frequently said he was wasting his time, and answered questions in a sarcastic and condescending manner.

After several unproductive sessions, the therapist learned that John had a collection of classic rock-and-roll records, which he had enjoyed listening to with his grandmother. He was encouraged to talk about this collection, and this led to lively discussions about his interest in music and his aspirations to be a disk jockey. After his initial resistance was overcome through limit setting on his disruptive behaviors and consistent reinforcement of his positive responses, the therapist was able to explore his unresolved feelings of grief over the loss of his grandmother, who had been very supportive of his schoolwork and interests. The working alliance was further strengthened when the therapist consulted with John's school counselor about developing a work-study plan that would enable him to work part-time at a radio station while taking courses more closely related to his vocational interests.

Issues in Individual Treatment. Clinical treatment of Black adolescents must recognize the impact of the social and political environment on these youth, as well as the culturally patterned coping strategies and defensive behaviors they have developed in response to their chronic levels of environmental stress (Franklin, 1982). Once the working alliance has been established, the clinician must remain continuously alert to the interaction of the intrapsychic, interpersonal, and environmental aspects of the problem. The clinician should encourage clients to describe their problems or issues as they view them, to explore the subjective effects of the problems and the impact of their behaviors on others, and to identify specific ways to alleviate the symptoms or ameliorate the problems. The problem-solving strategies should be reasonable and achievable within each adolescent's social context. The following cases provide examples of how these factors interact and influence the therapeutic interventions with Black adolescents. These three cases illustrate frequent issues presented by these clients: delinquent behavior, management of sexuality, and aggressive behavior.

Bobby, a 16-year-old high school dropout living in a group home, was referred by his probation officer. Bobby had been involved with the juvenile court system since age 14, when he was first arrested with two older boys for burglarizing houses in his neighborhood. In treatment Bobby was very "streetwise," manipulative, and defensive, avoiding discussion of his chaotic family and his failures in a succession of schools. When the clinician learned that Bobby was a natural leader in the group home, he was able to support his efforts to obtain some athletic equipment and games for the residents. As he gained more confidence by organizing activities in the home, he became less defensive and was able to talk about his feelings of never having nice things and never being able to depend on his parents for anything. At age 13 he had been recruited into a neighborhood gang, which became his substitute family. The male clinician provided him with a model of warmth, acceptance, and consistency, as well as providing an expectable environment and setting limits on his manipulative behavior. A few weeks after he confronted Bobby on the discrepancy between his obvious ability and his school failures, Bobby announced that he was going to go back to school "just to show these teachers and my parents that they were all wrong about me. I ain't dumb, I just didn't feel like working too hard." By challenging Bobby's negative self-image and supporting his competent behaviors, the clinician was able to help Bobby raise his self-esteem and his educational aspirations.

Juanita, a 15-year-old high school sophomore, was referred by her parents because she had recently become very depressed and withdrawn and had seemed to lose interest in everything. Juanita was overweight and very mature-looking, but she seemed listless, slightly sullen, and unmotivated for treatment. In exploring the reasons for Juanita's recent mood change, the therapist noted that she was very uncomfortable discussing the topics of boys and social life but became more animated when she talked about one special girlfriend. Through careful probing, her confused feelings about this relationship emerged. After the therapist spent one session generally discussing the importance of having a "best friend" and normalizing her feelings, Juanita revealed that she was "turned off" from boys after a party where she had smoked some marijuana and been fondled by two boys, who later bragged about it to their friends. She had felt very ashamed but was grateful to her girlfriend, who was supportive. Following this session, Juanita formed a very positive relationship with the therapist, whose warmth and empathy contrasted with her mother's punitive and critical manner.

Andrew, a 19-year-old sophomore in a private "elite" college, was referred to the counseling center for assaulting a White male student in his dormitory. After initially acting very suspicious and hostile toward the female therapist, he eventually formed a good working alliance with her, facilitated by a positive transference, which was not interpreted. Andrew reported that he had attacked the student after a series of incidents in which several students had made fun of his southern accent, his Afro haircut, and his clothes, all of which he interpreted as racist comments. The short-term treatment focused on helping Andrew to express his feelings about being a "token" Black who was always under a microscope, his doubts about his ability to achieve in the highly competitive environment, and his anger about being rejected by a White girlfriend. The therapist enhanced his self-esteem and feelings of competence by encouraging him to identify the talents and skills that had gained him admission to college and to review his actual college performance, which was above average. In addition, his own ambivalence toward socializing with other Black students was explored, and he was able to reevaluate and to reframe his social options. Finally, the therapist helped Andrew to recognize situations that particularly triggered his rather explosive temper and to develop more socially acceptable ways of channeling his anger.

Family Treatment

Family treatment, increasingly viewed as an important modality for Black adolescents, has been described by several authors (Harris and Balgopal, 1980; Hines and Boyd-Franklin, 1982; Sager, Brayboy, and Waxenberg, 1970; Weaver, 1982). Since many teenagers are struggling to separate from their families and to function autonomously, the clinician must make a careful assessment of the advantages and disadvantages of family therapy for a given client. It can be especially appropriate for pregnant teenagers and for those who are delinquent or predelinquent, depressed and suicidal, or engaging in substance abuse, where the self-destructive behaviors may be symptomatic of a dysfunctional family system, a scapegoated teenager, or a breakdown in family communication.

An eclectic blend of structural and strategic techniques is useful for Black families, wherein attention is focused both on restructuring family roles and on modifying family communication patterns (Hines and Boyd-Franklin, 1982; Minuchin and others, 1967). Frequently parents have singled out one child to bear the brunt of their own frustrations and feelings of victimization, scapegoating the adolescent by projecting all of their own anxieties and displacing their anger toward society onto this particular child. The adolescent, in turn, has responded by acting out the negative impulses in a way that both reinforces her unworthiness in the family and confirms her negative identity in the community.

The following case illustrates a teenager's response to her parents' authoritarian rules, which reflected their anxieties about social status and social mobility for their daughter.

Debbie, a pregnant 16-year-old school dropout, was referred by a counselor at her alternative high school because of depression. Debbie, who had a good academic record, had been pressured into a sexual relationship by her older boyfriend, who had dropped her soon after she discovered her pregnancy. Against her parents' wishes, she had decided to have the baby, and she now felt that she had no emotional support. Debbie's parents were an upwardly mobile working-class couple who wanted her to go to college and were quite angry about her "lower-class behavior."

Family treatment, which was recommended after Debbie's evaluation, focused on helping Debbie and her parents to express their mutual feelings of anger, disappointment, and shame over her pregnancy, to explore alternative options for the baby, and to reevaluate Debbie's educational and vocational goals. After her parents recognized that Debbie's pregnancy was partly a response to their rigid rules and excessive expectations, their anger dissipated, and they were able to show her more positive concern and support. When Debbie understood that her academic success was symbolic of upward mobility to her hard-working but poorly educated parents, she actively engaged with them to make plans to obtain child care while she returned to her regular high school and pursued her plans to attend a local community college.

Group Treatment

Group treatment is a popular modality for adolescents in both outpatient and residential settings. There are some special factors to consider in forming groups for Black adolescents: whether the group should be mixed by gender, by race, and by social class; whether the therapists should also be mixed by gender and race; and whether the group members should be selected by diagnostic category or balanced to reflect a diverse range of problems.

Psychoeducational groups are especially appropriate for delinquents, school dropouts, and other troubled Black youth who need a comprehensive treatment program that includes counseling, remedial education, and vocational training (Franklin, 1982; MacLennan and Felsenfeld, 1968). Such groups are an integral part of many alternative high schools and residential treatment centers; they are also a core element in the "street academies" pioneered by the National Urban League in the 1970s.

Group leaders should foster a sense of cohesiveness and support in addressing the similar problems of the group members, encourage the development of appropriate problem-solving skills to replace acting-out and self-destructive behaviors, and promote an identification with constructive role models. Preferably, Black males with sexual identity problems, impulse disorders, or acting-out problems should be assigned to groups with Black male therapists who can serve as positive role models and will not be intimidated by aggressive or seductive behaviors. Black females can benefit from relating to a Black female clinician who can offer an alternative model for identification other than teenage motherhood as a route to adulthood.

Crisis Intervention

Crisis intervention is a particularly appropriate modality for adolescents who cannot control their violent impulses, those who suffer toxic effects from alcohol or drug abuse, those who are physically or sexually abused, those who are extremely depressed or suicidal, and those who have psychotic symptoms (Miller, 1980; Landau-Stanton and Stanton, 1985).

Black teenagers who have experienced a severe trauma or have decompensated because of drugs or alcohol may present with extreme anxiety and paranoid symptomatology. As Ridley (1984) points out, many Black patients have a degree of "healthy cultural paranoia" owing to their marginal status in society; yet, this paranoid outlook tends to become more pronounced under stress. Thus, Black patients in crisis situations may appear very fearful and suspicious of the clinical staff, withhold pertinent information, engage in verbally abusive and threatening behaviors, and refuse medication or treatment. For those Black youth who are severely depressed and/or suicidal, the hospital emergency room may be a very frightening experience.

Sexual abuse and sexual exploitation of Black adolescents will probably increase as their ranks increase in the homeless population. As more Black youth become addicted to "crack," the derivative of cocaine, there will be greater numbers of victims of drug overdoses and drug-related violence (Brunswick,

1988). It is important for emergency room doctors to refer these youth for follow-up counseling to help them to deal with their feelings of anger, shame, low self-esteem, worthlessness, helplessness, and despair.

In crisis intervention with Black youth, the clinician's task is not only to allay the immediate symptoms of distress and restore the clients' ability to function but also to assess the family environment and social support system available to clients when they return home. Effective treatment will often require the clinician to intervene in a number of systems that impinge on the lives of Black adolescents, including the family, the school, the workplace, the juvenile justice system, and the social welfare system.

The following case illustrates a comprehensive approach to crisis intervention for an older female adolescent.

Mona, an 18-year-old high school dropout, was brought to the emergency room by her boyfriend after a suicide attempt. Mona had taken an overdose of sleeping pills, but she was conscious and she recovered after emergency treatment. She was admitted to the hospital on a forty-eight-hour hold for evaluation and follow-up. Mona had been very depressed for several weeks because of a number of traumatic events. First she had had a miscarriage after being beaten by her boyfriend, then she lost her job as a grocery clerk, and then her boyfriend threatened to leave her, so that she felt her life was hopeless and she could no longer cope with all her losses. The team of clinicians who evaluated her developed a plan that included four major aspects: she was referred for outpatient counseling to deal with her grief over losing the baby; she was referred for vocational counseling to discuss job training programs; she was referred to a social service agency for temporary financial assistance; and she and her boyfriend were encouraged to discuss the problems in their relationship, and her boyfriend made a commitment to stay with her until the immediate crisis was resolved.

Crisis intervention obviously requires rapid assessment skills, sensitivity to the client's social and psychological problems, and knowledge of community resources that are accessible and affordable for Black clients.

Summary and Conclusions

It is clear that Black youth are more likely to be identified for psychosocial than for psychological problems, although there is a close relationship between these two types of presenting problems. Since Black youth are more likely than White youth to be identified through the juvenile justice system, they are also less likely to undergo a thorough psychological assessment, less likely to receive a psychiatric diagnosis, less likely to obtain therapeutic treatment, and more likely to experience long-term psychological impairments and behavioral and social deficits or dysfunctions.

Knowledge of the multiple risk factors for Black youth, as well as the impact of social and cultural experiences on their values, norms, and behaviors, will give clinicians a better grasp of this group's attitudes and beliefs about mental health, symptomatology, patterns of defense and coping strategies, help-seeking patterns, utilization of services, and responsiveness to therapeutic treatment.

The psychological and psychosocial problems of Black adolescents in America have increased rather than decreased in the past twenty-five years. These problems have been exacerbated by poverty, discrimination, economic dislocation, and social changes that have had disproportionate effects on the Black community. Many of these problems could be reduced or eliminated by a coordinated effort of federal, state, and local governments to develop comprehensive and humane social and economic policies to strengthen vulnerable families and provide adequate health and social services for all children and youth. In the absence of such policies and programs, Black youth will continue to need a wide range of social and mental health services to address their psychological and behavioral problems in a social environment that is far less than optimal for their psychosocial development.

References

Acosta, F. X., Yamamoto, J., and Evans, L. A. *Effective Psychotherapy for Low-Income and Minority Patients.* New York: Plenum, 1982.

"AIDS: A Complex New Threat to Children's Survival." *CDF* [Children's Defense Fund] *Reports,* 1988, *91* (12), 1–8.

Allen, W. R. "Black Family Research in the United States: A Review, Assessment and Extension." *Journal of Comparative Family Studies,* 1978, *9,* 167–189.

Aschenbrenner, J. *Lifelines: Black Families in Chicago.* New York: Holt, Rinehart & Winston, 1975.

Bartz, K. W., and Levine, E. S. "Childrearing by Black Parents: A Description and Comparison to Anglo and Chicano Parents." *Journal of Marriage and the Family,* 1978, *40,* 709–719.

Belle, D. (ed.). *Lives in Stress: Women and Depression.* Newbury Park, Calif.: Sage, 1982.

Beschner, G., and Friedman, A. (eds.). *Teen Drug Use.* Lexington, Mass.: Lexington Books, 1986.

Billingsley, A. *Black Families in White America.* Englewood Cliffs, N.J.: Prentice-Hall, 1968.

Bowman, P., and Howard, C. "Race-Related Socialization, Motivation, and Academic Achievement: A Study of Black Youths in Three-Generation Families." *Journal of the American Academy of Child Psychiatry,* 1985, *24,* 134–141.

Bronfenbrenner, U. *The Ecology of Human Development: Experiments by Nature and Design.* Cambridge, Mass.: Harvard University Press, 1979.

Brown, S. V. "Premarital Sexual Permissiveness Among Black Adolescent Females." *Social Psychology Quarterly,* 1985, *48,* 381–387.

Brunswick, A. "Black Youths and Drug Use Behavior." In G. Beschner and A. Friedman (eds.), *Youth and Drug Abuse: Problems, Issues, and Treatment.* Lexington, Mass.: Lexington Books, 1979.

Brunswick, A. "Young Black Males and Substance Use." In J. T.

Gibbs (ed.), *Young, Black, and Male in America: An Endangered Species.* Dover, Mass.: Auburn House, 1988.

Brunswick, A., and Messeri, P. "Drugs, Life Style and Health." *American Journal of Public Health,* 1986, *76,* 52–57.

Cahill, I. D. "Child-Rearing Practices in Lower Socio-Economic Ethnic Groups." *Dissertation Abstracts,* 1966, *27,* 31–39.

Cauce, A. M. "Social Networks and Social Competence: Exploring the Effects of Early Adolescent Friendships." *American Journal of Community Psychology,* 1986, *14,* 607–629.

Cauce, A. M., Felner, R., and Primavera, J. "Social Support in High-Risk Adolescents: Structural Components and Adaptive Impact." *American Journal of Community Psychology,* 1982, *10,* 417–428.

Chambers, B. (ed.). *Chronicles of Black Protest.* New York: New American Library, 1968.

Chestang, L. "Racial and Personal Identity in the Black Experience." In B. White (ed.), *Color in a White Society.* Silver Spring, Md.: NASW Publications, 1984.

Children's Defense Fund. *A Children's Defense Budget.* Washington, D.C.: Children's Defense Fund, 1985.

Children's Defense Fund. *Building Health Programs for Teenagers.* Washington, D.C.: Children's Defense Fund, 1986a.

Children's Defense Fund. *Welfare and Teen Pregnancy: What Do We Know? What Do We Do?* Washington, D.C.: Children's Defense Fund, 1986b.

Children's Defense Fund. *A Children's Defense Budget.* Washington, D.C.: Children's Defense Fund, 1987.

Chilman, C. *Adolescent Sexuality in a Changing American Society.* New York: Wiley, 1983.

Clark, K. B. *Dark Ghetto: Dilemmas of Social Power.* New York: Harper & Row, 1965.

Clark, K. B., and Clark, M. "Skin Color as a Factor in Racial Identification of Negro Pre-School Children." *Journal of Social Psychology,* 1940, *2,* 154–167.

College Entrance Examination Board. *Equality and Excellence: The Educational Status of Black Americans.* New York: College Entrance Examination Board, 1985.

Colletta, N. D., Hadler, S., and Gregg, C. H. "How Adolescents

Cope with the Problems of Early Motherhood." *Adolescence,* 1981, *16,* 499–512.

Comer, J. P., and Hill, H. "Social Policy and the Mental Health of Black Children." *Journal of the American Academy of Child Psychiatry,* 1985, *24,* 175–181.

Committee for Economic Development. *Children in Need: Investment Strategies for the Educationally Disadvantaged.* New York: Committee for Economic Development, 1987.

Cross, W. E. "A Two-Factor Theory of Black Identity: Implications for the Study of Identity Development in Minority Children." In J. Phinney and M. J. Rotheram (eds.), *Children's Ethnic Socialization: Pluralism and Development.* Newbury Park, Calif.: Sage, 1984.

Dancy, B., and Handal, P. "Perceived Family Climate, Psychological Adjustment and Peer Relationships of Black Adolescents: A Function of Parental Marital Status or Perceived Family Conflict?" *Journal of Community Psychology,* 1984, *12,* 222–229.

Davis, K., and Swartz, J. "Increasing Black Students' Utilization of Mental Health Services." *American Journal of Orthopsychiatry,* 1972, *42,* 771–776.

Dembo, R. "Delinquency Among Black Male Youth." In J. T. Gibbs (ed.), *Young, Black, and Male in America: An Endangered Species.* Dover, Mass.: Auburn House, 1988.

Dougherty, M. *Becoming a Woman in Rural Black Culture.* New York: Holt, Rinehart & Winston, 1978.

Durrett, M. D., O'Bryant, S., and Pennebaker, J. W. "Child-Rearing Reports of White, Black, and Mexican-American Families." *Developmental Psychology,* 1975, *11,* 871–878.

Edelman, M. W. *Families in Peril: An Agenda for Social Change.* Cambridge, Mass.: Harvard University Press, 1987.

Erikson, E. H. *Childhood and Society.* New York: Norton, 1950.

Erikson, E. H. "Identity and the Life Cycle." *Psychological Issues,* 1959, *1* (1).

Felner, R. D., Aber, M. S., Primavera, J., and Cauce, A. M. "Adaptation and Vulnerability in High-Risk Adolescents: An Examination of Environmental Mediators." *American Journal of Community Psychology,* 1985, *13,* 365–379.

Field, T., Widmayer, S., Stinger, S., and Ignatoff, E. "Teenage, Lower-Class Black Mothers and Their Preterm Infants: An Intervention and Developmental Follow-up." *Child Development*, 1980, *51*, 426–436.

Foley, V. "Family Therapy with Black Disadvantaged Families: Some Observations on Roles, Communication, and Techniques." *Journal of Marriage and Family Counseling*, 1975, *1*, 29–38.

Foster, M., and Perry, L. R. "Self-Valuation Among Blacks." *Social Work*, 1982, *27*, 60–66.

Frank, J. D., and others. *Effective Ingredients of Successful Psychotherapy*. New York: Brunner/Mazel, 1978.

Franklin, A. J. "Therapeutic Interventions with Urban Black Adolescents." In E. E. Jones and S. J. Korchin (eds.), *Minority Mental Health*. New York: Praeger, 1982.

Franklin, J. H. *From Slavery to Freedom: A History of American Negroes*. New York: Knopf, 1967.

Frazier, E. F. *The Negro Family in the United States*. Chicago: University of Chicago Press, 1966.

Furstenberg, F., Jr., Lincoln, R., and Menken, J. *Teenage Sexuality, Pregnancy, and Childbearing*. Philadelphia: University of Pennsylvania Press, 1981.

Gardner, L. "The Therapeutic Relationship Under Varying Conditions of Race." *Psychotherapy: Theory, Research and Practice*, 1971, *8*, 78–87.

Gibbs, J. T. "Patterns of Adaptation Among Black Students at a Predominantly White University." *American Journal of Orthopsychiatry*, 1974, *44*, 728–740.

Gibbs, J. T. "Use of Mental Health Services by Black Students at a Predominantly White University: A Three-Year Study." *American Journal of Orthopsychiatry*, 1975, *45*, 430–445.

Gibbs, J. T. "Depression and Suicidal Behavior Among Delinquent Females: Ethnic and Sociocultural Variations." *Journal of Youth and Adolescence*, 1981, *2*, 159–167.

Gibbs, J. T. "Personality Patterns of Delinquent Females: Ethnic and Sociocultural Variations." *Journal of Clinical Psychology*, 1982, *38*, 198–206.

Gibbs, J. T. "Black Adolescents and Youth: An Endangered Species." *American Journal of Orthopsychiatry*, 1984, *54*, 6–21.

Gibbs, J. T. "City Girls: Psychosocial Adjustment of Urban Black Adolescent Females." *SAGE: A Scholarly Journal on Black Women*, 1985a, *2*, 28–36.

Gibbs, J. T. "Psychosocial Factors Associated with Depression in Urban Adolescent Females: Implications for Assessment." *Journal of Youth and Adolescence*, 1985b, *14*, 47–60.

Gibbs, J. T. "Treatment Relationships with Black Clients: Interpersonal vs. Instrumental Strategies." In C. Germain (ed.), *Advances in Clinical Social Work Practice*. Silver Spring, Md.: NASW Publications, 1985c.

Gibbs, J. T. "Assessment of Depression in Urban Adolescent Females: Implications for Early Intervention Strategies." *American Journal of Social Psychiatry*, 1986a, *6*, 50–56.

Gibbs, J. T. "Psychosocial Correlates of Sexual Attitudes and Behaviors in Urban Early Adolescent Females: Implications for Intervention." *Journal of Social Work and Human Sexuality*, 1986b, *5*, 81–97.

Gibbs, J. T. "Conceptual, Methodological and Sociocultural Issues in Black Youth Suicide: Implications for Assessment and Early Intervention." *Suicide and Life-Threatening Behavior*, 1988a, *18*, 73–89.

Gibbs, J. T. (ed.). *Young, Black, and Male in America: An Endangered Species*. Dover, Mass.: Auburn House, 1988b.

Glasgow, D. *The Black Underclass*. New York: Vintage Books, 1981.

Goodman, M. E. *Race Awareness in Young Children*. Reading, Mass.: Addison-Wesley, 1964.

Grier, W., and Cobbs, P. *Black Rage*. New York: Basic Books, 1968.

Griffith, M., and Jones, E. E. "Race and Psychotherapy: Changing Perspectives." *Current Psychiatric Therapies*, 1978, *18*, 225–235.

Gurin, P., and Epps, E. G. *Black Consciousness, Identity and Achievement*. New York: Wiley, 1975.

Gwyn, F. S., and Kilpatrick, A. C. "Family Therapy with Low-Income Blacks: A Tool or Turn-off?" *Social Casework*, 1981, 5, 259–266.

Halikas, J., Darvish, H., and Rimmer, J. "The Black Addict: I. Methodology, Chronology of Addiction and Overview of the Population." *American Journal of Drug and Alcohol Abuse*, 1976, 3, 529–543.

Hall, L. E., and Tucker, C. M. "Relationships Between Ethnicity, Conceptions of Mental Illness and Attitudes Associated with Seeking Psychological Help." *Psychological Reports*, 1985, 57, 907–916.

Hannerz, U. *Soulside: Inquiries into Ghetto Culture and Community*. New York: Columbia University Press, 1969.

Hare, B. R. "Black Youth at Risk." In J. D. Williams (ed.), *The State of Black America 1988*. New York: National Urban League, 1988.

Harris, D. C., and Balgopal, P. R. "Intervening with the Black Family." In C. Janzen and O. Harris, *Family Treatment in Social Work Practice*. Itasca, Ill.: Peacock, 1980.

Heiss, J., and Owens, S. "Self-Evaluations of Blacks and Whites." *American Journal of Sociology*, 1976, 78, 360–371.

Hendricks, L. E. "Unwed Adolescent Fathers: Problems They Face and Their Sources of Social Support." *Adolescence*, 1980, 15, 862–869.

Hines, P. M., and Boyd-Franklin, N. "Black Families." In M. McGoldrick, J. K. Pearce, and J. Giordano (eds.), *Ethnicity and Family Therapy*. New York: Guilford Press, 1982.

Honey, E. "AIDS and the Inner City: Critical Issues." *Social Casework*, 1988, 69, 365–370.

"Human Immunodeficiency Virus Infection in the United States." *Morbidity and Mortality Weekly Report* [Centers for Disease Control], 1987, 36, 801–804.

Jenkins, A. *The Psychology of the Afro-American*. Elmsford, N.Y.: Pergamon Press, 1982.

Jones, E. E., and Korchin, S. J. (eds.). *Minority Mental Health*. New York: Praeger, 1982.

Kandel, D. B., and others. "Antecedents of Adolescent Initiation into Stages of Drug Use: A Developmental Analysis." *Journal of Youth and Adolescence*, 1977, 7, 13–40.

Kaplan, S., Landa, B., Weinhold, C., and Shenker, I. "Adverse Health Behaviors and Depressive Symptomatology in Adolescents." *Journal of the American Academy of Child Psychiatry*, 1984, 23, 595–601.

Kasarda, J. "Urban Change and Minority Opportunities." In P. E. Peterson (ed.), *The New Urban Reality*. Washington, D.C.: Brookings Institution, 1985.

Kernan, C. "Language Behavior in a Black Urban Community." *Monographs of the Language Behavior Research Laboratory*, No. 2. Berkeley: University of California, 1971.

Kochman, T. E. *Rappin' and Stylin' Out*. Urbana: University of Illinois Press, 1972.

Kovar, M. G. "Health Status of U.S. Children and Use of Medical Care." *Public Health Reports*, 1982, 97, 3–15.

Krisberg, B., and others. *The Incarceration of Minority Youth*. Minneapolis: H. H. Humphrey Institute of Public Affairs, University of Minnesota, 1986.

Labov, W. *Language in the Inner City: Studies in the Black English Vernacular*. Philadelphia: University of Pennsylvania Press, 1972.

Ladner, J. *Tomorrow's Tomorrow*. New York: Doubleday, 1971.

Landau-Stanton, J., and Stanton, M. "Treating Suicidal Adolescents and Their Families." In M. Mirkin and S. Koman (eds.), *Handbook of Adolescents and Family Therapy*. New York: Gardner Press, 1985.

Lee, L. J. "Reducing Black Adolescents' Drug Use: Family Revisited." *Child and Youth Services*, 1983, 6, 57–69.

Leigh, J. W., and Green, J. W. "The Structure of the Black Community: The Knowledge Base for Social Services." In J. W. Green (ed.), *Cultural Awareness in the Human Services*. Englewood Cliffs, N.J.: Prentice-Hall, 1982.

Lewis, D., and Balla, D. *Delinquency and Psychopathology*. New York: Grune & Stratton, 1976.

McAdoo, H. *Black Families*. Newbury Park, Calif.: Sage, 1981.

MacLennan, B. W., and Felsenfeld, N. *Group Counseling and*

Psychotherapy with Adolescents. New York: Columbia University Press, 1968.

Mancini, J. K. *Strategic Styles: Coping in the Inner City.* Hanover, N.H.: University Press of New England, 1980.

Mayo, J. "The Significance of Sociocultural Variables in the Psychiatric Treatment of Black Outpatients." *Comprehensive Psychiatry,* 1974, *15,* 471–482.

Mays, V., and Cochran, S. "Acquired Immunodeficiency Syndrome and Black Americans: Special Psychosocial Issues." *Public Health Reports,* 1987, *102,* 221–231.

Mercer, J. "Psychological Assessment and the Rights of Children." In N. Hobbs (ed.), *Issues in the Classification of Children: A Sourcebook on Categories, Labels, and Their Consequences.* Vol. 1. San Francisco: Jossey-Bass, 1975.

Milazzo-Sayre, L., Benson, P., Rosenstein, M., and Manderscheid, R. "Use of Inpatient Psychiatric Services by Children and Youth Under Age 18, United States, 1980." *Mental Health Statistical Note,* No. 175. Washington, D.C.: U.S. Department of Health and Human Services, 1986.

Miller, D. "Treatment of the Seriously Disturbed Adolescent." *Adolescent Psychiatry,* 1980, *8,* 469–481.

Minuchin, S., and others. *Families of the Slums.* New York: Basic Books, 1967.

Myers, H. F. "Urban Stress and Mental Health in Afro-American Youth: An Epidemiologic and Conceptual Update." In R. Jones (ed.), *Black Adolescents.* Berkeley, Calif.: Cobb and Henry, forthcoming.

Myers, H. F., and King, L. M. "Youth of the Black Underclass: Urban Stress and Mental Health—Notes for an Alternative Formulation." *Fanon Center Journal,* 1980, *1,* 1–27.

National Institute of Drug Abuse. *National Survey on Drug Abuse, 1979.* Washington, D.C.: National Institute of Drug Abuse, 1979.

Neighbors, H. W. "Seeking Professional Help for Personal Problems: Black Americans' Use of Health and Mental Health Services." *Community Mental Health Journal,* 1985, *21,* 156–166.

Nobles, W. "Psychological Research and the Black Self-Concept: A Critical Review." *Journal of Social Issues,* 1973, *29,* 11–31.

Norman, J. S. "Short-Term Treatment with the Adolescent Client." *Social Casework,* 1980, *61,* 74–82.

Ogbu, J. U. "A Cultural Ecology of Competence Among Inner-City Blacks." In M. Spencer, G. Brookins, and W. Allen (eds.), *Beginnings: The Social and Affective Development of Black Children.* Hillsdale, N.J.: Erlbaum, 1985.

Omi, M., and Winant, H. *Racial Formation in the United States: From the 1960's to the 1980's.* Boston: Routledge & Kegan Paul, 1986.

Peters, M. F. "Parenting in Black Families with Young Children: A Historical Perspective." In H. McAdoo (ed.), *Black Families.* Newbury Park, Calif.: Sage, 1981.

Pinderhughes, C. "Racism and Psychotherapy." In C. Willie, B. Brown, and B. Kramer (eds.), *Racism and Mental Health.* Pittsburgh: University of Pittsburgh Press, 1973.

Powell, G. J. "Self-Concepts Among Afro-American Students in Racially Isolated Minority Schools: Some Regional Differences." *Journal of the American Academy of Child Psychiatry,* 1985, *24,* 142–149.

Pumariega, A., Edwards, P., and Mitchell, C. "Anorexia Nervosa in Black Adolescents." *Journal of the American Academy of Child Psychiatry,* 1984, *23,* 111–114.

Reed, R. "Education and Achievement of Young Black Males." In J. T. Gibbs (ed.), *Young, Black, and Male in America: An Endangered Species.* Dover, Mass.: Auburn House, 1988.

Ridley, C. R. "Clinical Treatment of the Nondisclosing Black Client: A Therapeutic Paradox." *American Psychologist,* 1984, *39,* 1234–1244.

Rivers, L. W., and others. "Mosaic of Labels for Black Children." In N. Hobbs (ed.), *Issues in the Classification of Children: A Sourcebook on Categories, Labels, and Their Consequences.* Vol. 2. San Francisco: Jossey-Bass, 1975.

Robinson, B. *Teenage Fathers.* Lexington, Mass.: Lexington Books, 1988.

Robinson, P., and Andersen, A. "Anorexia Nervosa in American Blacks." *Journal of Psychiatric Research*, 1985, *19*, 183–188.

Rosenberg, M. *Conceiving the Self.* New York: Basic Books, 1979.

Rosenberg, M., and Simmons, R. *Black and White Self-Esteem: The Urban School Child.* Rose Monograph Series. Washington, D.C.: American Sociological Association, 1971.

Sager, C., Brayboy, T., and Waxenberg, B. *Black Ghetto Family in Therapy.* New York: Grove Press, 1970.

Samuda, R. *Psychological Testing of American Minorities: Issues and Consequences.* New York: Dodd, Mead, 1975.

Schoenbach, V., and others. "Prevalence of Self-Reported Depressive Symptoms in Young Adolescents." *American Journal of Public Health*, 1983, *73*, 1281–1287.

Schorr, A. *Common Decency: Domestic Policies After Reagan.* New Haven, Conn.: Yale University Press, 1986.

Schulz, D. A. *Coming Up Black: Patterns of Ghetto Socialization.* Englewood Cliffs, N.J.: Prentice-Hall, 1969.

Shaffer, D., and Fisher, P. "The Epidemiology of Suicide in Children and Young Adolescents." *Journal of the American Academy of Child Psychiatry*, 1981, *20*, 545–565.

Skager, R. *A Statewide Survey of Drug and Alcohol Use Among California Students in Grades 7, 9, and 11.* Sacramento, Calif.: Office of the Attorney General, 1986.

Smith, E. "The Black Female Adolescent: A Review of the Educational, Career and Psychological Literature." *Psychology of Women Quarterly*, 1982, *6*, 261–288.

Snowden, L. R., and Todman, P. A. "The Psychological Assessment of Blacks: New and Needed Developments." In E. E. Jones and S. J. Korchin (eds.), *Minority Mental Health.* New York: Praeger, 1982.

Spencer, M. B. "Personal and Group Identity of Black Children: An Alternative Synthesis." *Genetic Psychology Monographs*, 1982, *106*, 59–84.

Stack, C. *All Our Kin: Strategies for Survival in a Black Community.* New York: Harper & Row, 1974.

Staples, R. "The Black American Family." In C. H. Mindel and

R. W. Habenstein (eds.), *Ethnic Families in America: Patterns and Variations.* (2nd ed.) New York: Elsevier, 1981.

Staples, R., and Mirande, A. "Racial and Cultural Variations Among American Families: A Decennial Review of the Literature on Minority Families." *Journal of Marriage and the Family,* 1980, *42,* 887–903.

Taylor, R. L. "Psychosocial Development Among Black Children and Youth: A Reexamination." *American Journal of Orthopsychiatry,* 1976, *46,* 4–19.

U.S. Bureau of the Census. *School Enrollment: Social and Economic Characteristics of Students, 1980.* Current Population Reports, Series P-20. Washington, D.C.: U.S. Government Printing Office, 1981.

U.S. Bureau of the Census. *Statistical Abstract of the United States: 1986.* (106th ed.) Washington, D.C.: U.S. Department of Commerce, 1985.

U.S. Bureau of the Census. *Statistical Abstract of the United States: 1987.* (107th ed.) Washington, D.C.: U.S. Department of Commerce, 1986.

U.S. Department of Health and Human Services. *Health, United States, 1986.* Washington, D.C.: National Center for Health Statistics, 1986.

Viadero, D. "Big-City Gang Culture Spreading to New Turf." *Education Week,* April 1988, 7, 1, 18–19.

Warshauer, M., and Monk, M. "Problems in Suicide Statistics for Whites and Blacks." *American Journal of Public Health,* 1978, *68,* 383–388.

Weaver, D. R. "Empowering Treatment Skills for Helping Black Families." *Social Casework,* 1982, *63,* 100–105.

Wilson, W. J. *The Truly Disadvantaged.* Chicago: University of Chicago Press, 1987.

7

Mexican American Children and Adolescents

Oscar Ramirez

Despite an accumulation of social science/mental health research spanning nearly thirty years, the knowledge base needed to guide and inform the process of providing effective mental health services to Mexican American youth and their families is small, fragmented, incomplete, and, in some areas, nonexistent. This chapter addresses this substantial void in the psychotherapeutic literature on Mexican Americans by presenting some cultural characteristics of Mexican American family life that therapists should be aware of in order to provide effective, relevant, and culturally sensitive therapeutic services.

The chapter is organized around the following topics: first, a demographic profile of the Mexican American population; second, an overview of specific cultural and familial char-

The author is deeply grateful to Robin A. Brill, Shannon E. Scott, Tina Ramirez Knoll, and Frank C. Paredes for their valuable and careful review, editorial comments, and suggestions on an early version of this chapter. I also want to express my gratitude to my friends and colleagues who provided me with clinical case material for use in this chapter: Tom Gaines, Anita J. Schacht, Shannon E. Scott. I am indebted to Nola Baker for putting together the statistics on diagnoses at the Community Guidance Center. I offer a very warm thanks to Ric Harvey for the technical preparation of this manuscript in all of its varying forms and stages.

acteristics of Mexican Americans; third, the epidemiological
research on the incidence/prevalence of psychological and behavioral disorders among Mexican American children and adolescents; fourth, the critical issues involved in providing effective and culturally relevant clinical intervention and treatment
services to these young people and their families; and finally, future directions for the delivery of mental health services to the
Mexican American population.

A Demographic Profile

In this chapter, a Mexican American is defined as any person who was born in Mexico or who is of Mexican descent. According to recent census figures, the Mexican American population in the United States comprises some 11.8 million people,
which represents a growth of 22 percent from 1980 to 1987.[1]
People of Mexican origin account for 63 percent of the Hispanic
population. The growth of the Mexican American population
can be attributed to a high fertility rate, as well as to improved
enumeration of illegal and undocumented individuals who continuously enter the United States from Mexico.

Mexican Americans tend to be younger than other groups
and are, in fact, the youngest among Hispanic groups, with a
median age of 23.3 years, compared with 24.3 years for Puerto
Ricans, 39.1 for Cuban Americans, and 31.9 for non-Hispanics.
The proportion of children and adolescents in this population is
even more striking. Minors aged 17 years and younger make up
39.1 percent of Mexican Americans. The comparable figures for
other groups are 37.1 percent for Puerto Ricans, 19.8 percent
for Cuban Americans, and 26.0 percent for non-Hispanics.

In 1984 the reported median income of Mexican American families ($19,200) was significantly lower than that of
non-Hispanic families ($27,000), lower than that of Cubans
($22,600), and higher than that of Puerto Ricans ($12,400). It
is generally acknowledged that larger families suffer the burden
of low income more severely. An earlier review reported that
Mexican American families with four or more children had lower

median incomes than Mexican American families with fewer or no children (Ramirez and Arce, 1981). The 1985 current population report indicated that the proportion of Hispanic families whose income fell below the poverty level was more than double that of non-Hispanic families. However, there were consistent differences within the Hispanic group. Puerto Rican families had the highest poverty rate, with 42 percent of family incomes falling below the poverty level, while only 13 percent of Cuban American and 24 percent of Mexican American family incomes fell below the poverty level.

Measures of educational attainment, a closely related socioeconomic variable, show that Hispanics, particularly Mexican Americans, have completed fewer years of formal education than non-Hispanics. The 1985 census reported that only 42 percent of Mexican Americans aged 25 and older had completed high school.

Geographically, the Mexican-descent population is largely concentrated in California, Texas, Illinois (primarily Chicago), New Mexico, Arizona, and Colorado. Two or three decades ago, Mexican Americans were characterized in the literature as being primarily a rural, agrarian subculture. However, in 1980 it was estimated that 55 percent of the Mexican American population now lives in the large metropolitan areas. Although this figure represents a major shift, it is highly significant that the remaining 45 percent of Mexican Americans continue to reside in smaller urban or rural settings.

In summary, recent demographic data indicate that Mexican Americans in the United States tend to be young, to be poor, to have high fertility rates, to live in large families, to have less than a high school education, and to confront problems of illiteracy and lack of facility in the English language. Even though a slight majority of Mexican Americans reside in large metropolitan areas, a substantial number continue to live in small urban and rural communities. This constellation of characteristics, as noted by Rogler, Malgady, Costantino, and Blumenthal (1987), makes this population highly vulnerable to the development of mental health problems. Thus, the need for culturally sensitive mental health services is clearly evident.

Mexican American Cultural Family Patterns

Although Mexican American families are quite diverse, an attempt will be made to outline some characteristic patterns and values. Keep in mind, however, that each family is unique and is at a different point on the continuum of acculturation, so that these patterns are secondary to the individual differences and diversity within this population.

Recent research suggests that Mexican American families are currently undergoing substantial changes. In a review of the contemporary Mexican American family, Ramirez and Arce (1981) examined multiple aspects of Mexican American family life and found a mixture of traditional and more contemporary patterns. Such traditional values as the primacy of the family and extended kinship ties remained strongly entrenched. The structure and function of Mexican American families continued to be characterized by a strong, persistent familistic orientation; a highly integrated extended kinship system, even for families three or more generations removed from Mexico; and a strong reliance on this extended family system, including *compadres* (godparents), for emotional and social support, child rearing, financial support, and problem solving (see, for example, Sena-Rivera, 1977, 1979; Keefe, Padilla, and Carlos, 1978a, 1978b, 1979; Baca Zinn, 1977; Mindel, 1980). To facilitate the functioning of this kinship network, traditional Mexican American values of affiliation and cooperation are stressed, while confrontation and competition are discouraged. As LeVine and Padilla (1980) state, "According to the traditional Hispanic values of *personalismo*, it is not ability but, rather, goodness and the quality of personal relationships that are important in life" (p. 34).

In contrast to these more traditional values, Ramirez and Arce (1981) found some interesting variations in the area of male and female roles and conjugal decision making. Traditionally, men assumed the instrumental role of provider and protector of the family, and women the expressive role of homemaker and caretaker of the children. To a certain degree this continues to be the dominant public norm (Falicov, 1982), and the concept of machismo continues to influence the role of the male and the patriarchal ideology in Mexican American families, though less so than in the past. Traditionally, this concept required men to be forceful and strong and to withhold tender or affectionate emotions. Ideally, it encompassed a strong sense of personal honor, family, loyalty, and care for the children; however, it also connoted exaggerated masculinity and sexual virility and aggressiveness (Trankina, 1983). When this concept was carried to an extreme, family problems and dissatisfactions often ensued. In contrast to the male, the female's role was one of self-denial and abnegation, and her personal needs were considered subordinate to those of other family members. Ramirez and Arce (1981) found that the concepts of machismo and absolute patriarchy currently have diminishing influence on the dynamics and structure of the contemporary Mexican American family; rather, joint decision making and greater equality of males' and females' roles and opportunities are apparent. Of major significance is the increased frequency of women's employment outside the home, which seems to enhance a wife's status within the family and in decision-making processes (Cromwell and Ruiz, 1979; Ybarra-Soriano, 1977; Baca Zinn, 1980).

Parent/Child Relationships. It is the existence of children that validates and cements a marriage. Within this culture, *el amor de madre*, motherly love, is considered a much greater force than wifely love. Since the parent/child relationship is considered more important than the marital relationship, the Mexican American couple typically enjoys little freedom from parental functions during the child-rearing stages.

During the family's early years, the home is usually child-centered. Both parents tend to be permissive and indulgent with the younger children. In spite of an emphasis on good behavior, parents give a great deal of nurturance and protection to young children and adopt a relaxed attitude toward the achievement of developmental milestones or the attainment of skills related to self-reliance. Generally speaking, Mexican American parents seem less pressured than Anglo-American parents to see that a child achieves developmental goals or to correct minor deviations from the norm. There is a basic acceptance of the child's individuality. Following this relatively permissive and indulgent phase, Mexican American parents begin to expect more responsible behavior from their children as they approach latency and the years beyond. During latency and adolescence, children are often assigned tasks or responsibilities in accordance with their age and ability. They are expected, for example, to help with housework, child care, cooking, and errands.

During the children's earlier years, the father is often playful and affectionate, but his primary role with older children is to discipline them and to expect obedience. This polarization of protective nurturance and authoritarian control between mother and father renders mother more accessible to the children and often places her in a position of mediator between father and children.

Sex-Role Socialization. Differences in sex-role socialization are clearly evident in this culture and become especially prominent at adolescence. The adolescent female is likely to remain much closer to the home and to be protected and guarded in her contacts with others beyond the family, so as to preserve her femininity and innocence. The adolescent male, following the model of his father, is given much more freedom to come and go as he chooses and is encouraged to gain worldly knowledge outside the home in preparation for the time when he will assume the role of husband and father. As Murillo (1971) notes, "During this period of development, the young male is likely to join with others of his age in informal social groups known as *palomillas.* Through such associations, he gains knowledge and experience in holding his own with other males" (pp. 104-105).

Psychological and Behavioral Disorders

Epidemiological studies conducted before 1980 found a lower prevalence of psychiatric disorder among Mexican Americans. In contrast, more recent epidemiological surveys (for example, Roberts, 1980) suggest that the prevalence of psychological distress among Mexican Americans is at least as high as in the overall population and, in some instances, higher. However, whether Mexican Americans are seeking mental health services at a rate commensurate with their actual prevalence of psychological disturbance remains an unanswered question.

Mexican American children and adolescents constitute

the most rapidly growing group of young people in the Southwest and one about which relatively little is known of mental health issues. Unfortunately, comparative surveys of the prevalence of disorder in Mexican American and Anglo young people are disparate in focus and use different measures and different methods of data collection, making comparisons difficult and resulting in inconsistent findings. These studies do not offer any clear, consistent evidence that Mexican American youth have either higher or lower rates of behavior problems or psychopathology than their Anglo counterparts. In addition, because these few studies are not true epidemiological studies, they do not offer accurate estimates of the incidence or prevalence of psychological disorders in this population group.

In the absence of systematic epidemiological studies, incidence rates are estimated from clinic-based research. In their study of Mexican American and Anglo children matched for sex and family income in three southwestern child guidance clinics, Stoker and Meadow (1974) found ethnic differences in the expression of behavior problems and psychopathology. Mexican American boys were more frequently described as more aggressive and acting out, Anglo-American boys more frequently as neurotic. Mexican American girls, who were referred to the clinics at a later age than subjects in the other three groups, showed more depression overall. Further, these researchers reported that clinicians viewed Mexican American children as generally benefiting less from treatment.

An informal analysis of the diagnoses given children and adolescents at a county guidance center where I practice reveals a similar distribution of diagnoses for the Mexican American and non–Mexican American groups (see Table 1). In both groups, the diagnosis most frequently given was dysthymic disorder (neurotic depression), followed by oppositional disorder and, third, overanxious disorder. Among these three diagnoses, Mexican Americans received a diagnosis of depression more often than non–Mexican Americans; non–Mexican Americans received a diagnosis of oppositional disorder more frequently than Mexican Americans; overanxious disorder was seen with equal frequency in the two groups. The diagnosis of conduct

Table 1. Selected Primary Diagnoses Given to Children and Adolescents
at the Community Guidance Center of Bexar County, Texas,
from January 1984 through April 1987.

Diagnosis	Mexican Americans	Non–Mexican Americans	Total
Dysthymic disorder	140 (31.7%)	202 (24.8%)	342
Oppositional disorder	58 (13.2%)	150 (18.4%)	208
Overanxious disorder	55 (12.5%)	105 (12.9%)	160
Adjustment disorder with mixed disturbance of emotions and conduct	32 (7.3%)	61 (7.5%)	93
Schizophrenic disorder	8 (1.8%)	22 (2.7%)	30
Affective psychosis	11 (2.5%)	17 (2.1%)	28
Attention deficit disorder without hyperactivity	8 (1.8%)	16 (2.0%)	24
Attention deficit disorder with hyperactivity	29 (6.6%)	85 (10.4%)	114
Conduct disorder, undersocialized, aggressive	20 (4.5%)	30 (3.7%)	50
Conduct disorder, socialized, aggressive	36 (8.2%)	41 (5.0%)	77
Conduct disorder, undersocialized, nonaggressive	6 (1.4%)	15 (1.8%)	21
Conduct disorder, socialized, nonaggressive	38 (8.6%)	71 (8.7%)	109
Total	441 (100%)	815 (100%)	1256

disorder (undersocialized or socialized, *aggressive)* was given
slightly more frequently to Mexican Americans than to non–
Mexican Americans, who were slightly more often given a diagnosis of conduct disorder, *nonaggressive.*

Substance Abuse. In his comprehensive report on drug
use in the United States and along the United States–Mexico
border, Adams (1986) notes that studies of drug use among Hispanics have been confined to small ethnic enclaves—that is, the
barrios (neighborhoods). He cites a study by Padilla and others
(1979) which reported that Mexican American adolescents were
at least fourteen times as likely to be abusing inhalants as their
Anglo counterparts in a national sample. He also describes a

pilot study conducted among eighth- and twelfth-graders in three small southwestern communities and notes the "relatively high prevalence of inhalants in these towns," ranging in size from 3,000 to 11,000 people, where the reported use of inhalants among high school seniors was *lower* than among eighth-graders, indicating the severity of drug use among younger Mexican American adolescents. When interpreting these studies, one must be careful not to generalize from school-based surveys to the entire Mexican American youth population, given the high dropout rate in the later school years. Adams also found that, in Texas, Hispanics account for almost 57 percent of heroin admissions and 88 percent of inhalant admissions to drug rehabilitation centers. Inhalant abuse is obviously a significant problem for the adolescent Mexican American population, especially those living in poor barrios, where the median age of first use among people admitted for treatment is about 14 to 15 years. Adams points to the isolation and relative poverty of some of these communities as important contributing factors, noting lower levels of education and higher levels of unemployment as two main indicators.

These observations are supported by Chavez, Beauvais, and Oetting (1986), who surveyed substance use among the youth of a small southwestern town. In this survey, Mexican American and Anglo youth were compared on drug-use variables and gender differences and then compared with a national sample and a group of urban barrio youth. Use of alcohol, stimulants, tranquilizers, and heroin was significantly higher in the small-town sample than in the national sample. There were two other significant differences between the Hispanic small-town sample and the barrio sample: A higher percentage of small-town subjects had tried alcohol and a lower percentage had used inhalants. The researchers concluded that Hispanic young people with physical or psychological problems should be assessed for possible drug involvement, particularly because they have been found to be more vulnerable to drug use than their Anglo peers.

Adolescent Mothers. Recently, deAnda (1985) studied the life experiences of Mexican American adolescent mothers aged 12 to 17 years who were pregnant or had delivered a child within the past twelve months. In general, deAnda found that, compared with the bilingual Mexican American group (N = 22), the Mexican American Spanish-speaking women (N = 19) received less support from their extended family; had fewer peer contacts; had more limited knowledge of child care, particularly about medical crises; and had lower incomes. Spanish-speaking subjects in this sample responded to upsetting situations with suppression of emotions and withdrawal, manifested by nervousness and somatic complaints, a pattern that has clinical implications.

Sociocultural Aspects of Assessment

In working with Mexican American patients, there are two sociocultural factors of particular importance in the assessment of the child and family: family structure and level of acculturation.

Family Structure. As noted previously, Mexican American norms emphasize the parent/child dyad over the marital dyad. Hence, during the initial stage of forming a therapeutic relationship, a focus on parent/child interactions will be accepted more readily than a focus on marital issues or on issues concerning the parents' families of origin. Furthermore, a therapeutic focus on individual needs over familial needs may meet with resistance. For example, Falicov (1982) indicates that it is unwise to try to convince a Mexican American mother that she needs time for herself in an attempt to decrease her involvement with her children, as this is contrary to the cultural ideal of maternal self-sacrifice.

It is important that the therapist respect the traditional family age/sex hierarchies of power and convey a sense of *respeto* (respect) by addressing questions to the father first, then to the mother, then to other adults, and finally to the older and younger children. A neutral opening allowing the family to choose its own spokesperson is also appropriate; however, if an adolescent son or daughter begins or dominates a session, it may be symptomatic of a weakened parental subsystem and contrary to the public sociocultural norms. In this situation, the therapist might want to redirect the session toward the parents in order to strengthen culturally consonant generational boundaries, as well as to build trust in the therapist. Viewed from another perspective, initiation or domination of the session by an adolescent son or daughter may indicate a considerable gulf between the parents' and the children's levels of acculturation. These children may have been functioning in a translator/negotiator role with the outside world for quite some time, and this fact is relevant and is important to explore with the family.

   Level of Acculturation. In addition to the usual family social and developmental history, it is important to obtain information on the patient's and family's immigration history and generational status in the United States. This information will influence interpretation of the data obtained throughout the assessment process. For example, a family who recently immigrated from Mexico may be unfamiliar with American customs and norms and may possess a distinctly traditional Mexican world view. In contrast, ethnic differences may be insignificant in a later-generation family.

   Family members often acculturate at different rates. Usually, children adapt to American values and norms more readily than parents, often stimulating intergenerational acculturation conflicts. Within the parental dyad itself, there may also be acculturation differences, often related to degree of adherence to traditional family and sex roles or to different ages at migration. For these reasons, the various complexities of acculturation within the family need to be carefully assessed.

Issues in Treatment

   Historically, Mexican Americans have shown low rates of mental health service utilization. In the past, this was partly explained by unfavorable attitudes toward these services. More recent studies have indicated that Mexican Americans in fact have a high positive regard for counseling and psychotherapy (Acosta and Sheehan, 1976; Karno and Edgerton, 1969). Explanations for low utilization have included language differences between

Mexican Americans and staff members of mental health services, social-class and cultural differences, insufficient numbers of mental health services in the barrios, widespread use of physicians for primary help with psychological problems, lack of awareness of available services, and the tendency of this population to defer seeking help for mental health problems (Acosta, Yamamoto, and Evans, 1982).

Given these obstacles to using mental health services, it is imperative to attend to those factors that will facilitate establishing a good therapeutic relationship with Mexican American patients. The following discussion focuses on the concepts of personal distance and self-disclosure in this relationship and special concerns in the entry phase of treatment. Clinical cases are then presented to illustrate such issues as differing identity crises and different treatment modalities. Throughout this section, the emphasis is on the family, as intervention with Mexican American children and adolescents invariably involves the entire family.

Personal Distance. Therapists should be aware of certain characteristics of verbal and nonverbal communication in their initial face-to-face encounters with a Mexican American family that will facilitate forming a positive therapeutic alliance. *Personalismo*, a Mexican American concept denoting a preference for personal contact and individualized attention in social interactions, contrasts with the Anglo preference for impersonal regulations and the organizational "chain of command." Mexican Americans expect less physical distance in personal interactions and are accustomed to frequent physical contact (LeVine and Padilla, 1980). Handshakes between acquaintances and embraces between friends are the norm upon meeting and separating (Padilla, 1981). Even Mexican American children have been observed to engage in more physical contact than Anglo or Black children and to use less space between themselves and playmates (Aiello and Jones, 1971). Thus, when exchanging initial introductions, it is appropriate for the therapist to stand close to the person, exchange a warm handshake, and perhaps even place a hand on the client's shoulder, all of which tends to reduce anxiety, to increase a client's comfort, and to facilitate openness in the early sessions. In greeting Mexican American clients, I find that I typically put my arm on the shoulder of the "identified child patient" and engage in casual conversation as the family and I walk toward my office. When this is not appropriate, as when an older teenager is the "identified patient," I usually engage one or both parents in casual conversation. These casual verbal exchanges offer vital information about language use and preference of the various family members and give important information on how to direct the session.

When the family are settling down in the office to begin the interview, they usually move their chairs so that they can sit very close together. The therapist may also find it effective to move his chair closer to the family member or members he is addressing.

Self-Disclosure. Self-disclosure among Mexican Americans in therapy is another issue to which therapists should be sensitive. LeVine and Padilla (1980) and Falicov (1982), who emphasize that Mexican Americans will disclose personal information very slowly, propose several ways in which a therapist can facilitate self-disclosure. For example, a social phase that transmits the therapist's interest in the persons rather than focusing on procedures is essential. Falicov (1982) suggests that disclosure can be facilitated when the therapist becomes a philosopher of life through storytelling, anecdotes, humor, analogies, and proverbs.

Entering Treatment. In exploring the presenting problem and gathering information about the family's referral, Acosta, Yamamoto, and Evans (1982) stress the importance of the therapist's showing a sense of personal interest—that is, friendliness and warmth. During the initial stages, as Falicov (1982) suggests, the therapist should not challenge the family's verbal statements that their life-style follows culturally prescribed norms, even if their actual behavior suggests otherwise. Falicov states: "For example, a wife may say that her husband is the 'boss' although the therapist and the rest of the family are all aware that she is dominating the therapy session and the family. These observations need to be placed in their cultural context and internally noted—but not verbalized" (p. 151).

In general, searching for strengths and praising the family's dignity will facilitate the development of a positive therapeutic alliance. Interpretations of dysfunction or direct confrontations tend to increase the Mexican American family's insecurity and may be perceived as disapproval rather than as a stimulus for change. Mexican American families usually provide enough information in the first interview to enable the therapist to formulate a working hypothesis that can be described summarily to the family. However, as Falicov (1982) warned, to close the first interview with an explicit "contract" may be too task-oriented for Mexican Americans, who tend to be person-oriented. There should be a general agreement about the proposed treatment approach and an estimate of the number of sessions needed; treatment objectives should be phrased clearly and focused either on the specific symptom or on improving parent/child relationships. In Burruel-Gonzalez's study (1975), Mexican American patients expected what they termed *pláticas-consejos* in therapy. *Pláticas-consejos* signified a mutual, sharing relationship between the therapist and patient that resulted in learning and growth for the patient. Therapy was perceived in psychological terms—insight, development of the self, and increased reasoning capabilities of the patient. Burruel-Gonzalez pointed out that this finding is "not supportive of the common belief that lower-income and minority people expect primarily direction, concrete assistance, and tangible results from a psychiatric setting" (p. 175).

Acosta, Yamamoto, and Evans (1982) stressed the importance of educating Hispanic patients to the process of psychotherapy by explaining the treatment plan, what is expected of the patient, and approximately how long the treatment is expected to last.

Because of the cultural emphasis on cooperation and respect for authority, many Mexican Americans feel it is impolite to disagree, a value that may interfere with formation of a positive therapeutic alliance. A Mexican American family may seem to accept the treatment contract suggested by the therapist even though they are covertly resistant to the treatment plan, as in the following vignette.

Ana, a 14-year-old oldest daughter, was brought to the clinic by her parents for "rebelliousness"—namely, that she was "boy crazy" and wanted to talk on the phone with boys, go to parties, and meet them at the mall. Ana's parents, who had moved to the United States ten years earlier from Mexico, had learned a little English but preferred to use Spanish in the sessions. Ana's father, who served as the family spokesperson, preferred to direct his answers to the Anglo male therapist, even though questions typically were asked of him by the Mexican American female therapist.

Ana and her siblings were extremely polite and reserved during the family interview, occasionally smiling as they were discussed. Ana's mother was also reserved and tended to agree with her husband's view of the problem. When seen alone, Ana described herself in a manner that reflected attitudes and interests typical for a girl her age reared in a predominantly Anglo culture. She talked a lot about socializing at school with both boys and girls and wished that her parents would allow her to have contact with her friends outside school. She spoke enviously of her 13-year-old brother, who was being given considerably more freedom by their parents. She exhibited some guilt that her interest in boys went against her parents' wishes; on the basis of her interactions with peers, however, she perceived this interest as normal.

When the therapists met with the family after the assessment to provide feedback and recommendations, they discussed Ana's conflict between her parents' wishes and her peer culture. They recommended that Ana be seen individually by the female therapist to discuss her conflict, after which a family therapy session would be planned. The parents tentatively agreed with these recommendations but did not follow through. Neither Ana nor the family returned for therapy.

This vignette brings up two important issues that are worth commenting on—one cultural and the other practical. The cultural issue, which apparently was not addressed adequately in formulating a treatment plan, was the substantial difference between Ana's level of acculturation and that of her parents. Certainly, when viewed from an Anglo perspective, her behavior and attitudes appear typical for a girl her age; however, when viewed from a traditional Mexican American cultural perspective, her behavior would be considered very deviant, almost to the point of bringing shame on the family. If the difference in levels of acculturation between the parents and the daughter had been made explicit, so that the parents felt supported in their cultural values, a more mutual understanding might have been reached by the end of this initial assessment. Practically, the patient should be encouraged to discuss with the therapist any disagreements with the therapeutic plan. The family's apparent resistance to the treatment plan was not addressed— neither by the family nor by the therapists. The therapist should actively encourage any questions or uncertainties on the part of the patient or family, as well as encourage the patient to make specific requests, statements of need, and self-disclosure and reward the patient for doing so.

Language is another important variable to consider when working with the Mexican American population. Language facility and preference are important indicators of level of acculturation. The various language preferences within a family may reflect significant family dynamics and points of acculturation and intergenerational conflicts or harmony. Whether the family speaks Spanish or English, however, the Mexican American linguistic style tends to vary between public and private situations (Falicov, 1982; Paz, 1961). In public, it is prone to allusions, indirect statements, and guardedness, while in private conversations—reserved only for intimate relationships—it may be bolder, more straightforward, and more direct.

Treatment Modalities. The case vignettes that follow illustrate different treatment modalities to emphasize that a particular approach may be required for a particular problem. These vignettes highlight some common themes of conflict that frequently occur among Mexican youth and their families.

LeVine and Padilla (1980) stated that family therapy offers particular promise with Mexican Americans because of the importance of, and the support inherent in, kinship ties. In addition, Falicov (1982) has concluded that Mexican American families of lower socioeconomic levels tend to respond best to a brief and problem-oriented approach that redefines the problem in interactional terms centered on the relationship between parents and children. The cultural emphasis on hierarchies within the family lends itself to a structural family therapy approach that emphasizes generational boundaries (Minuchin, 1974).

The following case illustrates these issues and highlights a theme of conflict common among Mexican American youth that goes beyond the common identity issues of "Who am I?" In this particular case, the conflict manifests itself as an acculturational and generational problem between parents and children.

Sergio (age 15), Laura (age 13), and their family were seen because of the parents' concern about Sergio's "bad temper" and Laura's sexual behavior. The parents complained about Sergio's anger, poor impulse control, and self-destructive behavior and Laura's overt interest in boys. Sergio, Mr. C. (43, migrated from Mexico to the United States 13 years before), Mrs. C. (34, born and raised in the United States), and Laura attended the first session. The Anglo intake therapist had reported that mother was the family spokesperson, but later it was determined that father spoke only Spanish, and the therapist was not Spanish-speaking. Accordingly, the family was transferred to the author for subsequent treatment.

Mother reported that father was having difficulty as the children reached adolescence and began to assert themselves more, which he viewed as blatant disrespect. Both teenagers reported that they were doing well in school and related very well to the interviewer. Mr. C. was emotional and articulate as he complained about his children's exposure to values and standards of morality that were considerably "lower" than what he wanted for them and what he had learned from his strict father. Sergio agreed that his father accurately described their defiant attitudes toward his values, and he explained that he and Laura constantly felt torn in two opposite directions. On the one hand was his father's strict, "old world" view of family life, in which children unquestionably accept the high moral and ethical standards set for them; on the other, the constant peer pressure to "go along with the crowd." The adolescents pleaded with the therapist to help their father understand that they felt very conflicted emotionally and had resorted to hurting themselves as a way of releasing their tension and frustration. The therapist ended the session by translating for the father what his children had said in English and assuring him of their loyalty, love, and respect for him but also explaining the pressure they felt to be accepted by their peers at school. The therapist made three recommendations to the family: first, that all corporal punishment cease immediately; second, that the family members discuss in Spanish how they had been feeling so that father could understand his children's emotional dilemma; and finally, that Sergio be allowed to stay temporarily with someone in the extended family in order to reduce the immediate tension in the home.

Over the next several sessions, the family improved dramatically, the level of tension decreased significantly, and there were no outbursts of aggression by anybody. Family therapy involved finding some middle ground for each teenager between father's rules and the peer pressure to do "illicit" things for group acceptance. Mother, who was more modern in her views, acted as a mediator between her husband and the children. Finally, father was encouraged to express nurturance and support toward his teenagers, whose earlier views of him as playful and affectionate had been replaced by experiences with him as angry and disapproving.

The complexity of the problems that Mexican American families present to a therapist often necessitates that the therapist play more than just a therapeutic role. For example, families who are referred for counseling are often involved with some other agency, such as the legal system or the child protective division. In order to work effectively with the family, the therapist must not only be the traditional clinician but must also work as a mediator, advocate, and resource finder. These roles are particularly critical when the "outside" agents are un-

familiar with and insensitive to Mexican American culture. The
following vignette offers a good example of the delicate interplay between these issues.

Susana, age 5, was referred for therapy with her mother,
a 44-year-old single parent, after the child had been sexually
abused by two teenage neighbors and two years earlier by a former boyfriend of the mother's. Susana was in foster placement,
and mother's service plan with the Department of Human Services (DHS) required that she recognize the seriousness of Susana's victimization, the child's needs, and mother's responsibility to protect her. Although mother and daughter had a close
relationship, mother clearly lacked adequate parenting skills,
evidently stemming from her own experience of inadequate
parenting and protection (she, too, had been victimized as a
child and young adult) and possible limited intellectual ability.

By conducting the sessions in Spanish, the therapist was
able to elicit much more emotional material in treatment. Using
Spanish also enabled mother to maintain some sense of privacy
from an Anglo DHS child advocate attorney who was vigorously
seeking termination of parental rights. The therapist agreed with
mother that the grounds for seeking termination of her parental
rights were culturally biased and insufficient to warrant such action. Examples of these were that no playground was located
close to mother's home; that mother worked and would not be
home when Susana got out of school (she had arranged for a
competent sitter); and that mother would not be able to provide Susana with the kind of life-style she had in her Anglo foster home.

In this case, the therapist was a mediator between mother
and DHS, as well as an advocate, protecting mother's interests
and privacy and working with her toward fulfilling the DHS re-
quirements that would allow Susana to return home.

In working with younger children or severely traumatized
children, individual play therapy may be the modality of choice.
Intensive and individually focused therapy is absolutely vital to
help the abused child work through the severe trauma and to re-

duce the probability of perpetuating the abuse syndrome in the next generation, as often happens. In the following case example, the therapist was an Anglo female with considerable experience with Mexican Americans.

Alma, a 9-year-old Mexican American girl, was referred for individual therapy by the Child Protective Services after she had been severely physically abused by her stepfather, Javier, a Nicaraguan exile who had lived with the family for one year. The abuse occurred after Javier discovered Alma playing with his gun. He punished her brutally over a period of three days, breaking an arm and ribs and burning her palms by holding them over a stove burner.

Alma's hands were severely scarred, and she wore mittens throughout her therapy to keep scar tissue from constricting the extension of her fingers. Alma was seen for thirty individual play therapy sessions over a year.

When Alma started therapy, she was extremely frightened and shy, spoke little, initiated little, and had difficulty following through in her play. The therapist took a nondirective approach to the play therapy, participating as directed by Alma and asking questions or reflecting feelings as seemed appropriate. Early play involved issues of authority, submission, and self-assertion. For example, Alma played games in which she held the position of authority (such as teacher or therapist) and told the therapist to pretend she was Alma. In the process of therapy, she moved from an "abusive authority/submissive other" stance to a more "moderate authority/assertive other" stance, appearing to model the behavior of the therapist. In her anger with Javier, she initially denied that she was Hispanic, viewing her mother and Javier as Hispanic and as "bad" and not wanting to identify with them. The therapist pointed out that her natural father, whom she liked, was also Hispanic (a fact she sometimes denied), and both her therapist and her Anglo foster mother encouraged Alma to be proud of her Hispanic heritage. She gradually became more comfortable with her ethnicity, no longer appearing to equate this with abusiveness.

In treatment, she frequently reenacted a drama in which

she and the therapist alternated roles between a vicious, devouring wolf and a terror-stricken child. As Alma gradually developed the ability to tolerate and manage these powerful feelings, she also began using realistic problem-solving strategies in which she called the police or found other ways to escape or thwart her persecutors. Notable in these dramas, in contrast to Alma's early play, was her ability to organize and carry through a play theme involving two persons and her comfort with assertiveness in both organizing and playing the parts. Around this same time, Alma began attempting to do chin-ups on the clothing bar in the closet, trying to get stronger despite the pain to her scarred hands.

Generally, by the time of termination of therapy, Alma's fear and anger appeared to be at manageable levels. She was more cognitively organized and more able to problem-solve. She had internalized an image of a nurturant adult who was moderate in her use of power and authority, and she had developed a healthy self-esteem that included acceptance of her ethnicity and enabled her to be assertive about getting her needs met and protecting herself.

Conclusions and Future Directions

It behooves clinicians to operate from a philosophical framework that presumes that nothing about a culture is sacred or exempt from clinical and adaptational analysis. For example, I myself consider traditional Mexican American norms that confine women to the status of lesser human beings to be dysfunctional and to be targets for change within psychotherapy. Differential (and discriminatory) socialization of Mexican American boys and girls is completely antithetical to successful living in a highly complex technological society that requires the full talents of all persons, regardless of gender. I make this personal value orientation explicit to my patients, "when the time is right." Some patients actively oppose this position, and their view is respected; others respond favorably and enthusiastically.

Along these same lines, Rogler, Malgady, Costantino, and

Blumenthal (1987) state, "It is our contention that when therapy modalities are modified to address the needs of Hispanic clients, the adapted therapy need not isomorphically reflect the client's cultural characteristics" (p. 569). Isomorphic reinforcement of cultural traits by therapists implies that those traits are adaptive, while departures from this position imply that some cultural traits serve as an obstacle to therapy and that acculturation to the values and norms of American society is an additional and valid standard of adjustment. The ultimate aim of psychotherapy should be relief from psychological distress and the adaptation of Mexican Americans to American society in such a way that ethnic identity and pride are not negated or diminished.

The clinical case examples offered in this chapter suggest that the therapeutic process can be facilitated greatly when the therapist is bilingual and bicultural. Unfortunately, there are not enough professionally trained bilingual and bicultural therapists to meet the mental health needs of the ever-growing Mexican American population. It is highly unlikely that this situation will change dramatically in the near future. However, there are other options: Non–Mexican American, monolingual clinicians serving a Mexican American clientele can be trained, both didactically and experientially, through supervision and consultation with bilingual and bicultural Mexican American clinicians, to work more effectively with their clients. The sociocultural and socioeconomic gulf between the Mexican American client and non–Mexican American clinician may not be eradicated entirely, but it can be bridged by education and training and by providing clinicians with experience in culturally sensitive research and service delivery (Acosta, Yamamoto, and Evans, 1982; Malgady and Rogler, 1987).

Priorities should be refocused to include a renewed commitment to primary prevention programs. Low-income, predominantly Spanish-speaking, undocumented Mexican Americans are at high risk for the development of general health and mental health problems. The need for early intervention with this group is clearly established. Fortunately, there already exists a model for such a primary prevention program—the Houston Parent-Child Development Center (H-PCDC), as reported by Johnson and Walker (forthcoming). The H-PCDC has been in operation since the early seventies, and its success in the area of prevention has been impressive. This center has had its greatest impact on conduct disorders, problems that clinicians have found the most difficult to treat. These children tend to go on to more antisocial acts in adolescence and as adults. Prevention, as described in the H-PCDC program, is not coercive, but it frees the individual to participate harmoniously and autonomously in society.

Finally, in an excellent paper that offers an epidemiological perspective on the mental health of individuals of Mexican origin, Roberts (1986) proposes that future research efforts should include rigorous, large-scale epidemiological studies of the mental health of Mexican-origin children and adolescents. "First, and foremost, if we are interested in primary prevention of diseases that are the product of lifelong interactions of risk factors, the earlier such preventive efforts begin, the likelier they will have an impact. Both the design of intervention programs and the assessment of their impact require knowledge of incidence, prevalence, and putative risk factors in the target population" (p. 14).

In conclusion, I urge all clinicians working directly with Mexican American children and adolescents and their families to publish and share their clinical experiences. In this way, we can begin the important process of dialogue around the critical issues of providing these clients with the effective and culturally sensitive clinical services they need.

Note

1. The demographic profile of Mexican Americans is based on primary data from the following U.S. Bureau of the Census documents: *The Hispanic Population in the United States: March 1986 and 1987* (advance report), Series P-20, No. 416; *Persons of Spanish Origin in the United States: March 1985*, Series P-20, No. 403, Dec. 1985; *Persons of Spanish Origin by State: 1980 Census of Population, Supplementary Report PC80-S1-7*, Aug. 1982; and *Condition of Hispanics in America Today*, 1980.

References

Acosta, F. X., and Sheehan, J. "Preferences Toward Mexican-American and Anglo-American Psychotherapists." *Journal of Consulting and Clinical Psychology*, 1976, *44*, 272–279.

Acosta, F. X., Yamamoto, J., and Evans, L. A. *Effective Psychotherapy for Low-Income and Minority Patients.* New York: Plenum, 1982.

Adams, E. H. "An Overview of Drug Use in the United States and Along the U.S.-Mexico Border." Paper presented at the U.S.-Mexico Border Public Health Association Conference, Monterrey, Mexico, Apr. 28, 1986.

Aiello, J., and Jones, W. "Field Study of the Proxemic Behavior of Young School Children in Three Subcultural Groups." *Journal of Personality and Social Psychology*, 1971, *19*, 351–356.

Baca Zinn, M. "Urban Kinship and Midwest Chicano Families: Review and Reformulation." Paper presented at annual meeting of the Western Social Science Association, Denver, Colo., Apr. 23, 1977.

Baca Zinn, M. "Employment and Education of Mexican-American Women: The Interplay of Modernity and Ethnicity in Eight Families." *Harvard Educational Review*, 1980, *50* (1), 47–62.

Burruel-Gonzalez, G. "The Definitional Process Among Mexican Americans and Its Effect on Utilization of Mental Health Services." Unpublished doctoral dissertation, Graduate School of Social Work, University of Denver, 1975.

Chavez, E., Beauvais, F., and Oetting, E. R. "Drug Use by Small-Town Mexican-American Youth: A Pilot Study." *Hispanic Journal of Behavioral Sciences*, 1986, *8*, 243–258.

Cromwell, R., and Ruiz, R. A. "The Myth of Macho Dominance in Decision-Making Within Mexican and Chicano Families." *Hispanic Journal of Behavioral Sciences*, 1979, *1* (4), 355–373.

deAnda, D. "The Hispanic Adolescent Mother: Assessing Risk in Relation to Stress and Social Support." In W. A. Vega and M. R. Miranda (eds.), *Stress and Hispanic Mental Health: Re-*

lating Research to Service Delivery. Rockville, Md.: National Institute of Mental Health, 1985.

Falicov, C. J. "Mexican Families." In M. McGoldrick, J. K. Pearce, and J. Giordano (eds.), *Ethnicity and Family Therapy.* New York: Guilford Press, 1982.

Johnson, D. L., and Walker, T. "The Primary Prevention of Behavior Problems in Mexican-American Children." *American Journal of Community Psychology,* 1987, *15,* 375–385.

Karno, M., and Edgerton, R. B. "Perception of Mental Illness in a Mexican American Community." *Archives of General Psychiatry,* 1969, *20,* 233–238.

Keefe, S. E., Padilla, A. M., and Carlos, M. L. *Emotional Support Systems in Two Cultures: A Comparison of Mexican Americans and Anglo Americans.* Occasional Paper No. 7. Los Angeles: Spanish Speaking Mental Health Research Center, University of California at Los Angeles, 1978a.

Keefe, S. E., Padilla, A. M., and Carlos, M. L. "The Mexican-American Extended Family as an Emotional Support System." In J. M. Casas and S. E. Keefe (eds.), *Family and Mental Health in the Mexican-American Community.* Monograph No. 7. Los Angeles: Spanish Speaking Mental Health Research Center, University of California at Los Angeles, 1978b.

Keefe, S. E., Padilla, A. M., and Carlos, M. L. "The Mexican-American Extended Family as an Emotional Support System." *Human Organization,* 1979, *38,* 144–152.

LeVine, E. S., and Padilla, A. M. *Crossing Cultures in Therapy: Pluralistic Counseling for the Hispanic.* Pacific Grove, Calif.: Brooks/Cole, 1980.

Malgady, R. G., and Rogler, L. H. "Ethnocultural and Linguistic Bias in Mental Health Evaluations of Hispanics." *American Psychologist,* 1987, *42* (3), 228–234.

Mindel, C. H. "Extended Familism Among Urban Mexican Americans, Anglos, and Blacks." *Hispanic Journal of Behavioral Sciences,* 1980, *2* (1), 21–34.

Minuchin, S. *Families and Family Therapy.* Cambridge, Mass.: Harvard University Press, 1974.

Murillo, N. "The Mexican American Family." In N. W. Wagner

and M. J. Haug (eds.), *Chicanos: Social and Psychological Perspectives.* St. Louis: Mosby, 1971.

Padilla, A. M. "Pluralistic Counseling and Psychotherapy for Hispanic Americans." In A. J. Marsella and P. B. Pedersen (eds.), *Cross-Cultural Counseling and Psychotherapy.* Elmsford, N.Y.: Pergamon Press, 1981.

Padilla, E. R., and others. "Inhalant, Marijuana and Alcohol Abuse Among Barrio Children and Adolescents." *International Journal of the Addictions,* 1979, *14,* 943–964.

Paz, O. *The Labyrinth of Solitude: Life and Thought in Mexico.* New York: Evergreen Books, 1961.

Ramirez, O., and Arce, C. H. "The Contemporary Chicano Family: An Empirically Based Review." In A. Baron, Jr. (ed.), *Explorations in Chicano Psychology.* New York: Praeger, 1981.

Roberts, R. E. "Prevalence of Psychological Distress Among Mexican Americans." *Journal of Health and Social Behavior,* 1980, *21,* 134–145.

Roberts, R. E. "An Epidemiologic Perspective on the Mental Health of People of Mexican Origin." Paper presented (under the auspices of the Hogg Foundation for Mental Health) at fifth Robert Lee Sutherland Seminar, San Antonio, Texas, Sept. 24–26, 1986.

Rogler, L. H., Malgady, R. G., Costantino, G., and Blumenthal, R. "What Do Culturally Sensitive Mental Health Services Mean? The Case of Hispanics." *American Psychologist,* 1987, *42* (6), 565–570.

Sena-Rivera, J. *La Familia Chicana as a Mental Health Resource: A Trigenerational Study of Four Mexican Descent Extended Families in the Michigan-Indiana-Illinois Region.* Advance report, Department of Sociology and Anthropology, University of Notre Dame, 1977.

Sena-Rivera, J. "Extended Kinship in the United States: Competing Models and the Case of La Familia Chicana." *Journal of Marriage and the Family,* 1979, *41,* 121–129.

Stoker, D. H., and Meadow, A. "Cultural Differences in Guidance Clinic Patients." *American Journal of Social Psychiatry,* 1974, *20,* 186–202.

Trankina, F. "Clinical Issues and Techniques in Working with Hispanic Children and Their Families." In G. J. Powell, J. Yamamoto, A. Romero, and A. Morales (eds.), *The Psychosocial Development of Minority Group Children.* New York: Brunner/Mazel, 1983.

Ybarra-Soriano, L. "Conjugal Role Relationships in the Chicano Family." Unpublished doctoral dissertation, Department of Sociology, University of California at Berkeley, 1977.

8

Puerto Rican Adolescents

Jaime E. Inclán
D. Gloria Herron

In order to present issues in the assessment and treatment of Puerto Rican adolescents from an ecologically oriented point of view, this chapter begins by providing a picture of the unique sociocultural experience of Puerto Ricans living on the United States mainland. Against this background, the experience of mainland Puerto Rican adolescents is highlighted, followed by special considerations in the psychosocial assessment process. The chapter concludes with a presentation of clinical considerations in ecologically oriented individual, group, and family therapy with these adolescents.

Demographic Data

The U.S. Bureau of the Census (1985) estimated that in 1985 there were 16.9 million Hispanics in the United States (excluding Puerto Rico). This represents 7.2 percent of the U.S. population. The largest subgroup of Hispanics is Mexican Americans (11.8 million), followed by Puerto Ricans (2.6 million). The increase of Puerto Ricans since the 1980 census was over 500,000, based on estimates of net movement of persons to and from Puerto Rico.

Puerto Ricans reside in every state, approximately 75 percent of them in urban areas. The highest concentrations are

251

found in New York and New Jersey (total of 61 percent) (Perez, 1985). In 1980 Puerto Ricans represented 14 percent of the total Hispanic population of the United States. However, in New York State they represented 59.4 percent of the state's Hispanic population of 1.7 million. Of New York City's 1.4 million Hispanics, 61.2 percent were Puerto Rican (Governor's Advisory Committee, 1985).

Almost 42 percent (260,000) of Puerto Rican families (or households of two or more people) lived below the poverty level in 1984, compared with 11.6 percent of the total population (U.S. Bureau of the Census, 1985). Of Puerto Rican families headed by females, 74.4 percent were below the poverty level. In 1984 the median family income of Puerto Ricans, $12,371, was the lowest of all Hispanic subgroups, because of such factors as family composition, educational level, and employment status of family members.

The Hispanic population is younger than the non-Hispanic population; median ages are 25 years for the former and 31.9 years for the latter, with the difference due to higher fertility levels among Hispanics. The median age of Puerto Ricans is 24.3 years, with 10.6 percent under age 5 and 26.5 percent between the ages of 5 and 17. Only an estimated 2.7 percent of Puerto Ricans are over 65 (U.S. Bureau of the Census, 1985).

In 1985 the mean family size among Puerto Ricans was 3.62 persons, compared with 3.23 in the general population and 3.18 for all non-Hispanics. Families of three persons or more accounted for 59.6 percent of all families, 58.5 percent of non-Hispanic families, and 75.6 percent of Puerto Rican families. Further, among Puerto Ricans, a three-member family was very likely to be a mother with two children, rather than two parents with one child, since 44 percent of Puerto Rican families were headed by a female with no male head of household present. This is in sharp contrast to 16.2 percent in the general population and 15.7 percent among non-Hispanics.

In 1985 only 46 percent of Puerto Ricans older than 25 years had completed high school (compared with 74 percent in the total U.S. population); 13 percent had completed less than five years of school. The median number of school years completed was 11.2. Of Puerto Rican males 16 years and over, 15 percent were unemployed, compared with 7.8 percent of the total population. The figures for females were 13.3 percent and 7.4 percent, respectively.

Population projections used by the Census Bureau (Spencer, 1986) are based on varying estimates of fertility, life expectancy, and yearly net immigration. Projections for the Hispanic population in the year 2000, based on 1982 population figures, vary from 23.1 million to 31.2 million. The Census Bureau projects that Hispanics, who represented about 7 percent of the U.S. population in 1982, will account for over 9 percent of the population in the year 2000.

Epidemiological Data

The majority of mainland Puerto Ricans reside in the greater metropolitan New York area. It is primarily this group that will be the focus of this chapter. Unfortunately, despite the size of the mainland Puerto Rican population and its unique sociocultural problems, data on mental health issues are scarce.

One of the few studies of Puerto Rican children using mental health clinics in the New York area was conducted by the Hispanic Research Center at Fordham University (Canino, Earley, and Rogler, 1980). This study was based on cases reported to the New York State Department of Mental Hygiene during the fiscal year 1976–77. Puerto Rican children under 13 years of age were represented in all fourteen of the most commonly indicated psychiatric problem categories. Among these 4,196 children, the percentages were as follows: antisocial attitudes, 5 percent; social withdrawal, 7 percent; dependency, 7 percent; speech articulation problems, 9 percent; sleep problems, 10 percent; depressed/inferiority, 11 percent; other physical problems, 15 percent; anger/belligerence, 16 percent; anxiety, fears, phobias, 17 percent; agitation/hyperactivity, 17 percent; social relations with other than family, 21 percent; social relations with family, 22 percent; inadequate intellectual development, 22 percent; social performance in school, 44 percent. In ten of these categories, percentages were higher for Puerto

Rican children than for White children. The investigators advise caution in interpreting these data owing to the tendency to underreport cases and the difficulties of cross-cultural diagnoses; nevertheless, it seems valid to conclude that Puerto Rican children in New York are overrepresented in a significant number of psychiatric categories.

In a more recent study of Hispanic ($N = 96$) and Black ($N = 53$) children seen at a New York City hospital outpatient clinic, Canino, Gould, Prupis, and Shaffer (1986) found the children to be experiencing high levels of stress and family problems, as well as physical disorders. For the Hispanic group, Spanish was predominantly spoken in the home, and a high percentage of the children's mothers were homemakers born outside the United States. Twenty-two symptoms were examined for both groups. In the five categories in which the two groups differed significantly, a higher proportion of Hispanics than Blacks had symptoms of morbid depression, fears and phobias, anxiety and panic, school refusal, and disturbances of relationships with other children. Thirty percent or more of the Hispanic children were represented in the following categories: withdrawal, disinhibited, disturbance of relationship with mother, disturbance of relationship with father, restlessness and fidgetiness, disobedience, and disturbance of sleeping.

Comprehensive epidemiological studies specific to the mental health of Puerto Rican adolescents are lacking, but clinical reports have begun to identify typical problems in this population. Hardy-Fanta and Montana (1982) describe the impact of migration on female Hispanic adolescents as manifesting itself as "either sexual or aggressive acting-out or as depressed withdrawal or excessive withdrawal or excessive conformity. . . . rebelliousness, poor school functioning, and impulsively established male-female relationships" (p. 352).

Social indexes provide additional information indirectly related to the mental health of Puerto Rican youth. In 1986 the New York City Mayor's Commission on Hispanic Concerns reported that 47 percent of Puerto Rican households had incomes of less than $7,500. Almost one third of Hispanic families had dependent children under age 18, and 20.5 percent of the

100,000 registrants in the city's Child Health Program were Puerto Rican. In that program, the most common problems were iron deficiency anemia, growth problems, asthma, and English language difficulties. With the economic reality of Puerto Rican mothers needing to work outside the home, unable to afford child care, and leaving children unattended, accidents were found to be the single largest cause of death for Puerto Rican children under the age of 16 years.

Nationwide, 13 percent of adult and adolescent AIDS cases reported from June 1981 to November 1987 were Hispanic. During the same period, 23 percent of the reported cases in children under age 13 were Hispanic. Of the adult and adolescent cases with the single risk factor of intravenous drug abuse, 35 percent were Hispanic, compared with 5 percent who were White and not Hispanic (Centers for Disease Control, 1987).

Birth statistics for 1980 and 1981 indicate that 32 percent of American-born Puerto Rican women giving birth were under age 20 and 50 percent were unmarried. These data compare with 15 percent teenage mothers and 20 percent unmarried mothers in the total population (Ventura and Taffel, 1985).

Migration and Transculturation

Migration from Puerto Rico to the United States mainland began slowly early in the 20th century. Mass migration did not begin until after World War II. In 1967 there was a net migration of 26,000 people, but a total of 3 million people had actually moved between Puerto Rico and the mainland. By 1970 the mainland Puerto Rican population was 1.5 million, about half of the island population, and New York City had a larger Puerto Rican population than San Juan, the island's largest city. There was negative migration again from 1972 to 1977. Growth of the mainland population continues and is now a function of early marriages and high fertility rates (Sowell, 1981).

Migration served the interests of capitalism in Puerto Rico as well as in the United States. In Puerto Rico, it served to alleviate the structural problem of massive unemployment. In the United States, the immigration of Puerto Rican workers, like that of previous ethnic groups, helped to keep wages low. Puerto Ricans, migrating in search of job opportunities, assumed low-level jobs that nobody else wanted, with correspondingly meager salaries.

An understanding of the identity conflict experienced by Puerto Ricans in the United States is facilitated by a developmental evolutionary view of their migration and transculturation. The authors' observations in this regard coincide with those of others who have studied various ethnic groups and of family theorists (Bowen, 1976) who contend that change takes place over the generations—in particular, that it takes at least three generations for substantive change to be effected. In this evolutionary progression, the second and third generations, currently the numerical majority of Puerto Ricans, experience the most profound difficulties.

The first generation tends to uphold its culture of origin and values when in the new host culture. For Puerto Ricans, these traditional values include a family structure with very strong ties and great importance placed on the extended family. There is also a *compadrazgo* system of godparents and coparents. The nuclear family is patriarchal. The role of the husband is to protect and provide. *Machismo* is a virtue that encompasses courage and romanticism. The wife's primary role is to hold the family together. *Personalism* upholds the dignity of the individual. It calls for the development of inner qualities to attain self-respect and gain the respect of others. Children are taught the importance of respect and the proper way to relate to others on the basis of age, sex, and social class. Aggression is to be controlled. Socially sanctioned channels for expression of anger include somatization, alcohol consumption, verbal threats, and loud discussions. Catholicism is the predominant religion, and the individual experiences a personal relationship with God. Many adhere to *spiritism*, which is a belief in good and evil spirits that can affect one's life. Time orientation is in the present, and "being" is valued above "doing" and "having" (Garcia-Preto, 1982).

First-generation migrants exhibit predominantly traditional values. In the new host environment, the family experiences culture shock, to which the first generation reacts by attempting to make the family a tighter unit and by holding more strongly to those values. As a response to this culture clash, "barrios" come into being where the native culture is re-created and preserved in the new environment.

The second and third generations, starting in adolescence and preadolescence, must cope with and adapt to the language, culture, and values of the new environment (Inclán, 1985). These constitute groundbreaking efforts where stress, failure, and defeat are not uncommon. In clinical practice, many of the families and youths seen are victims of this culture clash.

At the macrosystemic level, there is a dearth of Puerto Rican institutions, business enterprises, labor unions, and political, cultural, and community groups that can reach out to this upcoming generation. In this vacuum, to whom can youth turn for role models, for material assistance? There are few apprenticeship possibilities that are easily reached through familial or community ties. Some can find opportunities outside their primary group, but then what are the consequences for family cohesion and personal identity?

Successful utilization of out-of-group resources implies a process of acculturation, the development of new and different sets of values and orientations, and an integration of new and old cultural values. Frequently this involves a stressful distancing from one's family, which, lacking the framework to understand the desirability of the individual's movement, is likely to devalue and censure this development. For example, although many first-generation parents enjoy and take pride in their adolescent children's development of occupational and economic competence, they also find it difficult to accept the resocialization, the new values, and the behavior changes associated with success and acculturation. First-generation parents often interpret their children's acculturated life-style as less caring of them, more selfish, and reflecting a preference for peers over family (Inclán, 1985).

At the family microsystemic level, similar dilemmas ensue. The parents present a model of success through nonassertive, loyal compliance that, they trust, will be rewarded by the benevolence and appreciation of superiors, usually "the boss" (Inclán, 1979). These values, adaptive in an agrarian, highly structured, and hierarchal society, are not conducive to success in the industrial, competitive, impersonal environment that exists in American urban centers. To compete in this society, young people must experiment with behaviors for which they lack role models and for which the parents, primary guidance figures, cannot provide support. Again, the subjective experience for the adolescent is one not of progression and support, but of discontinuity and isolation. A compromise for these youth often involves modulating the pace of acculturation over the generations in order to maintain the necessary familial connection.

This process of value transformation influences the frequency and pattern of use of mental health services. Although there is disagreement on the prevalence of psychiatric symptoms in the Puerto Rican community, there is general agreement that this population underutilizes services (Daykin, 1980). A recent nationwide report (Centers for Health Education and Social Systems Studies, 1985) provides epidemiological data obtained during the decade 1970–1980. Hispanics were found to underutilize mental health facilities, with the exception of inpatient use of public general hospitals. It appears that when symptoms are severe, the likelihood that mental health facilities will be used is greater. Less-than-severe symptoms are customarily dealt with in the family or within an informal support network. In addition, structural barriers may discourage use of service institutions unless the need is great. These barriers include geographical inaccessibility of services, ethnic and racial discrimination, language, and clinicians' unfamiliarity with the cultural diversity of Hispanic patients.

Rodriguez (1987) reviewed the literature on service utilization by Hispanic, Black, and White residents in a low-income section of New York City. Results of the study supported two competing theories used to explain underutilization. The barrier theory suggests that people may want and need a service, but their cultural values render bureaucratic agencies unattractive. Rodriguez found that acculturated Hispanics were more likely to use services than the unacculturated. The alternative-resource theory assumes that people want and need help but turn to providers in their own natural support system. Among Hispanics and Blacks, it appeared that the support network encouraged utilization of formal services for serious psychiatric problems and viewed the informal system as an alternative for those with less serious symptoms.

Issues in Assessment

A valid psychological assessment of Puerto Rican adolescents requires an understanding of relevant sociocultural issues. The experience of these adolescents often differs significantly from that of mainstream White American adolescents, and needless to say, there is wide individual variation among Puerto Rican adolescents. However, one can begin to conceptualize the experience of these adolescents as a series of interrelated "clashes"— that is, cultural, generational, socioeconomic, and developmental clashes.

The cultural clash has its roots in the political relationship between Puerto Rico and the United States. Until 1917, Puerto Rico had been a colony of the United States. When citizenship was conferred on Puerto Ricans, the questions of cultural and political identity arose for the population. As American citizens, Puerto Ricans have voting privileges, benefit from entitlement programs, and have ease of travel between the mainland and the island. However, they have no congressional representatives, speak a different language, maintain a different culture, uphold different values, and are targets of constant racial and political discrimination. The question of political identity— Puerto Rican or American—is an ongoing dilemma. For adolescents, the juxtaposition of these two contrasting cultures renders self-definition an especially difficult process. The separation/ integration conflict on the political level indirectly influences the conflicting cultural pulls on adolescents.

The generational clash is reflected in the schism between first-generation parents and their offspring, particularly adolescents. Moral standards and cultural practices of the parent generation differ greatly from those of American adolescents, who rapidly become the reference group for Puerto Rican youth on the mainland. Sex-role differences, attitudes toward sexuality, and standards for drug and alcohol use are widely discrepant between the parental and the adolescent generations, rendering parental guidance and supervision ineffective. Peer pressures and the culture of the streets and the ghetto gain important influence over the adolescent's behavior and development. Whereas the generational clash is evident in many subgroups within the United States, it is intensified for Puerto Ricans by socioeconomic realities.

The socioeconomic clash refers to the contiguity of wealthy, affluent, mainstream communities and poor, disadvantaged ghetto communities. This clash incorporates Lewis's (1965) controversial concept of a "culture of poverty"[1] that coexists and competes as a framework for identity and success with the mainstream culture, which often reflects the aspirations of first-generation parents.

At the level of the individual, the "culture of poverty" includes a primary orientation to the present time mode, failure to postpone gratification, a tendency toward action and impulsivity, a sense of fate as predetermined and unchangeable, resentment of authority, a sense of being blamed, a feeling of aloneness and an inability to trust others, an underemphasis on rigor, discipline, and perseverance, and a tendency toward dependency. For Puerto Rican adolescents, the underlying fears and concerns are often characterized by this query: "Why compete and struggle through school when I see no light at the end of the tunnel?"

When working with Puerto Rican adolescents, therapists need to be aware of their own values and experiences and how these may influence their approach. Whereas for therapists the issue might present itself as *how* to succeed in the mainstream world, for their adolescent clients the issue may be a more basic one of "*Should* I aim for the mainstream world as a framework for success?"

The choice is not an easy one for the adolescent who is cognizant of the barriers to success for Puerto Ricans in mainstream society. The culture of poverty offers a here-and-now reward and access to status and commodities that might otherwise be out of reach. In our experience, recognizing and dealing with the dilemmas of this "choice" enable therapists to engage and more effectively treat Puerto Rican adolescents, who, consequently, experience their therapist as respectful and understanding of them.

It is also against this backdrop of the "culture of poverty" that therapists must operate when working with parents of Puerto Rican adolescents. In a middle-class culture, a therapist may view adolescence as a time for parents to relax their guidance and control in order to allow the children to find their way in society. However, in a community where the culture of poverty prevails, the therapist would need to be sympathetic with, and at times supportive of, the parents' demand for greater vigilance and control. At this juncture, concerned parents often call for military school, enlistment in the army, relocation to Puerto Rico, or other measures that may clash with a middle-class-oriented therapist's values. The therapist must be able to understand this request as an attempt to thwart the attractions of the "culture of poverty."

The fourth clash involves the process of individual development. Adolescence, as a discrete developmental stage, is a relatively recent concept (Erikson, 1963). This concept has been incorporated into the American ethos and is characteristic of a modern industrial society. However, for an agricultural economy, as Puerto Rico was in the 1960s, an apprenticeship model of passage into adulthood is functional and adaptive. Apprenticeship models of adolescence foster family cohesion and devalue individuality. When adolescence is conceived as a period of developing individualism and distancing from the family of origin, it is counterproductive to the labor demands of an agrarian economic system developed within a capitalist framework. The family's survival and economic growth require that the children stay within the family boundary and expand the productivity already achieved by the previous generation. Although Puerto Rican migrants live and work in the United States, and especially in its urban centers, they have not fully accepted the model of adolescence that is adaptive in this context.

Figure 8.1 presents the agrarian and industrial patterns of transition into adulthood. We have found this model helpful in

Figure 8.1. Agrarian and Industrial Patterns of Transition to Adulthood.

understanding the difficulties often present in the therapy of Puerto Rican adolescents and their families. First-generation parents operate within a framework that considers offspring to be children, regardless of age or responsibilities, until they become adults. Adulthood is usually marked by marriage or leaving home, whichever comes first. Viewed as children, adolescents are expected to subordinate their views and interests to those of the parents, to show respect, and to follow the guidelines of behavior and etiquette that the parents provide. Therapists who are unaware of the social and historical roots of this point of view often find themselves quickly and simplistically blaming the parents for being overly controlling and restrictive with their adolescents. This "blame the parent" position can be exacerbated, as pointed out earlier, when the therapist fails to recognize the larger social dynamics of the ghetto. Puerto Rican adolescents reared in the United States and exposed to its socializing influences begin to expect and demand an "adolescence," with its freedoms. This is an especially stressful demand to make for female Puerto Rican adolescents, whose requests are viewed within the cultural double standard that encourages sexual activity and increased freedom for the males and abstinence and overprotectiveness of the females.

Puerto Rican adolescents of both sexes are often referred for treatment when the pattern of "irresponsibility," as defined by traditional norms, has escalated. At these times, a vicious, mutually reinforcing cycle between repressive parents and acting-out youth becomes entrenched.

Treatment Modalities with Puerto Rican Adolescents

In this section we present ecologically oriented individual, group, and family treatment considerations. The interventions we describe are based on existing theory and techniques but are modified in order to be more relevant to Puerto Rican adolescents and their families. Specifically, values, migration history, and sociocultural factors are introduced as significant intervening variables in treatment. This expanded point of view includes a historical and social-systems perspective of problems. Furthermore, it uses and manipulates these variables for therapeutic effect. This approach to the understanding and treatment of problems most closely approximates the ecological model of therapy proposed by Auerswald (1968, 1987).

The Context of Treatment. In work with Hispanic adolescents and families, the treatment setting is an important factor that can facilitate engagement in treatment. The Roberto Clemente Family Guidance Center was developed with this consideration in mind. This center is an outpatient public mental health facility that operates under the direction of a public health hospital in New York City. The center has its own storefront in the midst of the Hispanic community.

The center's characteristics include the following:

• *Culturally sensitive care.* Operationally, this means two things. First, the physical plant itself reflects the community it serves. Maps of Caribbean countries and Central and South America, as well as Latino posters and community-donated artwork reflecting the diversity and richness of the Hispanic cultures, adorn its walls. The center is named after a Puerto Rican hero, Roberto Clemente. Second, the staff at the center reflects the Hispanic community. All members are bilingual and bicultural. Currently, out of a total staff of twelve, seven nationalities are represented.

• *Systems-oriented therapy.* The general orientation of services at the center is an ecological-systems model, with emphasis placed on the family. The issues that patients present are analyzed and treated within the context of changing culture, history, family values, and multisystem involvements.

• *Community orientation.* Not only is the center in the midst of the Hispanic community, but it is a participant in consortia and community networks. It has offered training opportunities for others in the community, participates in street and health fairs, and is continually active in community life.

• *Training and education.* Through its internship, externship, special seminar, field placements, and volunteer programs, the center provides training for Hispanic and other professionals who wish to further their skills in this area of work. The benefit is mutual, since new input and creativity are in turn made available to the center.

Although the concept of the "treatment setting" has often been ignored, especially in work with Hispanics and other minorities, the atmosphere, character, and staff of a center that serves poor and minority clients greatly influence its utilization rate.

Individual Treatment. Psychotherapy with poor Hispanic adolescents must reflect an awareness of the four intersecting clashes discussed earlier, as the presenting mental health problems are often embedded in complex sociocultural contexts. Immigrant status, cultural differences, and consuming poverty combine to isolate Puerto Ricans from mainstream society. Economically impoverished Puerto Rican adolescents recoil from integration into mainstream society, attempting to avoid the psychological disequilibrium associated with cultural conflict and with juxtaposing the familiar with the unfamiliar. However, this integration of the old with the new is the underpinning of psychological intervention and guides such issues as the nature of the setting, the choice of therapists, and the content of therapy.

At the Roberto Clemente Center, the physical setting embodies this concept. Maps, flags, and artwork, depicting different historical eras and cultures, convey the notion that the world is complex and varied and that one's reality can be set within a larger geographical, cultural, and historical perspective. Similarly, the center's therapists, though all bilingual and bicultural, are of different nationalities and social classes. Inherent in this staff composition is the potential for dissension and conflict as well as identification with the comfortable and familiar. This balance of the old and the new is often an objective of the therapeutic intervention. For example, Puerto Rican adolescents are more likely to reject the introduction of new ideas, values, or behaviors if they feel that their current ecological reality is not understood or validated by the therapist. Two examples from actual therapy situations serve to illustrate this point.

In the first case, premature termination of treatment occurred after the second interview with Eric, an 18-year-old Puerto Rican adolescent. Examination of the therapeutic interaction revealed that the therapist, aware of Eric's involvement in lucrative yet illegal activity, had failed to understand the socioeconomic realities of the youth and his family and was ignorant of the attractions of the ghetto's underground economy. Instead, he had engaged Eric in a mild-mannered dialogue about the benefits of returning to school and using education as a tool to attain future economic sufficiency and autonomy. Clearly, the therapist's agenda was strikingly remote from the realities of the adolescent. Without identification with the client's realities, interjection of new strategies may be futile.

In a second, somewhat similar case, the therapist successfully engaged Ricardo, a 16-year-old Puerto Rican known to be involved in highly profitable, illicit street business. The therapist engaged Ricardo in a thorough exploration of the ghetto subculture, of the means to quick money, of the difficulty of resisting peer pressures, of the lack of rewards that Ricardo's father had experienced after twenty-two years of working two forty-hour jobs, of the racism and institutional discrimination that impede the success of minorities and the poor, of the bankruptcy of the community political leadership, and so on. This acknowledgment became the foundation for a therapeutic relationship that would eventually permit the introduction of new ideas and more constructive strategies for helping Ricardo to negotiate within society.

Therapists who work within this framework are encouraged to be active in relation to their clients, not only as role models but also as bridges between the familiar and the new.

The clinical example of Sara and Noel, a young Puerto Rican couple, will highlight this process.

The presenting problem was that Noel had threatened Sara with physical abuse and Sara had threatened to divorce Noel. Penetrating beneath the presenting problem, the therapist observed the marked values differences and cultural polarizations in this couple's relationship. Noel maintained very traditional Puerto Rican values, while Sara was equally entrenched in American middle-class values.

The therapy proceeded first as couples therapy, then individual therapy, and finally reconvened as marital therapy. The couples' therapist facilitated a process of problem redefinition that enabled the blame and frustration to be shifted from the individuals to the process of acculturation. This was a first step toward diffusing the potential for violence. Individual therapy, with same-sex therapists, focused on the process of acculturation and the differences in level of acculturation and values transformation between the spouses. After eleven individual sessions with the husband and fourteen with the wife, the therapists reconvened the marital therapy. The couple reported symptom relief and increased understanding of themselves and each other.

This case underscores the role of the therapist as a bridge between the old and the new. The female therapist assisted the wife in crossing the bridge to the "old" set of values, while the male therapist helped the husband consider the "new" values set.

Group Therapy. The center's group therapy program adheres to an educational psychotherapy model, based on the assumption that migrant minority group populations need information and education as well as therapy. Oftentimes the clients' emotional problems are exacerbated by serious problems of living and real-life experiences. In this sense, the mental health professional is viewed not only as a therapist but also as an educator, adviser, and advocate who assists clients in dealing with individuals and agencies. Such multidimensional intervention requires that therapists be familiar with the real-life situation of their clients, that they use an active, directive therapeutic stance, which has been shown to be effective with this population, and that they divide therapy into time-limited segments (Acosta, Yamamoto, and Evans, 1982).

The educational psychotherapy group for adolescents is a time-limited group experience. Each of the ten ninety-minute sessions focuses on a particular theme: (1) introduction and getting acquainted, (2) family and independence, (3) sexuality, (4) cultural identity, (5) school issues, (6) peers and peer pressure, (7) racism and discrimination, (8) jobs and job interviewing, (9) alcohol and drugs, and (10) self-revelation, trust, and therapy. During the first half of each session, the therapist presents selected stimulus materials, such as films, on the session theme. An unstructured discussion follows this guided presentation. Objectives of this group format include "breaking the ice" to facilitate group exchange and discussion, providing concrete information, generating a shared data base for group members, normalizing contextualization of feelings, and facilitating engagement in ongoing therapy. Highlights from an actual group session will illustrate this process.

Before we developed the group program, issues of sexuality were particularly problematic in individual therapy with adolescents. Clinic therapists reported that the adolescents professed to know all about sex but wanted to share nothing. Ambivalence toward this topic was quite prominent. Sexuality was selected as the topic for Session 3 of the group program. Presentation of a film or video proved very effective in opening the discussion. Group members were able to focus on the film and talk about sexuality without experiencing the anxiety and resistance previously associated with personal disclosure. It was also clear that, contrary to their professed knowledge, there existed information lacunae, which the film addressed directly and indirectly, making subsequent discussion possible. Some members, typified by one young female, found great relief in normalization and contextualization of feelings about sexuality. This 15-year-old Puerto Rican teenager, Rosa, identified most with the feelings of guilt, isolation, and shame portrayed in the film. Until she viewed the film, Rosa had felt blemished and alone among her peers in having engaged in particular sexual acts. Group discussion revealed she was not alone in having had these experiences or in feeling inadequate because of them.

Most important, however, was the group discussion that followed the film. Two general themes surfaced, which the group discussed intensely and with little guidance from the group leaders. One theme can be described as a group recalibration of the biological, peer, and social pressures for and against sexual behavior. What males and females desire, differences between short-term and long-term effects of sexual activity on acceptance and esteem, questions of responsibility versus allocation of blame, feedback relative to peer perceptions of sexually active youngsters, and reactions to such perceptions were among the issues discussed.

The other important theme of the discussion was the adolescent/parental dynamics around questions of emerging sexuality. Surprisingly, when in a group context, the adolescents were able to verbalize explicitly an understanding of changing values between their parents' generation and their own. More challenging was the question of what to do about the differences. The group was divided between those who opted for "respect" for the parents and accommodation to their values and experiences and those who posited the need to act in accordance with individual beliefs and contemporary values. Their belief was that the parents needed to accommodate to them and the new morality. Rather than identifying a specific right or wrong position, the therapists highlighted and endorsed the group's framing of the problems within a context of familial and evolving values.

The ten-session educational psychotherapy group experience is designed to be a complete program in itself; however, it may also serve as an introduction to and preparation for continued therapy. Following the ten-session program, the adolescents are offered the opportunity to continue group treatment in an ongoing group. Adolescents who choose to continue in group therapy often make use of and refer to the more structured experience of the educational psychotherapy group. Thus, an added advantage of the educational psychotherapy group is the minimizing of differences in therapeutic experience among participants in ongoing group therapy.

Ecologically Oriented Family Therapy. The family therapy literature includes some references to treatment issues in work with Puerto Rican families (Garcia-Preto, 1982; Inclán, 1985). In this section we discuss three issues of importance in treating poor Puerto Rican adolescents in the context of their families: value differences, the importance of siblings, and questions of role hierarchy.

Although all families experience value conflicts between the parent and child generations, this clash of values is exacerbated in poor migrant families and becomes most intense at adolescence (Inclán, 1985). This added stress for migrant families must be understood by the therapists who treat them.

When working with Puerto Rican adolescents and their families, therapists have found the technique of "cultural reframe" useful (Falicov and Karrer, 1984). In this technique the experience or demand that a parent or adolescent makes is analyzed in relation to the cultural values that constitute the background for the demand or expectation. For example, a mother's request that her daughter interact less frequently with peers is viewed as expressing a value that the family takes priority over the individual. The adolescent's demand for greater peer contact is viewed as expressing a value of individuality over family. Each value is understood to be functional, or adaptive, within its social context: The traditional value of the family over the individual is implicit in the mother's definition of the situation, while the middle-class American value of the individual above the group is implicit in the adolescent's request (Inclán, 1985).

Cultural reframe allows one to shift the focus of blame from the person to the acculturation process, which places different demands on the parent and adolescent generations. Contextualization of the problem is achieved when blame of the other has been dissipated or transferred to blame of the acculturation process as it relates to adolescent expectations. Once this is attained, the therapist may proceed to the next stage of therapy, which involves presenting an objective and impartial model for family progression through the stages of adolescence. This model is based on the process of exchange and negotiation between parent and adolescent, for greater freedom, trust, and responsibility (Haley, 1980). For most families with adolescents, this is the normal developmental task, and it often needs clarification and therapeutic assistance. As discussed earlier, the Puerto Rican parent may view adolescence and its associated freedoms quite differently, making modifications of treatment necessary.

For example, in the family treatment of Carmen, a 15-year-old Puerto Rican girl who was angry and at odds with her parents, the therapist, through individual and family meetings, was able to sustain the girl's responsible behavior (no truancy or staying out beyond the agreed time) for a two-month period. Following this, the therapist supported Carmen in her "earned" request for greater freedom. Although the parents resisted at first, discussions resulted in permission for her to stay out later on weekend nights. At the same time, the rule governing exchange of privileges and responsibilities was further clarified and reinforced. Although Carmen observed the guidelines the first weekend, she failed to do so on the second one. As a result, the therapist insisted (to parents who were now, ironically, resistant) that a temporary curtailment of her new curfew privilege was indicated according to the previously agreed-on rule guiding the exchange of responsibilities and privileges. This second stage of therapy, described by Haley (1980), is useful in work with families where adolescent problems are present.

Because first-generation parents have limited ability to serve as a bridge between the old and new cultures, sibling relationships are very important in poor Puerto Rican migrant families. This is an underutilized resource in family therapy in general and in the therapy of minority adolescents in particular. Family dynamics and role distributions are usually such that some family member is able to differentiate from the family of origin earlier and/or more successfully than others. Often young women feel greater pressure to remain at home and help out than male Puerto Rican adolescents. The sibling who has been able to differentiate successfully from the family of origin can be enlisted in family therapy to serve as a bridge between the parent's and children's generations, as in the following case example.

In one Puerto Rican family of very traditional working-class parents who were distraught over and unable to cope with their son, Eluid's, use of drugs, the therapist used the older brother, Tomas, as a broker between the parental and young adolescent worlds and values. The parents, who operated within a very closed-system definition of family and trust, were helped to surrender surveillance and guidance functions to Tomas. This move detriangulated the conflict and provided a successful approach to dealing with Eluid's drug problem.

Therapists need to be aware of the importance of siblings in family therapy and move beyond their initial reluctance to include well-differentiated siblings in treatment. Although these siblings often live elsewhere, are asymptomatic, hold jobs, and have families and other pressing commitments, they remain loyal to the family and tend to respond readily when an appeal is made for their assistance.

Marta, age 17, had become maladaptively entrenched in the role of executive of the family system, a role she had assumed as a result of the hospitalization of the male head of household and her mother's very limited social competence. Exploration revealed that an older brother, Ernesto, had moved out of the home but maintained good family ties. Efforts to engage him in the therapy were successful, and Ernesto was instrumental in helping his younger sister reconnect with developmental tasks, issues, and priorities. Together, they were able to redefine self and family needs, as well as restructure family affairs so that family functioning could be maintained *and* Marta's autonomy and differentiation pursued.

Similarly, work with poor migrant Puerto Rican families suggests that traditional approaches to the question of hierarchy within the family be reviewed. In these families the adolescents often have a greater mastery of the language, behaviors, and social mores of the new culture. Thus, they have sources of power within the society. A therapist who focuses on the family without considering its acculturative context may operate within a family model that assumes a generational hierarchy that is actually contradicted by the social and familial reality.

Family therapy with poor Puerto Rican adolescents and their families may require a more flexible and operational, as opposed to generational, basis of role relationships within the family. Although it is standard to support generational hierarchies, the process of rapid social transformation makes the substantive basis for this hierarchy tenuous in many migrant families, where children can quickly surpass parents in technical knowledge and expertise, status, marketability, and income.

Some adolescents, owing to level of acculturation, social achievement, or developmental maturity, are able to assume executive or other functional leadership within the family. The clinical criterion to be observed in such situations is whether this role is assumed with the implicit sanction of the parents or in a manner that undermines parental status and role, thus generating family dysfunction and psychopathology. Specifically, a socially contextualized family role for a functional and well-differentiated adolescent in a poor Puerto Rican migrant family is one of great responsibility for the family unit as a whole and for the parental and sibling subsystems in particular. In our experience, it is the lack of these types of family responsibilities and expectations that tends to correlate positively with antisocial behavior and social anomie. This view appears counter to the mainstream view of adolescence as a time when youngsters pay less attention to family affairs and seek out an identity of self in the social world. This view is framed by an unquestioned value on individuality that constitutes a social-class and cultural bias which is nonadaptive socially and contraindicated therapeutically for Puerto Rican adolescents.

Summary and Conclusions

Puerto Rican adolescents are a significant and expanding, at-risk population group. Sociohistorical, cultural, and migration characteristics differentiate Puerto Rican migrants from previous arrivals. Their role as second and third generations in the larger process of transculturation is to begin the integration of two cultures, value sets, and traditions. A significant number of adaptational problems can be expected at this stage. Mental health practitioners must be prepared for the challenge that providing services to Puerto Rican adolescents and their families constitutes.

Cultural factors, values, and clashes between parental and adolescent generations cannot be overemphasized as necessary considerations in the assessment and treatment of minority group adolescents and Puerto Rican adolescents in particular. Neglecting to pay attention to the processes of value orientation and value clashes can lead to an overemphasis on intrapsychic or family dynamics that may limit the effectiveness of treatment. An ecologically oriented approach expands and complements the training in individual, group, and family assessment and treatment of Puerto Rican and minority adolescents. It argues for the need to expand clinical areas of competence to include contextual issues of migration, history, social class, and the role of the community.

Like cultural and value orientation factors, social-class issues have been underemphasized in mental health treatment. The need to overcome this neglect in the field becomes most evident when one works with Puerto Rican adolescents. Therapists working with poor minority adolescents need to understand that more than one world view competes for these clients' attention as a viable life course (Inclán and Ferran, forthcoming). Failure to understand this tends to result in ineffective therapies for minority groups.

Training of professional staff, Hispanics and others, to work with this large and growing at-risk population is a most important priority at this time. There is evidence of a decrease in training of Hispanic professionals in all the mental health disciplines. There is an equally alarming trend in the field toward the decontextualization of psychotherapy. Instead, "specialized" and biomedical approaches seem to be gaining acceptance. The combined effect of these two trends for the delivery of care to minority adolescents is of great concern. The system of organized therapy and training, in moving toward specialization and biotechnologies, may well be moving counter to the needs of Puerto Ricans and other minority populations whose interests are best met by an ecologically oriented and contextualized treatment approach.

Community-based services and agencies for mental health care for minority groups are models for service delivery that are gaining prominence as cultural sensitivity is emphasized in the Hispanic mental health community (Rogler, Malgady, Costantino, and Blumenthal, 1987). These services could play an expanded role in training and research. The experiences obtained could, in turn, serve to develop further a mental health system that effectively addresses the needs of all segments of the population. Greater exploration and expansion of the roles and possibilities inherent in culturally sensitive community mental health centers would be opportune, given the accelerated increase in migration from countries and cultures with values very different from the American norms. Although many of these groups are currently first-generation immigrants, it can be expected that the second and third generations, as in the case of Puerto Ricans, will experience more difficulties and dysfunctions.

Note

1. Lewis's concept includes phenomenological description and etiological implications, the latter being controversial when introduced in 1965. Our experience partly supports Lewis's findings of a culture of poverty. We observe it in a subculture of the ghetto, not in the ghetto as a whole. With regard to etiological implications, we believe, with Lewis, that societies that espouse a set of values for the dominant class which stresses the accumulation of wealth and property and simultaneously explains low socioeconomic status as the sole responsibility of the individual tend to foster a culture of poverty. For further elaboration, see Inclán and Ferran (forthcoming).

References

Acosta, F. X., Yamamoto, J., and Evans, L. A. *Effective Psychotherapy for Low-Income and Minority Patients*. New York: Plenum, 1982.

Auerswald, E. H. "Interdisciplinary Versus Ecological Approach." *Family Process,* 1968, 7 (2), 202–215.

Auerswald, E. H. "Epistemological Confusion in Family Therapy and Research." *Family Process,* 1987, *26* (3), 317–331.

Barry, H., III, Child, I. L., and Bacon, M. K. "Relation of Child Training to Subsistence Economy." *American Anthropologist,* 1959, *61,* 51–63.

Bowen, M. "Theory in the Practice of Psychotherapy." In P. J. Guerin, Jr. (ed.), *Family Therapy: Theory and Practice.* New York: Gardner Press, 1976.

Canino, I. A., Earley, B. E., and Rogler, L. H. *The Puerto Rican Child in New York City: Stress and Mental Health.* Monograph No. 4. Bronx, N.Y.: Hispanic Research Center, Fordham University, 1980.

Canino, I. A., Gould, M. S., Prupis, S., and Shaffer, D. "A Comparison of Symptoms and Diagnoses in Hispanic and Black Children in an Outpatient Mental Health Clinic." *Journal of the American Academy of Child Psychiatry,* 1986, *25* (2), 254–259.

Centers for Disease Control. *AIDS Weekly Surveillance Report— United States* (Nov. 16, 1987). Atlanta, Ga.: Centers for Disease Control, U.S. Department of Health and Human Services, 1987.

Centers for Health Education and Social Systems Studies. *Health Status of Minorities and Low-Income Groups.* Washington, D.C.: U.S. Government Printing Office, 1985.

Daykin, D. S. *Social and Community Support Systems in Hispanic Neighborhoods in New York City: A Public Policy Analysis.* Mental Health Policy Monograph Series, No. 3. Nashville, Tenn.: Center for the Study of Families and Children, Institute for Public Policy Studies, Vanderbilt University, 1980.

Erikson, E. H. *Childhood and Society.* (2nd ed.) New York: Norton, 1963.

Falicov, C. J., and Karrer, B. M. "Therapeutic Strategies for Mexican-American Families." *International Journal of Family Therapy,* 1984, *6* (1), 18–30.

Garcia-Preto, N. "Puerto Rican Families." In M. McGoldrick,

J. K. Pearce, and J. Giordano (eds.), *Ethnicity and Family Therapy.* New York: Guilford Press, 1982.

Governor's Advisory Committee for Hispanic Affairs. *New York State Hispanics: A Challenging Minority.* Albany, N.Y.: Governor's Advisory Committee for Hispanic Affairs, 1985.

Haley, J. *Leaving Home: The Therapy of Disturbed Young People.* New York: McGraw-Hill, 1980.

Hardy-Fanta, C., and Montana, P. "The Hispanic Female Adolescent: A Group Therapy Model." *International Journal of Group Psychotherapy,* 1982, *32* (3), 351–366.

Inclán, J. "Family Organization, Acculturation, and Psychological Symptomatology in Second Generation Puerto Rican Women of Three Socioeconomic Class Groups." Unpublished doctoral dissertation, New York University, 1979.

Inclán, J. "Variations in Value Orientations in Mental Health Work with Puerto Ricans." *Psychotherapy,* 1985, *22* (2S), 324–334.

Inclán, J., and Ferran, E. "Poverty, Politics, and the Family." In M. Myrkin (ed.), *The Social and Political Context of Family Therapy.* New York: Gardner Press, forthcoming.

Lewis, O. *La Vida: A Puerto Rican Family in the Culture of Poverty—San Juan and New York.* New York: Vintage Books, 1965.

Mayor's Commission on Hispanic Concerns. *Report of the Mayor's Commission on Hispanic Concerns.* New York: City of New York, 1986.

Perez, R. "The Status of Puerto Ricans in the United States." Paper presented at third National Puerto Rican Convention, Philadelphia, June 1985.

Rodriguez, O. *Hispanics and Human Services: Help-Seeking in the Inner City.* Monograph No. 14. Bronx, N.Y.: Hispanic Research Center, Fordham University, 1987.

Rogler, L. H., Malgady, R. G., Costantino, G., and Blumenthal, R. "What Do Culturally Sensitive Mental Health Services Mean? The Case of Hispanics." *American Psychologist,* 1987, *42,* 565–570.

Sowell, T. *Ethnic America: A History.* New York: Basic Books, 1981.

Spencer, G. *Projections of the Hispanic Population of the United States: 1983 to 2080.* U.S. Bureau of the Census, Current Population Reports, Series P-25, No. 995. Washington, D.C.: U.S. Government Printing Office, 1986.

U.S. Bureau of the Census. *Persons of Spanish Origin in the United States: March 1985 (Advance Report).* Current Population Reports, Population Characteristics, Series P-20, No. 403. Washington, D.C.: U.S. Government Printing Office, 1985.

Ventura, S. J., and Taffel, S. M. "Childbearing Characteristics of U.S.- and Foreign-Born Hispanic Mothers." *Public Health Reports,* 1985, *100* (6), 647–653.

9

Southeast Asian Refugee Children and Adolescents

Larke Nahme Huang

"Stranger in a strange land" is a theme played over and over again in the lives of refugees. Whether these refugees have fled their homes because of natural disasters such as drought or famine or because of political, religious, or racial repression, they enter host countries as aliens with mixed emotions of fear, anticipation, joy, and loss. By definition, refugees are subject to severe stress and problems of adjustment. In contrast to other people who migrate and resettle in foreign lands, refugees generally lack positive motives for abandoning their homes. As one Southeast Asian refugee succinctly stated, "We are not immigrants looking for a place where the grass is greener. For us refugees, the grass under our feet was burning" (Ferguson, 1984, p. 3).

Estimates of the number of refugees worldwide range from 10 to 15 million (Cohon, 1981; Loescher and Scanlan, 1986). It is generally estimated that children make up half the refugee population, although the proportions of children vary with the different waves of refugees (Huyck and Fields, 1981).

Since April 1975, over 800,000 Southeast Asian refugees have entered the United States as part of the aftermath of the Vietnam War and the civil wars in Cambodia and Laos. Within this population are three groups of refugee children: slightly over 2,000 orphans from Operation Babylift of April 1975, 7,637 unaccompanied minors (U.S. Department of Health and Human Services, 1987), and an untabulated number of children who entered with members of their families. Although the numbers are inexact, it has been estimated that children constitute 40-60 percent of the entering refugee population (Ahmed, Tims, and Kolker, 1980; Lee, 1987).

Consistent with the omission of youth in general in the psychological literature on refugees, systematic investigation of Southeast Asian refugee youth remains minimal. This is also evident in social policy documents, as reflected in the 1980 report by the Indochinese Refugee Consultation to the U.S. Department of Health and Human Services (Nguyen, Long, and Aylesworth, 1980). This report includes detailed and well-substantiated recommendations for training, service, and research programs but no recommendations specific to the issues, needs, and developmental concerns of refugee youth. Given that few crises are as traumatizing as rapid uprooting and forced migration due to war, it is important to understand the effects of this event on the development and mental health of children and adolescents.

This chapter focuses on these issues for refugee youth from Southeast Asia. Although the geopolitical term *Southeast Asian refugee* usually designates refugees from Vietnam, Cambodia, and Laos, in this chapter it will include only refugees from Vietnam and Cambodia, as these are the groups with which I have had the most clinical and research contact. Current demographic, epidemiological, and cultural information will be presented toward the goal of deeper understanding of these groups and development of appropriate psychosocial assessment and intervention strategies. When considering interventions, one must bear in mind that interventions for this group are not "proven" or well established, and to date, one cannot definitely declare the "right" way to generate positive outcomes for these children, many of whom have experienced nightmares in real life beyond what helping professionals can even begin to imagine.

Demographics of the Southeast Asian Refugees

The United Nations 1951 Refugee Convention defined refugees as persons outside the boundaries of their own countries who were not firmly resettled elsewhere and who maintained a well-substantiated fear of persecution based on race, religion, nationality, social class, or political opinion in their own country (United Nations, 1951). The Refugee Act of 1980, passed by the U.S. Congress, conformed to this international definition and clarified the legal parameters for refugee status (U.S. Department of Health and Human Services, 1987). However, this act did not readily translate legal definition into an organized resettlement policy at the national level. In contrast to well-defined, albeit fluctuating, policies for immigrants, who generally enter according to a system of preferences and do not feel the pressure of persecution in their homeland, U.S. government intervention with refugees has historically been piecemeal, lacking in continuity, and spearheaded by a few dedicated individuals influenced by humanitarian and political coalitions. These short-term rescue efforts have not evolved into a thoughtful long-range policy.

By the end of 1986, there were 806,000 Southeast Asian refugees in the United States. Vietnamese continue to be the majority group among these refugees, although there is increasing ethnic diversity in the entering population. Vietnamese form 63 percent of the entering total, Laotians 19 percent, and Cambodians 17 percent (U.S. Department of Health and Human Services, 1987). Estimated crude birthrates, to calculate the number of children born to refugees in the United States, yield a current population estimate of 1.026 million, consisting of 654,000 Vietnamese, 205,500 Laotians, and 166,900 Cambodians (Gordon, 1987). On the basis of these estimates, the Vietnamese are the fourth-largest Asian American group, after the Chinese, Filipinos, and Japanese.

The age and sex composition reveals a relatively young population, 55 percent male. The median age of the refugees is 25 years. In 1986, 3.5 percent were preschoolers, 27 percent were school age, and 19 percent were young adults, ages 18–24.

Twenty-one percent of the Cambodians who arrived in 1986 were children under 5 years old, many of them born in refugee camps (U.S. Department of Health and Human Services, 1987).

Geographically, Southeast Asian refugees are concentrated in the West, with 316,200 (39.2 percent) in California, 61,100 (7.6 percent) in Texas, and 37,500 (4.7 percent) in Washington. Although refugees reside in every state, about 85 percent reside in 18 states (U.S. Department of Health and Human Services, 1987). The initial government plan was to disperse refugees throughout the country in order to prevent an excessive burden on any particular community. However, secondary migration, in combination with the tendency of later refugees to seek already-existing refugee communities, worked against this plan. Secondary migration was spurred by employment opportunities, the pull of an established ethnic community, more desirable welfare benefits, better training opportunities, reunification with relatives, or a more attractive climate.

Turning to economic adjustment, refugee labor-force participation in 1986 was lower than in the general population, and the unemployment rate was higher. Forty-one percent of sampled refugees aged 16 and over were in the labor force, compared with 65 percent for the U.S. population as a whole. Of those, 84 percent had jobs, compared with 93 percent for the U.S. population. The jobs that refugees found in this country usually differed in type and status from jobs held in their country of origin. Whereas 37 percent had held white-collar jobs previously, only 19 percent were currently holding similar jobs in the United States, and significantly more refugees had blue-collar jobs or service jobs here than in their native countries. In 1982 the median family income for 1975 arrivals was $14,232, and for 1976–1979 arrivals it was $8,803. In 1984 these figures had increased to $16,377 for 1975 arrivals and $11,105 for 1976–1979 arrivals (U.S. Department of Health and Human Services, 1987).

Migration History

In order to comprehend the experience of the refugee, it is necessary to understand the conditions in the country of origin that necessitated flight, the sometimes circuitous and life-threatening journey, and the conditions and attitudes of the host country. For the three waves of Southeast Asian refugees, these circumstances were quite variable. The first wave of refugees were primarily Vietnamese who fled during the fall of Saigon in April 1975. These refugees and other Vietnamese who left before 1975, though a socioeconomically heterogeneous group, were generally well-educated white-collar workers and professionals who knew English and had had close contacts with Americans in Vietnam. Only 32 percent had been blue-collar workers in Vietnam (Aylesworth, Ossorio, and Osaki, 1980). Many were Roman Catholics from urban areas. With the pending collapse of the South Vietnamese government, the U.S. Congress agreed to evacuate 140,000 Vietnamese who were considered "allies" of the United States and whose lives would be endangered as a result of their contact with Americans during the war. Of this group, 50,000 were children under age 14 (Le, 1983; Vietnamese Children's Resettlement Advisory Group, 1975). These refugees were received at military bases in the United States, where they were given medical examinations and an orientation to American customs and then assigned to one of nine voluntary agencies that assumed the task of locating sponsors to assist in resettlement (Loescher and Scanlan, 1986). Following a short-lived enthusiasm, public support for these refugees, who represented America's obligation and "legacy of guilt" (Loescher and Scanlan, 1986, p. 112), rapidly dissipated. A Gallup poll taken in May 1975 indicated that Americans were opposed to the resettlement of Vietnamese by 54 percent to 36 percent ("The New Americans," 1975). The United States was in an economic recession in mid-1975, and the reasons for opposition were ostensibly economic: Refugees would take jobs from Americans, aggravate the already high unemployment, and compete for limited social services and federal assistance.

The second wave of refugees occurred in fall 1975 and fall 1978. Many of these refugees were "high risk" persons, those who had fought in the South Vietnamese army or had been associated with the United States or South Vietnamese government and had been unable to escape in April 1975. This group included many middle-class and politically elite persons, but the vast majority represented a broader cross-section of the population than in the previous wave of refugees. Thousands of peasants uprooted by the war also managed to flee. In Cambodia, civil war resulted in the death of one seventh to one half of the nation's population. Under the Pol Pot regime from mid-1975 to 1978, it is estimated, 1 to 3 million Cambodians died of executions, preventable malnutrition, disease, and exhaustion from forced marches and compulsory labor (Loescher and Scanlan, 1986). Pol Pot's Khmer Rouge army destroyed large segments of the middle and upper classes and forced the relocation and flight of the peasant classes. These conditions generated a steady stream of refugees to Thailand and subsequently to the West.

The third wave of refugees occurred between 1978 and 1980. The Communist restructuring of society in Vietnam and the elimination of a private entrepreneurial class stimulated the flight of many ethnic Chinese who had constituted the business class. Other Vietnamese, in anticipation of being sent to "re-education centers" or "new economic zones," began to flee. Many parents, realizing their children would have no future in Vietnam, arranged for the children's escape while they themselves remained behind. These refugees came to be known as the "boat people," as they escaped by sea, usually to Malaysia, Indonesia, Singapore, or Hong Kong, where they were given temporary asylum in prisonlike holding centers. In August 1978, the number of Vietnamese seeking asylum elsewhere in Asia averaged about 6,000 per month. By spring 1979, this had reached 65,000 per month (Reimers, 1985).

Simultaneously, in Cambodia, the bloodbath was intensifying with the Vietnamese invasion in 1978. All segments of the population were fleeing on foot to Thailand, which begrudgingly established refugee camps on the Thai/Cambodian border. These land refugees were arriving exhausted, malnourished, brutalized by the army. At least 50 percent had already experienced the death of a family member. Currently, nearly 300,000 refugees are in camps along the border, still extremely vulnerable to disease, robbery, rape, and extortion from inside and outside the camps (Oberdorfer, 1987).

The "boat people" and "land refugees" experienced more difficulties in adjustment to the United States than the first wave of refugees. Their conditions and methods of flight were harsher; they also came with less education and fewer employment skills, were predominantly rural, and had had little contact with Americans in their own countries. Overall, they experienced greater culture shock, which was exacerbated by direct entry into American communities without the orientation of the U.S. camp experience, which had been provided only for the first wave of refugees. On arrival in the United States, the refugees were entitled to government assistance for two years as a result of the 1975 Indochinese Migration and Refugee Assistance Act.

An Ecological Perspective

Understanding the experience of the refugee is an extremely complex process, as it involves numerous systems, sometimes competing, sometimes complementary, all at different levels of proximity and awareness to the refugee. The social systems transcend national boundaries, often involve international law and politics, and blur humanitarian and political ideologies. On a more immediate level, the refugee has to maintain the family system in the context of a new cultural system, negotiate employment and educational systems, comprehend the intricacies of migration and naturalization laws, and maneuver through an impersonal social service system. Underlying all this is the need to master a new language, a new culture, and a new set of behaviors and expectations. Additionally, the refugee needs to integrate the experience of flight and the abandonment of homeland and loss of family and friends into his or her current state of existence. For professional helpers interacting with refugees, where do they begin? How do they start to understand the refugee's shattered world, the physical and psychological torment, and the attempt to construct a new, acceptable world view? Can a professional helper, whose life experiences are so extremely different from those of a refugee, be truly helpful?

Bronfenbrenner's (1979) concept of the ecology of human development, as discussed in Chapter One, provides a conceptual framework that may help in organizing the vast complexities of the refugees' experience. This framework focuses on the reciprocal interaction of individual and environment, where the environment consists of immediate microsystems such as family, work, and school settings, more remote systems such as funding committees for English-language classes or legislative committees determining duration of federal assistance, and macrosystems, the "consistencies" or "blueprints" (Bronfenbrenner, 1979, p. 26) or cultural attitudes underlying the various systems.

An ecological perspective also takes into consideration the less tangible, psychological systems of the refugee. For example, in Asian cultures, the extended family is a vitally important structure, and usually one thinks of the extended family as visible and accessible. For many refugees, however, the extended family has become an inaccessible system, as many members actually remain in the homeland but are psychologically, and sometimes disturbingly, present to the refugee in the new country. Thus, many refugees are plagued by worry and regret about relatives left behind, while confronting hostile communities who resent the competition for jobs and housing, well-meaning sponsors who are ignorant of the refugee's culture and behaviors, and established ethnic communities who resent an influx of bedraggled fellow countrymen.

Mental Health Issues for Southeast Asian Refugee Youth

To date, there are few systematic studies of either the psychological and behavioral disorders or the positive adaptation and successful coping strategies of Southeast Asian youth. This may be attributed to several factors: Until the early seventies, Asians in general had not been the focus of extensive psychological research, and so there was little precedent or methodology for investigation of people from these cultures; second, the refugees are recent arrivals, and adults, not children, seemed to be the more immediate targets for investigation; and finally, the language problem has posed a significant impediment for most researchers. The studies that have been conducted have been primarily clinical observations by mental health consultants working in refugee camps and clinics or descriptive studies of adolescents in the foster care system.

The functioning of the significant adults in a refugee child's environment may have implications for the child's sense of well-being (Garmezy and Rutter, 1983). For this reason, studies of Southeast Asian adult refugees will be briefly reviewed before a more detailed discussion of the literature on refugee youth.

Studies of Adult Refugees. In a three-phase longitudinal study of 115 Vietnamese refugees, Lin, Masuda, and Tazuma (1982) documented high levels of physical and psychological dysfunction during the first two years of resettlement. Loss and culture shock seemed to be the primary components of the refugee experience and, when sustained for a prolonged period, seemed to result in clinically significant depression and anxiety. Paradoxically, refugees seemed to become more psychologically vulnerable when their lives had become concretely more manageable and within their control. This finding is consistent with other studies of migration that report an early stage of heightened activity focusing on survival and satisfaction of daily needs followed by a period of emotional distress, depression, and increasing anxiety (Sluzki, 1979). Lin, Masuda, and Tazuma (1982) also reported a disproportionate frequency of psychosomatic disorders and somatization, which may reflect the Asian concept of unity of mind and body and the tendency to avoid the stigma of mental illness. Frequent marital conflicts resulting in physical violence were also reported and were attributed to the breakdown of traditional age and sex roles due to the different rates and imperatives of acculturation within the family. Some reactive psychoses were reported; however, these individuals were usually symptom-free within several months.

In a survey of fifty Vietnamese families recently resettled in the South, Vignes and Hall (1979) concluded that most of the refugees were adjusting well in spite of a number of specific sociological stresses: loss of role identity and self-esteem, social isolation due to language barriers, local prejudice directed toward the Vietnamese, and Vietnamese prejudices and suspicion of the local community, helping agencies, and the federal government. The individuals who seemed to have the poorest adjustment were those from the higher socioeconomic strata in both Vietnam and the United States (income greater than $10,000), as they were least able to accept their downward mobility in occupation and status.

In an epidemiological study of refugees in Santa Clara County, California, Meinhardt, Tom, Tse, and Yu (1985–86) surveyed 378 Cambodians, 563 Vietnamese, 120 Chinese, and 620 nonrefugee Chinese and arrived at the following conclusions: (1) A poverty-level income was associated with refugee status, the median family income for Cambodians being $7,200; for refugee Chinese, $8,500; for Vietnamese, $10,000; and for nonrefugee Chinese, $31,005. (2) Cambodians as a group seemed to have experienced the most life-threatening trauma; 91 percent of Cambodians reported that their lives had been in danger "three or more years." (3) Depression and demoralization were repeated themes in the interviews. The post-1975 Vietnamese and Chinese refugees reported slightly higher mental health needs than that of the general county population at 4 percent, and 17 percent of the Cambodian population reported highly elevated needs for intensive help, including outpatient, day treatment, and inpatient services for extreme psychological distress and dysfunction. (4) Group differences in help-seeking patterns emerged. Cambodians (28.3 percent) used social workers, family counselors, and religious counselors to a significantly greater degree than the other Asian groups (4.1 percent). All the Asian groups reported greater use of spiritualists and natural healers than the general population.

Studies of Child and Adolescent Refugees. The earliest studies of Southeast Asian refugee children emerged from camps set up for the first wave of Vietnamese refugees. After examining these children, Harding and Looney (1977) concluded that those who had departed with their families seemed to adapt well to their new environment. These children received the strong, steady emotional support characteristic of multigenerational families. The orderly sense of roles in the family kept the children occupied with duties and responsibilities and guarded against boredom, anomie, and antisocial behavior in the camps. There was no evidence of severe psychological disorder. In contrast, children who had fled without family members or significant adults, the unaccompanied minors, seemed to fare less well and were at much higher risk for psychological problems. These children ranged in age from 18 months to 18 years, were predominantly boys, and varied in background from the illiterate lower class to the most privileged upper class. Psychological and physical examinations found that many of these children were significantly depressed, manifesting somatic complaints, sleep disturbances, violent antisocial behavior, tantrums, and withdrawal. A general sense of sadness and hopelessness was observed in these youth (Harding and Looney, 1977).

Williams and Westermeyer (1983) studied the adjustment of twenty-eight Southeast Asian adolescent refugees who were seen at a psychiatric clinic. Six of these adolescents received a diagnosis of functional psychosis and six were diagnosed as mentally retarded; however, all twelve had exhibited these problems before migration. The migration process intensified these disorders and led to more flagrant psychoses, suicide attempts, disruptive behavior, and school crises. Other diagnoses of adolescents in this sample included depression, conduct disorder, somatic disorder, personality disorder, learning disorder, and no diagnosis. This last category included intergenerational conflicts typical of migrating families. Adolescents usually acculturate to a new society more rapidly than their parents, thus creating differences in behavioral and cultural expectations. While parents attempt to retain the language and ways of their home culture, adolescents are more actively exploring the roles and behaviors of the host culture and gradually reshaping their values and self-concepts. Intergenerational conflict was most severe in refugee families who had settled in rural areas isolated from their cultural peers and in single-parent families, usually widowed mothers and their children (Williams and Westermeyer, 1983). In these situations, the parents were lacking a culturally similar and mutually supportive network.

Developmentally, adolescents are confronted with identity issues. From an ecological perspective, this task is intensified for the refugee adolescent, who must negotiate between family, peer, and societal expectations to resolve the question "Who am I?" Given the unpopularity of the Vietnam War and the intense emotionality associated with it, Southeast Asian adolescents may have a particularly difficult time integrating a bicultural identity when confronted by the hostility and negative memories of the American mainstream society. Although they may begin to internalize "being American," fears of rejection by Americans may lead to emotional conflict. Similarly, though dependent on American aid, they may simultaneously despise the Americans for their role in the war that generated the need to flee. This ambivalence may complicate formation of an identity and a positive self-concept. They may chronically feel they are "unwelcome guests" in someone else's home.

Carlin and Sokoloff (1985) have suggested that the concept of posttraumatic stress disorder applies to these refugee youth. Like the American veterans for whom this disorder has been recognized, these youth have undergone major stresses, have witnessed atrocities, terrifying losses, and torture, and now need to adjust to a Western, technological society. Unexplained fears and night terrors may be expected, as well as an initial "psychic numbing" to block out these experiences.

Sokoloff, Carlin, and Pham (1984) conducted a five-year follow-up study of Vietnamese refugee children and concluded that developmental reversal of physical problems was quite rapid. Similarly, behavioral and emotional problems, nightmares, and generalized fears were initially severe in frequency and type; however, by the end of the first year, these had noticeably diminished. The older children in foster care showed more adjustment problems. Though functioning better than expected, they evidenced a high incidence of "acting out" behaviors.

To date, the literature has not identified severe, long-term problems for refugee children. For the most part, these children show incredible resilience and healthy adaptation to a new environment. In contrast to many of the clinical studies, which tended to focus on maladjustment, Huang and Huang (1984) examined perceived competence in a comparison study of twenty-three Vietnamese refugee children and twenty-three

White American children. They found no significant difference between the two nonclinical groups in reported levels of perceived competence in the cognitive, physical, and social domains and no difference in general self-worth. Although this study started from a different set of assumptions, its findings were consistent with those in the clinical literature.

In my study of a nonclinical sample of fifty-one Vietnamese, Chinese, and Cambodian refugee school-age children, extensive interviews revealed serious concern about parents and their well-being. The children rated themselves as happier with the relocation than their parents and viewed their mothers as the least happy in the United States and the least adaptive to being American. Fathers were rated as slightly more willing to "Americanize." The role of ethnicity in self-concept shifted with the children's situation. In the context of their home, they clearly viewed themselves as more ethnic; in school, more American; and with "good friends," equally ethnic and American. This finding echoes DeVos's (1980) hypothesis that peers play an important role in mediating acculturation. Furthermore, these shifts in identification depending on the social context did not seem to affect feelings of general worth or competence.

When asked about the problems of most significance and difficulty for them, 32 percent cited physical altercations with peers in school, 20 percent indicated social interactions with peers, 20 percent described experiences of or concerns about physical injury such as being hit by a car, earthquakes, or being stabbed in the neighborhood, 15 percent reported problems within the family, and 10 percent cited worries about family members, primarily grandparents, remaining in Vietnam. Again, the role of peers was especially significant. Surprisingly, cognitive and language difficulties were reported only when I specifically asked about problems related to school. The high reported incidence of physical altercations with peers was reiterated in testimony by California researchers before Congress ("Asian Immigrants . . . ," 1987). They reported that racial tension and brawls had become a regular aspect of school life for Asian children in California and that all the Asian immigrants interviewed reported being punched, mimicked, harassed, or robbed by non-Asian fellow students.

In contrast to the children and adolescents who migrated with parents or other adult relatives, the youth at most risk are clearly the unaccompanied minors. Some became separated from their families before or during their escape; others were sent away by their parents in order to avoid induction into the Communist army or assignment to the "new economic zones," which are noted for their extreme hardship and lack of any economic or social future. Still others escaped under the auspices of another family; however, when these families realized that sponsorship would be found earlier for smaller families, they relinquished these children to camp authorities. The vulnerability of unaccompanied minors is exacerbated by their longer stays in refugee camps. Observers have noted that these youth are depressed, restless, often hyperactive, and lacking in concentration. They are often grieving for their family and homeland while trying to adapt to a new, unfamiliar environment without the presence of familiar support systems. In their foster homes, their behavior often vacillates between periods of cooperativeness and periods of anger, aggressiveness, or withdrawal (Mortland and Egan, 1987; Redick and Wood, 1982).

Bachyun Nguyen, a Vietnamese social worker with the Catholic Charities of St. Paul and Minneapolis for thirty unaccompanied minors from Vietnam, ranging in age from 5 to 18, cited the following as major problems for these youth (personal communication, 1987): (1) handling problems with foster parents, such as feeling unloved and "just a source of money," not being understood, and ambivalence toward forming an attachment to these parents while retaining a hope of being reunited with their biological parents, (2) having experienced the hardships of Communism and feeling that nobody really understands this, (3) harboring questions of "Who am I?" and "Where do I belong?" which usually emerge after two years of rapid assimilation, and (4) integrating two disparate cultures and learning to "flip-flop" according to the situation.

During extensive clinical experience with refugee youth, Nidorf (1985) observed severe depression, hysterical conversion reactions, high levels of agitation, and antisocial and acting-out behaviors among unaccompanied adolescents. Lacking meaningful support from close adults and longing for parental nurturance, they remained vulnerable to feelings of shame, despair, and humiliation and a sense of being an outcast because of their lack of a "family." In Asian cultures, the concept of family and filial piety is essential for organizing one's experiences, social reality, and identity. Nidorf (1985) hypothesized that certain events during the adolescent's escape may lead to specific types of maladjustment. The most traumatic aspect of the escape for many youth was physical and sexual assault by sea pirates, resulting in deep psychological wounds and traumatic memories. Adolescent females who experienced this may later present as chronically suicidal, withdrawn, uninterested in social relationships, or rejecting of the cultural expectation of marriage. Still others, identifying with the aggressor in order to survive, may present as sexually promiscuous and inappropriately seductive. Adolescent males, overwhelmed by fear, shame, and rage, may present as physically or psychologically impotent, apathetic, phobic, or anxiety-ridden.

Nidorf (1985) also indicated that unaccompanied minors are at a higher suicide risk than other refugees. They are more vulnerable to maladaptive behaviors for which they may lose face, and suicide may become an alternative for resolving issues of shame. Survivor guilt may also be a determinant of suicidal behavior. In some cases, survivor guilt is extremely reality-based, as with one child whose mother died of starvation in a refugee camp, having given her food to her children so that they would survive. This child literally watched his mother die. Alienation in a strange culture and in the absence of one's family, and depression accompanied by the frustration and pressures of adaptation, may similarly play a role in the etiology of suicide.

In metropolitan areas with large populations of refugees, gangs of Vietnamese youth have recently become more prominent (Kelley, 1987). These youth, detached from their native culture and unable to secure a niche in American society, group together for reasons of identity, protection, and economics. These gangs include youth with and without families, but the latter are more vulnerable to the lure of gang membership, which becomes a substitute for the absent family. The hierarchy and loyalty expected within the gang resemble those of previous family roles. Additionally, the communal experiences and family separations under Communist rule, in labor camps, and in the refugee camps have provided precedents for this type of group bonding. Nidorf (1985) reports that the youth attracted to gangs have limited educational and vocational skills and are drawn by the prospect of a sense of belonging, excitement, gaining otherwise unattainable material possessions, and enjoying freedom and sexual experiences without adult constraints. Formation of gangs, though ostensibly providing protection for their members, also provokes interracial tensions and endangers the members.

One other high-risk group is the Amerasians, the half-Vietnamese, half-American children fathered by U.S. servicemen during the Vietnam War. It is estimated that there are 8,000 to 12,000 Amerasians, whose average age is 17.5 years, living in Vietnam (Hiebert, 1988). Some 4,000 Amerasians have been resettled in the United States under a program administered by the United Nations. With their dual ethnic identity, they are considered outcasts in Vietnam and unwanted reminders of the war. They are deprived of economic, educational, and social opportunities available to other Vietnamese. Some live with families, but many are homeless street children. After much negotiating with members of the U.S. Congress, the Vietnamese government recently agreed in principle to an airlift of these children and their families to the United States (Hiebert, 1988). These youth, enduring ostracism and discrimination for over a decade, living in a Communist country in transition, lacking a father in a culture where the family unit is paramount, will confront a new set of stresses in the United States, including racism and discrimination and, at best, reluctant acceptance. The plight of these youth and its effect on their psychological well-being remain to be examined.

In general, current studies of Southeast Asian refugee youth are consistent with previous investigations of children living in violent, war-torn conditions (Garmezy and Rutter, 1983). Children separated from their families sustained the uprooting more poorly than those evacuated with their families. A prime factor in how children react to the stress of war is the behavior of their parents or significant adults, as the adults model the ability to exert control in the midst of crisis or upheaval. Thus, the confidence of the adult community may have a significant impact on the well-being of the children.

These findings have mixed implications for Southeast Asian refugee children. In addition to relocations, their families undergo major sociocultural changes. Children and adolescents view the transformation of their parents from previously competent, autonomous caretakers to depressed, overwhelmed, and dependent individuals. Like children of other immigrants, refugee children more rapidly acculturate to the new country. The confidence of the parents is inevitably undermined when they become so dependent on their children, who more quickly acquire facility with the new language and customs. Extrapolation from earlier studies might predict poor adaptation of these children, who lose the critical resource of a strong parent to rely on. This may be the case for some youth. However, for others, the assumption of parental responsibilities may engender a sense of importance and competence and ward off feelings of despair and helplessness.

Sociocultural Issues in Assessment

The assessment approach to be presented here is based on an ecological framework, which focuses on interconnected systems dynamically interacting with an individual. Ecological transitions occur when an individual's position in these systems is altered by a change in role, setting, or both; the transitions are the joint function of individual and altered environmental circumstances (Bronfenbrenner, 1979). On the positive side, this process of mutual accommodation between the individual and the environment represents the process of growth and change. However, ecological transitions are inherently stress-producing and may lead to maladaptive outcomes as well. For refugees, fleeing one's homeland, migrating to unfamiliar places, and accommodating to a new society all represent major ecological transitions with the potential for substantial growth or disorder.

The psychosocial assessment of Southeast Asian refugee youth, as of other refugee groups, must take into consideration at least three ecological contexts: premigration, migration, and postmigration (Kinzie, 1981; Nidorf, 1985). Within each context, the assessment includes larger, "macrosystem" issues, such as culture and societal expectations, as well as more focused microsystem structures, such as the family.

Premigration Period. The youth's perceptions of the world and ways of handling the environment are, to a large degree, influenced by cultural values. Although Vietnamese and Cambodians share some general characteristics of Asian cultures, the basic foundations of their respective cultures differ, leading to important cultural distinctions. The culture of Vietnam is based on Confucian traditions as imported from China during its early history of Chinese domination. Roman Catholicism, introduced by French missionaries and traders, became more widespread with the French conquest in 1958 (Chi, 1980). In contrast, Cambodia has been much more influenced by Buddhism and isolated from Western influences.

In accord with Confucian traditions, the family is the basic social unit of Vietnamese society. As in Chinese culture (see Chapter Two), the extended family and family interdependence are of critical importance. The family hierarchy and associated roles and responsibilities are clearly delineated; filial piety and respect for elders, teachers, and authority are socially expected behaviors. Regardless of social status, children represent the future of the family, and both children and adults feel a sense of inferiority if children do not achieve goals set by the family. Shame and loss of face are collectively shared by one's family, and avoidance of this is the motivator for much of one's behavior. Stoic attitudes, self-control, and avoidance of direct expression of emotions are highly valued. Harmony in interpersonal relationships is accomplished through tact, delicacy, and politeness, sometimes at the cost of honesty and forthrightness (Le, 1983).

The premigration culture of an Amerasian refugee may be quite dissimilar from that of other refugee youth. In a society where family is of primary importance, the experience of these youth is one of rejection and degradation. They are scorned by most Vietnamese and lack the all-important sense of belonging. They and their families, usually mothers and siblings, are out-casts in an ethnically homogeneous country and devoid of the priceless commodity, family. Thus, the premigration culture of an Amerasian refugee may instill values of self-preservation and basic survival, possible disdain for authority, and ambivalence toward one's country, culture, and family.

Cambodia is primarily a rural country whose society was influenced by the teachings of Buddhism. The society was pa-triarchal, with the father the head of the family, but his was not an all-powerful role. His rights over the family were counterbal-anced by duties prescribed by Buddhist morality and sanctioned by civil law. In many cases, husband and wife shared authority (Garry, 1980). In contrast to other Asian cultures, Cambodia is a more open society where the individual is not necessarily sub-ordinate to the family or social group. Although the extended family is acknowledged, family structure is based more on the couple relationship. From Buddhist teachings, the Cambodian people derived a respect for life in all its forms, a tolerance, gentleness, and honesty, and an indifference to material wealth (Garry, 1980). Buddhism suggests that all life involves suffering; however, one can influence this by morally upright behavior and thoughts and good deeds. In contrast to Vietnam, Cambodia had less exposure to Western technological societies and remains a less modernized, underdeveloped country. For example, the stringent examination system for education and the strong values of competition in Vietnam are not as apparent in Cambodia.

These cultural attributes of Vietnam and Cambodia are, by necessity, generalizations. One can expect wide individual and social-class variation. Additionally, these historical patterns are becoming increasingly challenged and diluted as new values are introduced or imposed by Western countries.

Another relevant aspect of the Vietnamese and Cam-bodian cultures is attitude toward mental health. In general, the conceptualization of mental disorders is bimodal. The less severe emotional and behavioral disorders were believed to reflect a combination of youthfulness, life circumstances, and unusual and excessive problems in living. Whenever possible, these disorders were handled within the family to avoid embarrassment and shame. When the family could no longer contain the confusion, agitation, or acting-out behavior, outside assistance was usually sought from priests and village elders or shamans and fortunetellers (Aylesworth, Ossorio, and Osaki, 1980). The more severe psychopathological disorders were believed to be of mysterious origin and were also handled within the family whenever possible. These abnormal behaviors were sometimes believed to be a result of some physical ailment, and occasionally help from a physician was sought. More likely, the family would contact the traditional cultural healers. Only as a last resort would the individual be taken to a psychiatric helper or admitted to a psychiatric facility.

Understanding the resources available to the youth's family in their homeland is also important, as this may significantly affect the psychological and practical coping capabilities of the refugee (Nidorf, 1985). Occupational status in the homeland has been considered a predictor of socioeconomic status in the country of resettlement as well as a weak predictor of psychological adjustment (Vignes and Hall, 1979).

Further, the child's age at the time of departure has implications for how the child comprehends and copes with the emigration experience. Preschoolers and adolescents are in particular need of a stable, predictable environment as they undergo significant physiological changes and major psychological upheavals. Preverbal memories of terror and disrupted language patterns may plague the preschooler, and the identity crisis of the adolescent may be intensified (Le, 1983).

Determining the age at departure may also provide important information on the youth's experiences in the homeland. Youth who remained in Vietnam or Cambodia after the Communist regimes became entrenched, around 1977, endured numerous hardships, such as disintegration of the family unit, witnessing of torture, forced internment in labor camps, and conscription into children's armies, events not experienced by those who left earlier (Nguyen, 1982; Sheehy, 1986).

Migration Period. Of critical importance in the assessment

is the microsystem of flight: with whom the youth migrated
and who was left behind. As seen in the studies reviewed earlier, whether or not one is accompanied by an intact family during the migration process will affect later psychosocial development.

Examination of this microsystem also includes the process
of flight—preparation for and means of escape and any danger-
ous situations or losses encountered during the escape. The
trauma incurred during flight may significantly transform a
youth's perception of self, others, and the world in general.
Many children, often for reasons of safety and security, were
not informed of the plans to leave. For example, one child in
my study was told that they were going to his grandmother's,
only to find that they were escaping by boat at night and he
would never see his grandmother again. Subsequently, this child
harbors obsessive concerns about his grandmother, and several
years after resettlement the intensity of his desire to see her has
not subsided. Children and adolescents who witnessed or experienced brutality at the hands of pirates or soldiers often feel a
betrayal of their expectation that adults, particularly family
members, will protect them. Their trust in the goodness and
predictability of the world has been deeply wounded, and their
sense of powerlessness in the world deeply accentuated. For
parents, these incidents of brutality, including repeated rapes
and beatings, underscored their inability to perform the sacred
duty of protecting their children. Their sense of rage and helplessness is apparent to the children. For many of the youth and
the adults, the fleetingness of life becomes a reality, and subsequently, many of these children, like other traumatized children (Terr, 1979), do not view life as long.

In an ecological framework, the refugee camp can be considered another microsystem affecting the development of refugee youth. The camp experience was characterized by over-
crowded, unsanitary conditions, makeshift shacks overrun by
rats, frequent outbreaks of bubonic plague, tuberculosis, and
malaria, food and clothing shortages, absence of privacy, and
prolonged periods of boredom (Borton, 1984). Nevertheless, it
provided a psychosocial respite during which refugees were able

to put their escape in perspective and begin to worry about the future. My brief observations at Camp Jubilee in Hong Kong in 1980 found the young children to be hungry and poorly clothed but playful and curious. Even in the squalor and poverty of the camp, the children played in small groups and converted the meager resources of the camp into instruments of play. In contrast, the adolescents seemed more remote and distant. They eyed the visiting observers warily and seemed to spend much of their time in bed listening to music. There were few activities for them, and their idleness and boredom were particularly striking.

In assessing the camp experience, one must be sensitive to the quality of the experience as it is subjectively viewed by the youth (Nidorf, 1985). Although media reports describe horrendous conditions, for the youth the camp may have been a safe haven from the previous horrors of their flight. Conversely, it may represent the first context for recognizing one's loss of family, home, and homeland and thus may be associated with the deepest sense of pain and tragic memories. While remaining attuned to the youth's subjective experience, one must also be cognizant of the tendency to idealize or vilify the camp experience.

The macrosystem phenomena within the migration period can be considered a "trauma culture." Straddling the uncertain line between life and death and between freedom and captivity, many refugees develop behaviors that would be uncharacteristic of them in normal situations. Basic survival skills, such as scrounging for food and shelter, become preeminent. Vigilance and mistrust become ubiquitous. When confronted with life-threatening situations, people are often forced to do things they would normally consider unacceptable; eventually, these behaviors must be integrated into an acceptable self-concept. Anticipating the role of victim and readily capitulating to more dominant personalities are behaviors associated with a trauma culture. The degree to which an individual remains immersed in a trauma culture is related to the duration and intensity of the traumatic events and the disruption of normality. This is especially pertinent for unaccompanied minors and Amerasian children, whose lives have usually been the most shattered and disrupted. Though occasionally adaptive, the learned behaviors from this stage may interfere with normal development and adjustment to a new society.

Postmigration Period. The categories of assessment for refugee youth may be similar to those used with nonrefugee youth: age, general appearance and size, speech and language, affect, interpersonal relatedness, level of anxiety, patterns of defense, and management of aggression and sexuality. However, the interpretation of these data needs to incorporate cultural and experiential differences. For example, determining the true age of the individual, usually considered a simple and routine question, may be quite difficult. For many refugee children, the age stated on official documents is several years lower than the child's actual chronological age. The rationale for this deception has to do with survival and resources. In refugee camps, younger children were usually given priority for food and shelter, and in the countries of resettlement, they would receive educational and welfare benefits for a longer period. In school, however, this age deception may be a source of problematic behavior, as, particularly for adolescent males, the 16-year-old in a class with 12- and 13-year-olds may feel isolated and awkward (Nidorf, 1985).

In the other assessment categories, judgments about the range of normality may be subject to cultural bias. For example, the form and intensity of affect may be more constricted and halting, as dictated by cultural norms. Interpersonal relatedness may be guarded and unusually cautious owing to emigration experiences of betrayals, multiple losses, and loss of faith in adult providers. The interviewer must be cautious in interpreting the assessment data and must carefully distinguish between culturally determined behavior and maladaptive psychopathological behavior.

When considering the family microsystem, the clinician must remember that refugee families are families in transition, presenting a wide range of issues: culture, communication, depression, grief, disorganization, and separation (Lappin and Scott, 1982). The hierarchy of roles within the family is often in disarray as children more readily acculturate to the host country and become emissaries for the parents with the outside world. Additionally, wives are often forced to work for economic survival. These age-role and sex-role reversals upset the prescribed distribution of power within the family, leading to tension and conflict. In addition, there is the stress of family members left behind. The efforts toward family reunification are relentless and time- and resource-consuming.

Refugee youth assigned to foster families encounter yet another set of stresses that needs to be included in any assessment. The expectations of the youth and the foster family need to be carefully examined. The child's hopes and dreams of America had often been a sustaining influence during the emigration. Inevitably, these idealizations will be met with disappointment with the reality. Similarly, foster parents' excitement and good intentions may become tarnished as they encounter a bewildered youth who is psychologically numbed, emotionally distant, and distrustful. Frequently the youth's anger toward the biological parents for abandonment is displaced onto the foster parents. In Asian cultures, the concept of foster parenting has no counterpart, as this task is usually assumed by the extended family. Consequently, refugee youth may have difficulty comprehending this Western form of "family" and determining their role in this structure. Cultural clashes are to be expected and need to be assessed. For example, the primacy of the youth's biological family may be hurtful to the foster family, who, for example, may resent the youth's sending money and medicine to the family in Asia. Meanwhile, the refugee youth may be struggling with divided family loyalties. Underlying these potential areas of conflict is the ever-present language difficulty, a source of repeated frustration and continual misunderstandings.

For these foster families, there are predictable times of stress that may trigger increased anxiety in the refugee youth (Rudnick and Harmatys, 1987). Receiving letters from home may raise feelings of guilt and depression; ethnic holidays, such as Tet, the Vietnamese New Year, may similarly trigger intense affect. School events, such as beginning a new academic year, meeting new teachers, or taking exams, may be particularly difficult for the refugee. American holidays, when all the children come home to "one big, happy family," intensify the refugee youth's loneliness and isolation, and school vacations present the refugee with much unstructured time to ruminate about personal losses and worry about the future and the family back home.

Another important microsystem is the school. For children and adolescents, the school is the most frequent source of referral to mental health agencies. It behooves the mental health worker to obtain a thorough assessment of the youth's functioning in the school, including cognitive and social skills.

The ethnic/racial composition of the school has implications for the refugee child's adjustment and acculturation. The presence of other ethnically similar children may ease the refugee's transition. However, it must be kept in mind that ethnic sameness does not guarantee a support system for the refugee. Earlier refugees or American-born ethnic Chinese, Vietnamese, or Cambodians, wishing to acculturate to mainstream America and disregard memories of a painful past, may be reluctant to associate with newer refugees. School-age children, driven by the need to belong and to be accepted, tend to avoid the unusual or unfamiliar. Amerasian children may be especially vulnerable targets of hostility, given their often unknown parentage and their physical features and color, which set them apart from other groups. These difficulties in ethnic/racial identity, in combination with significantly different school histories and pervasive language problems, give rise to not only academic but emotional and behavioral problems as well.

A final area of assessment is societal issues. Despite federal provision of funds for refugee resettlement, the public has been less than receptive to the refugees. Although this country was built on the concept of an "open door," refugees of color seem to be only reluctantly welcomed. Southeast Asian refugees also bear the stigma of association with the United States' "lost war" and deep dissension and divisiveness in the country.

In recent years, the United States has experienced a resurgence of racial tension and violence that had been subdued following the civil rights gains of the late 1960s. The refugees encounter racism from multiple directions, often stemming from economic and political tensions and cultural ignorance. At many inner-city schools, daily verbal and physical clashes between Southeast Asians and other racial minority groups have become habitual (Fong, 1987). Many of the refugees, coming from rural, racially homogeneous countries, had no previous contact with Blacks or Hispanics or with urban life-styles. As the refugees moved into predominantly minority communities, cultural clashes were inevitable. In Davis, California, racial tensions between Southeast Asian students and White students escalated without intervention, resulting in the stabbing death of a Vietnamese refugee high school student in the spring of 1984. Although the incidents of violence remain isolated, they are becoming disturbingly more frequent and routine. Children and adolescents do not remain impervious to this atmosphere of increasing interracial tension, and their developmental experiences may be directly or indirectly affected.

Intervention and Treatment

In developing an intervention approach with Southeast Asian refugee youth, several critical issues should be considered: (1) The concept of mental health is alien to these youth, and associated treatments are viewed warily. (2) Disclosure of problems beyond family boundaries is considered inappropriate and damaging to the reputation and integrity of the family. (3) Trust in professionals, whether ethnic or nonethnic, is usually only superficial, given the history of misunderstandings, bureaucratic entanglements, and repeated disappointments. (4) A request for help places one in the culturally eschewed position of "debtor." These issues form major impediments to effective intervention and therefore need to be acknowledged if one is to engage the refugee client in treatment.

An ecological perspective is the basis for the intervention strategies to be presented here. Identifying the pertinent systems that intersect with the individual provides the beginning points for intervention. For the child or adolescent, these invariably include the family, the school system, social service agencies that facilitate welfare benefits, such as Aid to Families with Dependent Children, or self-help, social support groups, such as mutual aid associations, within the community. The therapist needs to have a conceptual map of the individual's ecological niche and may need to work simultaneously with different systems. Essential to the therapist's successful engagement with the refugee are two elements: the therapist's credibility and the development of a working relationship based on an "active exchange."

As noted by Sue and Zane (1987), the therapist enters the situation with an "ascribed" credibility based on such characteristics as age, sex, ethnicity, and status in the agency. To sustain the refugee client in the treatment relationship, the therapist must attain a higher "achieved" credibility, which is based on effective therapeutic skills and a feeling of progress on the part of the client. Although one can delineate the traits that contribute to ascribed credibility, it is not always possible to predict the direction of influence. For example, many agencies automatically assume that a Southeast Asian refugee client would prefer an Asian therapist. In some instances, this assumption is correct. However, one Vietnamese client, for example, was deeply offended when assigned a Chinese therapist. This client harbored much hatred toward Chinese, reflecting the history of antagonism between these two ethnic groups in Vietnam. He resented the economic domination of the ethnic Chinese in Vietnam and more recently despised the role of Chinese Communists in the political situation in his homeland. For the client, the assignment of a Chinese therapist dramatically reflected the agency's insensitivity to him and confirmed his preconceptions that they would neither understand nor help him.

Matching client and therapist ethnicity does not guarantee augmenting the therapist's credibility. Some refugees are hesitant to interact with a therapist of their own ethnicity because of differing stages of loyalty to their ethnic group, fears of breaches in confidentiality if the therapist lives or works in their community, or reluctance to confront reminders of a painful past. Other refugees, though, find comfort in a shared culture and history with the therapist, and language obstacles may be minimized.

The combination of a White therapist with a refugee client similarly has its advantages and disadvantages. The refugee, ascribing higher status to the White therapist, may be more cooperative with a treatment plan, believing that this therapist possesses the power or expertise to obtain the desired resources or resolve the presenting problem. Conversely, the refugee may have much ambivalence toward Caucasian Americans stemming from their role in escalating the war in Vietnam, abandoning the country, and then begrudgingly providing assistance to refugees. The refugee may seriously question the trustworthiness and motives of the therapist.

An alternative to the usual combinations is a cross-cultural team approach that employs a nonrefugee American therapist and a bilingual refugee trained as a mental health paraprofessional. DeMonchy and Pin-Riebe (1987), a cross-cultural counseling team in the Department of Mental Health in Boston, report that bicultural teams are a visible symbol to their clients of the interaction between two worlds. The ethnic therapist provides familiarity with the culture, the language, a shared history, and an example of "making it" in the new country. In addition, this therapist may possess important knowledge and contacts within the ethnic community and may be instrumental in linking the client with a system of social support. The nonethnic therapist provides a link to the social service system, knowledge of laws and policies, and support and energy from a less traumatized perspective. Often this therapist is able to instill new hopes and dreams. Advocates of this method suggest that the integration and process between the team members are essential for effective intervention and are a critical model for the refugee clients.

A second critical component of the helping relationship with refugee clients is the concept of "active exchange." For many refugees, unfamiliar with Western mental health practices, the efficacy of "talking" is not readily apparent. Rather, the refugee client expects some form of advice, advocacy, immediate symptom relief, or change in the problematic situation. When this does not occur, the clients, as documented with minority groups in general (Acosta, Yamamoto, and Evans, 1982; Sue and McKinney, 1975), often terminate the relationship prematurely. Most clients are familiar with the physician/patient relationship, which entails a brief encounter, a series of questions from the doctor, concrete answers from the patient, and subsequently some sort of symptom relief. Refugee and minority clients often generalize from this relationship to that with the mental health worker. When these expectations are not met, the client becomes disillusioned with the process. To establish a working alliance with the client, the therapist or mental health worker needs to engage the client in an "active exchange," where the client perceives giving and receiving on the part of both client and helper. This reciprocal exchange enables the client to experience tangible gains as a result of participation in the interaction. As discussed in Chapter Two, components in this exchange, on the client's side, include willingness to meet with the helper, self-disclosure and receptivity, and some form of payment for the services, be it a nominal fee or a third-party payment. The therapist demonstrates a willingness to meet with and listen to the client, sharing personal credentials or qualifications, empathizing with the client's emotional pain or frustration, and acknowledging the client's explanations for the problem. On a concrete, practical level, the therapist may also provide specific information about social services, refugee resources, and social support groups in the community.

Construing the working relationship as an "active exchange" also serves to counter the notion of the client as debtor. Inherent in most Asian cultures is the unwillingness to incur obligation. The fear of being indebted to someone often drives Asian clients from a helping relationship. The active exchange promotes a sense of "partnership" in the helping process and transforms the client from a passive recipient to a more active participant, attempting to regain control over one's life situation.

The following two cases represent composites from my clinical and research experience. The objective of these presentations is to provide a sense of the refugee youth's experiences and presenting problems and to illustrate the concepts of therapist credibility and active exchange in the helping process. The first case focuses on a refugee child experiencing a psychological disorder akin to posttraumatic stress disorder, and the second highlights issues for unaccompanied minors in foster care.

Thuy, a 12-year-old Vietnamese girl, was referred to the child and adolescent unit of a community mental health center by her teacher and counselor. Her teacher had noticed a marked deterioration in her academic performance and noted that she frequently complained of headaches and asked to leave the class, seemed to lack energy, showed a loss of appetite, and nonverbally conveyed a general feeling of hopelessness. During the past six months she had changed from a good student, actively involved with peers, to a withdrawn, depressed preadolescent. Most recently, for days at a time, she would not talk unless pressured to and frequently stared off into space.

Thuy was from a middle-class family in Saigon, where until the downfall of South Vietnam, her father had been a lower-level clerk with the army. He fled Saigon with his family, a wife and three children, in 1978; however, during the escape, the family became separated and the wife and two younger children remained in Vietnam. Thuy and her father escaped by boat. Their boat was intercepted by Thai pirates, and Thuy's father was beaten and several women were raped. Although Thuy observed this, she herself was not physically assaulted. Eventually they reached Malaysia, where they remained in a refugee camp for nearly a year until they located relatives in the United States. They have been in the United States for two years and reside in a small apartment with a cousin's family of five in the inner city of a West Coast metropolitan area.

Thuy's father has had a particularly difficult time adjusting to the United States. He struggles with English classes and has been unable to maintain several jobs as a waiter. He attributes these difficulties to the assault during his escape, saying blows to the head impaired his memory and crippled him physically.

Just before the onset of Thuy's problems, she received a letter from her mother informing them of the death of her 5-

year-old brother. Complications from a childhood disease combined with malnutrition had contributed to his death. Thuy remained impassive on receiving this news, while her father wept
uncontrollably, mourning the loss of his only son. Soon after
that, her father was fired from yet another job, seemed to lose
interest in English classes, and just languished around the small
apartment.

At the insistence of the school and accompanied by her
father, Thuy came to the clinic most reluctantly. She was reticent and scowling. Her father immediately began to plead with
the therapist to help Thuy because she was all he had and he de-
pended on her to make it in this country. He vacillated between
sadness and anger toward Thuy. The therapist decided that
father and daughter needed to be seen separately and arranged
for the father to see another therapist, ostensibly to deal with
Thuy's problems, but also to address his own issues.

This case is not atypical of the refugee children who present at mental health clinics. Their histories are replete with
losses, trauma, and unrelenting family pressures. They are also
usually very young.

In this case, establishing credibility took a long time.
Thuy was initially quite distrustful of the therapist, assuming
the therapist to be yet another adult putting pressure and demands on her. Lacking knowledge about "therapists," Thuy assumed she was another teacher or tutor for remedial students.
Additionally, Thuy questioned the motivation of the female
therapist, who was Asian and not Vietnamese and who simultaneously reminded her of her distant mother. The therapist
gave Thuy permission to "not trust" her, recognizing that mistrust was a healthy reaction in this situation and that she would
have to earn Thuy's trust. Noticing Thuy's reticence and her
tendency to doodle during the early sessions, the therapist made
pencils, markers, and paper available. Thuy was too old for the
playroom, but simple art supplies could promote nonverbal
symbolic expression. The doodling seemed to be an outlet for
some anxiety, and Thuy began to banter with the therapist, first
about seemingly inconsequential matters such as objects in the

office, bus routes, and procedures in her classroom. The therapist addressed these issues at face value, realizing they were questions about American ways. The beginning of an "active exchange," a reciprocal relationship, was occurring; though remaining silent in the early sessions, Thuy continued to come. In turn, the therapist gave her time, patience, no pressure, and concrete materials—paper, markers, pencils—with no explicit expectation. Each party was contributing to the interaction. On the next level, Thuy shared her perplexity about American ways; the therapist reciprocated with education about customs, behaviors, and attitudes of Americans. They then moved on to more disturbing matters, such as racial incidents on the bus and harassment by other children in her classroom. Over the next two months, Thuy experienced the therapist as dependable, regular, genuinely listening, and, when asked, willing to give advice and suggestions for handling different experiences in the new country.

Of critical importance to the intervention with refugees is allowing them to "tell their story" (Carlin and Sokoloff, 1985; Kinzie, 1981; Rudnick and Harmatys, 1987). Refugee youth rarely have the opportunity to do this, as family rules implicitly advocate "Don't talk about it." Community pressures to keep "the secrets" hidden and not incur shame for unavoidable events similarly inhibit disclosure about the emigration. However, the ventilation of their often remarkable and horrifying stories of flight may be cathartic and essential to the building of trust. Thuy eventually recounted her story of flight, which included severe deprivations of food and water when on the boat as well as in the camp and severe brutality by sea pirates. Although Thuy herself was not attacked, she cringed in fear, hearing the screaming, and cried out for her own mother. The details of the stories are not as important as the accompanying emotions and associations. Thuy was only 9 years old at the time of the pirate attack; however, she still has nightmares about it and currently associates the women's screaming with the plight of her mother in Vietnam. Until the notice of her brother's death in Vietnam, Thuy had maintained a positive image of her mother, believing that she was safe, comfortable, and happy in Vietnam, much as Thuy remembered prior to their flight. Thuy firmly wanted to believe this; however, her brother's death penetrated this denial, and her fears and longing for her mother reemerged. She held much disdain for her father's perceived weaknesses: failure to bring the entire family out of Vietnam, inability to thwart the pirates, inability to maintain a job and save money to achieve family reunification, and excessive reliance on her.

Adhering to a model of "active exchange," what did the therapist give? With the child's continued disclosure, the therapist provided consistency, predictability, and support, things currently absent in this child's life. She was an attentive listener and acknowledged the child's pain and suffering. Of particular importance at this point is the careful monitoring of one's reactions to the child's story of horror and inhumanity. The therapist was careful not to show natural feelings of revulsion or to act on tendencies to be outraged at the persecutors or overidealizing of the refugee's endurance. Strong emotions from the therapist may inhibit the child's own expression of emotion.

For many refugee children, the opportunity to grieve over significant losses is inhibited. This was the case with Thuy, who on arrival in the United States, was immediately thrust into the role of caretaker for her father and "hope of the future" for her family. The therapist facilitated the delayed grief process for Thuy, for her losses of her brother, her homeland, and her mother and sister. This was begun with gentle yet firm questioning about her life in Vietnam. Thuy's grief was manifest as anger and rage toward her father for breaking up the family and failing to adequately protect her. Expression of these feelings was particularly difficult for Thuy, as it is culturally unacceptable to speak disrespectfully of one's father or other family members. However, when these feelings were legitimized by the therapist's acceptance and reassurance that many children in this situation would have similar feelings, Thuy seemed noticeably relieved. Thus, in the process of "active exchange," the therapist gave Thuy permission to grieve; in turn, Thuy entrusted the therapist with culturally prohibited feelings. Working through the grief also involved instilling hope for the future. For refugees, the grief process often remains incomplete because the prospects for family reunification are uncertain. In these circumstances, the therapist gives the youth ways to cope—for example, to anticipate and prepare for the feelings associated with receiving a letter from home or to anticipate the anxiety around birthdays or ethnic holidays.

The outcome of the intervention with Thuy was not complete symptom relief. Her presenting symptoms did subside and her schoolwork improved. However, she continued to have nightmares occasionally and felt anxiety in new situations. Some days her intense longing for her mother became so painful that she sank into periods of despair and weeping. However, she had discovered ways to live with her memories and the sense of disconnectedness in her life, so that her daily functioning was considerably improved.

In addition to the individual work, the therapist had regular contact with Thuy's teacher, who said Thuy had been indirectly involved in several interracial skirmishes at school. With the assistance of the mental health clinic, the school was initiating interracial student panels to address cultural differences and discuss reasons for racial hostility. Thuy was selected to participate in these panels.

Thuy's family situation had also improved. Her father, though still unemployed, periodically saw a therapist and had become more involved in the community mutual assistance association. His physical symptoms and complaints, the culturally acceptable manifestation of psychological distress and anxiety, had diminished. The emerging difficulties in the family revolved around cultural and generational conflicts. Thuy acknowledged the cultural imperative to respect and obey one's father; however, given her superior competence in American society relative to her father's diminished coping, this became a point of conflict. As Thuy became more bold, assertive, and self-initiating, adopting more Western behaviors, her father viewed this as a repudiation of her cultural heritage and family identity. Thuy received the confusing message that she was expected to succeed in America but to avoid becoming American.

This case discussion has focused primarily on the process

of "active exchange" in the individual therapy. In addition, the intervention was ecologically focused, targeting several systems pertinent to Thuy's life.

Sann, a 15-year-old Cambodian male, came to the attention of the community mental health clinic through the Department of Social Services. Sann had a history of poor school performance and truancy and had been in three foster homes in two years. Most recently, he was apprehended by juvenile authorities for petty theft.

Sann had been in the United States for two years. He had come in 1982 as an unaccompanied minor. His family had been middle-class residents of Phnom Penh until driven to the countryside by Khmer Rouge guerrillas under the Pol Pot regime. During this forced march, his mother, who had recently given birth, the newborn baby, and a younger sister died of starvation, dehydration, and exhaustion. Sann, his older sister, and his father were sent to a labor camp for nine months, where they witnessed regular beatings and deaths, until their escape, which involved walking across Cambodia into Thailand. During this escape, Sann's father was killed by a land mine, and Sann and his sister became separated. To this day, he is unsure of the whereabouts of his sister or even whether she is alive. Sann spent two years in refugee camps in Thailand, where he learned rudimentary English.

Entering foster care at age 13, Sann found it difficult to accept his new parental figures. He resented their authority and concern, and he reacted with sullenness and suspicion. His caseworker described both sets of foster parents as highly motivated, caring couples who were unable to develop a relationship with Sann and requested his reassignment after he was caught stealing money from them. Similar problems were occurring in his third placement.

The caseworker described Sann as a highly intelligent yet very vigilant and mistrustful child suffering from severe depression related to his traumatic and tumultuous life experiences. He vacillated between a sense of hopelessness and a strong will to survive. His coping skills were derived from his escape and camp experiences and had not been modified to fit his current living situation. He was a loner and seemed uninterested in peer relationships.

Mollica (1987), of the Indochinese Psychiatry Clinic in Boston, suggests that therapeutic objectives with refugees are (1) to increase the client's ability to cope in family, community, school, and work settings, acknowledging that the symptoms and memories from the trauma may last indefinitely and (2) to assist the client in re-creating a future that was destroyed by the trauma. For Sann, it would also have been ideal to regain some of the childhood that had been destroyed; however, connecting him with new elements in his present society took precedence. Adhering to an ecological model, the intervention with Sann was multifocused. In contrast to the work with Thuy, the individual therapy was a much smaller component of the intervention. The therapist occasionally met with Sann, but her role was more that of a resource broker. She linked him with a therapy group for Cambodian refugee adolescents, consulted with the caseworker who was doing family work with the foster family, advocated for a special tutorial program as he was struggling in school, and connected him with refugee community agencies who could assist him in a strategy to determine his sister's whereabouts.

Initially, credibility was not an issue for the therapist: In Sann's eyes, she had none. However, Sann knew that she had authority and that in order to avoid juvenile hall, he had to comply with the treatment program. The turning point for Sann was brought about by the group program. The refugee adolescents had the opportunity to share their stories with others who could understand on a personal level. After initial hesitation, they began to readily discuss events in their homeland, life before the political disruptions, and incidents during the escape. Their growing camaraderie, built on shared experiences and shared memories, tended to dissipate the powerful grip and intrusiveness of these traumatic memories. The Cambodian adolescents, all males and in foster placements, were on the verge of regaining a sense of positive control in their lives.

The issues in the foster family system included differing expectations, cultural misunderstandings, and conflicts around independence and control. Sann's foster family was a middle-class Caucasian American family associated with a church organization that sponsored refugees. Finances were a first source of conflict. As a survivor, Sann existed by looking out for himself and taking whatever he could get. His efforts to gain money and material possessions were thwarted by the foster family. Each month there was conflict over the disposition of the foster care stipend. This is an issue that seems common to many refugees' foster care arrangements (Mortland and Egan, 1987). Second, there was continual conflict over Sann's role in the family. Still bewildered by American customs and confused about his own identity, Sann resisted integration into the family. He remained distant and aloof, uncommunicative, and erratic in complying with family chores and responsibilities. Sann assumed the role of an uninvolved boarder, which made the family feel unappreciated, used, and annoyed. In their frustration, the foster parents became less sensitive to Sann's emotional needs and inadvertently belittled his heritage with such comments as "You should consider yourself lucky you're in America; a lot of kids your age are still living in primitive conditions in Cambodia." Third, after being on his own since age 11, Sann had difficulty accepting the authority of the foster parents and the infringement on his independence. Like other refugees in foster care (Mortland and Egan, 1987), he resented family rules, inability to handle his own federal stipend, and being forced to adapt to a family that was not really his. Sann felt angry and ashamed that he did not have his own family, and he resented the family in which he had been involuntarily placed. With consultation from the therapist, the caseworker addressed these issues with the family and tried to develop contractual agreements between Sann and the family. The caseworker tried to prepare the family for emotional assaults stemming from Sann's displacement of anger about his own family and situation onto the foster family. Clarification of roles, of the cultural meanings of family, and of the preconceptions of each other's cultures were addressed by the caseworker.

The intervention with the school was unsuccessful, as neither the school nor Sann was motivated. The counselor felt that Sann's needs were beyond the school's limited and already strained resources and that his age would soon make him "eligible to drop out." Although his school was racially and ethnically mixed, he felt like an outcast. He was embarrassed to be in classes with students several years younger and avoided contact with other refugees because of his status as a "foster kid," a refugee without a family. In his life experiences, he could find little to share with his nonrefugee peers. In spite of the joint efforts of the therapist and counselor to devise a special program, Sann eventually dropped out.

Sann's withdrawal from school coincided with his increased involvement in the group of Cambodian adolescents and entry into the refugee community. At the therapist's insistence, Sann enrolled in English-language courses and became active at a community center serving Cambodian refugees. Here he made contacts and learned of refugee agencies that could assist him in locating his sister. Sann was beginning to assemble pieces for a future. While acknowledging that she might have died, Sann could at least begin to talk about her, his longing for her, and his fears for her demise. And, most important, he had become reconnected with his culture and his community.

In order to reengage Sann, the concept of "active exchange" was applied repeatedly and in various settings. He was retrieved from his isolation by the mutuality in the group program for Cambodian adolescents; the caseworker negotiated the give-and-take with the foster family; and the ethnic community gave him a sense of belonging and hope for the future in exchange for his renewed motivation and contributions to the center. In essence, the overall intervention represented a balance and reciprocity between helpers and client.

Conclusions

With few exceptions, Southeast Asian refugee youth have spent a significant portion of their lives in violent conditions, experiencing serious loss, fear of the unknown, prolonged periods of waiting, and discontinuities in their schooling and health care. The escape from their homeland was usually precipitous, with little warning or time for preparation and farewells. The journey itself was often traumatic and, at times, life-threatening. These experiences were intensified by the dynamic interaction of these frightened children with their traumatized parents or other accompanying adults (Huyck and Fields, 1981). In general, the dramas of refugee youth are extreme and tragic, and their stories are a testimony to both the brutality of human beings and the resilience of the human spirit. Professionals in a range of fields can learn much about survival and coping from these children.

This chapter has presented the developmental and psychosocial conflicts of Southeast Asian refugee youth in the context of their unique migration and sociocultural histories. Although many of these children and adolescents have adapted well to their new life circumstances in the United States, some are still struggling with memories of the past, psychological wounds from the trauma, and new intercultural and intergenerational dilemmas. The effects of war and uprooting are subject to individual variation, ranging from major disruptions in development to incidental annoyances. The degree of risk for psychological disturbance also varies and seems correlated with economic and familial resources. The common finding in many studies identifies unaccompanied minors and Amerasian children as higher-risk groups.

An ecological model for intervention is based on the assumption that an individual's development is both the cause and the effect of multiple system interactions. The task for the therapist working with refugee youth is to identify the unique systems and cultural frameworks to be incorporated into the intervention. In this sense, one's role may range from individual therapist to school consultant to advocate; the arenas for investigation may be not only the individual and family but also schools, work settings, social service agencies, and community organizations. In my experience, therapist credibility and active exchange are essential ingredients in a working relationship. Because there are no definitive routes to successful outcomes, therapists must be innovative in developing appropriate interventions for this unique population.

References

Acosta, F. X., Yamamoto, J., and Evans, L. A. *Effective Psychotherapy for Low-Income and Minority Patients.* New York: Plenum, 1982.

Ahmed, P., Tims, F., and Kolker, A. "After the Fall: Indochinese Refugees in the United States." In G. Coelho and P. Ahmed (eds.), *Uprooting and Development: Dilemmas of Coping with Modernization.* New York: Plenum, 1980.

"Asian Immigrants Say Schoolmates Harass Them." *San Francisco Chronicle*, Mar. 28, 1987.

Aylesworth, L., Ossorio, P., and Osaki, L. "Stress and Mental Health Among Vietnamese in the United States." In R. Endo, S. Sue, and N. Wagner (eds.), *Asian-Americans: Social and Psychological Perspectives.* Vol. 2. Palo Alto, Calif.: Science and Behavior Books, 1980.

Borton, L. *Sensing the Enemy: An American Woman Among the Boat People of Vietnam.* New York: Doubleday, 1984.

Bronfenbrenner, U. *The Ecology of Human Development: Experiments by Nature and Design.* Cambridge, Mass.: Harvard University Press, 1979.

Carlin, J., and Sokoloff, B. "Mental Health Treatment Issues for Southeast Asian Refugee Children." In T. Owan (ed.), *Southeast Asian Mental Health: Treatment, Prevention, Services, Training, and Research.* Washington, D.C.: U.S. Department of Health and Human Services, 1985.

Chi, N. H. "Vietnam: The Culture of War." In E. Tepper (ed.), *Southeast Asian Exodus: From Tradition to Resettlement—Understanding Refugees from Laos, Kampuchea and Vietnam in Canada.* Ottawa: Canadian Asian Studies Association, Carleton University, 1980.

Cohon, D. "Psychological Adaptation and Dysfunction Among Refugees." *International Migration Review*, 1981, *15* (1), 255–275.

DeMonchy, M., and Pin-Riebe, S. "Cross-Cultural Team Therapy with Cambodian Trauma Survivors." Paper presented at third annual meeting of the Society for Traumatic Stress Studies, Baltimore, Oct. 1987.

DeVos, G. "Ethnic Adaptation and Minority Status." *Journal of Cross-Cultural Psychology*, 1980, *11* (1), 101–124.

Ferguson, B. "Successful Refugee Resettlement: Vietnamese Values, Beliefs, and Strategies." Unpublished doctoral dissertation, School of Social Welfare, University of California at Berkeley, 1984.

Fong, T. "Cultural Dialogue Program Eases Tensions Between Blacks and SE Asians at Oakland's Fremont High." *East/West News*, June 18, 1987, p. 6.

Garmezy, N., and Rutter, M. (eds.). *Stress, Coping and Development in Children*. New York: McGraw-Hill, 1983.

Garry, R. "Cambodia." In E. Tepper (ed.), *Southeast Asian Exodus: From Tradition to Resettlement—Understanding Refugees from Laos, Kampuchea and Vietnam in Canada*. Ottawa: Canadian Asian Studies Association, Carleton University, 1980.

Gordon, L. "The Missing Children: Mortality and Fertility in a Southeast Asian Refugee Population." Paper presented at annual meeting of the Population Association of America, Chicago, May 1987.

Harding, R., and Looney, J. "Problems of Southeast Asian Children in a Refugee Camp." *American Journal of Psychiatry*, 1977, *134* (4), 407–411.

Hiebert, M. "Hanoi Said Ready to Speed Amerasians' Exit." *Washington Post*, Jan. 21, 1988, p. 1.

Huang, K.H.C., and Huang, L. N. "Perceived Competence and Self-Worth in Vietnamese Refugee and Caucasian-American Children: A Comparison Study." Unpublished paper, 1984.

Huyck, E., and Fields, R. "Impact of Resettlement on Refugee Children." *International Migration Review*, 1981, *15* (1), 246–254.

Kelley, B. "Vietnam's 'Lost Generation' of Youth New Focal Point for Racial Conflicts." *East/West News*, Apr. 30, 1987, p. 4.

Kinzie, J. "Evaluation and Psychotherapy of Indochinese Refugee Patients." *American Journal of Psychotherapy*, 1981, *35* (2), 251–261.

Lappin, J., and Scott, S. "Intervention in a Vietnamese Refugee Family." In M. McGoldrick, J. K. Pearce, and J. Giordano (eds.), *Ethnicity and Family Therapy.* New York: Guilford Press, 1982.

Le, D. "Mental Health and Vietnamese Children." In G. J. Powell (ed.), *The Psychosocial Development of Minority Group Children.* New York: Brunner/Mazel, 1983.

Lee, E. "Assessment and Treatment of Southeast Asian-American Survivors of Mass Violence." Paper presented at third annual meeting of the Society for Traumatic Stress Studies, Baltimore, Oct. 1987.

Lin, K. M., Masuda, M., and Tazuma, L. "Adaptational Problems of Vietnamese Refugees: Part III. Case Studies in Clinic and Field: Adaptive and Maladaptive." *Psychiatric Journal of the University of Ottawa*, 1982, *7* (3), 173–183.

Loescher, G., and Scanlan, J. *Calculated Kindness: Refugees and America's Half-Open Door, 1945 to the Present.* New York: Free Press, 1986.

Meinhardt, K., Tom, S., Tse, P., and Yu, C. Y. "Southeast Asian Refugees in the 'Silicon Valley': The Asian Health Assessment Project." *Amerasia Journal*, 1985–86, *12* (2), 43–66.

Mollica, R. "A Worldwide Survey of the Psychological Impact and Treatment of Refugee Trauma and Torture." Paper presented at third annual meeting of the Society for Traumatic Stress Studies, Baltimore, Oct. 1987.

Mortland, C., and Egan, M. 'Vietnamese Youth in American Foster Care." *Social Work*, 1987, *32* (3), 240–245.

"The New Americans, Are They Welcome? A Refugee Referendum." *Gallup Poll Index*, May 1975, pp. 2–5.

Nguyen, N. N. *The Will of Heaven: A Story of One Vietnamese and the End of His World.* New York: Dutton, 1982.

Nguyen, T., Long, P. B., and Aylesworth, L. *The ADAMHA Role in ADM Service, Training and Research for Indochinese Refugees.* A Report by the Indochinese Refugee Consultation to the Alcohol, Drug Abuse, and Mental Health Administration. Washington, D.C.: Indochinese Refugee Consultation, 1980.

Nidorf, J. "Mental Health and Refugee Youths: A Model for Diagnostic Training." In T. Owan (ed.), *Southeast Asian Mental Health: Treatment, Prevention, Services, Training, and Research.* Washington, D.C.: U.S. Department of Health and Human Services, 1985.

Oberdorfer, D. "Indochinese Americans Seek Help for Refugees." *Washington Post,* Mar. 3, 1987, p. A18.

Redick, L. T., and Wood, B. "Cross-Cultural Problems for Southeast Asian Refugee Minors." *Child Welfare,* 1982, *61* (6), 365–373.

Reimers, D. *Still the Golden Door: The Third World Comes to America.* New York: Columbia University Press, 1985.

Rudnick, J., and Harmatys, J. "The Young Immigrants: Treating PTSD in Refugee Adolescents." Paper presented at third annual meeting of the Society for Traumatic Stress Studies, Baltimore, Oct. 1987.

Sheehy, G. *Spirit of Survival.* New York: Morrow, 1986.

Sluzki, C. "Migration and Family Conflict." *Family Process,* 1979, *18* (4), 379–390.

Sokoloff, B., Carlin, J., and Pham, H. "Five-Year Follow-up of Vietnamese Refugee Children in the United States. Part I." *Clinical Pediatrics,* 1984, *23,* 565–570.

Sue, S., and McKinney, H. "Asian-Americans in the Community Health Care System." *American Journal of Orthopsychiatry,* 1975, *45* (1), 111–118.

Sue, S., and Zane, N. "The Role of Culture and Cultural Techniques in Psychotherapy: A Critique and Reformulation." *American Psychologist,* 1987, *42* (1), 37–45.

Terr, L. "Children of Chowchilla: A Study of Psychic Trauma." *Psychoanalytic Study of the Child,* 1979, *34,* 547–623.

United Nations. *U.N. Convention Relating to the Status of Refugees, 1951.* No. 2545, 189 UNTS (U.N. Treaty Series) 137, Article 1A (1), July 28, 1951.

U.S. Congress. *Refugee Act of 1980.* Public Law 96-212. Hearings, 96th Congress, Mar. 17, 1980.

U.S. Department of Health and Human Services. *Refugee Reset-*

tlement Program: Report to the Congress. Washington, D.C.: U.S. Department of Health and Human Services, 1987.

Vietnamese Children's Resettlement Advisory Group. *Recommendations of the Vietnamese Children's Resettlement Advisory Group.* Unpublished report submitted to the Interagency Task Force for Indochinese Refugees (Senator Edward Kennedy, Chairperson), Washington, D.C., 1975.

Vignes, J., and Hall, R. "Adjustment of a Group of Vietnamese People to the United States." *American Journal of Psychiatry,* 1979, *136* (4A), 442–444.

Williams, D., and Westermeyer, J. "Psychiatric Problems Among Adolescent Southeast Asian Refugees: A Descriptive Study." *Journal of Nervous and Mental Disease,* 1983, *171,* 79–85.

10

Biracial Adolescents

Jewelle Taylor Gibbs

Since the early 1960s, American society has undergone some profound social, cultural, and demographic changes. As a natural consequence of the civil rights movement, the counterculture movement, and the Vietnam War protests, conventional social barriers were weakened and contacts between diverse racial and ethnic groups greatly increased. As social interactions among members of different ethnic groups expanded, interracial marriages and partnerships inevitably increased (Cretser and Leon, 1982; Stuart and Abt, 1973; Washington, 1970). These mixed marriages have produced a growing number of biracial children, many of whom are now adolescents and young adults.

This chapter describes biracial adolescents as an emerging population of young people who have some unique characteristics, some potential problems, and some special needs, all of which are related to their ambiguous ethnicity and their need to define their identities in a society where race has always been a significant social dimension. As this group has increased in the population, there has been a concomitant blurring of racial distinctions and an increasing societal tolerance toward interracial marriage (Cretser and Leon, 1982; Ladner, 1977). Despite these changes, we lack information about these biracial youth, who are faced with the developmental task of integrating two ethnic identities and, frequently, two distinct cultural heritages. Since adolescence is the stage during which these issues emerge as

322

major psychosocial tasks, it is important for mental health clinicians, educators, and other human service professionals who serve youth to understand the impact of biracial identity on the attitudes, behaviors, and problems of these youth.

Demographic data on the population of biracial children are subject to a number of statistical biases because the validity of self-professed racial labels on marriage applications and birth certificates is questionable, particularly for children born out of wedlock. Since the federal government has collected statistics on Black/White interracial marriages for the longest period, this chapter will focus on adolescents who are offspring of Black/White unions.

In 1986 there were over 827,000 interracial married couples in the United States, including 181,000 Black/White couples (U.S. Bureau of the Census, 1987). Although Black/White married couples constituted only 22 percent of all interracial married couples in 1986, the actual number had nearly tripled from 65,000 in 1970. The majority of these families reside in urban areas of the North, Midwest, and West Coast, where they have found less overt racial prejudice and greater tolerance for diversity in family structures and life-styles. Metropolitan areas with a significant number of interracial families are New York, Boston, Chicago, Minneapolis–St. Paul, Denver, Seattle, San Francisco, and Los Angeles (Collins, 1984).

Estimates of the number of biracial children and adolescents in the United States range from 600,000 to 5 million, but these estimates include offspring of other interracial unions, such as Asian/White and Indian/White (Collins, 1984). Since "Children of the Rainbow's" estimate of 1 million biracial youth was based on 1980 population data, it is probably reasonable to assume that currently there are 300,000–500,000 Black/White biracial offspring, many of them still in adolescence or young adulthood.

A recent series about interracial families in the *Los Angeles Times* (Njeri, 1988) described the experiences of these families, the varied ways in which they cope with their uniqueness, and the complex challenges faced by biracial teenagers in their efforts to separate from their families and establish their own identities. Quoting from several of these articulate young people, Njeri noted the emerging sense of community among biracial persons and the perceived need for a new racial category to describe themselves, a view also advocated in a study of interracial families by Gay (1987).

Historical Background

Interracial families are a relatively recent phenomenon in American society, primarily because of three historical factors. First, many states passed laws before and after the Civil War prohibiting marriage between Whites and non-Whites. As Gay (1987) points out, these laws were based on theories of white supremacy and myths about racial mixing that were frequently supported by conservative political and religious writings. Second, even after the Supreme Court declared these antimiscegenation laws unconstitutional in 1967, social sanctions continued to operate against interracial marriages, and the costs of defying these sanctions were very high, including family disapproval and alienation, social exclusion, and discrimination in housing, employment, and public accommodations (Gay, 1987). Third, social and economic discrimination against Blacks and other non-Whites resulted in the development of two essentially separate, castelike communities, so that Blacks and Whites had few opportunities for social relationships and shared activities. Thus, although informal contacts and nonmarital sexual liaisons between Blacks and Whites occurred despite these barriers, marriages between these groups were relatively rare before World War II.

After World War II and the Korean War, Black soldiers brought home European and Korean war brides. Coinciding with a number of other significant changes in American society, these interracial couples settled in communities that seemed more hospitable to them and were generally more open to the other postwar innovations in economy, technology, and social structure. These communities included the newly expanded suburbs with housing developments tailored to the needs of returning veterans with low-interest mortgages, such as the Levittown planned communities in the Northeast, which were among the first to promote integrated middle-income housing.

During the postwar period of the late 1940s and early 1950s, landmark Supreme Court decisions also overturned many of the legal underpinnings of discrimination in housing, public accommodations, and education, further generating a social climate of tolerance and equal opportunity that was beneficial for interracial couples as well as for all non-Whites (Omi and Winant, 1986).

After the Supreme Court outlawed school segregation in 1954 and the Montgomery, Alabama, bus boycott began in 1955, the South witnessed a remarkable alliance between young Blacks and Whites who mounted a successful decade of civil rights protests, which culminated in two major federal civil rights bills in 1964 and 1965 (Chambers, 1968). Although these protests and the ensuing legislation met with much resistance, the important legacy of this era was the breaking down of institutional barriers to Blacks, as well as the opening up of greater opportunities for interracial social interaction in educational, employment, recreational, and cultural settings. These opportunities inevitably led to more interracial dating and more interracial marriages, as can be inferred from the dramatic increase in the Black/White marriage rate in less than fifteen years (Porterfield, 1982).

As noted earlier, the social upheaval brought about by the counterculture movement of the late 1960s and 1970s, the Black student protests on White college campuses, and the Vietnam War protests was accompanied by significant shifts in Black/White relationships and radically different norms of social behavior regarding sexuality, drug use, and marital patterns. Antiestablishment attitudes and massive rejection of middle-class norms among young Whites and Blacks fostered an environment of social and political experimentation, including interracial relationships, communes, and political organizations. In some liberal communities and on many college campuses, it became a sign of "radical chic" to date interracially, so that the incidence of Black/White affairs and marriages rose, with a corresponding increase in biracial children (Cretser and Leon, 1982; Pope, 1985).

In more recent years the trend toward interracial marriages appears to have increased, perhaps for a number of reasons, including the greater number of unions between Black females and White males, the weakened sanctions against unions between Black males and White females, and the general decrease in societal disapproval of interracial marriage. In fact, a Gallup-poll analysis of changes in American attitudes toward interracial marriage found that, between 1968 and 1983, the proportion of people who expressed disapproval decreased from 72 percent to 50 percent. Although half of the American public may still disapprove of interracial marriage, the trend is clearly toward a more liberal viewpoint.

Social and Cultural Issues

One of the major issues for interracial families is the transmission of a coherent sense of a cultural heritage and an ethnic identity to their children. In contrast to other minority families, these parents do not share the same racial or cultural heritage even if they are from the same socioeconomic background and educational level. Whites and Blacks in America have different historical roots, have different social experiences, and are reared in different subcultural contexts. As the descriptions in Chapters Five and Six clearly show, the predominant influences shaping the experiences of Blacks in America have been slavery, discrimination, and poverty. Blacks were forced to develop a "separate and unequal" set of social institutions (for example, churches, schools, social and health services, small businesses, and fraternal, social, and political organizations) and have maintained many of these institutions even after segregation was legally abolished. This quasi caste system required most Blacks to become familiar with the institutions of the dominant society to the extent that this knowledge facilitated their educational or economic activities, but few Whites found it necessary or useful to acquire any knowledge about Black cultural or social institutions. Even for most middle-class Blacks, this legacy has left its imprint in many social, psychological, and behavioral characteristics that reflect an adaptation to prejudice and social exclusion (Jenkins, 1982; Pierce, 1970; Pinderhughes, 1982; Willie, Brown, and Kramer, 1973).

By contrast, Whites came to America voluntarily as immigrants or refugees and so were able to maintain much of their cultural heritage while adjusting to a new country. Regardless of their country of origin, White immigrants were eventually able to become fully acculturated and assimilated into the mainstream society through educational and economic mobility. Thus, while few Blacks have enjoyed the full benefits of citizenship, most Whites have been able to enjoy at least a part of the American dream. This disparity in social and cultural backgrounds sometimes makes it quite difficult for Whites and Blacks to communicate and to understand each other's viewpoints. More relevant to interracial families, it poses a special challenge to parents, who must transmit to their children knowledge about their family history and continuity, a positive sense about their dual cultural heritage, and an integrated sense of an ethnic identity. As McGoldrick (1982, p. 5) asserts, "Ethnicity is a powerful influence in determining identity. A sense of belonging and of historical continuity is a basic psychological need. We may ignore it or cut it off by changing our names [and] rejecting our families and social backgrounds, but we do so to the detriment of our well-being."

Despite evidence of more liberal societal attitudes toward interracial marriage, studies of these couples and their children suggest that they frequently encounter problems of family approval, community acceptance, job discrimination, and social isolation (Gay, 1987; Porterfield, 1978; Stuart and Abt, 1973; Washington, 1970). Biracial children and adolescents are particularly vulnerable to differential treatment by their parents and relatives, social rejection by their peers, and ambivalent attention in their schools and communities. These experiences have been described in the few ethnographic, social, psychological, and clinical studies of this group reported in the literature, which establish a framework for viewing the mental health issues for biracial youth.

Mental Health Issues for Biracial Adolescents

Biracial children and adolescents have legitimate claims to majority and minority ethnicity, and yet society forces them to define and label themselves as members of a minority group. The existence of a dual racial identity and a dual cultural heritage poses dilemmas for these youth as they enter adolescence. Erikson (1959) proposed that the central task of adolescence is to form a stable identity, which he described as "a sense of personal sameness and historical continuity." He delineated a series of developmental tasks to be successfully negotiated in the development of a healthy and positive identity: development of a personal identity (sense of uniqueness and self-esteem), establishment of a sense of autonomy and independence from parents, development of the ability to relate to same-sex and other-sex peers, and commitment to a vocational choice.

Several authors have pointed out that identity formation for Black adolescents may be a more difficult and problematic task, particularly in view of the messages they receive from the dominant society that they are members of a disadvantaged and devalued minority group (Erikson, 1968; Jenkins, 1982; Logan, 1981; Taylor, 1976). Chestang (1984) notes that Blacks must integrate a "personal" and a "racial" identity in order to form a cohesive total identity. Recent history offers numerous examples of Black youth who have overcome barriers of discrimination and the social devaluation by Whites to achieve remarkable accomplishments that reflect an internal sense of purpose and personal worth, for example Bill Cosby, Carl Lewis, Jesse Jackson, Barbara Jordan, and Alice Walker.

Empirical studies of biracial children indicate that their racial attitudes and self-concepts develop differently than those of either Black or White children (Gunthorpe, 1978; Logan, 1981; Payne, 1977). In one study, accurate racial identification decreased as skin color darkened, suggesting that the darker children had a more negative self-concept. However, the findings of these studies have been challenged by other studies that found biracial children to have equivalent or higher self-esteem compared with their nonmixed peers (Chang, 1974; Duffy, 1978; Jacobs, 1978).

If identity formation is more problematic for Black than White adolescents, then one can hypothesize that it would be even more difficult for adolescents with a biracial background (Sommers, 1964; Piskacek and Golub, 1973). By their teen years, these youth are fully cognizant of the differential prestige accorded to Blacks and Whites in America, the differential opportunities available to each racial group, and the advantages and disadvantages of belonging to each. Moreover, their normal identity conflicts will inevitably be exacerbated by their feelings of love and loyalty to each parent, especially when they can easily attribute ambivalent feelings toward either parent as a sign of racial rejection rather than as an expression of the normative separation process (Adams, 1973; Lyles and others, 1985; Sebring, 1985).

Community surveys of biracial children and adolescents have also produced conflicting findings. Whereas earlier researchers focused on the incidence of low self-esteem, confused racial or ethnic identity, and psychological or behavioral problems among these youth (Benson, 1981; Gordon, 1964; Henriques, 1974; Ladner, 1977; Piskacek and Golub, 1973), more recent authors have emphasized their adaptability, resiliency, and creativity (Gay, 1987; Johnson and Nagoshi, 1986; Poussaint, 1984). Positive outcomes are predicted for those youth who are reared in supportive families, have a sense of competence and high self-esteem, and are involved in supportive social networks (Adams, 1973; Lyles and others, 1985; Sebring, 1985).

Biracial children in school settings have also been characterized as having a high incidence of academic and behavioral problems as well as identity conflicts (McRoy and Freeman, 1986). Further, these problems have been noted among Black or racially mixed children who have been adopted by White parents (McRoy, Zurcher, Lauderdale, and Anderson, 1984; Simon and Alstein, 1977; Silverman and Feigelman, 1981). Although the majority of these adopted children appear well adjusted, those who do have problems are more likely to reveal them as they enter adolescence.

Clinical studies of biracial children are sparse, but a pioneer study by Teicher (1968) noted that these children had problems of identification with the minority parent, sexual-identity conflicts, and problems of adjustment to a predominantly White environment. These observations have been supported by reports of clinicians who have treated a variety of biracial children, adolescents, college students, and interracial families (Adams, 1973; Faulkner and Kich, 1983; Gibbs, 1973; Lyles and others, 1985; Sebring, 1985). In addition, these latter studies have described a range of psychological and behavioral problems in these youth, including conduct disorders, substance abuse, academic problems, psychosomatic disorders, depression, and suicidal behaviors.

Finally, in a 1986 survey of fifty social service, mental health, special education, and probation agencies located in the San Francisco area, 60 percent of the thirty-one responding agencies reported that referrals of biracial adolescents had increased during the past ten years and that this group was overrepresented among their adolescent client population (Gibbs, 1987). These clients had been referred for a broad spectrum of problems similar to those earlier described in the clinical literature. Not only had the incidence of referrals in this group increased, but their presenting symptoms had also become more severe.

Despite the obvious limitations of clinical studies and the difficulty of drawing any generalizations from so few studies of biracial children and adolescents, some issues have been identified across a wide range of studies, as well as some themes of potential problems and protective coping mechanisms. First, these biracial youth must integrate dual racial and/or cultural identifications while also learning how to develop a positive self-concept and sense of competence. Second, as they enter adolescence, they must synthesize their earlier identifications into a coherent and stable sense of a personal identity as well as a positive racial identity. In accomplishing this task, they must deal effectively with the related tasks of developing peer relationships, defining their sexual orientation and sexual preference, making a career choice, and separating from their parents, all of which may be more problematic for this group.

In conceptualizing the process of identity development for biracial adolescents, I have proposed that they may experience conflicts in their efforts to resolve five major psychosocial tasks: (1) conflicts about their dual racial/ethnic identity, (2) conflicts about their social marginality, (3) conflicts about their sexuality and choice of sexual partners, (4) conflicts about separation from their parents, and (5) conflicts about their educational or career aspirations (Gibbs, 1987; Gibbs and Moskowitz-Sweet, 1986). Both clinical studies and community surveys indicate that these conflicts may be expressed in a variety of psychological and behavioral symptoms, ranging from mild symptoms of anxiety and depression to moderate symptoms of academic underachievement and peer conflicts to severe symptoms of delinquency, substance abuse, and suicidal behaviors. At the milder end of the spectrum, these symptoms reflect a pattern of identity confusion, while the moderate level of symptomatology reflects a form of identity diffusion or foreclosure and the severe symptoms reflect the formation of a negative identity (Hauser, 1972).

The consensus of clinicians is that those teenagers who experience difficulties in negotiating this identity process are those most likely to be referred for assessment and treatment (Adams, 1973; Lyles and others, 1985; Sebring, 1985). Further, some clinicians would predict that biracial adolescents are at greater risk for problematic outcomes because of their potential vulnerability to conflicts in each of the central developmental tasks. Although there are no epidemiological data to support this hypothesis, clinical evidence suggests that an understanding of this important developmental process in biracial adolescents will increase clinicians' sensitivity to their unique concerns and will enable them to serve this emerging group more effectively.

In the following section these identity conflicts will be illustrated with case vignettes and guidelines for assessment. The case examples are drawn from my experiences over an eighteen-year period as a clinician, consultant, and supervisor in college mental health clinics, outpatient psychiatric clinics, and private practice. The clinical material is supplemented by interpretations of the developmental, empirical, and clinical studies summarized earlier.

Conflicts and Coping Strategies of Biracial Adolescents

In this section I propose that the central issue for the clinician to assess in evaluating biracial adolescents is their underlying attitudes toward their dual racial/ethnic heritage, which must be successfully integrated before they can resolve the developmental tasks in the four related areas of identity achievement. The defense mechanisms and coping strategies employed by these teenagers to handle these conflicts are also described. An ecological framework is used to examine four other important domains of assessment, encompassing individual, family, school, and peer areas.

Conflicts About Racial/Ethnic Identity. Racial identity is the most widespread conflict encountered by clinicians when treating biracial adolescents, who describe themselves variously as "half and half," "Heinz 57 varieties," or "Oreos." The basic question in this area is *"Who am I?"* In these cases there has been a partial or complete failure to integrate both parental racial backgrounds into a cohesive racial/ethnic identity. These teenagers may identify with the White parent as the symbol of the dominant majority, rejecting the Black parent even if there is a closer physical resemblance. Typically, the mixed teens seen by clinicians express ambivalent feelings toward the racial/ethnic backgrounds of both parents, alternately denigrating and praising the perceived attributes of both groups (Benson, 1981; Lyles and others, 1985; Sebring, 1985).

Adolescent females are more likely to feel ashamed of their Black physical traits, such as dark skin, curly hair, or broad facial features. As a consequence of incorporating negative attitudes and stereotypes about Blacks, they often try to distance themselves from Black peers in school and social situations, and they may reject any identification with Black culture as it is expressed in the music, dance, and dress styles of those peers.

When biracial teens have overidentified with their Black parents, the similar phenomenon of rejecting White culture and White friends is played out. This overidentification may take the form of adopting the attitudes, behaviors, styles of dress, and styles of speech stereotypically associated with low-income Blacks rather than with their own middle-class life-style. Since many of the biracial adolescents referred for treatment are from middle-class families, these behaviors not only are quite dissonant with the family life-style but also tend to result in a negative identity formation. That is, the negative identity is associated with the dissonant and devalued social status of the Black parent's culture, which is not congruent with the reality of these clients' life experiences.

Thirteen-year-old Marcia, born out of wedlock to a White mother and Black father, was referred by her White adoptive parents because of rebellious behavior, truancy, and stealing from family members. The parents also suspected she was sexually active and using drugs. In individual sessions, Marcia, who had very light skin but Black facial features and hair, spoke of always feeling inferior to her younger sister, who was part Asian and had always been favored by the adoptive parents. Her behavioral problems had surfaced when she entered junior high school and felt she did not belong with any of the cliques, was rejected by former White neighborhood friends, and drifted into a group of "dopers" who were alienated from school and society. In family sessions it was clear that Marcia had assumed the role of the "bad child," identifying with the negative stories she had been told about her Black father, who had been imprisoned for drugs and burglary, and playing out an unspoken script to fulfill the negative expectations communicated to her by her parents. Marcia tried to resolve her racial identity conflict through assuming a negative identity and seeking out deviant peers whose antisocial behaviors reinforced that identity. By "acting just like my dad," Marcia was identifying with her natural Black parent while also punishing her adoptive White parents for their ambivalence toward her "Blackness."

Conflicts About Social Marginality. A conflict about social marginality is inextricably related to the core identity conflict, but it can be assessed as a separate problem. The basic

question in this area for these biracial teens is *"Where do I fit?"*
This question is especially salient as they enter adolescence and
begin to participate in heterosexual social and extracurricular
activities. During this phase of development, teens are particularly vulnerable to the twin terrors of anxiety about social acceptance and fear of social rejection.

In elementary school these children may have had a close-
knit peer group and satisfying social relationships. However, social problems will often emerge when they enter junior high
school and later go to high school. Typically, girls seem to experience more anxiety than boys about social acceptance, because
they are more often excluded from social activities and extracurricular school activities.

In a stage where conformity is expected and valued, these
biracial teens are often rejected by both majority and minority
peer groups because they are neither fish nor fowl, their physical appearance is "exotic" or unusual, their family background
is unorthodox, and they often feel torn between two competing
sets of cultural norms and values (Benson, 1981; Ladner, 1977;
Porterfield, 1978; Stuart and Abt, 1973).

Jill, the 19-year-old daughter of a Black mother and
White father, was from a well-to-do eastern family. After growing up in a White neighborhood and attending an exclusive prep
school, she enrolled in a West Coast university for a "change of
scenery." Her first year was difficult because she preferred to
socialize with the White students from similar backgrounds but
felt that the Black students were very hostile to her. After an
unsuccessful affair with an older White male who physically
abused her, she became very depressed and stopped going to
classes. She was brought into the student mental health clinic
by her roommate after she took an overdose of sleeping pills,
and she was hospitalized for several days. Jill confided in the
therapist that she felt as if she had a foot in two worlds but
couldn't stand on both feet in the White world or the Black.
She was very angry at her parents "for treating me like I was
White and not preparing me for the real world as a Black person."

Conflicts About Sexuality. Conflicts about sexuality emerge in tandem with the conflicts of racial identity and social marginality. The basic question in this area is *"What is my sexual role?"* This conflict finds expression in several ways—in issues of sexual orientation, gender identity, choice of sexual partners, and patterns of sexual activity. Uncertainties about gender identity and/or sexual orientation sometimes seem to be an extension of a more general identity confusion of biracial adolescents. Females may exhibit very masculine mannerisms in speech, dress, and behavior long beyond the normal "tomboy" stage; males may appear effeminate and engage in traditionally feminine activities. Sexual orientation is a conflictual issue with some of these teens, particularly those who failed to make appropriate sex-role identifications during the oedipal phase of development, perhaps as a result of negative feelings toward the Black parent of the same sex.

Choice of sexual partners and patterns of sexual activity are also highly charged issues for these teens. Biracial females often perceive that their dating options are limited to Black males, a group toward which they are often ambivalent and from which they frequently feel alienated. Although Black males feel they have a broader range of options, they are also acutely aware of the risk of rejection from White females.

Patterns of sexual activity also tend to be an "all or none" situation. Sexual promiscuity represents for some biracial adolescents a negative identification with their Black heritage, while others choose the path of celibacy and avoid the risks of sexual relations.

Brenda, a 16-year-old eleventh-grader, was the daughter of a White mother and a Black father who had divorced when she was ten. She physically resembled her father, with light brown skin and dark, curly hair, but streaked her hair blond like her mother's. After she entered high school, she became friendly with a group of older teens who liked to party, were using drugs, and were sexually active. When she became pregnant after a casual date, she told her mother that boys expected her to have sex with them because she was Black. She was referred for counseling from a family planning clinic.

Conflicts over Autonomy. Biracial adolescents may experience an exaggerated version of the normative adolescent separation/individuation conflict over the balance between autonomy and dependency in parent/teen relationships. The basic question in this area is *"Who is in charge of my life?"*

Particularly vulnerable to external assaults on their self-esteem, these adolescents are often overprotected by their parents, who try to shelter them from the social realities of prejudice and discrimination. They may respond either by becoming overly dependent on their parents and using home as a haven against the mixed signals of society or by rebelling and establishing their independence prematurely.

Adolescents who prolong their dependency on their parents are usually also more immature physically and socially, as expressed in their tendencies to be more obedient, more conforming, and more passive in their relationships with adults and peers. Clinically, this group appear to be more depressed or emotionally constricted and do not seem to be handling the task of separation very effectively, accepting the parental message that they need protection from a potentially hostile society.

The more rebellious adolescents assume an overt posture of pseudosophistication and maturity, engaging in more assertive, more confrontational, and more risk-oriented behaviors. More frequently involved in delinquent behaviors, school problems, and interpersonal conflicts with parents, siblings, and peers, these teenagers challenge society to acknowledge them and to validate them, refusing to accept parental discipline or protection.

Conflicts over Educational and Occupational Aspirations. The source of conflicts over aspirations for many of these adolescents is their ambivalence toward achievement and upward mobility. The basic question for them is *"Where am I going?"* Some biracial teens, fearing rejection by their Black peers if they are perceived as "bookworms" or "nerds," lose interest in school achievement or activities. Others become involved in truancy and deliberately fail their courses. For those teens who identify with White middle-class culture, academic achievement may be one area in which they excel in order to prove that they are as smart as their White peers. In the clinical setting, the more typical pattern is nonachievement, negative attitudes toward school, and unclear or unrealistic career aspirations.

The aspirations of many of these teens seem to be shaped by their unstated awareness of prejudice and discrimination toward their racial or ethnic minority group. In some cases, they apparently impose self-limiting constraints on their educational achievement and mobility aspirations in response to these perceptions.

David, a 17-year-old high school senior, was the son of a German American woman and a Black soldier. He had grown up on army bases in Europe until he moved to the States to complete high school. David had attended base schools where there were children of many nationalities, and he thought of himself as a "military brat." A good student, he particularly enjoyed athletics and tried out for several teams. His teammates were friendly at school but rarely included him when they went out on weekends after games. White girls rejected his overtures to date, and he gradually withdrew and lost interest in school. His parents encouraged him to apply to college, but he said he couldn't make up his mind about what he wanted to study. When his counselor referred him for treatment, he was quite apathetic and refused to talk. After a few sessions, he confided that he had always felt "more White than Black" because he spoke German and had very light skin. He said he didn't like living in the States because "you have to choose to be something you would rather not be." He didn't want to go to college at this point because "most Black people don't go to college, and anyway nobody expects me to set the world on fire."

In summary, these cases illustrate the types of identity conflicts experienced by biracial adolescents who are referred for psychological treatment. These conflicts may be mild, resulting in some level of identity confusion and maladaptive behaviors, or moderate, resulting in more symptoms of identity diffusion or identity foreclosure, or severe, resulting in a negative identity with more serious behavioral problems.

It is important to emphasize, however, that clinicians should not assume that psychological or behavioral problems presented by biracial adolescents are necessarily responses to conflicts over their ethnic identity. In fact, clinicians must be particularly cautious in inferring a causal relationship between biracial ethnicity and psychosocial maladaptation. Adolescents of all races may experience emotional distress because of normative developmental and social experiences, interpersonal relationships, academic problems, family conflicts, and a host of other causes. In assessing biracial adolescents, clinicians must rule out all these usual stressors before concluding that their psychological symptoms are the result of ambivalence or rejection of their dual racial heritage.

Defense Mechanisms and Coping Strategies. Given the adolescent's task of developing a stable identity, a biracial background can create anxiety and confusion. If the ethnic identities of both parents are not integrated, the adolescent may feel pressure to assume one identity at the expense of the other, precipitating anxiety or guilt over rejecting one parent and identifying with the other.

The defense mechanisms and coping strategies employed by these adolescents to deal with anxiety may be maladaptive or adaptive, depending on their context and the function they serve in the adolescent's overall psychological adjustment. Many of the behavioral strategies are aimed at protecting the adolescents' low self-esteem and warding off the anxiety associated with their feelings of identity diffusion. To cope with their conflicts over racial/ethnic identity and social marginality, they employ denial (for example, "I'm not Black, I'm mixed"), reaction formation ("I don't like to hang around with the Black kids at school because they always segregate themselves"), and over-identification with the idealized racial group ("I prefer to go to White parties").

Their fears of social rejection may result in social withdrawal as "loners" or in overconformity to group norms. They may be especially vulnerable to peer pressure to become involved in delinquency in order to achieve group membership and social acceptance.

To cope with their sexual identity conflicts, they employ two contrasting sets of defense mechanisms and behaviors. On the one hand, some exhibit a pattern of repression (for example, asceticism and lack of any interest in sexual activity) or sublimation (for example, excessive involvement in sports or extracurricular activities); on the other hand, others exhibit a pattern of promiscuity and, in a few instances, experimentation with homosexuality, bisexuality, or prostitution.

To cope with their autonomy/dependency conflicts, they also adopt contrasting defenses and behaviors. Those teens who use reversal to deal with their anxieties about separation from their parents behave in a pseudomature manner, insisting on independence from parental supervision and rejecting parental rules and values. This pattern may occur more frequently in single-parent homes and adoptive homes where the teenager is defending against fears of abandonment in a problematic or unstable family situation.

For those teens who employ regression as a defense, excessive dependency emerges, and they appear childish, clinging, and fearful. In families where parents have been extremely overprotective, teens may unconsciously choose to delay their second separation/individuation process.

Biracial teens also use rationalization and projection or intellectualization and identification with the aggressor to cope with their conflicts over educational and career goals. Rationalization ("I'm not going to waste my time studying because I probably won't be able to get a good job anyway") or projection ("None of the teachers like me because I'm different") is used more frequently by underachievers. This group are also more likely to be negatively invested in their Black identity, to have problematic relationships with their teachers, to blame external causes for their erratic academic record, to have a record of truancy and/or acting-out behaviors in school, to express low aspirations for college, and to have no clearly articulated career goals.

Intellectualization ("I spend all my time studying and don't have energy to worry about what people think of my race or color") and identification with the aggressor ("White people run the country because they are smarter than Blacks") are sometimes employed as defenses by those teens who are consistent overachievers. This group are more likely to be positively invested in their White identity, to feel committed to academic achievement, to be "super-students," to be heavily involved in extracurricular activities, and to express high aspirations for college and future career plans.

In evaluating this spectrum of defense mechanisms and coping strategies, three trends emerge. First, those teens who assume a negative identity tend to exhibit more primitive defense mechanisms (for example, denial, acting out), and their coping strategies are more maladaptive and socially dysfunctional (for example, sexual promiscuity, low school achievement). Second, those teens who develop a negative identity usually identify with the most devalued and deviant stereotypes about their Black heritage and then pattern their behaviors to achieve a self-fulfilling prophecy. Third, those teens who identify with their White racial heritage tend to maintain an overt façade of adaptation to the majority culture but experience some degree of identity confusion, which exacts a high psychic cost. Thus, they are more likely to be sexually and emotionally inhibited, over-enmeshed in their families, and perfectionistic in school and community contexts.

Sociocultural Issues in Assessment

In the assessment of biracial adolescents, it is important to evaluate four specific areas: (1) age-appropriate developmental behaviors and concerns, in contrast to identity conflicts and problems, (2) parental and family attitudes toward their biracial identity, (3) school and community resources and social networks, and (4) peer relationships. As McRoy and Freeman (1986) suggest, assessment of mixed-race children should have two goals: to isolate the factors that influence the child's racial identity and to identify environmental supports to reinforce a positive racial identity.

Age-Appropriate Behaviors and Concerns. Normal adolescents have a host of concerns that may induce periods of transitory anxiety or depression, minor rebelliousness in the family, and some fluctuations in school performance, peer relationships, and community activities. Such symptoms and mood shifts are not indicative of severe pathology or maladjustment (Oldham, Looney, and Blotcky, 1980).

However, more severe psychological or behavioral problems should not be confused with age-appropriate developmental behaviors and concerns. These behaviors should be evaluated for evidence of successful identity achievement, in contrast to identity foreclosure, identity diffusion, or negative identity. As described earlier, the latter three outcomes tend to be expressed in exaggerated, deviant, or self-destructive behaviors in the areas of personality functioning, family and peer relationships, school achievement, and antisocial activities.

These adolescents call attention to themselves because they are *oversocialized* (overachieving, constricted, and overconforming) or *undersocialized* (impulsive, antisocial, and alienated). Even if they are superficially adapted, they may be paying a high psychological price for their external conformity. Alternatively, their behaviors may be dysfunctional and maladaptive to the environment in which they are living.

Parental and Family Attitudes. Biracial adolescents often receive conflicting messages about their identity from parents and family members on both sides (Adams, 1973; Benson, 1981; Lyles and others, 1985; Porterfield, 1978). This may be particularly true of White parents who cannot accept society's definition of their children as "Black" and give them mixed messages about their skin color and non-White physical appearance. Some parents handle their child's biracial identity through denial, while other parents assume a Pollyannish attitude, behaving as if the society were truly "color blind" and minimizing evidence of differential treatment.

Assessment of parental racial attitudes is especially important in family treatment so that these attitudes can be confronted and clarified in order to provide clear, consistent, and positive feedback to their children about both sides of their racial heritage. It is also essential to determine what steps parents have taken to expose their teens to both racial/ethnic backgrounds.

In this connection, attitudes of relatives and close family

friends must also be assessed. Relatives sometimes treat the child in an ambivalent, demeaning, or rejecting manner, or they may express their ambivalence by teasing the child or making racist statements about either parent's racial background.

School and Community Resources. Several researchers have proposed that biracial children and adolescents are happier and better adjusted in schools and neighborhoods where there are other mixed families and minority families with similar socio-economic backgrounds, primarily because they can identify with other children who look like them and have similar family compositions (Ladner, 1977; Porterfield, 1978; Stuart and Abt, 1973).

In addition to the racial and socioeconomic composition of the school's student body, it is important to evaluate the racial/ethnic balance of the faculty and staff and their experience in teaching from a multicultural perspective, as well as dealing with children of varied racial and cultural backgrounds. Further, the community should be evaluated for its educational, cultural, and social resources that would be helpful to interracial families in supporting their efforts to develop positive identities in their adolescents.

Peer Relationships and Social Networks. Since relations with peers are a particularly critical area for biracial teens, it is important to evaluate not only the size and cohesiveness of the current social networks but also the group dynamics to determine whether the adolescent is playing an unhealthy role or being scapegoated in order to be accepted by the group.

The adolescent's self-perception in relation to peer groups in the neighborhood and the school should be assessed. If the current relationships are not satisfactory, alternative group experiences such as youth organizations that promote multicultural goals and focus on building self-esteem and competence should be sought.

Implications for Intervention and Treatment

The clinician must first develop a working relationship with the teenager, following the general principles of short-term, ego-oriented adolescent treatment (Norman, 1980). In addition, the clinician must be particularly sensitive to the possibility of mistrust and hostility based on racial factors in the therapeutic relationship (Gardner, 1971; Gibbs, 1985; Jones and Seagull, 1977). In the case of Marcia, for example, the Black female therapist had to explore Marcia's negative transference feelings toward her and confront her testing behaviors, simultaneously establishing a therapeutic climate of warmth and nonjudgmental acceptance to elicit Marcia's trust.

Second, the clinician must permit these teenagers to ventilate feelings about their biracial identity and its meaning in our society and must be able to provide confirmation and assurance that those feelings are not irrational or paranoid (Lyles and others, 1985; Sebring, 1985). In these sessions the clinician must demonstrate cognizance of the social realities and must be aware of his or her own attitudes and feelings about majority/minority race relations. In the case of Jill, for example, the therapist's knowledge of the particular problems of middle-class Black students on integrated college campuses was useful in establishing rapport and encouraging Jill to express her ambivalence and anger toward both her White and Black classmates.

Third, the clinician should help these teenagers to build up their self-esteem as unique individuals by identifying and supporting their positive coping mechanisms, their abilities, and their interests that are independent of their racial heritage (Adams, 1973; Lyles and others, 1985; Sebring, 1985). In this process, the clinician will have to help these teenagers distinguish between their own personal interests and abilities and those they have adopted out of a stereotyped notion of their racial identity. In David's case, for example, the therapist encouraged him to describe his interests in sports and languages. By reinforcing his basic feelings of competence and exploring his individual aspirations, she was able to help him sort out his own interests as distinct from the negative ethnic stereotypes he had internalized.

Fourth, the clinician must help these teens to see the link between their confusion over their racial identity with their confusion in other areas of behavior or developmental tasks (Gibbs, 1987; Sebring, 1985). It is important to challenge those with foreclosed or negative identities so as to unlock their potential for growth in a positive direction. They should be encouraged to discuss alternative scenarios for their current behaviors and to project reasonable options for their future; they should also be confronted with the realistic fact that continued dysfunctional or antisocial activities will result in a self-fulfilling prophecy for their negative or foreclosed identities. Brenda's self-destructive behaviors, for example, though motivated by a need for social acceptance, represented a negative identification based on a stereotype of Black female sexuality. The therapist focused on helping Brenda to understand this connection and to channel her considerable energies into more constructive activities.

Fifth, the clinician should encourage these teens to explore both sides of their racial heritage in order to form a positive sense of identification with their ethnic and cultural roots (Lyles and others, 1985; Sebring, 1985). They can be assigned "homework" to read and report on heroes and achievements of both groups for school essays; assisted in drawing a family tree to illustrate the various facets of their heritage; encouraged to put together scrapbooks about their family, friends, and neighbors to illustrate the cultural diversity in their lives; and urged to participate in holiday celebrations and other community activities that recognize the contributions of both of their racial groups.

Finally, parents and siblings should be involved in treatment if at all possible, particularly so that one child can avoid being stigmatized as the family problem (Adams, 1973; Lyles and others, 1985). If the teenager is seriously confused about his racial identity, he has probably received mixed signals from his immediate family. By exploring the parental attitudes toward race in general and toward the teenager specifically, the therapist can attempt to clarify and modify attitudes so that a more supportive family environment can be developed.

In addition, the clinician can involve the entire family in activities that will promote individual self-esteem and family pride, such as recreational and cultural activities involving ethnic themes, church-based interracial activities, and political activities to enhance the status of the Black minority group.

Other strategies that are effective in working with these teenagers to help them consolidate their identities and to improve their self-esteem include roleplaying, keeping diaries to record feelings and concerns, expressing conflictual feelings in creative writing or other forms of creative endeavor, storytelling about the past, and fantasizing about the future. More traditional psychodynamic techniques can also be supplemented by behavioral techniques such as contracting for short-term behavioral goals, giving "homework" assignments for specific behavioral change, and self-monitoring of negative attitudes and feelings.

Implications for Clinical Training and Practice

The increase of biracial children and adolescents in the community poses a new set of challenges for mental health professionals. Given the inadequacy of classroom and clinical training in minority mental health in most professional schools, it will be necessary for clinicians to expand their knowledge in this area through continued education, workshops, in-service training, and consultation. It is also important for clinicians to examine their own attitudes toward interracial relationships so that they can confront their own prejudices in working with these youth and their families.

Graduate training programs for mental health professionals need to strengthen their course offerings in the area of minority mental health, integrate this information into their regular curriculum, sponsor colloquia on these topics, and provide clinical opportunities for students to gain experience and skills in working with these clients.

Demographic trends suggest that rates of marriages between Blacks and Whites will increase as the two groups come into closer contact and as social attitudes continue to become more cosmopolitan. Intermarriage between Whites and other non-White groups will also increase as the proportion of non-Whites increases in the population because of immigration, high birthrates, and lower mortality rates. Thus, the proportion of biracial children in our society will continue to rise, and as they enter adolescence, they may prove to be particularly vulnerable to the vicissitudes of this developmental stage. This chapter offers a conceptual framework for the understanding of the special issues these teenagers face as well as a set of therapeutic goals and techniques for the effective treatment of these clients. As these biracial youth increase in the population, many will manage to achieve truly integrated identities, while others will experience chronic identity conflicts. This latter group will pose a growing challenge to mental health professionals in the twenty-first century.

References

Adams, P. "Counseling with Interracial Couples and Their Children in the South." In I. R. Stuart and L. E. Abt (eds.), *Interracial Marriage: Expectations and Reality.* New York: Grossman, 1973.

Benson, S. *Ambiguous Ethnicity.* London: Cambridge University Press, 1981.

Chambers, B. *Chronicles of Black Protest.* New York: New American Library, 1968.

Chang, T. "The Self-Concept of Children of Ethnically Different Marriages." *California Journal of Educational Research,* 1974, *25,* 245–253.

Chestang, L. "Racial and Personal Identity in the Black Experience." In B. White (ed.), *Color in a White Society.* Silver Spring, Md.: NASW Publications, 1984.

Collins, G. "Children of Interracial Marriage." *New York Times,* Mar. 20, 1984, p. 17.

Cretser, G. A., and Leon, J. J. (eds.). *Intermarriage in the United States.* New York: Haworth Press, 1982.

Duffy, L. K. "The Interracial Individual: Self-Concept, Parental Interaction, and Ethnic Identity." Unpublished master's thesis, University of Hawaii, 1978.

Erikson, E. H. "Identity and the Life Cycle." *Psychological Issues,* 1959, *1* (1).

Erikson, E. H. "Race and the Wider Identity." In E. H. Erikson, *Identity, Youth and Crisis.* New York: Norton, 1968.

Faulkner, J., and Kich, G. "Assessment and Engagement Stages in Therapy with the Interracial Family." *Family Therapy Collections*, 1983, *6*, 78–90.

Gardner, L. "The Therapeutic Relationship Under Varying Conditions of Race." *Psychotherapy: Theory, Research and Practice*, 1971, *8*, 78–87.

Gay, K. *The Rainbow Effect: Interracial Families.* New York: Franklin Watts, 1987.

Gibbs, J. T. "Black Students/White Universities: Different Expectations." *Personnel and Guidance Journal*, 1973, *51*, 463–469.

Gibbs, J. T. "Treatment Relationships with Black Clients: Interpersonal vs. Instrumental Strategies." In C. Germain (ed.), *Advances in Clinical Social Work Practice.* Silver Spring, Md.: NASW Publications, 1985.

Gibbs, J. T. "Identity and Marginality: Issues in the Treatment of Biracial Adolescents." *American Journal of Orthopsychiatry*, 1987, *57* (2), 265–278.

Gibbs, J. T., and Moskowitz-Sweet, G. "Clinical and Cultural Issues in the Treatment of Biracial and Bicultural Adolescents." Paper presented at the National Association of Social Workers Clinical Conference, San Francisco, Sept. 1986.

Gordon, A. *Intermarriage.* Boston: Beacon Press, 1964.

Gunthorpe, W. "Skin Color Recognition, Preference and Identification in Interracial Children: A Comparative Study." *Dissertation Abstracts International*, 1978, *38* (10-B), 3468.

Hauser, S. "Black and White Identity Development: Aspects and Perspectives." *Journal of Youth and Adolescence*, 1972, *1*, 113–130.

Henriques, F. *Children of Conflict: A Study of Interracial Sex and Marriage.* New York: Dutton, 1974.

Jacobs, J. "Black/White Interracial Families: Marital Process and Identity Development in Young Children." *Dissertation Abstracts International*, 1978, *38* (10-B), 5023.

Jenkins, A. *The Psychology of the Afro-American.* New York: Pergamon Press, 1982.

Johnson, R. C., and Nagoshi, C. J. "The Adjustment of Offspring Within Group and Interracial/Intercultural Marriages: A Comparison of Personality Factor Scores." *Journal of Marriage and the Family*, 1986, *48*, 279–284.

Jones, A., and Seagull, A. "Dimensions of the Relationship Between the Black Client and the White Therapist: A Theoretical Overview." *American Psychologist*, 1977, *32*, 850–855.

Ladner, J. A. *Mixed Families*. New York: Anchor Press, 1977.

Ladner, J. A. "Providing a Healthy Environment for Interracial Children." *Interracial Books for Children Bulletin*, 1984, *15*, 7–8.

Logan, S. L. "Race, Identity and Black Children: A Developmental Perspective." *Social Casework*, 1981, *62*, 47–56.

Lyles, M., and others. "Racial Identity and Self-Esteem: Problems Peculiar to Bi-Racial Children." *Journal of the American Academy of Child Psychiatry*, 1985, *24*, 150–153.

McGoldrick, M. "Ethnicity and Family Therapy: An Overview." In M. McGoldrick, J. K. Pearce, and J. Giordano (eds.), *Ethnicity and Family Therapy*. New York: Guilford Press, 1982.

McRoy, R. G., and Freeman, E. "Racial Identity Issues Among Mixed-Race Children." *Social Work in Education*, 1986, *8*, 164–174.

McRoy, R. G., Zurcher, L. A., Lauderdale, M. L., and Anderson, R. E. "The Identity of Transracial Adoptees." *Social Casework*, 1984, *65*, 34–39.

Njeri, I. "A Sense of Identity." *Los Angeles Times*, June 5, 1988, p. C-1.

Norman, J. S. "Short-Term Treatment with the Adolescent Client." *Social Casework*, 1980, *61*, 74–82.

Oldham, D. G., Looney, J. G., and Blotcky, M. "Clinical Assessment of Symptoms in Adolescents." *American Journal of Orthopsychiatry*, 1980, *50*, 697–703.

Omi, M., and Winant, H. *Racial Formation in the United States: From the 1960's to the 1980's*. Boston: Routledge & Kegan Paul, 1986.

Payne, R. "Racial Attitude Formation in Children of Mixed Black and White Heritage: Skin Color and Racial Identity." *Dissertation Abstracts International*, 1977, *38* (6-B), 2876.

Pierce, C. M. "Offensive Mechanisms." In F. Barbour (ed.), *The Black 70's*. Boston: Porter Sargent, 1970.

Pinderhughes, E. "Afro-American Families and the Victim System." In M. McGoldrick, J. K. Pearce, and J. Giordano (eds.), *Ethnicity and Family Therapy*. New York: Guilford Press, 1982.

Piskacek, V., and Golub, M. "Children of Interracial Marriage." In I. R. Stuart and L. E. Abt (eds.), *Interracial Marriage: Expectations and Reality*. New York: Grossman, 1973.

Pope, B. R. "Black Men in Interracial Relationships: Psychological and Therapeutic Issues." *Journal of Multicultural Counseling and Development*, 1985, *5*, 10–16.

Porterfield, E. *Black and White Mixed Marriages*. Chicago: Nelson-Hall, 1978.

Porterfield, E. "Black Intermarriage in the United States." In G. A. Cretser and J. J. Leon (eds.), *Intermarriage in the United States*. New York: Haworth Press, 1982.

Poussaint, A. "Study of Interracial Children Presents Positive Picture." *Interracial Books for Children Bulletin*, 1984, *15* (6), 9–10.

Sebring, D. "Considerations in Counseling Interracial Children." *Journal of Non-White Concerns in Personnel and Guidance*, 1985, *13*, 3–9.

Silverman, A. R., and Feigelman, W. "The Adjustment of Black Children Adopted by White Families." *Social Casework*, 1981, *62*, 529–536.

Simon, R. J., and Alstein, H. *Transracial Adoption*. New York: Wiley, 1977.

Sommers, V. "The Impact of Dual Cultural Membership on Identity." *Psychiatry*, 1964, *27*, 332–344.

Stuart, I. R., and Abt, L. E. (eds.). *Interracial Marriage: Expectations and Reality*. New York: Grossman, 1973.

Taylor, R. "Psychosocial Development Among Black Children and Youth: A Reconsideration." *American Journal of Orthopsychiatry*, 1976, *46*, 4–19.

Teicher, J. "Some Observations on Identity Problems in Children of Negro-White Marriages." *Journal of Nervous and Mental Disease*, 1968, *146*, 249–256.

U.S. Bureau of the Census. *Statistical Abstract of the United States, 1988.* (108th ed.) Washington, D.C.: U.S. Department of Commerce, 1987.

Washington, J. R. *Marriage in Black and White.* Boston: Beacon Press, 1970.

Willie, C., Brown, B., and Kramer, B. (eds.). *Racism and Mental Health.* Pittsburgh: University of Pittsburgh Press, 1973.

11

Multicultural Perspectives on Two Clinical Cases

Larke Nahme Huang
Jewelle Taylor Gibbs

Perceptions of reality are, in part, shaped by ethnicity, culture, and social class. In contrast to a singular valid truth, a given event or circumstance may generate multiple perceptions and multiple truths. This concept has often been called the "Rashomon" model, after the famous Japanese movie in which various characters present their own interpretations of a particular incident. This phenomenon, or perhaps reality, is what we will attempt to illustrate in this chapter.

We presented a child or adolescent clinical case to the contributing authors in this book and requested that they comment on the case from a particular ethnic and sociocultural perspective. In the two cases, the details of the presenting problems remained constant for all discussants; only the youth's ethnicity and migration history differed. The discussants were asked to address three topics: issues of referral, assessment, and treatment.

Referral issues included the following questions: What questions would you ask concerning the pattern of referral to the clinic? What data would you gather about previous attempts to resolve the problem? What attitudes and beliefs would you evaluate concerning the client's symptoms and how they should be treated?

Assessment issues included the following: What is a valid

theoretical framework for evaluation of the symptoms and behaviors? In what ways are these behaviors adaptive or maladap- ⚹
tive? What cultural norms need to be considered? What are the
developmental norms to be considered? How does this interplay
with the ethnic minority status of the child or adolescent? What
are the hypotheses regarding the areas of impaired functioning?
What are the issues of differential diagnosis?

Treatment issues included the following: What intervention would you recommend for this client? What approach would
be most culturally relevant? Who or what systems should be involved in the treatment? What modifications or innovations in
treatment would be indicated and what strategies would be
inappropriate or contraindicated?

Our objective in this chapter is to demonstrate multicultural perspectives on a given stimulus, this stimulus being the
clinical case material. When we set out to do this chapter, we
did not know how the various discussants would respond to the
material. We remained receptive about the areas of similarity or
difference and were hopeful that the final product would eluci-
date the themes presented in the earlier chapters, generating a
useful comparative analysis of clinical material across cultures
and across ethnic groups.

The child case and the adolescent case in this chapter are
each discussed from three different ethnic vantage points. The
primary discussant in each case is of a similar ethnic background
to the child or adolescent. Presenting issues in each case are
typical of the age group. The child case is presented first, followed by three discussions that treat the child as Native American, Black, or Japanese American. The adolescent case is then
presented, followed by three discussions that view the adolescent as Black, Puerto Rican, or Chinese American. The discussions are grouped by referral, assessment, and treatment issues,
and each section is followed by our brief commentary.

The Child Case

John is a 9-year-old [Native American/Black/Japanese
American] boy who was referred by his school to the psychol-

ogy clinic for evaluation in January. His fourth-grade teacher complained of unmanageable behavior, including fighting with other children, disruptive noises and talking during class, angry outbursts, and uncooperative behavior. He seemed to have trouble concentrating on assigned tasks, and his schoolwork had rapidly deteriorated during the past three months. He showed no motivation or interest in improving his performance.

John's parents also reported a change in his behavior in the past several months. He seemed more easily frustrated at home, displayed more temper tantrums, and fought continually with his siblings. When he wasn't being angry and hostile, he tended to seclude himself in his room and remain uncommunicative or wander off with a friend for long periods of time, often coming home late into the evening. According to his parents, John stole money and small items from his siblings and evidenced persistent lying.

[For Black/Native American cases]: John lives with his parents, his grandmother, his aunt, two older sisters, and one younger brother. His parents relocated to an urban area from a primarily rural district two years ago, and his grandmother and aunt migrated last year and immediately moved in with the family. John's parents and his aunt work in skilled labor positions, while the grandmother stays home with the children.

[For the Japanese American case]: John, his parents, his aunt, and his two older sisters were born in this country. John and his sisters are Sansei, or third-generation Japanese American, while his parents and aunt are Nisei, from the second generation. The grandmother immigrated to the United States in the early 1900s. Although his grandmother and aunt recently came to live with the family, they are not recent immigrants from Japan. John's parents and aunt speak in English but can understand Japanese. The grandmother speaks only Japanese and understands some English, while John speaks English but does not understand Japanese. John's family has recently moved from one community to another. John's parents and his aunt work in skilled labor positions, while the grandmother stays home with the children.

In contrast to John, his siblings are described as "model children." They are good students, well liked among peers, easily managed, and well behaved and respectful at home. They have been a source of pride to their parents, but John has been disappointing and frustrating.

According to John's mother, his developmental history is normal, with developmental milestones attained within the expected time period and no unusual illnesses or problems during his early years. Prior to this year, John had been an average student and well behaved and obedient at home.

Referral Issues

[*LaFromboise and Low (Native American)*]: Several questions arise regarding John's referral. First, although it is clear that the referral came from John's school, it is not clear who referred him. Did a school counselor evaluate John's behavior? If so, valuable information might be available from this liaison. Second, the level of family involvement should be assessed. How supportive is John's family of the referral? Are they willing to participate in therapy or a behavioral program with John? Third, was the referral an attempt to avoid serious dysfunction or adjustment problems, or was John referred because he can no longer function in the classroom context? Fourth, the therapist should ascertain the ethnic composition of the school and the class and solicit information about classroom structure and management that might be relevant.

Information about previous attempts to resolve the problem is crucial, particularly any previous therapeutic experiences. In addition, the degree of involvement of his extended family in these interventions should be documented. Because John has recently relocated to an urban area, information regarding the amount of contact with the reservation and potential tribal resources would be helpful. If other interventions have been tried, some measure of their effectiveness is crucial.

The therapeutic problem may be defined at a number of different levels. First, it is important that John's conceptualization of the problem be elicited, with particular attention to the attitudes of his family and his culture toward acting out, misbehavior, rebellion, and disrespect. Finally, the therapist must evaluate the family's attitude toward psychotherapy, and specifically, the level of cooperation and compliance they are realistically able to offer.

[*Majidi-Ahi and Allen (Black American)*]: The teacher's chief complaints—disruptive behavior, deterioration in academic work, concentration problems, and attention-seeking behavior—are symptoms one sees in many children diagnosed as attention deficit disorder (ADD) with hyperactivity. Has this child been tested before? If yes, were there any signs of attention deficit or any indication of learning disabilities? We would recommend a complete neuropsychological evaluation aimed at assessing the child's learning impairments, if any. One question to investigate thoroughly is whether there was a *sudden change* in John's classroom behavior and academic performance, or are his preexisting difficulties more elaborate and evident now? Usually, around fourth grade there is a shift in what is expected from a student from learning skills to performing and producing. Often learning impairments become more pronounced around this time. Previous test and school reports should shed light on this question.

If there has been a sudden change within the past three months, a medical evaluation and a neurological exam for the presence of tumors or other neurological deficits is strongly recommended. The nature of the "disruptive noises" and "angry outbursts" should be investigated in relation to the presence of a neurological condition.

Finally, a history of the family's attempts to seek help for John's problem behaviors should also be obtained. We would want to assess the family's experiences with formal mainstream services and helpers within the Black community. Given the frequent dissatisfaction and distrust among Blacks regarding their experiences with formal services and predominantly White institutions and schools, it would be important to assess this family's particular experiences and attitudes. This may provide useful information regarding their attitudes about the present referral.

[*Nagata (Japanese American)*]: Referral information for this case indicates that although John's parents had noticed a change in his behavior, they did not seek services themselves prior to the school referral. This is not surprising given their cultural background and should not be interpreted as a sign of defensiveness or resistance to therapy. However, because John has now been referred to the psychology clinic by the school, it is possible that his parents will experience a sense of shame and embarrassment about this. Japanese American culture emphasizes the belief that an individual's behavior reflects upon his entire family, and so John's parents might feel that the referral indicates their own failure to raise their son properly. To investigate these possibilities, it is important to explore the significance of the referral to the parents and to John himself. For example, does he also see the referral as an indication of personal failure, or does he show relief in receiving services?

It is also important to know how John and his parents conceptualize the referral problem itself. Many Japanese Americans feel that difficulties can be overcome through hard work and dedication, and John's parents may view his problem behavior as something that he could change on his own if he tried hard enough. If so, their previous attempts to deal with the problem may have been focused on his motivation rather than on more emotional or systemic issues. Assessment of previous intervention strategies should also explore the potential role of the extended family. The presence of multiple generations may have influenced the degree to which previous interventions have been attempted, encouraged, or discouraged. Since John's grandmother lives with him, it is quite possible that she, being the eldest family member, has a great deal of power in influencing the children's upbringing. For example, even if John's mother wanted to talk to him about his emotional difficulties, his grandmother might instead suggest that the best way to handle John is to impose restrictions or exclude him from family activities. If his grandmother is from the paternal side of the family, John's mother may defer to her, since a deferential role is culturally expected of a daughter-in-law.

Commentary. In their discussions of referral issues, LaFromboise and Low and Nagata focus on understanding the presenting behavior in a cultural framework. They place much emphasis on the family's reaction to the referral and the meaning of such a referral given their cultural belief systems and their understanding of John's behavior.

LaFromboise and Low highlight the importance of the ethnic composition of John's school and, more particularly, his classroom and encourage the clinician to determine the familial and cultural attitudes toward acting-out behavior. Nagata follows a similar line of thought, focusing on how both John and his parents conceptualize the problem. She also underscores the role of multiple generations in the referral process and the potential for conflict given John's extended family situation. In contrast, Majidi-Ahi and Allen devote less attention to family and referral issues, focusing instead on developmental processes and the importance of ruling out neurological or organic factors in John's behavior. Secondarily, to understand the family's attitude about the present referral, they suggest assessing the family's history and experience with help seeking in both the mainstream White and Black communities.

Assessment Issues

[*LaFromboise and Low (Native American)*]: The selection of specific assessment strategies is difficult to make on the basis of the available information. We assume that John's move from a rural/reservation environment two years before and the recent arrival of members of the extended family have created some cultural dissonance for John. Initially, the therapist should assess the level of acculturation among various members of John's family and the level of cultural congruity between John's family and the new community in which they live. John may be trying to maintain a cultural identity in direct conflict with his family or his community environment.

Clearly, John is aggressive, acting out, and having difficulty controlling his impulses. Without knowing more about the surrounding circumstances, it is difficult to formulate a diagnosis based on this information. There may be circumstances (for example, a very hostile school environment, a prejudiced teacher) where such acting out may be adaptive. Misbehavior is not adaptive in an Indian home, however, where children are expected to be socially responsible, kind, and honest and to represent an extension of the reputation and pride of the entire family. John's position in the birth order should be examined, along with his level of responsibility in the family and his relationship with various family members, particularly with the grandmother responsible for his care. Almost any Indian child having difficulty in school should be tested for hearing loss and language difficulties. Having recently come to an urban area, John may have difficulty with English or with Anglo classroom learning styles. If he is repeatedly asked to read aloud or overtly demonstrate expertise in class, he may feel awkward and anxious. Developmentally, a 9-year-old is acquiring concrete operations and learning important verbal and mathematical skills. So it is important that John have some success at this stage to facilitate literacy and the acquisition of related skills.

In order to formulate a working diagnosis, the therapist should rule out physical problems, learning disabilities, and attentional problems (hyperkinetic behavior). If these organic and developmental issues can be eliminated during assessment, we would conclude that John is acting out as a result of cultural conflicts. For example, there may be cross-generational conflicts (for example, the grandmother and parents may disagree on his upbringing); there may be differences between John's early childhood cultural experiences and his current environment; and finally, John himself may have trouble "deciding" which behaviors are appropriate in the school setting.

[*Majidi-Ahi and Allen (Black American)*]: It is reported that parents have noted a change in John's behavior at home, too. How much is change versus how much is an elaboration of preexisting problems needs to be investigated. The statement "John has been disappointing and frustrating" leads us to think that John has had problems all along, as a sudden appearance of behavior problems does not usually result in such a global statement. What was the nature of those problems? What changes have taken place in the demands on John at home that may have contributed to his acting out? When parents say, "He had been well behaved and obedient," what do they really mean? In other words, we need to reevaluate the parents' assessment of how normal he has been until now.

With regard to the stealing and lying behaviors, we need to assess parents' observations; specifically, how long has this been going on? In addition, it is useful to consider and evaluate the possibility of drug involvement, which may account for John's stealing, lying, seclusive behavior, and staying out late with friends, patterns that are not uncommon in urban inner-city neighborhoods.

It is important to evaluate the family system: Have there been any recent changes in the patterns within the family system to which John may be reacting? How did he react to the family relocation that occurred two years ago and to the move of his aunt and grandmother into their home one year ago? If John's behavior changes are sudden and recent—what changes have occurred at home or in the family system? Have there been any changes in authority or in new demands? Does John exhibit any behavior indicative of physical or sexual abuse? Is he secluding himself in his room or coming home late to avoid something unpleasant in the household? Is his acting out at home and school his cry for help?

[*Nagata (Japanese American)*]: John's presenting problem requires the evaluation of many additional questions. Among these are: What are the roles expected of John and others in this extended family household, of males and females, sons and daughters, the young and the old? Are the aunt and grandmother relatives of the father or mother, and how is their presence accommodated by the nuclear family? To what degree is Japanese spoken in the home, and is this a potential source of embarrassment for John? Were one or more of John's parents, aunt, or grandmother in internment camps during World War II?

Information concerning the changes precipitated by the family's recent move is also clearly significant. John may have moved from a predominantly Japanese or Asian American community to one in which there are no or few Asian Americans and he may feel pressures (for example, from peers) to minimize his Japanese heritage. In this situation, although John's behaviors appear to be maladaptive, they may also be viewed as adaptive. His disruptiveness and poor school performance are a far cry from the "model" Japanese American child but may indicate an attempt to establish his own identity and/or need for acceptance in the new community. As the eldest son, John is likely to have experienced particular pressures to carry on the family name, reputation, and responsibilities. His recent seclusion from the family, disruptive behavior, and wandering off with friends could, again, reflect a separation from his cultural and family identity. Since verbal challenging of parents and elders is rare or minimal in Japanese American families, John may not have felt comfortable confronting his family with verbal expressions of distress, but instead may demonstrate his emotional struggle through overt actions.

A preliminary *DSM-III-R* diagnosis based on the sketchy case information is clearly difficult. While John does not meet the full criteria for conduct disorder, an alternative diagnosis might be adjustment disorder with disturbance of conduct. However, the case does not include a clearly identifiable stressor three months prior to John's change in behavior. One problem with the *DSM-III-R* classification is that it does not take into account cultural variables when specifying the time frame in which a stressor needs to have occurred to create a significant impact. In John's case, it is possible that aspects of his Japanese American background (for example, keeping emotions within and not troubling others with one's own concerns) may have delayed the overt display of stress-induced behavior precipitated by his family's move and the arrival of his grandmother and aunt.

Commentary. Perhaps the most striking similarity among the various discussions on assessment is the tendency of each discussant to examine the presenting behavior in a cultural context and to consider the "adaptiveness" of this troublesome behavior in the pertinent sociocultural environment. LaFromboise and Low address the need to assess the cultural congruity between John's family and the new community as well as the level of acculturation among family members, with the explicit assumption that cultural dissonance may be involved in the etiology of his disturbing behavior. Similarly, Majidi-Ahi and Allen raise the hypothesis that the presenting behaviors reflect socio-environmental problems common to urban inner-city neighborhoods. Nagata further raises the possibility that the behavior reflects identity issues and a need for acceptance in the new community. She emphasizes the possibility that John's disturbing behavior may reflect personal and familial acculturation conflicts, a hypothesis that needs to be examined in the assessment process.

Interestingly, the discussants arrive at different tentative diagnoses. LaFromboise and Low, as well as Majidi-Ahi and Allen, raise the possibility of attention deficit disorder, although the former two discussants mention this primarily as a diagnosis to rule out, instead strongly emphasizing cultural and cross-generational conflicts. Similarly, Nagata proposes an adjustment disorder with disturbance of conduct, while acknowledging the limitations of the diagnostic criteria for different ethnic groups. Two of the three sets of discussants mention the need to evaluate and rule out the possibility of organic or neurological causes for John's problematic behaviors.

Treatment Issues

[*LaFromboise and Low (Native American)*]: A family systems approach, including the extended family members who interact with John, is recommended. The goals of therapy would be to identify cognitions, communication patterns, and family roles that are maladaptive; to enhance communication between John and his family; and to reduce John's acting-out behaviors. Extended family members who could provide John with support and direction even from afar (for example, letters, phone calls, visits) might be mobilized. If acculturation is a problem for this family, the "talking circles" intervention, which clarifies family roles in the context of the larger community, would be helpful. In addition, we would offer to do some consultation with John's teachers, including classroom observation. If these interventions do not facilitate change, nonconfrontational individual therapy techniques like mutual storytelling could be employed to facilitate the exploration of John's cognitions and behaviors. Social cognitive interventions designed to increase John's confidence and ability in school (see our chapter) might also be employed in therapy. One-on-one psychodynamic approaches or client-centered therapies would be contraindicated in this case.

[*Majidi-Ahi and Allen (Black American)*]: Once a diagnostic evaluation is completed, treatment alternatives can be considered for John. If ADD is diagnosed, the primary intervention is an appropriate school placement and an individualized educational plan plus the possibility of stimulant medication on a trial basis. Parent guidance work in such a case is often useful. Individual play therapy may also help the child work through some of the emotional problems which often accompany or result in learning difficulties, such as low self-esteem. If the child, as the identified patient, represents the psychopathology of the family system, family treatment is strongly indicated. If the child's behavior problems are in reaction to a change or dysfunction in the family system, then the intervention must address the system and not the individual.

[*Nagata (Japanese American)*]: Early on, the therapist for this case should actively work to elicit the concerns and questions John and his parents have about therapy and address those concerns as clearly as possible. The therapist should also identify a time frame for the therapy and adopt an active, rather than a passive, role. Given the central role of the family in Japanese American culture, family sessions would be especially useful. However, sensitivity to the multigenerational issues present in John's family is also crucial. For example, if assessment information reveals the existence of tension between the grandmother and others, simply counseling the parents to have the grandmother move out could be countertherapeutic, since Japanese American culture stresses an indebtedness and responsibility to one's elders. Likewise, instructing John's parents to disregard the grandmother and implement their own intervention strategies could be threatening. A more sensitive approach might include the enlistment of the grandmother's support in carrying out interventions within the family and providing a role for her in the change process.

Finally, the therapist should be especially attentive to both verbal and nonverbal messages from John and his family. Since many communications within Japanese American families are unspoken, the therapist must recognize that the dynamics of family interaction during therapy may not be overt.

Commentary. The section on treatment issues elicited the

most variation among the discussants. A full range of treatments was suggested, including individual and family treatment, school consultation, and medication. The common element in all the treatment recommendations was the need for family intervention. Specifically, LaFromboise and Low recommended a family systems intervention as the primary treatment of choice; Nagata proposed this as well, though less emphatically; and Majidi-Ahi and Allen recommended this in conjunction with a primary emphasis on school consultation, involving determination of an appropriate school placement and an individualized educational plan.

The Adolescent Case

Maria is a 15-year-old female, the oldest daughter in a middle-class [Black/Puerto Rican/Chinese American] family. Her father is a salesman, and her mother works part-time as a sales clerk. Maria's parents have moved frequently for better opportunities for their children. [*For Puerto Rican and Chinese American cases, this sentence reads*]: Maria's parents have recently immigrated to the United States for better opportunities for their children. Until recently, Maria has been a "model child," helping her mother with the household chores and care of her three younger siblings, doing average work in school, and spending time with her friends at a neighborhood youth center.

In the last six months, Maria's behavior and moods have radically changed. She is moody and irritable much of the time, quarrels constantly with her mother, and has lost interest in her schoolwork. She also complains about sleeping and doesn't have much appetite, so she has lost some weight. She has begun to stay out late with a new group of older friends, whom her parents don't like. Maria's teacher called her mother and requested that the parents come to the school for a conference. Maria's parents were surprised to learn that she had been truant several times, was failing in several classes, and was hanging around with a group of teenagers who were known to be involved with drugs and delinquent activities. The teacher suggested that Maria needed counseling because she was "headed for trouble." The teacher addressed her comments primarily to Maria's mother, virtually ignoring the father.

Maria's parents reacted very differently to the teacher's disclosures. Her father was very angry and threatened to discipline her very harshly "to bring her into line," but Maria's mother felt that she was just getting adjusted to a new school and that she would "get back to herself soon." The teacher referred the family to a local mental health center, but they seemed very reluctant to comply.

Referral Issues

[*Gibbs (Black American)*]: The case of 15-year-old Maria includes a number of issues that would be viewed with particular concern by a Black clinician.

First, the clinician would want to explore the feelings of Maria and her parents toward the teacher's referral for counseling. It would be important to ascertain whether or not Maria's parents had consulted with any other members of their family, their minister, or their family doctor before finally following through on the referral. If so, the clinician should encourage them to discuss their feelings of ambivalence over the referral, their attitudes toward being stigmatized by their friends, and their need to seek information and support from significant members of their family and professionals in the Black community about counseling. This information will enable the clinician to evaluate parental attitudes and beliefs about mental health problems and their solutions, to identify prior sources of help with the problem, and to verbalize their fears and anxieties about the treatment process. Questions to be asked about the referral include the following: (1) How did they initially feel when the teacher recommended counseling for Maria? How did Maria herself feel? (2) How did they view Maria's behavior before the discussion with her teacher? After the discussion? (3) What did they do to deal with Maria's behavior before the teacher called them in? What have they done since the meeting?

(4) What alternative sources of advice or help did they seek for Maria before the referral? After the referral?

[*Inclán (Puerto Rican)*]: In view of Maria's acting-out behaviors and personality changes, the teacher's decision to refer this family for treatment was a correct one. The fact that she called for a parent meeting to discuss the referral is equally commendable. It is more common in a middle-class Puerto Rican family like Maria's for both parents to attend the meeting than in a poor family. However, the teacher made an error of process by addressing the mother exclusively. Cultural awareness and sensitivity dictate either addressing father first or both parents equally in Puerto Rican families. This subtle behavior is an important one that may influence the father's, and subsequently the family's, engagement in treatment, and so it is important for teachers and therapists to acknowledge these cultural patterns.

[*Ying (Chinese American)*]: Since Maria's parents are recent immigrants to this country, they are unlikely to have much knowledge of counseling. Thus, they are likely to view the teacher's recommendation as an accusation that they have been bad parents and that their daughter is "crazy." The referral, as well as Maria's behavior, certainly represents a major loss of face for the family, and so it is understandable that the parents would feel most reluctant to follow up on the teacher's referral.

It is important to assess how Maria and her parents understand her change in behavior. Did they view the change as reflective of physical problems or difficulty adjusting to the new environment? It is likely that Maria's bad temper and loss of interest in schoolwork have been most disturbing to her parents, since obedience and respect toward one's parents and academic excellence are expected from children in Chinese culture. It is unclear whether Maria is experiencing difficulty in school because of difficulties with English, and so it would be important to talk with Maria and her parents separately about what they view as the cause of her behavior change and how they have tried to deal with it. Have they sought help from other family members or Western and/or traditional Chinese doctors? It is unlikely that they would be willing to go to a mental health clinic unless other avenues for help have been exhausted.

Commentary. In their discussions of referral issues, Gibbs, Inclán, and Ying are in general agreement regarding the appropriateness of the referral and the importance of including the family in the intervention. Gibbs and Ying focus on understanding the meaning of the referral for the family in a sociocultural context and suggest that a history of their help-seeking behavior be obtained in order to determine what has been attempted before this referral, particularly since members of these ethnic groups often seek out informal and indigenous sources of help for psychological problems. Ying and Inclán additionally present specific cultural issues such as the role of language and generational and gender hierarchy within the family, all of which must be addressed in the assessment process.

Assessment Issues

[*Gibbs (Black American)*]: Assessment issues are also influenced by the social and cultural context of the family's socioeconomic status. The clinician would note that Maria is entering middle adolescence and is becoming more concerned about peer relationships, group norms, and heterosexual activities. Because her family has been very mobile, Maria may not have a strong sense of roots and/or an extended family to support her parents' child rearing. If she is living in a racially integrated neighborhood and attending an integrated school, she may feel pressure to identify with other Black teenagers, even if they come from lower class backgrounds. Alternatively, if she attends a primarily Black school and lives in a segregated neighborhood, she may be adjusting to a completely new racial environment in her school and neighborhood, and her behaviors may reflect some confusion over adapting to the norms of new peer groups.

The clinician should evaluate the norms of Maria's new neighborhood and peer group to determine whether parents exercise little supervision over their teenage children and whether many of the teenagers engage in minor delinquency as an adaptation to their social milieu. Further, the clinician should explore parental expectations for Maria to assume a mother's-helper role with her siblings. Are these expectations reasonable, or is Maria assuming the role of a surrogate parent? As the eldest daughter in a Black middle-class family, Maria may be rebelling against becoming a parent surrogate.

The level of Maria's self-esteem and her identity development as a minority adolescent should also be evaluated. Is her acting-out behavior a symptom of low self-esteem? Is she assuming a "negative identity" as a Black teenager in a White society? How have her parents handled her transition to puberty—that is, what discussions have they had with her about sexual feelings and learning how to respond to peer pressures about drugs and delinquent activities?

Maria's functioning is impaired in several major areas: mood changes, relationship with her parents, schoolwork, and impulse control. These symptoms and behavioral signs suggest that Maria is suffering from depression, perhaps as an adjustment reaction to her family's most recent move. Since her parents have moved frequently for better opportunities for their children, they may not be aware of the difficulties for Black adolescents of finding a supportive peer group and making an adjustment to a new school where teachers may have ambivalent feelings and low expectations for Black students. Further, Maria may have been ridiculed by other Black students in her school because of her previous academic achievements, so that she now experiences conflicts about being a good student.

A tentative formulation in this case is that Maria is depressed as a result of several factors, including her recent move, her excessive household responsibilities, and her parents' lack of empathy with her situation. Her acting-out behavior serves several functions. First, it is a way of externalizing her inner conflicts and warding off the depressive feelings that threaten to overwhelm her. Second, the delinquent behaviors may be a route to acceptance by a peer group whose approval she seeks. Third, her labile moods and her eating and sleeping irregularities are symptoms to alert her parents that she is very unhappy. Since they both work, it may be necessary for Maria to find multiple ways to express her depression in order to gain their attention and sympathy.

[*Inclán (Puerto Rican)*]: Assessment of this family situa-

tion is facilitated by an ecosystemic point of view that concep-
tualizes the young adolescent and her family, community, and
society as coevolving and mutually interacting. Maria is in mid-
adolescent development, and as the first-born daughter of working parents, she occupies an instrumental, mother-substitute
role at home. Following the usual pattern of acculturation of
migrants to the United States, the mother's adaptation to the
new host culture and its values precedes the father's. The family's migration, acculturation, and idiosyncratic coevolutionary
development take place in a society still evolving with regard to
male/female roles and their implications for work life, family
life, and power relations in general.

The initial working hypothesis in this case is that of a Hispanic family in transition from a preadolescent to an adolescent
stage, where transitional problems and symptoms are manifest
in the young adolescent. The family would be followed up in
therapy and observation to determine whether the problem sub-
sides and the family coevolves or the adolescent behavior rigidi-
fies into a conduct disorder.

Further assessment considerations would focus on the acculturation—that is, values incorporation—of the spouses. It
should be noted that social-class mobility usually involves the
incorporation of values, norms, and attitudes that go with that
social-class status. Moreover, the process of acculturation proceeds at different paces for male and female parents. This often
results in conflict and argument between parents with regard to
what each believes is appropriate and most functional for the
family.

[*Ying (Chinese American)*]: From an ecological perspective, Maria has recently undergone major changes. Along with
the physiological and cognitive changes of adolescence, Maria
finds herself in a new environment with conflicting values that
seriously burden the normal task of identity formation. The
family has been involved in a number of moves recently, possi-
bly hampering Maria's ability to form close peer relationships
crucial for the development of a sense of self during adolescence.
In addition, Maria's recognition of being an ethnic minority
member in a predominantly White society and the need to master a new language and adapt to a new peer culture may com-

pound the already difficult task of finding a comfortable niche for herself in her new world. Moreover, her parents have probably had to devote much of their attention to the financial and physical survival of the family and are less available to assist her in this difficult transition.

In Western societies, adolescence is generally recognized as a time of turmoil for the child and heightened parent/child struggles around independence. In Chinese culture, this developmental stage is much less well accepted or acknowledged. Although Chinese and Chinese American adolescents may also experience the urge to test their independence, it is often a covert process. Generally, they do not leave home, and they do not openly form romantic relationships. If they challenge authority, they are severely reprimanded. Overtly, they do what they have been expected to do all along—that is, to go to school, to do well, and to conform to the rules at home. They may be extremely idealistic and philosophical, but that is well tolerated as long as their behavior conforms to the above-stated norm.

In Maria's case, she may be struggling to make sense of these divergent views of adolescence and the greater tolerance for nonnormative behavior outside the home (which is not to say peer culture does not have its own set of norms). Finding herself now in a Western culture, Maria may be wishing for the independence she observes among her peers; yet, she is unable to reconcile her parents' disapproval of it. Her conflict is compounded by the fact that, as the first-born in her family, she is expected to implement the family norm and to serve as surrogate parent to her siblings during her parents' absence, particularly if they are working long hours struggling for the family's economic survival.

Maria's behavior and mood changes strongly suggest the presence of depression. Appetite and sleeping disturbances and irritability are common first signs of depression among Chinese. The severity and duration of the symptoms need to be assessed for major depression. It is, of course, important to rule out the presence of organic causes.

Commentary. In discussing assessment, Inclán focuses on the family as a coevolving system, a family in transition in its acculturation and its establishment of new cultural/social roles.

He arrives at a diagnostic formulation focusing on the family
system, identifying it as a family adjusting from the preadolescent to the adolescent stage of development. Maria's acting-out
behaviors are thus viewed as an expression of family disequilibrium, exacerbated by cultural conflicts.

Gibbs highlights other contextual and developmental factors within an ego-psychological framework that examines the
ongoing and new tasks of the adolescent. She also focuses on
the influence of social and ecological factors such as the family's socioeconomic status and the racial environment in which
Maria is functioning. She highlights the need to understand
Maria's symptoms in context, especially in the context of her
peer relations, and to evaluate her self-esteem and identity formation as a minority adolescent. Proceeding from a dynamic interpretation of Maria's behavior and symptoms, Gibbs arrives
at a tentative diagnosis of depression.

Ying examines the contextual stressors such as Maria's recent move, her ethnic minority status, the possibility of language difficulties, a change in the peer culture, and developmental changes consistent with adolescence. She also points to the
need to assess acculturation stresses and divergent cultural views
of the various generations within the family. Through a similar
analysis of Maria's symptomatology, Ying also arrives at a tentative diagnosis of depression.

The three discussants employ a developmental perspective emphasizing the tasks and pressures associated with adolescence. Ying, however, also focuses on the different meanings of
adolescence across cultures. While all three discussants attend to
Maria's mother-surrogate role and how this may conflict with
drives for her own autonomy, Ying points out that the different
cultural meaning of adolescence for some Chinese families may
compound the more conventional generational conflicts stimulated by emergence into adolescence.

Treatment Issues

[*Gibbs (Black American)*]: The treatment modality that
would be most appropriate developmentally and culturally for

Maria is a combination of individual and family treatment. The initial phase of treatment should involve the entire family so that the parents can clearly communicate their expectations and aspirations to Maria and, simultaneously, can become more sensitive to her developmental needs for greater autonomy and social relationships. The family needs to explore the multiple pressures that Black teenagers experience in integrated versus segregated school environments to determine whether Maria's rebellious behavior is a way of identifying with a specific Black peer group. Individual sessions should be time-limited and should focus on three issues: (1) helping Maria to express her ambivalent feelings toward her parents, (2) helping her to express feelings of insecurity and anxiety about being accepted in a new environment, and (3) helping her to develop a positive self-concept and coping skills that will enable her to resist peer pressures, to identify with her parents' aspirations, and to sublimate her energies into more constructive activities.

[*Inclán (Puerto Rican)*]: The whole family should be seen in treatment, particularly the father, mother, and Maria. Additionally, Maria should be referred to an adolescent-transition group where she may be able to work on developmental issues regarding family and self from the vantage point of her peers.

Treatment of the family would begin with engagement of the father. Then the therapist should focus on reaching a common understanding of the demands and issues involved in migration/acculturation and social-class transition. As suggested in our chapter, specific techniques such as a visual mapping-out process should be considered. Following this stage of therapy, a more focused discussion of the developmental issues facing Maria and her family, and the systemic triangulation that appears to be present, would be encouraged. Expected adolescent behaviors such as attending school would be examined from the privileges/responsibility continuum that was, again, discussed in our chapter.

Individual therapy for Maria would not be recommended at this time.

[*Ying (Chinese American)*]: It would be important to involve at least Maria and her parents in treatment. Given that Maria is an adolescent and likely to feel uncomfortable speaking openly in front of her parents, I would recommend a primarily individual orientation. However, if only she is seen and her parents are not, the treatment is very likely to fail. Maria's parents may be expected to sabotage the treatment if they are uninformed about what is being done with their daughter. Thus, it is important to involve the parents, especially initially, by engaging them as partners in the treatment process. I might exchange with them perspectives on what is going on with Maria to help them recognize normal developmental changes and the stresses and losses she and the family have suffered and to praise their efforts in providing for her. A major challenge for the therapist will be to maintain confidentiality within Maria's treatment and to convey successfully to the parents an openness when they feel a need to contact the therapist. Further, it would be important to assess Maria's immediate needs (for example, language) and her potential sense of estrangement from her current world.

    Commentary. The most striking difference among the discussants is in their recommendations for treatment. Whereas there was some similarity in their comments on assessment and their tentative diagnoses, they clearly differ on treatment formulation. This may be more a function of the discussant's philosophical and theoretical orientation and clinical training than of the ethnicity of either the presenting adolescent or the discussant. Inclán recommended an educationally and developmentally oriented family intervention. Gibbs would combine the family and individual modalities with different agendas for each form of intervention. Interestingly, she focused more explicitly on Maria's probable ambivalence toward the parents than either of the other discussants. Ying recommended an individually focused intervention, with Maria as the target of treatment and her parents as collaborators but not the identified "clients." All these discussants emphasize the need to develop a treatment plan that involves Maria's parents, reflecting their shared understanding of the importance of an ecological perspective and the crucial need for family involvement in the treatment of minority adolescents.

Conclusions

Our objective in this chapter was to begin to examine how different clinicians respond to the same clinical material with one varying attribute, that being ethnicity of the presenting child or adolescent. This was also an initial attempt to present a comparative analysis across clinicians whose ethnicity also differed. Of course, this was not a controlled study, and many factors besides ethnic/racial identity differed. For example, the clinician-discussants varied in their own training and professional backgrounds, their theoretical perspectives, their treatment expertise, their personal backgrounds, and their involvement with ethnic minority populations. Though not intended to be an experimental design, the comparative analysis can be viewed as a beginning exchange among clinicians who serve minority youth and their families.

Moreover, the discussants functioned under the following limitations: First, there was no dialogue between us and the discussants or among the discussants about the case; second, they were merely sent the case with a brief set of questions to which they were to respond; and third, they were given stringent limitations of space and time and asked to reach conclusions from limited data.

In spite of these limitations, we feel that some valuable information has emerged in this initial look at clinical responses to ethnic minority clients who are children and adolescents. Some similarities and differences emerged, although of course these may not be due solely to the ethnic variable but may reflect other factors, as noted above.

Each discussant assumed a primarily ecological perspective, examining the child or adolescent in the relevant sociocultural context. Less attention was given to individual psychodynamics independent of the familial and cultural environment, leading to a tentative conclusion that ethnic and sociocultural factors, as considered by this set of clinicians, are significant factors in the etiology of psychological problems, the symptomatology expressed, the familial attitudes toward these problems and symptoms, and the help-seeking patterns of these youth and their families.

In summary, among the factors to consider are understanding the presenting behavior in a cultural framework; determining the cultural and familial attitudes toward the problem and toward help-seeking behaviors and services; considering the adaptiveness of the presenting behavior in the ecological and developmental environments; assessing the cultural congruity among the child/adolescent, the family, and the community; considering the possibility of identity conflicts in culturally dissonant contexts; examining the appropriateness of the treatment in a cultural context; and applying, with caution, the conventional differential diagnostic criteria. Consequently, ethnic factors should be seriously and carefully considered in every phase of the assessment and treatment process.

Although it is clear that the Rashomon model is pertinent to clinicians and clinical data, the present chapter has also illustrated striking areas of similarity and commonality in the process of assessment and treatment of minority youth. The integration of these two perspectives has provided a useful glimpse into the clinical reasoning process within an ethnic/sociocultural context.

12

Future Directions: Implications for Research, Training, and Practice

Larke Nahme Huang
Jewelle Taylor Gibbs

The overall objective of this book has been twofold: first, to provide in-depth information about the mental health of youth from selected ethnic and racial minorities in the United States; and second, to present culturally appropriate and sensitive forms of mental health assessment and intervention. Although the primary focus has been on the individual child or adolescent, we have consistently examined this individual in his or her pertinent contexts. It is our contention that, just as in figure/ ground perceptual tasks, one cannot understand the child divorced from the environment, nor can one comprehend the environmental context devoid of the individual. Accordingly, throughout this book, we have tried to place each ethnic or racial group in a historical and societal context; this context, in turn, has provided the backdrop for understanding the individual in the more immediate and personal ecological system.

Emerging Themes

From the theoretical, empirical, and clinical material discussed in the various chapters, several themes emerge that have direct implications for ethnic minority youth: (1) the relation of changing demographics to social, economic, and mental health imperatives, (2) the balance between universalism and pluralism, (3) the resilience and adaptation of ethnic minority groups, and (4) minority status as a stressor on the growth and development of individual youth.

Changing Demographics. Although the ethnic minority population in the United States is increasing as a proportion of the total population, the patterns and directions of growth among the separate groups are quite variable. Blacks remain the largest minority group in the United States, nearly half of their population, 10.5 million, being youth under 19 years of age. This group experiences steady growth due more to fertility rates and intermarriage than to immigration. Key social indicators highlight a particularly dismal socioeconomic picture for Black youth in terms of education, employment, teen pregnancy, substance abuse, and delinquency (Gibbs, 1984). Additionally, in 1984, 46 percent of Black children, compared with 39 percent of Hispanic and 16 percent of nonminority children, lived below the poverty level (Children's Defense Fund, 1986).

Hispanics are the most rapidly growing minority group, primarily because of immigration and high fertility rates. It is expected that they will be the largest minority group within the next twenty-five years. Since 1970 the Hispanic population has evidenced a 6.1 percent annual growth rate, and in 1980 it numbered 16.9 million (U.S. Bureau of the Census, 1985). Approximately 41 percent are children under 17 years of age (Powell, Yamamoto, Romero, and Morales, 1983). This rapid population increase has significant implications for the allocation of health, mental health, and educational resources. For example, ethnic surveys of the Los Angeles Unified School District indicate 44 percent Hispanic enrollment, and in the elementary grades, over 50 percent (Los Angeles Unified School District, 1979). Mexican Americans are the most numerous in the Hispanic population, followed by Puerto Ricans. These two Hispanic groups are unique in their ease and frequency of movement between their homelands and the U.S. mainland. Thus, although statistics show an annual net growth, the actual composition of this group is quite fluid and the degree of acculturation is quite variable.

Asian Americans are the second-fastest-growing minority group, currently numbering nearly 4 million and comprising over thirty distinct ethnic and cultural groups (Wong, 1982). Thirty-two percent of Asian Americans are under 17 years of age (Powell, Yamamoto, Romero, and Morales, 1983). Growth for these various groups has been bidirectional. For example, Japanese Americans have a low fertility rate, minimal immigration, and high rates of outmarriage. Thus, their overall rate of growth is nominal. In contrast, the Southeast Asian American population is expanding rapidly over a short, concentrated period of time. Except for Japanese Americans, the largest Asian American groups are composed mainly of immigrants: 60 percent of Chinese Americans, 70 percent of Filipino Americans, and 98 percent of Southeast Asian Americans are immigrants (Wong, 1982). Within this minority group is the small, though currently highly publicized, group of Amerasian children from Vietnam. All these highly diverse groups fall under the designation "Asian American," but their needs and rates of acculturation are quite different.

According to the 1980 census, there are an estimated 1.6 million American Indians, which represents a doubling in size since the previous census (U.S. Bureau of the Census, 1983). This increase is more likely due to shifts in racial identification, a newly important social factor among American Indians, than to incorrect enumeration or high fertility rates (Passel, 1976). Nearly 40 percent of this population is under 21 years of age. Like other minority groups, American Indians are becoming increasingly urban.

Changing demographics influence the degree of sociopolitical attention accorded individual minority groups, which, in turn, is a determinant of the allocation of resources. As the needs of a particular group are highlighted, funds are channeled in that direction. However, the crisis-oriented approach characteristic of much of the distribution of federal funds renders one group a national priority and then, without warning, replaces this group with another. Such has been the situation with mental health funding, resulting in the expansion and contraction of services to minorities independent of careful assessment and consideration of need. Perhaps the next group to undergo such

a fate will be the Amerasians, currently in the news and attract-
ing much-needed public and congressional attention. Because of
their limited size and political voice, they will most likely fade
into the anonymous multicultural mix of American society, and
their unique mental health needs will go unattended.

About one in every five Americans is from one of the
four ethnic minority groups (Suinn, 1987). This minority population is younger as a group, with a higher proportion of youth,
than the nonminority population. Currently, nearly 40 percent
of public school students are minorities (Vobejda, 1987). Given
that the school system is the major source of referral to mental
health agencies for youth, it is likely that a significant number
of the referrals will be minority students, thus dramatically
changing the clientele of these agencies. Furthermore, a significant proportion of these children will live below the poverty
line and come from non-English–speaking families.

These changes in clientele will necessitate changes in mental health priorities and policies. This, in fact, was evident in the
recommendations of the President's Commission on Mental
Health (1978). The commission urged that attention be focused
on the needs and problems of racial and ethnic minorities and
that innovative strategies be developed, acknowledging the
unique cultural and racial experiences of Asians, Blacks, Hispanics, and Native Americans, in order to promote their mental
health and social well-being. As minority status emerged as a
priority in mental health care, funds were allocated for minority research centers, minority training centers, minority scholarships in mental health. The shift in demographics had signaled
changes in mental health care and delivery systems. Of course,
the funds were limited and the various minority groups strug-
gled among themselves for "pieces of the pie." With the changing political winds and the arrival of a new administration, however, mental health priorities once again shifted. Biological factors
were "in," social factors were "out." Thus, the changing demographics and the emergent political clout and visibility of these
minority groups had brought about a rearrangement of priorities, but this rearrangement was only short-lived.

Another result of growing ethnic and racial minority

populations is the increasing number of biracial and multicultural children. These children encounter a different set of problems and issues in development and, accordingly, may present different mental health needs and concerns (Gibbs, 1987; Ladner, 1977; Sommers, 1964). While these children may be symbolic of the harmonious and positive blending of cultures, they may also experience painful crises of identity and alienation. Mental health services will need to be attuned to the special problems and competencies of this unique group.

Balancing Universalism and Pluralism. The focus on evolving demographics serves to underscore the increasing diversity in American society. The Western European origins of this society are being challenged by new belief systems and cultures emanating from different parts of the world. The twenty-first century has already been declared the "Century of the Pacific" as Third World countries in Asia gain economic stature and prominence, thus redirecting American economic and sociopolitical interests from Europe to Asia (Kotkin and Kishimoto, 1988; Powell and others, 1988). As people, products, and joint business endeavors (such as New United Motor Manufacturing Association, the union of General Motors and Toyota in Fremont, California) are imported from Third World countries, the blending of new and old cultures is inevitable. Whether the relationship will be egalitarian remains to be seen.

These economic and population trends reawaken the continuing debate over universalism versus pluralism in the field of mental health (Berry, 1969; Draguns, 1981; Jones and Korchin, 1982; Sue and Morishima, 1982; Triandis and Brislin, 1984). The uniqueness of the various ethnic minority groups in the United States is reflected in their manifestation of psychological problems, in their understanding and explanations of these problems, in their problem-solving strategies, and in their help-seeking patterns. Proponents of pluralism contend that the mere application of mainstream services for these culturally and historically different populations is inadequate and unacceptable. Rather, programs and services tailored to the unique needs of these various groups are necessary. In part, pluralism has arisen in reaction to the universalist assumptions that human functioning is largely governed by uniform processes and modes of expression and that group-related differences are insignificant (Snowden, 1982).

In this book, our intent has been to highlight cultural diversity and to suggest that it is an important value in our society in general and in the mental health field in particular. We are not proposing that every racially or ethnically different group requires its own unique programs or mental health strategies. If this were so, the number and categories of intervention would become unwieldy, and this approach would obfuscate the important variation within minority groups, thus reducing them to unidimensional stereotypes. Rather, we are proposing that diversity be acknowledged and that a balance between universalism and pluralism be attained. In the past, diversity has been a difficult concept to accept, and in most fields, including education and psychology, attempts were made to fit people of different races and cultures into previously existing schemata. The homogenization of races and cultures has been a predominant American ethic (deAnda, 1984; Green, 1982). This was most clearly exemplified by the psychological testing movement, which used instruments standardized on White populations for all racial and ethnic minorities, totally ignoring the question of cultural relevance, appropriateness, and validity (Mercer and Lewis, 1978; Oakland, 1977; Samuda, 1975; Snowden and Todman, 1982). More recently, this has been an issue in college education. There has been increasing dissatisfaction on university campuses with the classical liberal education, which is viewed as too White, too male, and too Western (Nakao, 1987). Critics assert that changing demographics in the United States and growing internalization warrant a more globally oriented curriculum that better reflects human and cultural diversity, taking into consideration contributions of women, minorities, and other "nonelite" groups to Western culture. Our intent in this book has been to highlight the unique cultural characteristics of ethnic and racial minority groups and to suggest methods of assessment and intervention that reflect a blending of traditional, mainstream knowledge and techniques with innovative, culture-specific conceptualizations and strategies. The ability to differentiate the general and the specific, the universal and the unique, is critical to effective work with children of all cultures and backgrounds.

Each of the preceding chapters has included a discussion about the unique cultural and historical factors of the minority group and their role in the assessment and treatment process. These special considerations, however, have been presented in conjunction with established mainstream techniques. For example, LaFromboise and Low combine traditional American Indian techniques such as the "sweat lodge" and "talking circle" ceremonies with more conventional group and social cognitive therapies. In the chapters on Chinese Americans and Southeast Asian refugees, the concept of "active exchange" is presented in combination with conventional individual and family therapy to counter the stigma of obligation in these cultures. In the chapter on Puerto Rican youth, Inclán and Herron combine the established family therapy techniques of Jay Haley (1980) with the "cultural reframe" technique espoused by Falicov and Karrer (1984). And in the chapter on Black adolescents, Gibbs highlights the need to blend "interpersonal competence" with an instrumental, task orientation in order to overcome the Black youth's initial mistrust, an often justified product of previously negative experiences with bureaucracies and mainstream institutions.

Thus, the emerging theme reiterates Kluckhohn and Murray's (1956) observation that every individual is in certain respects like all other persons, in other respects like some but not all other persons, and in still other respects like no other person. One may emphasize either shared qualities or individual differences; however, a complete picture requires a balancing of universals and specifics.

Resilience and Adaptation of Minority Groups. A common thread in the history of these minority groups is the experience of racism and exclusion. Each group individually encountered violent to subtle acts of racism by segments of the dominant White community, and occasionally several groups were lumped together. In 1854 the California Supreme Court declared, in the case of *People* v. *Hall,* that Blacks, mulattoes, Indians, Chinese, or any other persons of color were prohibited from being witnesses against Whites (Heizen and Almquist, 1971). A few years earlier, President Rutherford Hayes had analyzed the "Chinese problem" in America, declaring the current Chinese labor invasion pernicious and destructive and likening this problem to that of the other "weaker races," the Negroes and Indians (Takaki, 1979, p. 220).

Three of these groups, the American Indians, the Blacks, and the Japanese, were subjected to forced removals and relocations with the intent of "protecting" the dominant White society and disempowering these groups by weakening their cultures and communities. The systematic removal of American Indians decimated entire tribes and vanquished them to reservations. The slavery of Blacks disrupted family and kinship ties and denied them their African language, culture, and even remembrance of their country. Alexis de Tocqueville, describing the White or European character, writes in *Democracy in America* ([1835] 1945): "The European is to the other races of mankind what man himself is to the lower animals; he makes them subservient to his use, and when he cannot subdue he destroys them" (p. 370). De Tocqueville predicted that Indians would perish in their refusal to conform to White civilization, whereas Blacks would continue to be dependent on and "fastened" to Whites but would not intermingle (Takaki, 1979). During World War II, Japanese Americans were dispossessed of their land and their belongings and forcibly interned in relocation camps (Bosworth, 1967; Daniels, 1971; Girdner and Loftis, 1969).

In spite of the attempts of the dominant White group to enslave or dispossess entire populations, these minority groups survived and eventually flourished. In the face of severe oppression and unrelenting efforts to disperse and divide communities, these groups maintained their culture and heritage. As minority groups coexisting in a predominantly White society, they have demonstrated impressive resilience and adaptation. Confronted with implicit or explicit attempts at segregation, they have developed their own communities and social structures, such as Black churches, Vietnamese mutual assistance associations, Chinese American family associations, Japanese-language schools,

Indian "bands" and tribal associations, and Mexican American *compadrazgo* (fictive kin) systems, simultaneously learning to negotiate with mainstream societal structures. In essence, they have mastered two cultures—two competing realities—and have developed competencies and strategies for dealing with an unaccepting oppressor. In the United States, race has been the persistent determinant of advantage and privilege throughout every generation in history (Duster, 1987); thus, the resilience and adaptation of these groups can teach us much about coping and survival in the face of overwhelming adversity. The dynamics of race and ethnicity must be viewed as potential sources of strength and resources. The negative experiences of racism, discrimination, and restricted access to goods and services have often resulted in the development of personal and group resources, such as a strong collective identity, a sense of personal and collective resilience, and creative and flexible coping strategies (Hill, 1972; Kitano, 1974; Myers, 1982; Stack, 1974).

The Stress of Minority Status. Moritsugu and Sue (1983) have described minority status as a stressor, suggesting that members of minority groups may encounter hostility, prejudice, and lack of effective support during crises and may develop ineffective cognitive coping styles as a result of these experiences. Minority status has been associated with alienation, social isolation, heightened stress, and decreased social structure resources. These characteristics have, in turn, been associated with increased psychological dysfunction in communities (Dohrenwend, 1978) and in youth (Garmezy and Rutter, 1983).

A number of studies, reviewed by Moritsugu and Sue (1983), have confirmed the relation between minority status and heightened risk of mental disorder. Bloom (1975) found that in Pueblo, Colorado, the 1970 psychiatric hospitalization rates for Spanish-surnamed individuals were highest where they were in a minority, and the same was found for the non-Spanish-surnamed when *they* were in a minority. Analyzing the relation between ethnic group size within a community and psychiatric hospitalization rates in New York City, Rabkin (1979) consistently found that, for Whites, Blacks, and Puerto Ricans, the smaller their group size was in an area, the higher their rate of hospitalization. Mintz and Schwartz (1964) found that Whites living in Black areas had a rate of psychosis 313 percent higher than Whites in White areas; Blacks living in White areas had a 32 percent higher rate than Blacks in Black areas. Numerous studies over several decades have supported this relationship. However, since most have been of a correlational nature, they do not establish cause and effect. It may be that disturbed persons, or those so predisposed, tend to live in communities where they are in the minority; or it may be that minority group status creates stress and related disorders. Although the direction of the relationship has yet to be determined empirically, Moritsugu and Sue (1983), drawing on the concept of stress, have provided a sound conceptual argument based on the latter hypothesis.

In addition, the evolving demographics of minority populations stimulate the potential for "clashes" on several levels. As upwardly mobile minority families begin to leave the cities and penetrate historically all-White neighborhoods, interracial tensions increase. Similarly, racial tensions and hostility flourish among the various ethnic and racial minorities as they each struggle for limited housing and employment opportunities and a fair share of the limited market. Clashes become inevitable as Korean family markets spring up in Black urban neighborhoods; as Vietnamese extended families displace Hispanic and Black apartment-dwellers; as the increasing enrollment of Asian students on college campuses is perceived as a threat to affirmative action policies by other non-White, minority students. Although race relations in the United States have historically been conceptualized as Black/White, this is no longer the sole combination of racial animosity. As Hispanics and Asians have increased in number and as Native Americans have crossed the boundaries of reservations, the visibility and mobility of these groups have brought them into contact not only with mainstream White society, but with one another as well. Depending on the circumstances, this contact has been variably harmonious or antagonistic. Children and adolescents are not immune to these experiences of racial and ethnic antagonism, which affect one's self-esteem and, in turn, mental health (Comer, 1972; Phinney and Rotheram, 1987).

Many minority youth suffer early traumas that can be attributed to the dynamics of race and ethnicity (Dohrenwend and Dohrenwend, 1970; Myers, 1982). Myers (1982) contends that patterns of early deprivation due to low-income and minority status continue throughout the youth's life experiences, which are characterized by instability and unpredictability as the fate of the individual and family are often controlled by factors beyond their influence and control (for example, unemployment due to cutbacks; changes in policies governing welfare, job training, language courses, immigration, and health care; changes in college admission quotas). On a more personal level, minority youth are often the targets of ethnic and racial prejudice, as discussed in the previous chapters. Allport (1954) outlines three levels of rejection aimed toward out-group members: verbal rejection, discrimination, and physical attack. These forms of behavior, as well as the perception of prejudice, have obvious negative effects on minority youth.

Thus, in addition to the normative tasks of development, ethnic minority youth need to master the stress of "being different" and to overcome the labels of "inferior" and "second class." They need to selectively internalize the range of "reflected appraisals" (Rosenberg, 1979) from their surroundings in order to establish a strong self-concept and positive self-esteem. They need to negotiate constantly between at least two distinct cultures and value systems and to modulate the attendant hostility from the social environment. Cross (1983) analyzed the commonplace parent/child activities that went on in the homes of Black and White families with young children and found that a White-oriented monocultural frame was found in most White homes and a dual cultural—that is, Black and White—perspective was found in Black homes. Black families, responding to social realities, seemed to be promoting the development of bicultural competence in their children.

Bicultural competence is the ability to understand and "step in and out of" two cultural environments, adjusting one's behavior to the norms of each culture in order to attain one's objectives (deAnda, 1984). While many minority youth attain a healthy bicultural identity, for others this is a particularly difficult and problematic task, especially in view of the disparaging messages received from the mainstream society (Gibbs, 1987). Many of these youth must develop and differentiate between a "personal" identity and an "ethnic" or "racial" identity in order to form a cohesive sense of self. In the past, biculturality was considered synonymous with a diffuse or marginal identity and was associated with insecurity, anxiety, distrust, hostility, and defensiveness (Paz, 1961; Stevenson and Stewart, 1958; Stonequist, 1935). More recent theories emphasize the benefits of dual socialization (McFee, 1968; Phinney and Rotheram, 1987; Ramirez and Castaneda, 1974). However, while suggesting that children with bicultural competence may have higher self-esteem, greater understanding, and higher achievement than others (Ramirez, 1983), these theories also acknowledge, as discussed in the chapter by Gibbs, the additional stress of straddling two disparate cultures (Welsh, 1988).

A Model for Mental Health Intervention

The themes discussed above underscore the need for changes in mental health intervention for minority youth and their families. The majority of these youth will probably not require such services, but the number that do come to the attention of mental health providers will be increasing (Hines and Boyd-Franklin, 1982). With the ethnic minority population in the United States growing from 17 percent in 1970 to 23.3 percent in 1980 (U.S. Bureau of the Census, 1973, 1983), mental health providers can expect to see more children and adolescents from these various groups. As pointed out in the previous chapters, each ethnic or racial group understands psychological disorder differently, manifests different help-seeking patterns, and encounters different barriers and facilitators to services. There are many similarities among the various groups, such as the value of interdependence over independence, the primacy of the group over the individual, the emphasis on extended family networks rather than nuclear family units, and the clashes of roles and values vis-à-vis the mainstream society. There are also significant differences, however, not all of which can be detailed here.

In view of these complexities, we are proposing a model of intervention that delineates a process of inquiry and investigation. Consistent with the ecological perspective represented throughout this book, this model draws heavily from Bronfenbrenner's (1979) model of the person in the environment. At the center of this model is the developing individual. This individual is embedded in a complex array of systems dynamically interacting with the individual and with one another. The individual and the environmental systems are mutually shaping systems, each changing over time and each adapting in response to changes in the other (Garbarino, 1982). The interaction is reciprocal and ongoing throughout development. Figures 12.1 and 12.2 depict the two orders of interaction. Figure 12.1 displays an ecological network for a developing child or adolescent, the sig-

Figure 12.1. An Ecological Framework for Intervention:
First-Order Interactions.

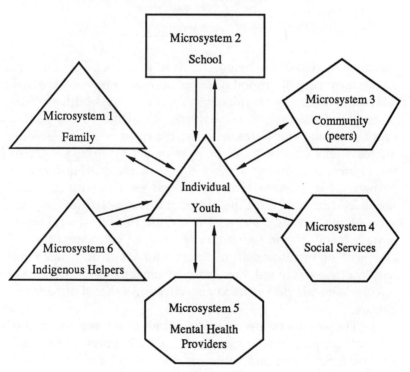

388 Children of Color

Figure 12.2. An Ecological Framework for Intervention:
Second-Order Interactions (Solid Lines).

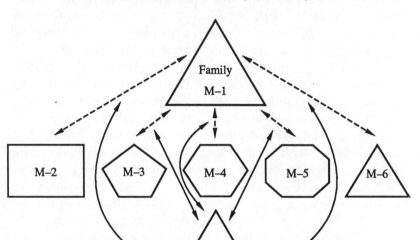

nificant microsystems being the family, the school, and the community (neighborhood or peers). For our purposes, we have added the indigenous helping system, the mental health provider system, and the social service system. For children and adolescents requiring the latter services, these systems also become microsystems affecting and being affected by these youth. As the bidirectional arrows symbolize, the direction of influence is two-way. The geometric shapes around each microsystem and the individual symbolize the different histories, origins, and cultures of the various systems. The culture of each system represents a blend of the subculture of race, of ethnicity, of social class and of institutionalism. Except for youth in foster families, the shape around the central individual and the family microsystem should be the same, reflecting a shared history and culture.

The shapes encompassing the individual and the microsystems are particularly significant, as they represent the basis for the functioning and values of the particular microsystems.

These shapes are distinct in order to highlight the differences and potential for conflict among the various systems. For example, returning to Figure 12.1, the individual comes from the "Culture of the Triangle," attends a school in the "Culture of the Rectangle," and participates in a community characterized by the "Culture of the Pentagon." In this sense, the child or adolescent negotiates among three distinct cultural systems. The values and beliefs of the school system, unlike this child's family, are founded on a "Rectangle" culture and the concept of institutionalism, which emphasizes the "organization" at the expense of other factors, including individual characteristics. To be successful in school, the child must accommodate to the norms of the "Rectangle" culture; to maintain harmony in the family, the child must adhere to the values and norms of the "Triangle" culture; and to gain acceptance in the community, the child must abide by norms of the "Pentagon" culture. Eventually, in order to develop a coherent sense of self, the child must meaningfully integrate these diverse cultural systems. The experience of this child would differ significantly from a child whose family, school, community, and peer systems all emanated from the same cultural basis. Obviously, this geometric description of a child's ecology oversimplifies the reality. However, it is parsimonious, provides a starting point for assessment and intervention, and reflects our assumption that race, ethnicity, and the associated culture form the foundation for one's values and perceptions and, therefore, attitudes and behaviors in the world. In working with ethnic minority youth, determining the ecological map and relevant cultural systems is of paramount importance.

This map also targets the points for intervention. It is particularly critical in working with children and adolescents that one identify the relevant systems impinging on the individual. Although the child or adolescent is most frequently the focus of the intervention, in some instances this may be inappropriate. Rather, the school, family, or peer system, or some combination of these systems and the individual, or even intersystemic interaction not actually involving the individual, may more appropriately be the target of an intervention. Again, this model presents the range of possibilities appropriate for a single or multipronged intervention. Figure 12.1 displays the first order of interaction between the individual and the various systems. Figure 12.2 shows the second-order interactions, or what Bronfenbrenner (1979) calls the mesosystem—that is, interactions between the various microsystems that have an impact on the individual and vice versa. For example, the interaction between the school and family system, whether mutually supportive, absent, or hostile, will have an impact on the child. Reciprocally, the child will also have an effect on this relationship. Similarly, the relationship between the family and the peer group or between the family and the mental health provider will affect the individual child or adolescent. As in the previous first-order interactions, the consonance or dissonance of cultures may affect the nature of these interactions. This is represented again by the various geometric shapes. The mental health provider must adequately assess these complex relationships, which may have a bearing on the problems presented by the individual youth.

This model of intervention, which focuses on the individual in an ecological context, is not a new idea, but it is a model particularly pertinent to ethnic minority youth for a number of reasons. First, it emphasizes the subjective field of experience for the youth, which may generate essential data not normally tapped by conventional, mainstream methods of inquiry. Second, it focuses attention on both the immediate and the more distant, albeit deeply embedded, cultural environment (Garbarino, 1982). Third, by focusing on intersystem relationships and their effects on the individual and vice versa, it reveals connections that might otherwise be overlooked and enables one to look beyond the immediate first-order interactions. In this sense, it also mandates an interdisciplinary perspective, which helps to minimize the "holes" in one's data. Fourth, this model cuts across theoretical orientations and modalities of treatment. It does not prohibit the psychodynamic theorist, banish the behaviorist, or ignore the social cognitive advocate. Rather, it provides a comprehensive, systematic way of viewing intervention. The provider may, in fact, use a psychodynamic approach with the individual while developing a psychoeducational consultation with the school. Similarly, this model does not limit the target of intervention. On the contrary, it renders the individual, the family, the couple, the group, or the institution equally appropriate targets of change, depending on the circumstances.

This model has important implications for the roles of mental health providers. The task for these providers working with ethnic minority youth is to identify the unique systems and cultural frameworks to be incorporated into the intervention. One's role may range from individual therapist to family therapist to school consultant to advocate; the arenas for intervention may be the individual, the family, the school, the work setting, the social service agency, or the community organization. Although a single provider may not be able to fulfill these various roles, it is critical to acknowledge the necessity of these functions and the need to work in multiple contexts and, if necessary, in multidisciplinary teams and with indigenous helpers. Most important, however, is the need to acknowledge one's own limitations given the demands of this model of intervention.

Preparing a "Wish List" and Understanding the Obstacles

A new model of intervention necessitates changes in the preparation of mental health service providers. This final section will address these recommended changes, some of which have been discussed in previous chapters. Many of these recommendations are not new and have already been implemented in some mental health settings. However, they do represent "ideals" and in some instances would require major reconceptualizing and restructuring in mental health settings and training arenas. We feel these are important directions that need to be delineated. In conjunction with this discussion, we will address some of the impediments to these recommended changes.

Multicultural Competence in Service Delivery. Throughout this chapter we have emphasized the balance between pluralism and universalism and the value of diversity, both on a larger societal level and at the individual level. Accordingly, this is a value that should be prominent in the foundations of a mental health care system and manifest throughout all levels of operation. It would involve integrating culture-specific beliefs and healing practices with conventional, mainstream treatments and increasing collaboration between cultural healers and mainstream service providers. The precise blend of these two components would be tailored to the needs of the client. In this sense, knowledge of different cultures is necessary but not sufficient; rather, this must be supplemented with an understanding of the client's unique and personal history of acculturation. For example, as Nagata implies, for the third-generation Japanese American client who is highly assimilated to American society and fluent only in English, conventional, mainstream approaches may be appropriate, while a different blend of services may be appropriate for that person's second-generation parents. In contrast, the recent Hispanic immigrant may require a bicultural, bilingual provider or intercultural team who, as Inclán and Herron state, can serve as a "bridge between the old and the new." The important point here is the *availability* of the different combinations of services, which, in turn, reflects the agency's or service provider's attitude toward diversity.

Multicultural competence in a helping service can be attained in a variety of ways, two of which are the recruitment of bicultural providers and the establishment of intercultural teams. The increase of ethnic minority providers in the mental health field was a priority of the 1960s and the 1970s; however, with the changing priorities and decreases of funds for minority training, much of this gain may soon be reversed (Korchin, 1976; Snowden, 1982). As Allen and Majidi-Ahi conclude, a "critical mass" of minority providers and trainees in the field is necessary in order to diminish the societal patterns and socioemotional pain of "tokenism." Among other obstacles, bicultural providers may experience difficulty locating a meaningful position in the field. Although they are representatives of a different race or ethnicity, in most instances their training has been predominantly mainstream. Accordingly, on completing their training, many of these young professionals struggle with conflicts of professional identity (Am I a minority professional? Am I a minority person trained only in White conventional methods?) and finding systems that will recognize and value their bicultural interests and competencies. This dilemma is akin to that of the scientist-practitioner in the field of clinical psychology. After the landmark Boulder Conference (Raimy, 1950) in which this model was established, training programs embraced this image of the psychologist. However, the eventual work settings for the graduates of this model were limited in number. Universities wanted the scientist-researcher and provided few incentives for the practitioner; clinical and community settings wanted the practitioner and provided minimal resources for the scientist. Thus, in some ways, this model remained more a state of mind rather than an actuality. We hope that this will not be the outcome for the bicultural provider.

Intercultural teams have been used in a variety of settings to address the needs of bicultural or biracial clients. As Huang described earlier, this has been a highly effective approach with Southeast Asian refugees. Using a combination of providers enables each helper to concentrate on his or her area of expertise so that the breadth and depth of the intervention are maximized. Intercultural teams, as well as bicultural helpers, are important role models for ethnic minority youth, who see and experience these minority individuals in positions of competence, authority, and expertise. The drawback of this approach is the tendency of intercultural teams to inadvertently reenact the political dynamics of the larger society. Rather than assuming positions of equality, the "leader" of the team is often from the dominant, White culture and is the "professional in charge"; the "helpers" are often the minority or bicultural providers, translators, or paraprofessionals. Many of the latter individuals have accumulated extensive experience in mental health that they cannot transform into policy or programs because they lack the necessary titles or influential positions (Muñoz, 1982). It is therefore imperative that these individuals be identified and given the opportunity for continued training and education, as this would move the mental health system toward the goal of multicultural competence.

The "Whole Child" Versus Professional Preciousness. As mentioned throughout this book, mental health providers working with children and adolescents need to be familiar with the total ecology of the child. Without knowledge of the settings that foster or impede psychological development, our understanding of youth, particularly ethnic minority youth, will remain limited and incomplete (Bronfenbrenner, 1979), and our system of service delivery will continue to be fragmented and poorly coordinated (Namir and Weinstein, 1982). For example, there are specialists who work with children in medical settings, in school settings, in recreational settings, in family settings, in community settings, in juvenile justice settings, and in advocacy. Rarely is a specialist trained or given the opportunity to work with the whole child or gain access to the child's total ecology. Services are created and delivered on the basis of pieces of the children's lives, and providers become setting specialists as opposed to child specialists (Namir and Weinstein, 1982). This serves to promote "professional preciousness" (Sarason, 1974), the conceptualizing of problems in ways that professionals have been trained to treat them; it impedes the coordination of multiple and disparate services; and it leads to further specialization and polarization.

The model of intervention that we have proposed requires that providers be familiar with the ecological map of an individual child or adolescent. This requires either familiarity with more than one setting or interdisciplinary collaboration, both in training and in service delivery, across settings. Providers must be sensitive to the cultural diversity of these various systems and the influence of economic, educational, and racial factors on the operation of these settings and the functioning of the children within these settings. Unfortunately, the value of these suggestions is readily apparent, but they are discouragingly difficult to implement. Professionals are entrenched in their specific body of knowledge and zealously guard their area of expertise, assuming that sharing resources and territories is antithetical to a well-delineated and protected professional domain. Thus, if these ideas are to be implemented, they need to be introduced early in a provider's training and professional development.

Systematic Changes in Curriculum and Training. The concepts of a multicultural perspective and interdisciplinary collaboration need to be part of the socialization of the mental health provider. Cultural diversity and interdisciplinary orientations should be integrated into the content and process of training and education.

A core curriculum in mental health should include knowledge not only from psychology, social work, and psychiatry but from the fields of education, public policy, sociology, anthropology, and history as well (Levine and Levine, 1970). This knowledge should be conveyed by experts in these related disciplines who can help relate their respective areas to the psychology of the developing child or adolescent. Similarly, training experiences should span a range of settings so that the provider will gain familiarity with the different approaches and priorities of the collaborating disciplines. As stated by Namir and Weinstein (1982), "Interdisciplinary collaboration in learning, as well as in the delivery of services, is a critical factor in the training of specialists of the whole child" (p. 65).

For the most part, culture and diversity have been accepted as legitimate topics of scientific inquiry and training. Ethnicity is recognized as an important independent and dependent variable and is associated with different value systems, learning histories, philosophical outlooks, social structures, life experiences, and behaviors (Suinn, 1987). The content areas include such topics as values and practices of minority cultures, historical experiences of minority groups, impact of institutional racism on child-rearing practices and psychosocial development of minority children, effects of discrimination and racism on the individual and the group, minority family structures and values, and identity development of minority individuals and groups. In the field, however, the continuing debate is how best to incorporate ethnic minority content into the education and training of mental health providers.

There are usually two options for curriculum development: (1) a single course or series of specialized courses focusing only on minority content or (2) an integration of minority content into the existing courses (Gibbs, 1985; Suinn, 1987). Obviously, the former option is easier to implement; however, the latter may be more effective in reaching a larger number of students and in socializing both ethnic minority and mainstream

White students to the value of diversity and cultural pluralism. Proponents of the specialized-course approach argue that faculty members cannot be expected to offer other than superficial coverage of ethnic topics and that, under the auspices of "academic freedom," they will proceed to teach their courses as they always have. Thus, until a new generation of instructors emerges, one that has been socialized in our increasingly multicultural society with the value of cultural diversity, little change will be possible.

It is our contention, however, that the faculty, like the curriculum, will have to evolve to meet the changing needs and demands of our society. Ethnicity is relevant to all instructors and all students, not just minority instructors and minority students. Suinn (1987) argues that education, as demonstrated by the curriculum and the faculty, imparts attitudes as well as knowledge. Students in research sequences learn the basic tools of statistics while also acquiring the attitude of investigative curiosity to guide future research endeavors. Similarly, ethnic content should convey the attitude that ethnicity is an important, integral part of a core curriculum, not a specialized subtopic of limited value. If ethnic content is distributed across all or most courses, students will accept it as valued, relevant academic material, as opposed to a "token" session on minority mental health or a perfunctory lesson on social awareness.

Research Directions. In the "best of all possible research funding worlds," the topics for investigation could fill several chapters! Acknowledging the limits of time, space, and resources, we will suggest three areas especially pertinent to the themes of this book.

What consistently emerges from each of the previous chapters is the need for epidemiological data to establish the incidence and prevalence of psychological and behavioral disorders among ethnic minority children and adolescents. Without this information, it is difficult to determine whom we are serving, whom we are underserving, and what directions we need to develop. This problem is embedded in a general lack of epidemiological data for all children and adolescents, which stems, in part, from the problems of definition, diagnosis, and differentiation between psychological disorder in childhood and cognitive or social lags in development (Achenbach, 1974; Namir and Weinstein, 1982).

Consistent with the themes of changing demographics, increasing multicultural contact and diversity, and recognition of minority status as a stressor, it is important to further our investigations of bicultural identity development and competence (deAnda, 1984; Phinney and Rotheram, 1987). It is critical to examine the developmental processes that facilitate or detract from bicultural competence in order to develop primary prevention programs for children in these situations of risk and more effective intervention strategies for children and adolescents already succumbing to the stresses and pressures of being ethnic or racial minorities in a White-dominant society.

Finally, research must focus on the helping relationship in the context of the child's or adolescent's ecological environment. The effectiveness of the proposed multicultural, multisetting model of intervention must be assessed so that limited resources in the field will be utilized most efficiently and effectively. This entails systematic investigation of inter- and intra-cultural helping relationships with youth.

Conclusion

The idea for this book arose from our frustrations as university professors who were repeatedly asked to teach graduate students how to provide mental health services to children and youth of color. Each year we would comb the literature and occasionally locate a relevant article or paper. Needless to say, we were dismayed at the lack of attention to this high-risk population and decided to try to begin to address this void. We have attempted to consolidate theoretical, clinical, and empirical information about major ethnic minority youth populations in the United States, drawing on experts in the field and our own clinical and research experience. What we have presented represents "sketches" of these youth, an initial attempt to increase our understanding of ethnic and racial minority youth, the problems they encounter, and the competencies they display. We have offered ways to intervene and a systematic method of inquiry. We have raised some significant issues and advanced a number of proposals in the hope that others will continue these efforts. As Edelman (1987) proclaims, children are the easiest people in America to ignore. The field remains wide open and there is much more to be done. Sketches are only a beginning; we remain a significant distance from the finished portraits. It is our hope that the momentum will be sustained and that the conclusions of our endeavor will provide the groundwork for new inquiry and investigation.

References

Achenbach, T. *Developmental Psychopathology.* New York: Wiley, 1974.

Allport, G. W. *The Nature of Prejudice.* Reading, Mass.: Addison-Wesley, 1954.

Berry, J. W. "On Cross-Cultural Comparability." *International Journal of Psychology,* 1969, *4,* 119–128.

Bloom, B. *Changing Patterns of Psychiatric Care.* New York: Human Science Press, 1975.

Bosworth, A. P. *America's Concentration Camps.* New York: Norton, 1967.

Bronfenbrenner, U. *The Ecology of Human Development: Experiments by Nature and Design.* Cambridge, Mass.: Harvard University Press, 1979.

Children's Defense Fund. *A Children's Defense Budget, 1986.* Washington, D.C.: Children's Defense Fund, 1986.

Comer, J. P. *Beyond Black and White.* New York: Quadrangle Books, 1972.

Cross, W. "The Ecology of Human Development for Black and White Children: Implications for Predicting Racial Preference Patterns." *Critical Perspectives of Third World America,* 1983, *1,* 177–189.

Daniels, R. *Concentration Camps U.S.A.: Japanese Americans and World War II.* New York: Holt, Rinehart & Winston, 1971.

deAnda, D. "Bicultural Socialization: Factors Affecting the Minority Experience." *Social Work*, 1984, *29*, 101–107.

Dohrenwend, B. S. "Social Stress and Community Psychology." *American Journal of Community Psychology*, 1978, *6*, 1–14.

Dohrenwend, B. S., and Dohrenwend, B. P. "Class and Race as Status-Related Sources of Stress." In S. Levine and N. Scotch (eds.), *Social Stress*. Hawthorne, N.Y.: Aldine, 1970.

Draguns, J. G. "Cross-Cultural Counseling and Psychotherapy: History, Issues, Current Status." In A. J. Marsella and P. B. Pedersen (eds.), *Cross-Cultural Counseling and Psychotherapy*. Elmsford, N.Y.: Pergamon Press, 1981.

Duster, T. "Purpose and Bias." *Society*, 1987, *24* (2), 8–12.

Edelman, M. W. *Families in Peril: An Agenda for Social Change*. Cambridge, Mass.: Harvard University Press, 1987.

Falicov, C. J., and Karrer, B. M. "Therapeutic Strategies for Mexican-American Families." *International Journal of Family Therapy*, 1984, *6* (1), 18–30.

Garbarino, J. *Children and Families in the Social Environment*. Hawthorne, N.Y.: Aldine, 1982.

Garmezy, N., and Rutter, M. *Stress, Coping and Development in Children*. New York: McGraw-Hill, 1983.

Gibbs, J. T. "Black Adolescents and Youth: An Endangered Species." *American Journal of Orthopsychiatry*, 1984, *54* (1), 6–21.

Gibbs, J. T. "Can We Continue to Be Color-Blind and Class-Bound?" *Counseling Psychologist*, 1985, *13* (3), 426–435.

Gibbs, J. T. "Identity and Marginality: Issues in the Treatment of Biracial Adolescents." *American Journal of Orthopsychiatry*, 1987, *57* (2), 265–278.

Girdner, A., and Loftis, A. *The Great Betrayal: The Evacuation of the Japanese-Americans During World War II*. New York: Macmillan, 1969.

Green, J. W. *Cultural Awareness in the Human Services*. Englewood Cliffs, N.J.: Prentice-Hall, 1982.

Haley, J. *Leaving Home: The Therapy of Disturbed Young People*. New York: McGraw-Hill, 1980.

Heizen, R. F., and Almquist, A. F. *The Other Californians*. Berkeley: University of California Press, 1971.

Hill, R. B. *The Strengths of Black Families.* New York: Emerson Hall, 1972.

Hines, P. M., and Boyd-Franklin, N. "Black Families." In M. McGoldrick, J. K. Pearce, and J. Giordano (eds.), *Ethnicity and Family Therapy.* New York: Guilford Press, 1982.

Jones, E. E., and Korchin, S. J. "Minority Mental Health: Perspectives." In E. E. Jones and S. J. Korchin (eds.), *Minority Mental Health.* New York: Praeger, 1982.

Kitano, H. *Race Relations.* Englewood Cliffs, N.J.: Prentice-Hall, 1974.

Kluckhohn, C., and Murray, H. A. "Personality Formation: The Determinants." In C. Kluckhohn (ed.), *Personality in Nature, Society and Culture.* New York: Knopf, 1956.

Korchin, S. J. *Modern Clinical Psychology: Principles of Intervention in the Clinic and Community.* New York: Basic Books, 1976.

Kotkin, J., and Kishimoto, Y. "America's Asian Destiny." *Washington Post,* July 3, 1988, pp. C-1, C-4.

Ladner, J. A. *Mixed Families.* New York: Anchor Press, 1977.

Levine, M., and Levine, A. *A Social History of Helping Services: Clinic, Court, School, and Community.* East Norwalk, Conn.: Appleton-Century-Crofts, 1970.

Los Angeles Unified School District, Los Angeles City Board of Education. *Integrated Educational Excellence Through Choice: Response to Court Order of February 7, 1978.* Submitted to the Los Angeles Superior Court, Mar. 12, 1979.

McFee, M. "The 150% Man, a Product of Blackfeet Acculturation." *American Anthropologist,* 1968, *70,* 1096–1103.

Mercer, J., and Lewis, J. *System of Multicultural Pluralistic Assessment.* New York: Psychological Corporation, 1978.

Mintz, N., and Schwartz, D. "Urban Ecology and Psychosis: Community Factors in the Incidence of Schizophrenia and Manic-Depression Among Italians in Greater Boston." *International Journal of Social Psychiatry,* 1964, *10,* 101–118.

Moritsugu, J., and Sue, S. "Minority Status as a Stressor." In R. Felner, L. Jason, J. Moritsugu, and S. Farber (eds.), *Preventive Psychology: Theory, Research and Practice.* Elmsford, N.Y.: Pergamon Press, 1983.

Muñoz, R. "The Spanish-Speaking Consumer and the Community Mental Health Center." In E. E. Jones and S. J. Korchin (eds.), *Minority Mental Health.* New York: Praeger, 1982.

Myers, H. F. "Stress, Ethnicity, and Social Class: A Model for Research with Black Populations." In E. E. Jones and S. J. Korchin (eds.), *Minority Mental Health.* New York: Praeger, 1982.

Nakao, A. "Western Culture Faces Decline—at Least on Campus." *San Francisco Examiner,* Apr. 5, 1987.

Namir, S., and Weinstein, R. "Children: Facilitating New Directions." In L. R. Snowden (ed.), *Reaching the Underserved: Mental Health Needs of Neglected Populations.* Newbury Park, Calif.: Sage, 1982.

Oakland, T. (ed.). *Psychological and Educational Assessment of Minority Children.* New York: Brunner/Mazel, 1977.

Passel, J. S. "Provisional Evaluation of the 1970 Census Count of American Indians." *Demography,* 1976, *13,* 397–409.

Paz, O. *The Labyrinth of Solitude.* New York: Grove Press, 1961.

Phinney, J. S., and Rotheram, M. J. *Children's Ethnic Socialization: Pluralism and Development.* Newbury Park, Calif.: Sage, 1987.

Powell, B., and others. "The Pacific Century." *Newsweek,* Feb. 22, 1988, pp. 43–51.

Powell, G. J., Yamamoto, J., Romero, A., and Morales, A. (eds.). *The Psychosocial Development of Minority Group Children.* New York: Brunner/Mazel, 1983.

President's Commission on Mental Health. *Report to the President of the President's Commission on Mental Health.* Washington, D.C.: U.S. Government Printing Office, 1978.

Rabkin, J. "Ethnic Density and Psychiatric Hospitalization: Hazards of Minority Status." *American Journal of Psychiatry,* 1979, *136,* 1562–1566.

Raimy, V. C. (ed.). *Training in Clinical Psychology.* Englewood Cliffs, N.J.: Prentice-Hall, 1950.

Ramirez, M. *Psychology of the Americas: Mestizo Perspectives on Personality and Mental Health.* Orlando, Fla.: Academic Press, 1983.

Ramirez, M., and Castaneda, A. *Cultural Democracy, Bicognitive Development, and Education.* Orlando, Fla.: Academic Press, 1974.

Rosenberg, M. *Conceiving the Self.* New York: Basic Books, 1979.

Samuda, R. *Psychological Testing of American Minorities: Issues and Consequences.* New York: Dodd, Mead, 1975.

Sarason, S. B. *The Psychological Sense of Community: Prospects for a Community Psychology.* San Francisco: Jossey-Bass, 1974.

Snowden, L. R. "Services to the Underserved: An Overview of Contemporary Issues." In L. R. Snowden (ed.), *Reaching the Underserved: Mental Health Needs of Neglected Populations.* Newbury Park, Calif.: Sage, 1982.

Snowden, L. R., and Todman, P. A. "The Psychological Assessment of Blacks: New and Needed Developments." In E. E. Jones and S. J. Korchin (eds.), *Minority Mental Health.* New York: Praeger, 1982.

Sommers, V. "The Impact of Dual Cultural Membership on Identity." *Psychiatry,* 1964, *27,* 332–344.

Stack, C. *All Our Kin: Strategies for Survival in a Black Community.* New York: Harper & Row, 1974.

Stevenson, H. W., and Stewart, E. C. "A Developmental Study of Racial Awareness in Young Children." *Child Development,* 1958, *29,* 399–409.

Stonequist, E. V. "The Problem of the Marginal Man." *American Journal of Sociology,* 1935, *41,* 1–12.

Sue, S., and Morishima, J. K. *The Mental Health of Asian Americans: Contemporary Issues in Identifying and Treating Mental Problems.* San Francisco: Jossey-Bass, 1982.

Suinn, R. M. "Minority Issues Cut Across Courses." *APA Monitor,* Mar. 1987, p. 3.

Takaki, R. *Iron Cages: Race and Culture in Nineteenth-Century America.* Seattle: University of Washington Press, 1979.

Tocqueville, A. de. *Democracy in America.* Vol. 1. New York: Knopf, 1945. (Originally published 1835.)

Triandis, H., and Brislin, R. "Cross-Cultural Psychology." *American Psychologist,* 1984, *39,* 1006–1016.

U.S. Bureau of the Census. *1970 Census of Population: Characteristics of the Population.* Washington, D.C.: U.S. Department of Commerce, 1973.

U.S. Bureau of the Census. *1980 Census of Population: Characteristics of the Population.* U.S. Summary, PC 80-1-B1. Washington, D.C.: U.S. Department of Commerce, 1983.

U.S. Bureau of the Census. *Persons of Spanish Origin in the United States: March 1985.* Washington, D.C.: U.S. Government Printing Office, 1985.

Vobejda, B. "Education Leaders Warn of Crisis for U.S. Youth." *Washington Post,* June 2, 1987, p. A-16.

Welsh, P. "The Black Talent Trap." *Washington Post,* May 1, 1988, p. C1.

Wong, H. Z. "Asian and Pacific Americans." In L. R. Snowden (ed.), *Reaching the Underserved: Mental Health Needs of Neglected Populations.* Newbury Park, Calif.: Sage, 1982.

Index

A

Abbott, E., 43, 63
Abbott, K., 43, 63
Abelson, W., 160, 178
Aber, M. S., 195, 215
Ablon, J., 118, 140
Abramson, P. R., 80, 107
Abt, L. E., 322, 327, 334, 342, 349
Academic achievement, 18–19; American Indians and, 117, 123–124; biracial adolescents and, 336–337; Black Americans and, 151, 185–186, 193, 199; cultural attitudes toward, 13–14; Japanese Americans and, 69, 76, 85; Mexican Americans and, 226; school adjustment and, 18–19; verbal skills and, 19
"Acculturation gap," in Chinese American families, 47–48
Achenbach, T., 153, 163, 173, 397, 398
Achievement tests, 18
Acosta, F. X., 23, 26, 94, 113, 162, 173, 201, 213, 234, 235, 236, 237, 247, 267, 306, 317
Acquired immunodeficiency syndrome. See AIDS
Active exchange: Chinese Americans and, 55–57, 58–60, 63; Southeast Asian refugees and, 305–306, 309, 310–311
Adams, E. H., 231, 247

Adams, P., 329, 330, 331, 341, 343, 344, 346
Affect, expression of, 13; Black American adolescents and, 193–194; Chinese American children and, 46; Japanese Americans and, 79
Affirmative action programs, backlash against, 183–184
Aggression, management of, 14
Ahmed, P., 279, 317
AIDS (acquired immunodeficiency syndrome): Black American adolescents and, 190; Puerto Ricans and, 255
"AIDS: A Complex New Threat to Children's Survival," 190, 213
Aiello, J., 235, 247
Albee, G. W., 169, 173
Alcohol abuse: American Indians and, 116, 118, 119, 135–136; Black American adolescents and, 189–190; Japanese Americans and, 74–75
Allen, L., 148, 153, 166, 169, 176, 355, 357, 358, 360, 361, 363, 392
Allen, W. R., 184, 213
Allport, G. W., 385, 398
Almquist, A. F., 382, 399
Alstein, H., 329, 349
Amerasians, 293
American Indian children and adolescents: academic achievement